The Greatest Beach

LALH
Library of American Landscape History

The Greatest Beach

A HISTORY OF CAPE COD NATIONAL SEASHORE

Ethan Carr

LIBRARY OF AMERICAN LANDSCAPE HISTORY   AMHERST, MASSACHUSETTS

THE UNIVERSITY OF GEORGIA PRESS   ATHENS

For Sarah and Marion

A volume in the series
Designing the American Park
Edited by Ethan Carr

Published by the University of Georgia Press
Athens, Georgia 30602
www.ugapress.org
in association with
Library of American Landscape History
www.lalh.org

Designed by Jonathan D. Lippincott
Set in Garamond 3
Printed and bound by Four Colour Print Group

Southern Highlands Reserve Publications

The paper in this book meets the guidelines for permanence and durability of the Committee on Production Guidelines for Book Longevity of the Council on Library Resources.

Printed in China
19 20 21 22 23 C 5 4 3 2 1

Library of Congress Control Number: 2018962516
ISBN: 9780820355580 (hardcover : alk. paper)

Frontispiece: American beach grass, Outer Cape dunes. Photo by M. Woodbridge Williams, c. 1965. NPS.

The Greatest Beach was made possible with the generous support of the following individuals:

Anonymous
Foundation for Landscape Studies
Mr. and Mrs. William Frederick Jr.

Robert and Joan Feitler, The Feitler Family Fund
Michael and Evelyn Jefcoat, in honor of Ethan Carr, FASLA
Thomas Lemann, The Azby Art Fund
Karen Madsen and John Furlong

Ann Mullins, Margaret A. Frank Fund at The Chicago Community Foundation
Nancy Newcomb and John Hargraves
James F. Olmsted
Lauren Stimson, ASLA, and Stephen Stimson, FASLA
Margaret Sullivan
Dana and Joe Woody
Dr. and Mrs. T. Price Zimmermann, Foundation for the Carolinas

Donald Albrecht
Anonymous, in memory of Duncan Wall
Randall J. Biallas
Charles Burnham
Dr. and Mrs. Charles Carroll IV
Laurence A. Clement Jr.
David B. Coleman
George W. Curry, FASLA
Dede Delaney
Rolf Diamant, ASLA, and Nora Mitchell, ASLA
Terese D'Urso, in honor of John Furlong
Elsbeth T. Falk
Nancy Fee, in honor of Cabot and Ingrid and Family
Frances Shedd Fisher
Elisabeth French
Alexander Goriansky
Mimi Gross, in memory of Renee and Chaim Gross
Bryan Haltermann, in honor of Mary Bryan Haltermann
Esley Hamilton
Margarete R. Harvey, ASLA
Katherine Koch
Francis R. Kowsky
Mr. and Mrs. Michael Loening
Richard Longstreth
Margaret Jean McKee
Jaqueline J. Melander, in honor of Jody Melander
Hugh C. Miller, FAIA
Mary Eugenia Myer
Darwina L. Neal, FASLA
Thomas Paine, ASLA
Monique Parsons
Dr. and Mrs. W. Scott Peterson, Connecticut Community Foundation
David Schuyler
Walter M. Spink
Robert A. M. Stern Architects, LLP
William H. Tishler, FASLA, in honor of Darrel Morrison
Wellington D. Watters
Judith Howard Whitney-Terry, Fidelity Charitable
Claire B. Willis
Louise A. Wrinkle

Contents

Preface

This book is the fourth volume in Library of American Landscape History's series Designing the American Park. The series was established to publish new and original research on this highly significant and often underappreciated form of American cultural expression. In particular, we have sought to highlight parks and park systems that have not received the scholarly attention they deserve, from the municipal park system of Buffalo, New York, to the segregated state parks of the Jim Crow era, to the unique and fascinating contributions of the landscape architect Arthur Shurcliff.

The Greatest Beach continues this undertaking by examining how U.S. national park making changed in the mid-twentieth century. The forces of change were both national and local, but the local influences were perhaps the most significant. Individually and through their town meetings and elected representatives, the residents of the six towns of the Outer Cape encouraged the National Park Service to think about landscape conservation in new ways—that is, if the agency hoped to remain a part of the discussion at all. To their credit, in 1961, the park service went along with the new "formula" or "model" that allowed for private property ownership within Cape Cod National Seashore. In doing so they altered the future of U.S. national park planning. The 1960 election of John F. Kennedy, who originally introduced the federal park legislation with fellow Massachusetts senator Leverett Saltonstall the year before, of course helped turned the tide. But the history of the national seashore is above all one of how the long-established (and by the 1950s very influential) communities of Cape Cod helped change the way national parks would be planned in the United States and, subsequently, in the world.

The Designing the American Park series illustrates the ability of park history to uncover and elaborate on important themes in American society which otherwise remain unexamined. More broadly, the same is true of the mission of LALH, which publishes books that educate the public on the heritage of designed landscapes and encourages their stewardship. The history of Cape Cod National Seashore is one of stewardship—never easy, always complex, and often contentious—and how citizens, park officials, and elected representatives devised new planning, design, and management priorities to achieve that stewardship in the context of rapid social and environmental change. A period of daring innovation, it was also one of unprecedented threats and challenges. More than any other national park of the era, Cape Cod National Seashore embodied the new approaches and changed policies that those conditions required.

This is a park that tells a larger story of the ever-changing relationship between the American public and the system of federal landscape reservations that are often described as one of the country's greatest achievements. A new kind of national park, Cape Cod National Seashore's greatest success was the revitalization of the national park idea and the demonstration of a renewed relevance for national park making. But its story is more than a transitional moment in park history; it captures aspects of the profound social and economic changes that characterized the mid-twentieth century, in general, and survives today as a living record of the highest hopes of generations of area residents, park managers, and conservation advocates. *The Greatest Beach* is therefore instructive beyond its immediate subject—the conservation of the Outer Cape—and addresses larger themes of landscape history that make it an appropriate addition to the Library of American Landscape History.

Acknowledgments

The sources for my research were drawn primarily from archives, newspaper accounts, and oral histories. As is the case with any park history, the assistance and interest of the managers and staff of the park—who know the story best—were essential for uncovering and sometimes correcting many details. I would like to acknowledge the National Park Service staff (past and present) and those who work with them in the six towns of the Outer Cape, the Cape Cod Commission, and other institutions not only for their efforts and dedication that sometimes spanned lifetimes, but also for the documentation of these efforts through letters, transcripts, and reporting. The Cape Cod National Seashore has benefited from the labors of a remarkable generation of residents and advocates who were also aware of the importance of their cooperative project and recorded it.

Library of American Landscape History selected this book as a volume in its series Designing the American Park, for which I am extremely grateful. The editorial and design expertise this group is able to muster, thanks to an outstanding board of directors and many individual contributors and granting organizations, is deeply appreciated by the author. In particular, I want to thank Sarah Allaback for her developmental editing of the manuscript and expansion of the illustration program. Carol Betsch not only provided editorial wisdom, but also produced an extraordinary portfolio of her own photographs specifically commissioned for *The Greatest Beach.* Jonathan Lippincott used these original photographs, and many other images gathered from archival sources, to design a book worthy of its subject. Robin Karson, executive director of LALH, has been the guiding force behind this work, the series of which it is a part, and the larger and successful efforts of LALH to achieve its mission of publishing new and meaningful research on the designed landscapes that form such a vital and overlooked dimension of our national experience.

The administrative records of the National Park Service are conserved by the National Archives as Record Group 79. The files belonging to this record group in the central archives in College

Park, Maryland, can be accessed with the help of an excellent finding aid, "Inventory of the Records of the National Park Service, Record Group 79," compiled by the park service in 2007. The park service also makes available a guide to writing administrative histories of the parks, "National Park Service Administrative Histories: A Guide" (2004), which includes valuable information on the location of park service records. Most of the federal records used in this study that directly concern the administration of Cape Cod National Seashore are kept at the Boston National Archives, the regional national archives facility in Waltham, Massachusetts. The regional archives in Philadelphia retain the records of the park service's Eastern Office of Design and Construction, which was important during the early years of the Cape Cod National Seashore. The National Park Service's Harpers Ferry Center also curates the NPS History Collection, including an extensive archive of national park images. Archivist Nancy J. Russell guided me through these collections. Two oral history projects were also used for this study. The first was undertaken in the 1970s by Francis W. Sargent, Robert F. Gibbs, and Francis P. Burling, who interviewed many of the people prominent in the legislative effort to establish the park. The transcriptions are kept at the national seashore offices. The second was undertaken as part of this project by Sara Patton, then a graduate student in the history department of University of Massachusetts Amherst. Thanks and acknowledgment are extended to her for her work, and to all those who generously participated in the oral history interviews, the recordings of which are also kept by the national seashore.

As is often the case, Cape Cod National Seashore also maintains its own archives relating to its administration and operation. Cultural Resources Program Manager Bill Burke contributed his time and expertise not only to make these files available, but also to point to numerous other sources and provide invaluable guidance. Burke's historical knowledge of the park and region provided a touchstone for this entire project.

The Greatest Beach

Dunes, Provincetown. Photo by Carol Betsch.

Introduction

The 1961 federal legislation that established Cape Cod National Seashore dramatically altered the trends and patterns of development of the Outer Cape landscape at a critical point in the region's history.[1] The mandate described in "An Act to Provide for the Establishment of Cape Cod National Seashore" set new precedents for policies and processes of landscape conservation in the United States and, by their influence and example, in the world. As it implemented the mission assigned to it, the National Park Service elaborated a vision for how a national park could be managed as a cultural landscape: the continuous history of human habitation and cultural practices in the region, together with its unique scenery and rich natural resources, would be understood as mutually influential and vital dimensions of the "landscape character" that the agency was charged with "preserving" from the effects of postwar population growth and rising recreational use. The mixed but highly instructive results of these efforts are the subject of this book.

Critical to the story is an understanding of the origins of what would come to be identified and valued as the character of the Outer Cape landscape. Cape Cod differed from other New England seaside resorts from the start. As Boston grew into a large city in the nineteenth century, wealthy merchants and professionals established colonies of summer houses around Boston Harbor, from Nahant to Nantasket, and on the shores north and south of Boston, from Beverly to Scituate. By the mid-nineteenth century, hotels and resorts were scattered along the New England coast from the Connecticut shore to southern Maine.[2] Resort towns developed new identities and economies associated with the urban centers they were linked with socially and geographically. They became part of the modern pace of life and rapid economic development of the nineteenth century.

Cape Cod remained remote from the metropolitan culture of these other seaside destinations. The few tourists drawn to the Cape in the first half of the nineteenth century found a somewhat desolate, sparsely populated landscape with a unique regional

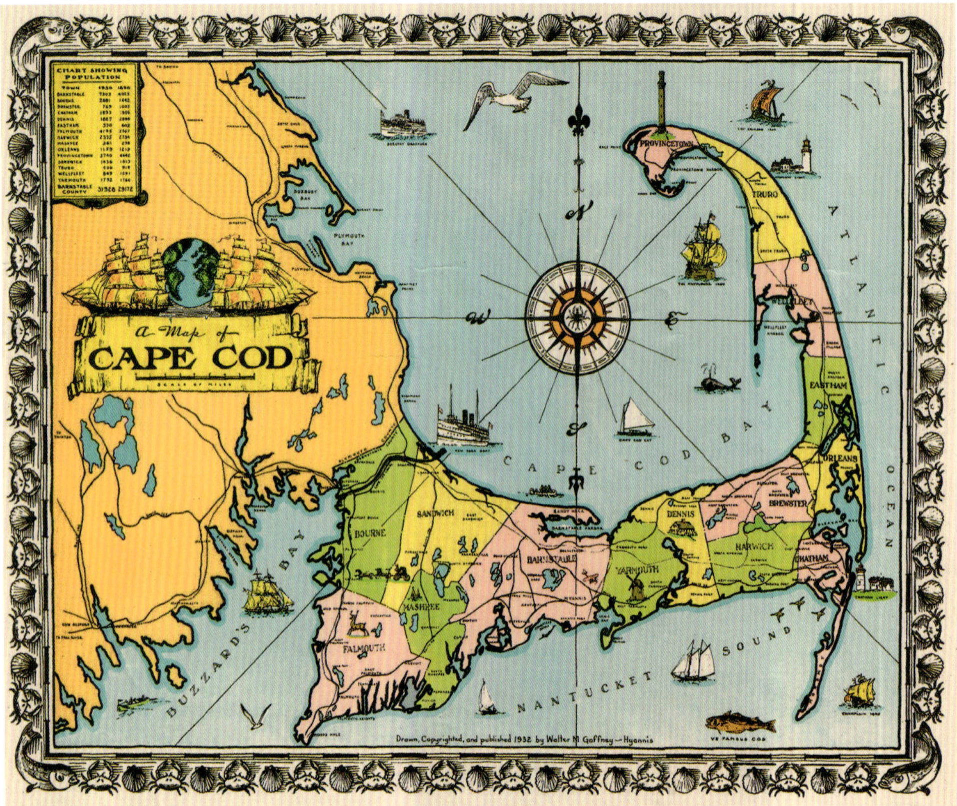

"A Map of Cape Cod," by Walter M. Gaffney, 1932. Wikimedia Commons.

history. The communities of the Cape were among the oldest in North America. The Pilgrims famously dropped anchor in Provincetown Harbor in 1620, and although they chose to establish their plantation across Cape Cod Bay at Plymouth, some members of the colony soon returned and created new towns at Sandwich, Yarmouth, and Barnstable by 1639, and at Eastham in 1644. As the settlements proliferated over the next century, the growing Cape population cleared forests and cultivated whatever land could support crops and livestock. The region's unique geographic situation soon encouraged maritime industries, such as whaling, shipbuilding, salt making, and fishing, all established by the time of the Revolution.[3]

For much of the nineteenth century, however, the economy and the population of Cape Cod waned. While Massachusetts as a whole experienced vigorous economic growth during the decades before and after the Civil War, many rural and coastal areas in New England did not. On Cape Cod, agriculture had long suffered from soil erosion, and the saltworks that covered many bayside shorelines began disappearing once salt mines were opened in upstate New York. Whaling and shipbuilding moved to other ports with larger, centralized facilities. Fishing increased in importance as other industries disappeared, but still declined later in the century. The population of Barnstable County had significantly decreased by the time the century drew to a close.[4] As New England became increasingly populous, industrialized, and urban, Cape Cod and its people persisted in rural isolation.

It was during this time of social and landscape change on the Cape that at least some hardy tourists began to define and value the region in new ways.[5]

Seine fishing from railroad wharf, Provincetown, 1907–9. NPS.

Governor Thomas Prence House, Eastham, before 1880. HABS.

Towns that had seen their economies collapse were "quaint" in the eyes of visitors who appreciated the vernacular architecture of earlier eras. Fields abandoned by farmers were growing into picturesque heathlands, covered in blueberries (*Vaccinium spp.*) and other shrubs, or into stunted forests of pitch pine (*Pinus rigida*) and oaks (*Quercus spp.*) The peculiar accents and ways of life of local people delighted (and in some cases dismayed) visitors, without apparent concern that these differences were the products of social seclusion and relative poverty. As the geographer John R. Stilgoe observes, sustained economic woes made much of coastal New England "almost a de facto historical preserve, a place in which old habits and things endured essentially because they could not be replaced."

Cape Cod, in particular, by the 1880s had become in the eyes of visitors and travel writers "almost antique, filled with 'historical associations,' essentially quaint."[6] Some tourists saw and valued other aspects of the Cape landscape in new ways as well. Fresh and saltwater wetlands were teeming with birds, some of great interest to sportsmen as well as naturalists. The incomparable Great Beach, famous as the scene of horrifying shipwrecks and lethal currents since the time of the Mayflower, could also be perceived as a unique, desolate, and Romantic landscape.[7] Extending for almost forty miles, the Great Beach of the Outer Cape was not only a "graveyard" for shipping but also a truly sublime landscape experience.

The attraction of Cape Cod would be, in other words, that of a cultural landscape, which embodied not only beaches and fresh air but older ways of Yankee life that had disappeared elsewhere. Windmills and lighthouses, blueberry heaths and cranberry bogs, the weathered and modest architecture that seemed so suited to the headlands and harbors all contributed to new constructions of the "character" of the Cape Cod landscape. Cape residents and their activities took on iconic significance. "Old salts" and fishermen, groups of women and children gathering berries for making pies and candles, and watermen working oyster beds and digging for clams were as much parts of the scene as sky, water, and sand. To a greater degree possibly than any other tourist destination in the country, the appeal of Cape Cod, for at least some visitors, combined people and place, cultural history and natural beauty.

The most important early tourist to Cape Cod was Henry David Thoreau, who in the fall of 1849 decided to visit the Cape and write about his experi-

The Great Beach. NPS.

Fishermen baiting longlines, n.d. NPS.

"The Cranberry Harvest, with the Scoop." *Cape Cod and the Old Colony,* 1921.

ences. He returned twice over the following years and delivered his observations as a series of public lectures and as articles for *Putnam's Magazine* and the *Atlantic Monthly*. These were assembled and published in 1865, three years after his death, and went into many later editions. Always as interested in people as much as in other species, in *Cape Cod* Thoreau gives an invaluable account of a cultural landscape on the verge of great change, a change that his own tourism and writing both indicated and helped bring about. "I did not see why I might not make a book on Cape Cod, as well as my neighbor on 'Human Culture,'" he wrote in his first chapter. "It is but another name for the same thing, and hardly a sandier phase of it."[8]

The book is replete with detailed descriptions of shorelines, dunes, wetlands, and harbors, as well as specific accounts of the plants and animals he observed. The narrative is even more notable, however, for the cheerful and often humorous encounters between the author and the "first people," or early residents, of the Cape.[9] These included "wreckers" salvaging the tragic remains of the brig *St. John,* the "retired sea-captains, in easy circumstances, who talked of farming as sea-captains are wont," a "broad, red-faced, Cape Cod man, who had seen too many storms to be easily irritated," and "the Wellfleet oysterman," among many others. Their appearance, dialect, and activities made colorful subjects for the author. Thoreau criticizes travel guides from earlier in the century which did not, in their prosaic descriptions of places and accommodations, adequately identify or appreciate the true beauty and interest of the Cape. He corrects this deficiency with his own vivid compositions of people, places, and natural history, as in this sketch of a bayside scene on the Upper Cape:[10]

> The windmills on the hills,—large weather-stained octagonal structures,—and the salt-works scattered all along the shore, with

> their long rows of vats resting on piles driven into the marsh, their low, turtle-like roofs, and their slighter windmills, were novel and interesting objects to an inlander. The sand by the roadside was partially covered with bunches of a moss-like plant, *Hudsonia tomentosa,* which a woman in the stage told us was called 'poverty grass,' because it grew where nothing else would.[11]

Thoreau anticipates the sensibility of generations of tourists to come. He also notes the desolation of many areas, which had been deforested and then farmed until the topsoil blew away. Thoreau's Cape Cod was largely treeless, with land that "no farmer in the interior would think of cultivating, or even fencing." The furrows of one field looked "white and yellow, like a mixture of salt and Indian meal." There is an elegiac tone to *Cape Cod,* a palpable sense that life there, as it had been, was fading. In its place, Thoreau reveals new fascinations for a visitor such as himself. On Cape Cod, he enthuses, "everything told of the sea, even when we did not see its waste or hear its roar." When he begins his trek on foot along the Great Beach, from Nauset Harbor to Race Point, he exclaims an awakening that many visitors (although probably fewer of his "first people") could appreciate:

> There I had got the Cape under me, as much as if I were riding it barebacked. It was not as on the map, or seen from the stage-coach; but there I found it all out of doors, huge and real, Cape Cod! as it cannot be represented on a map, color it as you will; the thing itself, than which there is nothing more like it, no truer picture or account; which you cannot go farther and see. I cannot remember what I thought before that it was.[12]

"Great Marshes of Barnstable." *Cape Cod and the Old Colony.*

"Many Like This on the Cape." *Cape Cod and the Old Colony.*

In his observations of the 1850s, Thoreau records both the imminent passing of one Cape Cod and a rising awareness of another. His experience was that of a modern tourist—an observer of the landscape—as opposed to that of the generations who had worked in and around it. Essential to this new mode of perception was the railroad, which had been extended to Sandwich in 1848, the year before Thoreau used it to facilitate his first excursion. But "the terminus of the 'Cape Cod Railroad,'" he notes, was "but the beginning of the Cape." From there, he proceeded by stage and on foot, as others wishing to make the journey would, on a barely maintained network of sandy, winding roads. The principal route along the length of the Cape he described as "a mere cart-track, in the sand . . . continually changing from this side to that, to harder ground, or sometimes to avoid the tide."[13]

Moonlight view of ocean, in winter, 1875. Stereograph by G. H. Nickerson, Provincetown. LC.

Conditions like these helped assure that Cape Cod did not become one of the fashionable seaside resorts of early nineteenth-century New England. As the historian Dona Brown points out, Martha's Vineyard, Nantucket, and coastal Maine had more early visitors than Cape Cod, which "lagged far behind neighboring areas in the development of tourist industries."[14] The apparent desolation of the treeless—to many, forbidding—landscape, and perhaps the social and economic conditions of Cape communities, discouraged early tourism. This remained the case on much of the Cape even when the Old Colony Railroad was extended all the way to Provincetown in 1873. William Cullen Bryant, the principal editor of *Picturesque America,* left Cape Cod entirely out of that 1874 compilation of descriptions and images of

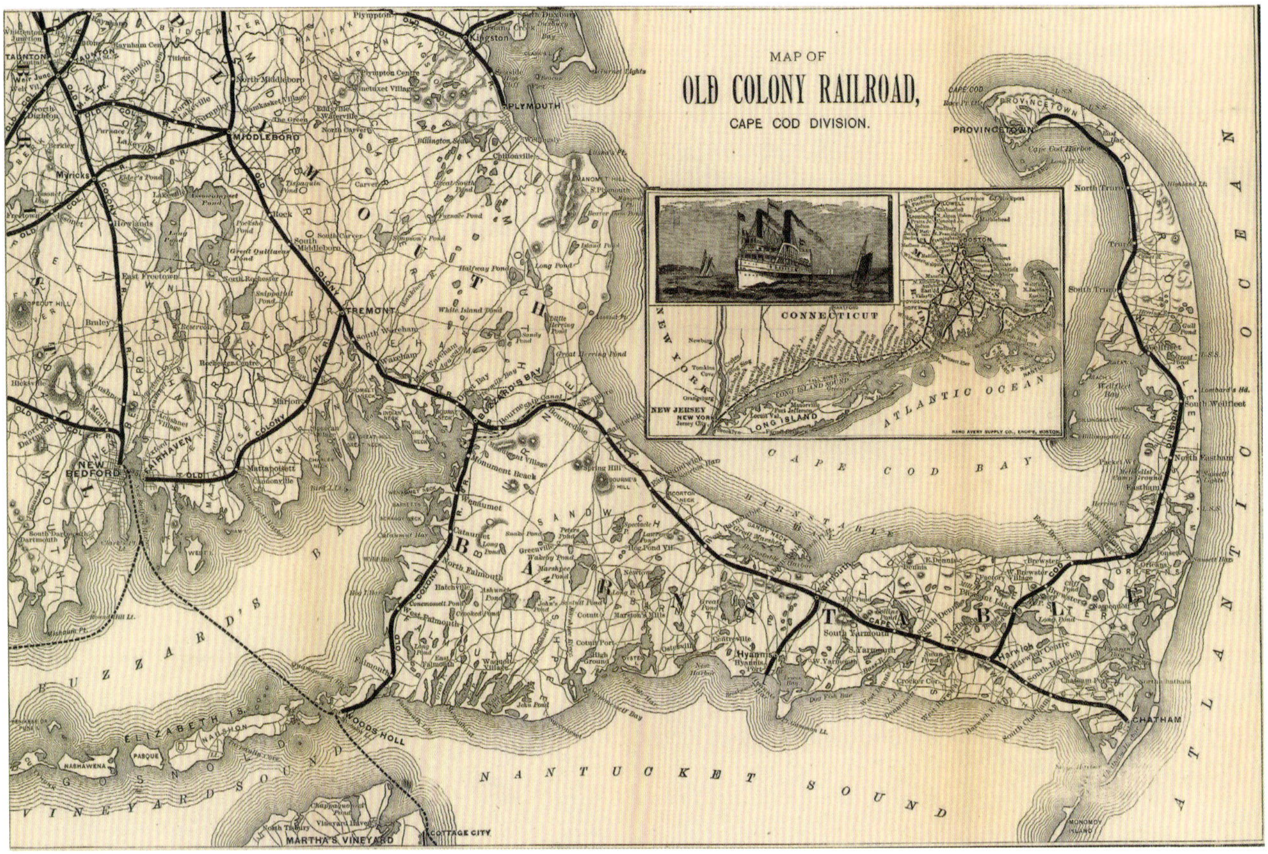

"Map of Old Colony Railroad, Cape Cod Division," 1888. Wikimedia Commons.

scenic places. This was a telling omission; the resort areas of coastal Maine and Mount Desert, the North Shore of Massachusetts, eastern Long Island, the Connecticut shore, and Narragansett Bay and Newport all were featured.[15]

Thoreau had predicted that it would be many years before Cape Cod would become a major destination for the "fashionable world," a fact that did not displease him. He had no love of contemporary spas and resorts, which was the reason he chose to visit and write about the Cape instead. Despite a growing and more affluent population in the Northeast looking for every opportunity for tourism, Cape Cod remained relatively isolated for decades. In several areas, including Sandwich and Monomoy, outfitters set up small hotels and hunting camps for sportsmen interested in shooting waterfowl. Religious camp meetings attracted large congregations in Yarmouth, Eastham, and Craigville, as they did on Martha's Vineyard and elsewhere.[16] But if significant in their own right, neither hunting camps nor tent revivals elevated the Cape to the itinerary of the "fashionable world," or to the catalog of *Picturesque America*. On the Great Beach, a visitor could indeed "put all America behind him," as Thoreau wrote, in more senses than one.[17]

The Upper Cape, closer to Boston, Providence, and New York, began to change first. The first large hotel on the Cape, Santuit House, opened in Cotuit in 1860. It was followed by other hotels, summer homes, and more modest cottages in areas on the warmer South Shore (or South Side, facing Nantucket Sound) of the Cape. By the 1890s, the region was established as a railroad tourist destination, with summer crowds received at hotels from Penzance Point in Falmouth to Hyannis Port in Barnstable and in the communities along the eastern shore of Buzzards Bay. These towns, at least, finally benefited from an expanding tourist economy that mitigated hard times.[18]

But if some parts of Cape Cod started to resemble other coastal resorts in New England, the region as a whole retained its peculiar geography and much of its local culture and historical identity. The cultural landscape remained distinct and somewhat removed. Distance was not the only reason; the Old Colony Railroad made the Cape as accessible as many other coastal areas. Geography did help preserve an older way of life on the Cape, but so did other factors. Cape residents guarded their tradition of independent self-government, exercised through town meeting. Towns controlled decisions over land uses and capital improvements that would open towns—or not—to increased real estate speculation and development. This tradition of municipal self-determination, dating back to the seventeenth century, may have significantly slowed the expansion of the tourist economy in the nineteenth century. Local governments, for example, apparently helped delay the extension of the railroad to Provincetown until 1873. Town meeting allowed wary farmers and other residents to prevent what they may have seen as an unwelcome intrusion.[19]

By the 1890s, however, much was changing. The Upper Cape was a well-known resort area, gaining a national prominence when President Grover Cleveland established his summer White House in Bourne. A new generation of Cape Codders determined to benefit from opportunities that the new century would bring. All of the attractions of the cultural landscape of Cape Cod were waiting to be exploited. They were still viewed alternately as intriguing and

New York, New Haven & Hartford Railroad station, South Orleans, postcard, c. 1900. Wikimedia Commons.

"Santuit Hotel and Cottages, Cotuit," brochure cover, n.d. Local Guide Book Collection, W. B. Nickerson Cape Cod History Archives, Cape Cod Community College.

Railroad wharf, Provincetown, n.d. NPS.

exquisite, and as magnificent and awesome, as Thoreau had described them. And they would finally be fully perceived and then coveted by an immense and more middle class American public—once that public acquired automobiles. In the years following World War I, the mobility made possible by cheap and reliable cars created unprecedented access to all of Cape Cod and opened the region to a distinctly twentieth-century form of tourism. Once tourists could drive Cape roads in their own vehicles, they discovered a new mode of landscape experience—and they discovered Cape Cod. If the Cape had remained obscure longer than other coastal areas, it was about to become the greatest beach of all.

Growing numbers of tourists in cars created an equally large demand for roadside accommodations and services suited to their needs. The construction of vacation cottages, tourist cabins, and roadside businesses drove up land prices. Cape communities that had seen their populations and economies dwindle since before the Civil War were ready to welcome not only automotive tourists but new opportunities to profit from land subdivision, speculation, and development.

Cape Cod would truly "become Cape Cod," as James C. O'Connell puts it in his history of the region's resort development, in the twentieth century. The "golden age" of tourism on the Cape—the era when it wholly assumed its distinct identity as a summer home and vacation mecca—coincided with the rise of the automobile and the recreational opportunities it enabled. Highway improvements and bridge construction sponsored by state and federal governments shaped the pattern and quickened the

Corn Hill, near Provincetown, tourist houses on left. Photo by Edwin Rosskam, August 1940. FSA/OWI.

pace of landscape experience. In the 1890s, the old stagecoach route between Bourne and Provincetown was macadamized, and the location of what would become Route 28 was established to the south. In the first decade of the twentieth century, what was by then called the "State Highway" was paved along the route of what is today Route 6A and the portion of Route 6 from Orleans to Provincetown. In 1935, the Sagamore and Bourne Bridges, subsidized by federal work relief appropriations, provided highway crossings of the Cape Cod Canal (completed in 1914). By that time, there were 136 miles of official state highway and more than 1,000 miles of other paved roads on the Cape. A framework of highway infrastructure was not only in place but was heavily used by thousands of visitors and summer residents in their cars.[20] Passenger rail began its inevitable decline.

The road building and property development well under way by the 1920s would continue through the century. The number of year-round residents in Barnstable County increased from 26,670 in 1920 to 37,295 in 1940, ending the long decline in population (and surpassing the previous highest census figure of 35,990 in 1860).[21] The statistic does not fully indicate the effects of seasonal tourism and new vacation homes, and the summer population probably swelled to several times that of winter. As in Florida and other coastal areas of the country during this period, speculators bought up land, subdivided, and reaped profits. Centered in Hyannis, the boom turned to bust toward the end of the 1920s. But a new economy had been born, based on the availability of undeveloped land and the market for it. Most

"Joining of waters," Cape Cod Canal, 1914. LC.

Sagamore Bridge, 2012. Photo by Matt H. Wade. Wikimedia Commons.

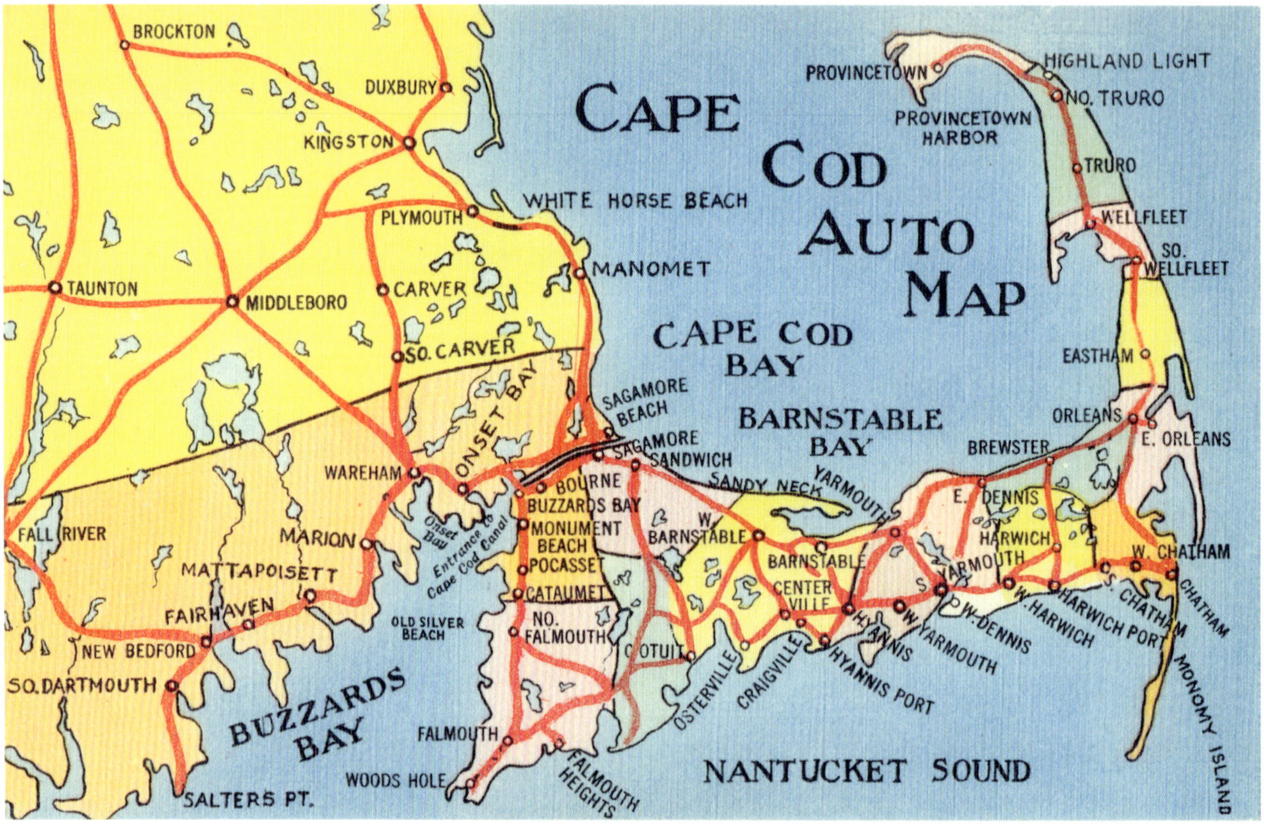

Map of early highways on Cape Cod, postcard, c. 1930–45. BPL.

A new development, Beach Point, North Truro. Photo by Edwin Rosskam, August 1940. FSA/OWI.

large resort hotels soon went the way of the passenger rail service that had been their source of clients. Roadside restaurants, tourist cabins, campgrounds for automotive tourists, vacation homes, and "tourist homes" (residences opened for boarders) replaced them.[22]

The needs and numbers of twentieth-century tourists reshaped the landscape of Cape Cod. The landscape, in turn, influenced a new, regional cultural life. The Cape became the summer residence—and the muse—of many of the greatest artists and writers of the era. Provincetown had been building its reputation as an art colony since Charles Hawthorne opened the

Tourist house, Truro. Photo by Edwin Rosskam, August 1940. FSA/OWI.

Art class, Provincetown. Photo by Edwin Rosskam, August 1940. FSA/OWI.

Cape Cod School of Art in 1899. By 1916 there were five art schools in the town. That year the Provincetown Playhouse opened and began a tradition of major theatrical productions staged in several locations. The Cape became identified with a generation of painters, poets, playwrights, and writers, many from New York, who in summer drew inspiration from the regional landscape and the solitude it afforded them.[23]

Perhaps the most significant creative work of the period, however, might be characterized as a communal reimagining of the Cape Cod cultural landscape itself. Not only artists, writers, and summer vacationers but also native residents, business people, real estate developers, and a new regional chamber of commerce together reinvented Cape Cod as they discovered—and imagined—its history, people, and places. The American public had finally arrived, as Thoreau knew they would, and the Cape Cod they represented and promoted had its origins in the sensibilities that that writer first evinced.

The interwar period produced a diverse and heightened awareness of regional history and landscape character. The three-hundredth anniversary of the Pilgrims' arrival at Provincetown was a cause for commemorative events, and the Cape Cod Tercentenary Commission spent thousands of federal and state dollars on memorials and markers. The interest in colonial origins and lineages was pronounced on the Cape and was an important part of the broader Colonial Revival movement in the United States. The study, restoration, and creative reinvention of historic architecture was a calling for new homeowners and scholars alike. Architects and historical organizations restored scores of historic buildings and structures, including windmills, notably the Eastham windmill in 1920. New inns and other

Commemorative plaque on Corn Hill, with tourist houses, Truro. Photo by Edwin Rosskam, August 1940. FSA/OWI.

The restored windmill, Eastham, 1935. HABS.

businesses adopted variations of Colonial Revival design, which was both popular at the time and deemed appropriate for the increasingly "historical" ambience being created in many towns. The region became an inspiration for architects all over the country, who reproduced the building types and furnishings of "old Cape Cod" for a wide variety of settings and purposes. The "Cape Cod cottage," which captured the public imagination during these years, would be adapted to become one the most common, mass-produced housing types in American history.

Documenting and defining the character of the Cape landscape was a literary as much as an architectural project. A large number of authors developed a place-based literature of guidebooks, histories, and novels. The Cape Cod of maritime industries and ancient origins—the insular society that Thoreau had described and that by now was almost completely gone—became the subject of elaborate reconstructions in an entire genre of historical accounts and fictional narratives that blended summer escapism with an intense interest in the bygone ways of life that had shaped the landscape. From the ethnographic approach of Elizabeth Reynaud, to the historical narratives of Henry C. Kittredge, to the novels of Joseph C. Lincoln, the character of the Cape emerged from the written page as much as it was embodied in sand dunes, beaches, cottages, and windmills.[24]

The economic boom of the 1920s was driven by capital investment attracted by the thousands of tourists who overran what had been until recently a depopulated, economically depressed area. But from the beginning, politicians, business leaders, and property owners also invested in the production and to some degree the preservation of the historical "charm" which they understood constituted, together with scenery, wildlife, and recreational opportunities, the area's unique appeal. The character of the Cape landscape was a subject of active concern and curation, as well as marketing. A 1934 Cape

Cod Chamber of Commerce brochure stated that their organization stood for "the protection of Cape Cod's natural beauties, and the preservation of its charm; for the development of its facilities in an orderly, conservative manner; for the preservation and remembrance of the Cape's glorious history since the Pilgrims landed here in 1620."[25] At that time, with the Great Depression suppressing new construction and the Cape enjoying its "golden age" as an expansive and not yet overcrowded vacation landscape, the balance of development and preservation may indeed have seemed attainable.

But Cape Cod, like many coastal areas in the United States, had only seen the first wave of automotive tourism wash onto its shores. After World War II, a more populous and affluent nation would have the leisure and the means to pursue summer vacations and outdoor recreation as never before. Once again, federal and state governments were quick to encourage the trend. The first section of the Mid-Cape Highway (the modern Route 6) opened in 1950 between Sandwich and Barnstable. Within ten years it was extended to the Orleans Rotary, and the first portion was doubled in capacity.[26] A network of modern highways encouraged new tourist and summer home development everywhere on the Cape, including interior areas as well as the shore. During a period when zoning ordinances and master plans were still controversial and only just gaining acceptance on the Cape, the prerogatives of home rule and town meeting now helped facilitate residential and commercial development on a scale and at a pace without precedent.

By the 1950s, the erosion of the "charm" of Cape Cod was evident to many. The scale and type of construction changed during the postwar era. Midcentury modernism became a dominant architectural idiom, and new, larger motels, restaurants, and other businesses lined busy highways. The numbers of tourists and the extent of roadside and residential construction transformed much of the Cape. Resi-

Atwood-Higgins House, Wellfleet. Photo by author.

Street scene, Provincetown. Photo by Edwin Rosskam, August 1940. FSA/OWI.

Tourists on the street, Provincetown. Photo by Edwin Rosskam, August 1940. FSA/OWI.

dents and summer visitors alike became more aware of the environmental damage that had already been done to fragile dune, wetland, shoreline, and forest ecosystems. At the same time, the "historic character" of the Cape—discovered, admired, and lovingly constructed in the first half of the century—was being overwhelmed. A much larger population of native residents and more recent arrivals faced one of the greatest preservation challenges in the country. At stake were the vital ecosystems and the historic features and characteristics of the entire cultural landscape of Cape Cod.

The resulting efforts by Cape communities, conservationists, and political figures to rescue Cape Cod would make history. Most significantly, Hyannis Port resident Senator John F. Kennedy would cosponsor legislation to authorize the Cape Cod National Seashore, and then sign the bill as president on August 7, 1961. The final legislation was a masterpiece of political compromise that defined a model for a new kind of national park. Some parts of the act were detailed, including the definition of complex boundaries, the rules covering the use of eminent domain in land acquisition, and the extent and type of recreational facilities the National Park Service would provide. In other ways the legislation left much to be decided regarding the seashore's management policies and even its fundamental purpose. The Cape Cod National Seashore Advisory Commission was specified as a means for the park service to collaborate with town governments, residents, and appointed representatives to determine some of these priorities. Their work together over the following decades is an instructive case study of U.S. national park management. Congress, the National Park Service, and the six towns of the Outer Cape (the towns directly affected by the creation of the national sea-

Hauling in a cod aboard a Portuguese fishing dory. Photo by John Collier Jr., Spring 1942. FSA/OWI.

White Crest Beach, Wellfleet. Panoramic view by Matt H. Wade, 2011. Wikimedia Commons.

shore) all entered into an experiment in landscape conservation that continues to this day.

The 1961 legislation stated that "the seashore should be permanently preserved in its present state" and also that its managers should "provide for the public enjoyment and understanding of the unique natural, historic, and scientific features of Cape Cod within the seashore."[27] This straightforward language did not come close addressing the complexities that would ensue. Landscapes always change, both through natural processes and through cultural activities, and the Outer Cape, with shifting dunes and shorelines, fragile habitats, and thousands of years of human history culminating in the postwar boom in tourism and vacation home building, could never be "permanently" kept in a specific moment in time. The many backers of the legislation agreed that the "character" of the Cape was being lost; but the exact qualities and aspects that constituted that character were not, and probably could not, be precisely enumerated in a legislative mandate. What preservationists hoped to save from destruction included not only headlands, dunes, beaches, and wetlands but less tangible resources as well. Since Thoreau's day, the appeal of Cape Cod involved certain experiences, ephemeral moments, chance encounters, and other ineffable qualities that constituted a unique sense of place. The concern and values that were expressed through the national seashore legislation extended to the region's history, occupations, architecture, and agriculture—in other words, to its people, their activities, and their "way of life."

The character of the Cape originally was a function of its isolation and relative poverty. Generations of native residents and visitors alike had then discovered, represented, and described the region as a landscape of leisure and fulfillment. For the thousands of people who spent many idyllic hours experiencing

Cape Cod, the landscape—and their memories of it—became part of their individual and group sense of identity and purpose in life. What the National Park Service, the Cape Cod National Seashore Advisory Commission, and the six towns of the Outer Cape were asked to "manage" in 1961 was a living cultural landscape, valued by many different people and groups, for just as many different reasons.

The experiment began during a period of intense social, environmental, and landscape change. There were precedents, proposals, and studies on which the park service would rely, but the demographic and technological contexts of the mid-twentieth century would challenge them all. "Old Cape Cod" by then was a representation of a representation, a memory of a memory; it had attained the allusive power of myth that remains today. But in a time of population growth and economic prosperity, how could anyone maintain the integrity of a changing landscape that evoked conditions and ways of life that had passed? The character of the Cape was tied to its rich ecologies and the experience of Romantic desolation so consonant with the spirit of Thoreau. Now thousands of Thoreaus combed the Great Beach for

The Great Beach. Photo by M. Woodbridge Williams, c. 1965. NPS.

inspiration, and tens of thousands arrived simply to lie in the sun, or swim, or fish, or drive over-sand vehicles. Could they all be managed? Would there still be room for nesting terns and plovers? These questions only begin to describe the challenges of administering the Cape Cod National Seashore from its inception. These challenges are worthy of study not only for their historical interest, but because they are still being addressed. The goals for the administration of the national seashore remain lofty, worthwhile, and only partially achieved.

Thoreau's *Cape Cod* was published the same year that another great work in the history of American landscape description and conservation was written. In 1865, the landscape architect Frederick Law Olmsted described the "union of the deepest sublimity with the deepest beauty" at Yosemite Valley, a landscape he considered "the greatest glory of nature."[28] Congress had acted the year before to grant the valley to the state of California as a public park. In his report to the new park commission charged with setting management policies, Olmsted described how Yosemite would one day be visited by millions, and therefore development should be as minimal as possible to allow the public to enjoy and appreciate the landscape fully without destroying it. He particularly objected to hotels and any other large buildings that would encroach on the scenery, suggesting that visitors camp instead. He explained that the wet meadows of the valley floor were delicate communities of native plants that would be easily destroyed by cultivation or simply by trampling. As any visitor to Yosemite National Park knows, his recommendations were not followed. His ideas did provide the intellectual framework and justifications for the future national park system in the United States, however, and his report expressed objectives for the preservation and public experience of Yosemite which are still compelling today.

Thoreau did not foresee, nor did he make recommendations for, Cape Cod as a protected, public landscape. His descriptions of the region, however, also contain an influential vision for what he hoped the experience of the Cape could be for visitors such as himself, even in the distant future. His vision was not implemented any more than Olmsted's. But there is no national park more closely associated with Thoreau's philosophy and writing. As in Olmsted's descriptions of Yosemite, Thoreau evokes ideals of the landscape's essential character, and of the public's experience of it, that are as relevant today as ever.

> The time must come when this coast will be a place of resort for those New-Englanders who really wish to visit the seaside. At present it is wholly unknown to the fashionable world, and probably it will never be agreeable to them. If it is merely a ten-pin alley, or a circular railway, or an ocean of mint-julep, that the visitor is in search of,—if he thinks more of the wine than the brine, as I suspect some do at Newport,—I trust that for a long time he will be disappointed here. But this shore will never be more attractive than it is now. Such beaches as are fashionable are here made and unmade in a day, I may almost say, by the sea shifting its sands. Lynn and Nantasket! this bare and bended arm it is that makes the bay in which they lie so snugly. What are springs and waterfalls? Here is the spring of springs, the waterfall of waterfalls. A storm in the fall or winter is the time to visit it; a light-house or a fisherman's hut the true hotel.[29]

PART I

Discovering the Seashore

Head of the Meadow Beach. Photo by Carol Betsch.

ONE

National Parks and National Seashores

The concept of a "national park" has always evoked large tracts of land set aside for the purpose of conserving them in as "natural" condition as possible for the benefit and enjoyment of the American people. The realities of the national park system—and the difficulties of managing its diverse and numerous units—are more complex. The scientific and cultural understanding of what exactly is "natural," for example, has hardly remained static. A generation of scientists and geographers have demonstrated the importance of human history in understanding the condition and functioning of ecological systems.[1] When people are considered part of nature, in this sense, "natural" conditions no longer can be defined simply as the absence of anthropogenic influence, and history must be an aspect of environmental research and management.

Historical research and education have, in fact, always been part of the mandate of the National Park Service. Congress established Mesa Verde National Park in 1906, the same year it passed an act for "the preservation of American antiquities." The Antiquities Act allowed the president to proclaim "national monuments" on federal land that contained "objects of historic or scientific interest."[2] The law led to the preservation of numerous archaeological sites, beginning a commitment at the Department of the Interior to manage cultural heritage. In 1916, Congress established the National Park Service (within the Department of the Interior) and specified the duties of the new bureau. A key portion of the bill, drafted by Olmsted's son, Frederick Law Olmsted Jr., stated that the "the fundamental purpose" of the parks was "to conserve the scenery and the natural and historic objects and the wild life therein and to provide for the enjoyment of the same in such manner and by such means as will leave them unimpaired for the enjoyment of future generations."[3] Over the decades, the number of archaeological and historic sites, battlefields, and other historic landscapes under the care of the park service multiplied. Today a majority of the units of the national park system—under a variety of specific designations—primarily conserve and interpret "historic objects" and cultural heritage.

The National Park Service also was charged with accommodating and facilitating "enjoyment," a term that implied some forms of public recreation. Deciding exactly which forms has consistently provoked contention. Federal designation as a unit of the national park system indicated a national interest in the value and public benefits of a place, a distinction the park service used to elevate the purpose and qualities of recreation planned for national parks. Municipal, county, or state parks were the appropriate places to provide for sports and games. Local governments could build ball fields, golf courses, skating rinks, or swimming pools wherever they were convenient to the populations they served. The primary recreational purpose of a national park involved the outstanding opportunities to appreciate scenery, wildlife, and history that federal designation signified.

National parks were not intended to serve local recreational needs, but rather offered specific experiences that could not be easily attained elsewhere. "Enjoyment" of these national landscapes profoundly affected individual well-being and sense of identity and contributed to national historical narratives supported through their creation. The fundamental theory behind these policies went back, again, to the ideas and writings of the elder Olmsted, who in his 1865 Yosemite report described the purposes of public landscape reservations in these terms. There were certain places, such as Yosemite Valley, which because of the extraordinary experiences of landscape beauty they offered needed to remain (or become) public property. (Fig. 1.1) Otherwise the benefits of such experiences—which Olmsted described as necessary for the well-being of society as well as of individuals—would be monopolized by the wealthy few, to the profound detriment of the nation.

In the 1920s, the park service accordingly organized its policies for managing the development and expansion of the national park system. The national parks needed to be open to the public, and by that time this was understood to mean a public in cars.[4] The design and development of roads, campgrounds, trails, accommodations, and park museums all suited to the needs of the automotive tourist became a primary objective for the new National Park Service. The bureau's landscape architects initiated the era of "rustic" architecture and site development which not only facilitated automotive tourism but created mediating landscapes that presented the scenery and history of the national park system through a consistent design idiom which itself became an identifying and appreciated dimension of the national park experience. Log and boulder buildings, scenic roads, and restored or reconstructed historic sites introduced and connected visitors to magnificent scenery, intricate ecologies, and deliberate histories.[5]

While at Cape Cod an analogous elaboration of the cultural landscape emerged independently, through artistic and literary production and chamber of commerce promotion, in the national parks the park service employed organized educational initiatives that were its second most significant early priority. The greater potential of park landscapes for public education was another attribute that set them apart from local parks and reservations. Educational programs were under way in several parks already by 1920, and three years later Stephen Tyng Mather, the first director of the National Park Service, created an "education division" and gave it an equal place in his agency's organizational structure with the other two main divisions, "landscape architecture" and "engineering." National park educational efforts at first emphasized natural history and, in parks such as Mesa Verde, ethnography and archaeology. (Fig. 1.2) After the transfer of jurisdiction of dozens of historic sites and monuments to the park service in 1933, however, historical research and education became necessary and critical tasks as the agency became the steward of some of the country's most

Fig. 1.1. Yosemite Falls, Yosemite National Park. Photo by Carol M. Highsmith. CHA.

Fig. 1.2. "Cliff Palace, Mesa Verde," Mesa Verde National Park. Photo by Photochrome Co., 1898. LC.

revered shrines. The Historic Sites Act of 1935 codified new research and education responsibilities for the agency and directed it to develop public educational programs pertaining to "historic and archaeological sites, buildings, and properties of national significance."[6]

By the 1930s, landscape conservation, the facilitation of recreation, and the interpretation of natural and cultural history were all integrated into the "master plan" approach that guided development and management in every unit of the national park system. From memorial battlefields to presidential homes, and from pre-Columbian archaeological sites to western mountain expanses, the park system exhibited a range of national landscapes. Within the geographic and typological variety, however, the centralized administration of the park service enforced consistent policies, administration, and design standards and details. This was what a "system" implied: a consistent set of values and approaches to management for a diverse and far-flung group of exceptional places.

The federal legislation that established each unit of the system individually bestowed a wide variety of specific designations and individual mandates. "National park" was only one such designation, and was used for reservations such as Platt (Oklahoma) and Hot Springs (Arkansas), as well as Mesa Verde, Yellowstone, and Yosemite. Congress was not consistent regarding nomenclature. Many units of the system began life as "national monuments," which could be proclaimed by quick presidential action, and later (in many cases, much later) could be made national parks when Congress passed the required legislation. Some places that clearly might be considered national parks still remain national monuments. Other categories were unique, such as Gettysburg National Military Park, while others were introduced, including "national historical parks" and "national memorials." (Figs. 1.3, 1.4) The establishment of national parks has always been a political process and has proceeded on a case by case basis, with a resulting diversity of official designations.[7] But as units of

Fig. 1.3. Gettysburg National Military Park. Photo by Carol M. Highsmith. CHA.

Fig. 1.4. Madison Museum, Yellowstone National Park (built in 1929), 1983. Photo by Jet Lowe. HABS.

the national park system, all were subject to a set of policies that allowed for public access, appropriate forms of recreation (hopefully), education (by the 1940s described as "interpretation"), and, above all, a commitment to conserve park landscapes and their natural and cultural resources "unimpaired" for future generations.

All units of the national park system, in other words, were "parks," in the sense that they shared the management objectives and overall standards and purposes of the system.[8] To a greater or lesser degree, they also all contained cultural as well as natural resources, and they all were open to the public for its "benefit and enjoyment." As the park system dramatically expanded in the 1930s, however, many additions to the system were clearly valued primarily for their historical associations, such as Civil War battlefields and historic houses. Others were engineered primarily to serve the growing appetite for what park planners called "outdoor recreation." Most park service officials saw this as a healthy expansion and strengthening of the system. Many historic sites were in the East, where most of the population still lived and where there had always been fewer national parks. And at least some forms of popular outdoor recreation—especially swimming, boating, and other water-related activities—were better served by areas developed specifically for these purposes, which might reduce pressure to accommodate them in less appropriate settings.

The catalyst for this expansion was the New Deal that President Franklin D. Roosevelt launched in 1933. The National Park Service, which had been preparing "master plans" for all of its parks, was in a unique position as "emergency conservation work" began in virtually every state and national park. As a result of federal spending and the natural fit between many New Deal programs and the park service's expertise and personnel, the national park system grew in size and variety, gaining responsibility for dozens of historic sites, battlefields, and national monuments. The bureau planned for the recreational uses of public lands under different jurisdictions, through cooperative relationships with other federal agencies and state and local park authorities. New kinds of parks were instituted, including the "recreational demonstration area," the "national recreation area," and in 1937, at Cape Hatteras (North Carolina), the first "national seashore."[9]

The expansion of the national park system to include areas that emphasized outdoor recreation was a result of the increased role of the park service in not only New Deal programs, such as the Civilian Conservation Corps (CCC), but the larger responsibility it assumed in "national planning" initiatives in Washington. The chief federal "recreational planner" was a young landscape architect, Conrad L. Wirth, who in 1933 was put in charge of the CCC planning and design work that the National Park Service supervised for state park commissions. (Fig. 1.5) Wirth was the son of the well-known Minneapolis park superintendent Theodore Wirth and had trained at the Massachusetts Agricultural College (now the University of Massachusetts Amherst) in the 1920s. In 1928, after his private practice declined with the economy, his father's friend Frederick Law Olmsted Jr. helped place him in a job with the National Capital Park and Planning Commission in Washington. From there he transferred to the National Park Service in 1931.

Fig. 1.5. Conrad L. Wirth (right) in 1937, speaking with CCC director Robert Fechner (seated). Harris & Ewing Collection, LC.

As his state park program grew after 1933, Wirth oversaw the expansion of dozens of state park systems and the development of hundreds of parks. Various New Deal programs contributed funds for the acquisition of land and the construction of park buildings. "Recreational demonstration areas" took several forms, but most accommodated organizations that operated summer camps for children. Most of these model state parks reverted to state jurisdiction in 1942. Wirth also collaborated with other federal agencies. In 1934, the Bureau of Reclamation was assigned nine CCC camps with the stipulation that the park service would oversee the development of recreational facilities and create "national recreation areas" around new reservoirs.[10] This was another significant departure for the agency. The park service had always fought against dam construction within the national park system as a particularly egregious form of "impairment." The new recreation areas were not in preexisting national parks but would become part of the national system as the reservoirs were opened to the public for swimming and boating. The potential was great; Lake Mead, which was slowly filling behind the new Boulder (Hoover) Dam, would eventually have 550 miles of shoreline offering recreational opportunities close to Las Vegas. The first national park of its type, in 1936 the area was designated the Boulder Dam (later Lake Mead) National Recreation Area.[11]

As the park service's mission expanded, so did Wirth's responsibilities. Now head of the park service's "branch of planning," he organized a national survey of "outdoor recreational resources" and a state-by-state plan for national, state, and local parks. Classes of "recreational areas" were described as a spectrum from "primitive" areas, or the most inaccessible wilderness, to "developed," such as the new recreation areas. The park planners assembled data on topography, geology, climate, biology, history, and social and economic factors to prepare their report on the potential of different regions for outdoor recreation of every kind.[12] The scope of this national land use survey and the resulting plan, published in summary form in 1941, were unprecedented.[13]

For the New Deal planners, "recreation" included all "constructive uses of leisure time." The settings of these activities were just as varied, from "far-away wildernesses" to "the nearby pastoral landscape." Wirth and his park service colleagues assembled data and created plans for a great deal more than state park systems, addressing the entire "problem" of preserving and providing a full range of opportunities for public outdoor recreation. The concept of a series of "national seashores" to be added to the national park system came out of this rich period of national planning for outdoor recreation. Wirth and his branch of land planning conducted studies of coastal areas along the Atlantic and the Gulf of Mexico in 1934 and 1935, and soon conducted a similar survey of the Pacific Coast. The result was a recommendation that twelve seashore areas—including Cape Cod—would qualify as new national parks, and another thirty as state parks. But in 1937, Congress authorized only one new seashore park, Cape Hatteras National Seashore.[14]

The expansion of the park service into new categories of parks alarmed some park advocates who feared that the original intent to preserve scenic and wild places would be undermined or even violated by the agency's embrace of federally funded park development. Robert Sterling Yard, Robert Marshall, and Rosalie Edge, among others, represented early environmental advocacy organizations that insisted that the park service should emphasize its responsibility to preserve "primeval wilderness" rather than focus on the opportunities to plan and develop new types of parks for outdoor recreation.[15] But for Conrad Wirth, and for most New Deal planners and park administrators, "recreation" was not so narrowly construed. It included all forms of leisure enjoyment, including hiking and stock trips in wilderness areas, as well as camping, boating, and other activities in more accessible locations.

National planning for recreation implied that some parks—such as the new state parks and national recreation areas—would be more heavily developed for large numbers of people arriving in cars to picnic, swim, hike, and pursue other outdoor activities. Other park areas would be rigorously protected from the development such uses implied. The goals were not antagonistic so long as planners bore in mind the distinction. And park service planners and landscape architects felt that they were specifically qualified to delineate master plans that assured the correct balance and appropriate types of use.[16]

The park service mandate, like that of the CCC and to some degree the entire New Deal, was to conserve both human and natural resources during a period that seemed to threaten both. Wirth and his planners saw no inherent conflict between recreation and preservation as long as both were provided for in comprehensive park master plans—and even a national plan—that they devised. From their point of view, critics who wanted to break up the national park system into primeval, recreational, and presumably historical systems may have had good intentions, but they had lost faith in the broader project of conceiving and enlarging comprehensive park systems. Planning for outdoor recreation was not part of a separate mandate; it was the mandate. And it included conserving wilderness areas and natural resources, as well as interpreting history and providing facilities for swimming, boating, and other increasingly popular forms of recreation.

Rather than divide the park system by the types of "enjoyment" the parks offered, New Deal planners were more concerned with making distinctions between what places possessed the resources and opportunities that qualified them to be part of the national system, and which were better managed by state and local park authorities. Comprehensive surveys of natural resources, scenery, and historical associations could be used to identify truly outstanding places that possessed these attributes to a degree of national significance. A national recreation area, for example, might remain part of the national system because it offered recreational opportunities at a national scale (and, of course, was already under federal jurisdiction because the Bureau of Reclamation had created the reservoirs). The state parks developed under park service supervision remained under state jurisdiction, or were transferred to the states if the land had been acquired through federal spending by other New Deal agencies. They possessed important scenic and historic resources as well, but not at the level of national significance; the landscapes themselves drew more of a local constituency of users and were not of outstanding or unique significance when considered in a national context. If this process established a standard for considering additions to the national park system, passing national park legislation nevertheless remained inherently political: a national park was, in the end, what Congress said it was.

In the case of seashores, rampant residential and resort development in Florida, the Gulf Coast, Cape Cod, and elsewhere had already made it difficult to consider many areas for public acquisition and park designation. The inherent limitation of the amount of coastline available made any remaining relatively undeveloped beaches especially crucial to consider for new national and state parks. Opportunities for recreation (whether at a local or national level) were only one part of the equation. Seashores appropriate for inclusion in the national park system would also contain rich natural resources and habitat, outstanding scenery, and important historical sites. They would be national parks, in the sense that they were intended to conserve and interpret resources of national significance, for the benefit and enjoyment of a national public. From the beginning, park service officials would debate a variety of names and purposes for "national beach parks," but in all cases they would insist that such additions to the national park system would not be limited to a narrow strip of popular beaches and their attendant recreational facilities. Such purely recreational areas should be left to states and municipalities to develop and manage. Federal designation would imply a balance between the conservation of nationally significant resources with the provision of recreational opportunities serving more than local visitors.

The Outer Banks of North Carolina became a proving ground for the National Park Service as it invented this new kind of national park. The long, narrow string of sandy peninsulas and barrier islands of the Outer Banks extends the length of the North Carolina coast, and in its northern portion reaches far out into the Atlantic, separated from the mainland by Pamlico Sound and vast marshes

Fig. 1.6. Aerial view of Okracoke Island, 2011. Photo by Karen L. M. Morgan / USGS.

teeming with fish and wildlife. (Figs. 1.6, 1.7, 1.8) There were many parallels to Cape Cod. Cape Hatteras, at an easternmost point of the Outer Banks, was a formidable menace to coastal shipping—another "graveyard of the Atlantic"—and as at Cape Cod, the federal government had erected early lighthouses and life-saving stations to mitigate the hazard. The Outer Banks was also a site of early English settlement, on Roanoke Island, where the ill-fated Roanoke Colony was established and quickly met its mysterious end in the 1580s.

But through its subsequent history, most of the Outer Banks remained far more isolated than Cape Cod, particularly in its remote northern portion. Ocracoke and Hatteras Islands, for example, were still without bridges or a paved road system in the 1930s, and the population of less than two thousand was concentrated in a few fishing settlements. Real estate prices had always been low, a fact that had encouraged a few wealthy families and sportsmen to acquire large tracts for private hunting and recreation. With the onset of the Depression land values fell even further, and some landowners were ready to sell or donate land for park purposes.[17] Up until then, at least, the North Carolina coast had yet to receive the onslaught of automotive tourism

Fig. 1.7. Cape Hatteras National Seashore, North Carolina. Photo by Carol M. Highsmith. CHA.

Fig. 1.8. Bayside wetlands, Cape Hatteras National Seashore, 2013. Photo by Jason Hollinger. Wikimedia Commons.

and resort development that so many other coastal areas had.

For these reasons, Roger W. Toll, the superintendent of Yellowstone National Park and one of the park service officials surveying coastal areas in 1934, considered the Outer Banks "most suited to development as a national ocean beach." Toll often investigated the suitability of proposed national park areas, and he reported that year that the region was "primitive in character," with few summer homes and no resort developments. Real estate values were correspondingly low, despite the fact that the area was within a day's drive from metropolitan areas such as Norfolk and Raleigh. Following Toll's report, the park service's chief landscape architect, Thomas C. Vint, visited the Outer Banks with architect Charles E. Peterson and assistant director Hillory A. Tolson. As important advisers to then–park service director Arno C. Cammerer, they concurred with Toll's observations, noting that "the Cape Hatteras area is decidedly interesting and important enough to justify its inclusion in the National Park system." They recommended acquiring a large area including all of Hatteras and Ocracoke (except the existing villages), replanting areas to control erosion, and limiting the construction of roads to preserve the "wilderness character of the area."[18] In addition to the significant scenery, natural resources, and recreational opportunities of the Outer Banks, the officials also remarked on the landscape's significant historical sites and associations. The Kill Devil Hills National Monument (later the Wright Brothers National Memorial) was created in 1927 to memorialize the site of the first sustained powered airplane flight, and Fort Raleigh, on Roanoke Island, was declared a national historic site in 1941.[19] (Fig. 1.9)

It remained unclear, however, how a "national coastal park," or "national beach park," would fit into the system and what fundamental purposes and management policies should be described for it. In

Fig. 1.9. Wright Brothers National Memorial, Kill Devil Hills, North Carolina. Photo by Carol M. Highsmith. CHA.

his history of the Cape Hatteras National Seashore, Cameron Binkley describes considerable dissension at the park service as planners and officials expressed different concerns and aspirations for how a federal role in coastal conservation should take shape. Arno Cammerer, for example, responded to his planners' report in 1935 by insisting that Cape Hatteras should be considered a type of recreational area, perhaps, but did not meet the qualifications of a "national park." Tolson disagreed, insisting that as "probably the outstanding example of a type of characteristic scenery not now preserved in a national park," it met the "standard prescribed for national parks." Park service scientists, such as George M. Wright, expressed concern that national park designation would inevitably lead to roads, parking lots, accommodations, and other plans that would diminish the wilderness character of the Outer Banks and damage fragile ecosystems.[20] Landscape architects such as Wirth and Vint would argue that an influx of tourists and cars was inevitable, and that by creating a national seashore park, conservation and recreation could be balanced to achieve both better preservation of resources and a more meaningful public experience than would occur if the area were left in private ownership.

In the meantime, local park advocates, notably the artist and local real estate agent Frank L. Stick, together with North Carolina state officials, supported the creation of a national park, which they knew would bring in CCC camps and other federal funds and programs to both conserve and develop the Outer Banks. Increased tourism would also be a welcome boost to the state's economy during the Depression. Stick was already acting to secure substantial gifts of land for park purposes from fellow property owners on the Outer Banks, and the North Carolina legislature passed a bill authorizing a state commission to begin acquiring property with the intent of later transferring it to the federal government. Soon several CCC camps were at work in dune stabilization and revegetation projects. (Fig. 1.10)

Stick promoted the historical, scenic, and natural resources of the area to the park service, urging that federal legislation be drawn up to create a "Cape Hatteras Coastal Park." Stick was an avid sportsman himself and emphasized the importance of waterfowl hunting as a major draw for the new park, causing further confusion for park planners since hunting was typically banned in national parks. But whatever qualms park service officials may have had, in 1935, both the North Carolina governor and the state's congressional delegation wanted the project to move forward quickly in order to take advantage of federal emergency spending programs. Representative Lindsay C. Warren worked with the park service to draft legislation, which he then introduced. In 1937, Roosevelt signed the act authorizing the "Cape Hatteras National Seashore."[21]

Cape Hatteras National Seashore was a first for the national park system and would set many important precedents, some of which still required further development and resolution before it would be clear exactly what the guiding policies of the new park would be. In his letter endorsing the national seashore, for example, Secretary of the Interior Oscar L. Chapman wrote that the new unit of the national park system would be "preserved as a primitive wilderness, except for swimming, boating, sailing, fishing, and other recreational activities of a similar nature," apparently confident that this language (taken from the legislation authorizing the park) did not present insurmountable conflicts. He noted that the 150-mile stretch of sand beaches had a powerful appeal for a large and diverse public, but that the area also comprised critical habitat for waterfowl and migratory birds. There were significant "historical values" in or near the new park, such as Kill Devil Hills and Fort Raleigh, but overall Cape Hatteras was "particularly adapted to concentrated

Fig. 1.10. Planting American beach grass on the Outer Banks in 1938. NPS, Cape Hatteras National Seashore.

use for water sports, so necessary for the densely populated sections of the central eastern seaboard."[22] An amendment to the legislation specified the extent of hunting to be allowed, and commercial fishing would continue from the villages of the Outer Banks, which were not included within park boundaries. The national seashore, as described in 1937, would clearly be a complex management challenge, and one with no precedent in the national park system up to that point.

But in one important way the legislation authorizing Cape Hatteras retained a well-established approach to creating new national parks: congressional appropriations for the acquisition of property were forbidden. The legal establishment of the park would therefore depend on the donation of land and structures from the State of North Carolina.[23] Congress, in fact, had never appropriated funds for the direct acquisition of private property to create a new federal park. Western parks had typically been set aside out of lands already in the public domain, simply by retaining them in federal ownership. But creating a new national park out of private lands (usually the case in the East) required that a state government (or individuals) first acquire the land and then grant it to the federal government. Shenandoah National Park in Virginia, for example, was authorized in 1926, along with Great Smoky Mountains and Mammoth Cave National Parks; but the establishment of the new park would not occur until a long and contentious process of land acquisition was completed by the State of Virginia, which then transferred jurisdiction to the park service in 1935.[24]

The delay in land acquisition at Cape Hatteras would be even longer, despite the low cost of land and the early work of Frank Stick in securing promises and donations from Outer Banks landowners. Once the authorizing legislation was signed, the State of

North Carolina held off making the necessary land purchases to reach the total minimum acreage required by the legislation for the official establishment of the park. The American entry into World War II brought an end to CCC activities, and still the state legislature had made little progress in land acquisition. After the war, the prospect of offshore oil wells and the potential of resort developments on the Outer Banks further complicated the political situation, prevented further land acquisition, and endangered the entire park project.[25]

Conrad Wirth, who became director of the park service in 1951, was forced to substantially reduce the size of the Cape Hatteras proposal because of postwar resort development and accompanying increases in land prices. Local interests in North Carolina also insisted on a more developed road system and other concessions as the national seashore proposal was significantly reconceived. In 1952, armed with redrawn and more realistic boundaries as well as cost estimates, Wirth overcame considerable local opposition to the establishment of the seashore and revitalized interest on the part of the state in acquiring the needed acreage. But he would not have succeeded without the fortuitous involvement of the philanthropist Paul Mellon, who contacted the park service director that year regarding potential funding for national park land acquisition in the Outer Banks region from the Mellon family's charitable foundations.

Mellon was a resident of Virginia and recognized that if the Cape Hatteras national park plans were delayed any longer, the opportunity would be lost forever. Wirth leveraged Mellon's offer to convince the governor and state officials in North Carolina to provide matching funds for land purchases. The project proceeded through a cooperative agreement in which the park service was in charge of the acquisition process using state and private funding. Once the legal minimum threshold of ten thousand acres under park service jurisdiction was finally surpassed, the bureau had the authority to establish the Cape Hatteras National Seashore, which it did at the beginning of 1953, while further acreage was still being acquired.[26]

Still, this was only the beginning of the creation of the new national park. Park visitor facilities, roads, and all the other aspects of park development still needed to be planned, designed, and funded. A new master plan was begun in 1954, but the moment was not an auspicious one for any ambitious construction plans. The New Deal programs, which had been a vast source of funding for park development and operation since 1933, ended abruptly with the American entry into World War II. After the end of the war, the park service struggled with the combined effect of the loss of New Deal spending and the CCC and flat or declining appropriations. At the same time, the national park system—along with many other scenic and recreational destinations—experienced greatly increased numbers of visitors.

Postwar Americans had more leisure time and the affluence to enjoy it, and the national parks experienced an era of exponential growth in visitors and popularity.[27] But the park service remained at prewar levels of funding, unable even to staff the now-inadequate facilities it had built mostly in the 1920s and 1930s. Congress, preoccupied with postwar priorities and then war in Korea, showed few signs of making an investment in the national parks anything like it had during the New Deal. The result was what park service director Newton B. Drury described in 1949 as "the dilemma of our parks": overcrowded and understaffed, the national parks often lacked even basic utilities and amenities adequate for the levels of use they were experiencing.[28]

Cape Hatteras required an entire program of buildings, utilities, roads, and other public facilities at a time when the condition of the park system had reached a nadir. The park service managed Cape

Hatteras during its first years as best it could, using available existing buildings for visitor contact and services. The Mellon family foundations also funded resource and management studies needed as a basis for devising the best policies for preserving the delicate shoreline and its ecosystems while facilitating large numbers of visitors who wanted automobile access and opportunities for recreation.[29]

But the situation for Cape Hatteras, and for the entire park system, was about to change radically. After years of suffering bad press about the poor condition of the park system and congressional indifference to the situation, Conrad Wirth organized a massive response to the postwar "dilemma" that was now his responsibility to address. In 1955, he gathered his staff in Washington and in a matter of months assembled an ambitious ten-year plan for the modernization and expansion of the entire national park system. Wirth called the plan "Mission 66," and brought it to the attention of President Eisenhower and Congress the next year, hoping to greatly increase his bureau's appropriations in order to achieve a complete rehabilitation and redevelopment of the park system by 1966, the fiftieth anniversary of the National Park Service.

The core of the proposal was a series of park "prospectuses," prepared by park staff but overseen and approved by Wirth and his planners, that detailed the outstanding needs of every national park, along with cost estimates and revised master plans. Over the next ten years, more than $1 billion was spent on national parks, making the period the most significant since the New Deal for the development and expansion of the national park system. To this day, many national parks still rely on the public buildings, roads, maintenance facilities, park housing, campgrounds, and utilities that Mission 66 made possible.[30]

Cape Hatteras was in a position to be an early prototype for the new master planning principles and design standards that would consistently identify Mission 66 park projects. The first national seashore now became one of the first parks to be planned and developed under the aegis of Mission 66. Typical of many of the initiative's prospectuses, the new plans called for increased automotive access and a series of "visitor centers," or combined visitor-contact and administration buildings. This new building type, developed by Wirth and his in-house staff of architects and landscape architects, was intended to supply basic services and interpretive programs efficiently to large numbers of people arriving in automobiles. (Fig. 1.11)

The visitor center acknowledged the reality of widespread automobile ownership and the public's desire to use their cars to facilitate vacations and recreational activities. While prewar park planning had often been centered on overnight lodges and other accommodations, Mission 66 prospectuses usually indicated a shift to "day trips" into the parks, with nearby (or "gateway") towns providing for the increased demand for motels, gas stations, and other tourist needs. The new visitor centers served day-trippers, in other words, by efficiently intercepting large numbers of people in cars and assuring that they all received orientation, contact with a park ranger, and other services intended to make their visit both meaningful and convenient. Other basic infrastructure was budgeted in the Mission 66 prospectuses, including paved roads and parking lots, park staff housing, maintenance areas, and visitor facilities including (in the case of Cape Hatteras) public beaches, restrooms, picnic areas, and campgrounds. As a result of Mission 66 annual budget increases, the basic infrastructure of Cape Hatteras National Seashore was in place by 1958, the year the park was officially dedicated (it was "established" in 1953) in a large opening ceremony attended by Wirth, Paul Mellon, North Carolina state officials, and other elected officials and dignitaries.[31]

Fig. 1.11. Wright Brothers National Memorial Visitor Center (1960), North Carolina. NPS.

By the time the country's first national seashore was officially up and running, the subject of coastal conservation had become one of the most important priorities for the expansion of the national park system under Mission 66. This was due in part, again, to the generosity of Paul Mellon and his sister Ailsa Bruce, who through their family foundations had funded a second park service survey of the Atlantic and Gulf Coasts in 1954. The results of the survey were completed the next year, just before Mission 66 planning began.[32] Of the areas recommended for public acquisition just twenty years earlier, all had been lost to private resort, residential, and commercial development, except two: Cape Hatteras National Seashore and the Great Beach of Cape Cod. (Fig. 1.12) Later printed in summary form under the title *Our Vanishing Shoreline,* the 1955 survey documented exactly that: the stunning pace of postwar development of coastal areas.[33]

And yet authorizing legislation for new seashore parks still did not occur. Unless Congress proved willing to break with tradition and fund the direct acquisition of land for the creation of new park areas, there was no way to proceed with ambitious plans for national seashores. The lesson of Cape Hatteras was clear in that regard. The complexities of multiple uses and priorities, local and state politics, and the economic pressures of other potential forms of development made such comprehensive park planning—and particularly land acquisition—extremely difficult in popular seashore destinations. The new coastal survey recommended sixteen new areas for consideration, including (again) Cape Cod. But at least during the initial phase of Mission 66, Congress passed no new seashore legislation, much to Wirth's frustration and despite his recommendations. "The lesson is all around us," he wrote in June 1961, with the experience of Cape Hatteras in mind and the future of the Outer Cape about to be decided. "We can no longer depend on private philanthropy, [and] State donations . . . to meet our park and recreational requirements. . . . We got our national park system the easy way. . . . From now on they are going to cost money, and a great deal of it. . . . The time is now. Ten years will be too late."[34]

Wirth knew that to implement national sea-

Fig. 1.12. Fencing and dunes, Cape Hatteras National Seashore. Photo by Elaine Leslie / NPS, 2007. Wikimedia Commons.

shore plans on a large scale, a major change would need to occur in Congress's attitude toward the creation of national parks: federal funds for direct land acquisition would need to be made available. Cape Cod, which was now prioritized as first on the new list of seashores to be conserved, would become that turning point. For Wirth, who had come to detest the "beg, borrow, or steal" system of park land acquisition (epitomized by Cape Hatteras), the Cape Cod legislation would be a "milestone." He wrote in his memoirs that "it took from March 1, 1872, the date Yellowstone National Park was established, until August 7, 1961, the date of authorization of Cape Cod National Seashore," for Congress finally to acknowledge that "the preservation of our national heritage for the benefit of the people, present and future, is an important federal responsibility that deserves spending federal money to buy the land that will make such preservation possible."[35]

The creation and development of the Cape Cod National Seashore would be inextricably tied to the successes and failures of the Mission 66 program. During its early years, Mission 66 was greeted as a tremendous boon. The carefully planned and budgeted proposal had loosened Congress's purse strings and allowed for the redevelopment of dozens of national parks. But by 1958, critics at the Sierra Club, the National Parks Association, and other early environmental groups had come to oppose what they felt was the "overdevelopment" of the national parks. Mission 66 was going too far to accommodate automotive tourism, they felt, without addressing critical resource management issues that threatened the integrity of the system. Beginning in January 1961, the changes brought about by the Kennedy administration, in particular by Kennedy's secretary of the interior, Stewart L. Udall, meant that Mission 66 proceeded under revised conditions.

In 1962, Udall created the Bureau of Outdoor Recreation within the Department of the Interior, an agency that assumed many of the recreational planning duties of the park service. Wirth would be forced into retirement in 1964, two years before his program was completed. The changed circumstances of the early 1960s both altered the trajectory of Mission 66 and made possible some of its most important accomplishments—notably the Cape Cod National Seashore legislation—which might have never have been realized if Kennedy had not been elected. At the same time, the "New Conservation" agenda initiated by Udall was the beginning of the end for Wirth and Mission 66. And yet the creation of the Cape Cod National Seashore, with its unprecedented federal funding for land acquisition, the use (and restrictions on the use) of eminent domain, and the other aspects of what would come to be called the "Cape Cod formula," or the "Cape Cod model," would be a signal achievement of Mission 66.

The success of this new model of landscape protection would lead to the establishment of eleven more national seashores, all of which had been planned under Mission 66. The long and difficult creation of Cape Hatteras National Seashore had been a transition: both the first of a new type and a last example of a traditional park service approach to park planning. Cape Cod would be the first of an entirely new method of large-scale landscape protection, one which directly influenced the largest recreational planning initiatives of the era and which established precedents that continue to shape such efforts to the present day.

The social and political contexts for conservation efforts were entirely different in Massachusetts from what they had been in North Carolina, and these differences greatly affected the nature of the legislation passed in 1961. The history and character of the Cape Cod region had been the subject of preservation concerns since, if not Thoreau's day, certainly since the 1890s, when the Province Lands, the state-owned area around Provincetown on the Outer Cape, was the subject of conservation plans and legislation initiated by a Massachusetts land trust, The Trustees of Public Reservations. The long and storied history of the communities and ways of life of Cape Cod—the awareness and concern for Cape Cod as a cultural landscape—shaped the preservation campaign of the 1950s in ways that had not been evident in the case of Cape Hatteras. The Cape Cod formula of landscape conservation would be crafted as much by local advocates and the congressional staff of the sponsoring legislators as it was by the National Park Service. The result would be both one of the great achievements in that agency's history and also a radical departure for it.

The success of the new model introduced nothing less than a new planning culture at the park service, one that would require real community outreach and partnership, an enhanced role for an official citizens' advisory commission, and more effective cooperation with the owners of private property within park boundaries. These and other initiatives described in the Cape Cod legislation were foreign to the planners and landscape architects at the park service. New occasions taught new duties. The National Park Service had to adapt to an entirely new way of doing business—breaking many of its traditional rules—in order to make Cape Cod and the other national seashore projects of the 1960s work. This was happening at a time when the culture of the park service was already changing, as Mission 66 came under fire and Wirth and his generation of New Deal recreational planners were retiring and losing influence. The experience of creating and managing Cape Cod National Seashore set the agency on new paths, and permanently changed how large-scale landscape conservation would be practiced in the United States thereafter.

View from Fort Hill Trail, Eastham. Photo by Carol Betsch.

TWO

Early Land Conservation on Cape Cod

There were many important differences between the Cape Cod and Cape Hatteras national seashore proposals, beginning with the history of advocacy for the creation of each of the parks. The first efforts to protect the landscape of Cape Cod predated the park service—and even the federal government—and arose from some of the earliest land conservation efforts in North America.[1] The Province Lands, a landscape of beach grass, dunes, and stunted pine forests north of Provincetown, was described in the 1622 narrative *Mourt's Relation* as "sand hils, much like the Downes in Holland, but much better; the crust of the earth a Spits depth, excellent blacke earth; all wooded with Okes, Pines, Sassafras, Juniper, Birch, Holly, Vines, and some Ash, Walnut."[2] At that point, much of Cape Cod was covered in forest, with the exception of beaches and dunes, salt marshes, and areas such as Fort Hill which indigenous people had cultivated for centuries.

In 1661, the governor of the Plymouth Colony asserted public ownership of the tip of Cape Cod as common land, following the colony's purchase of the area from the Nauset tribe in 1654. Plymouth Colony used its title as the basis for leasing fishing rights to the fishermen who operated out of Provincetown Harbor. In 1727, the Massachusetts General Court established the Town of Provincetown, which had grown along the wharves and slips of the harbor; but the court specified that Massachusetts still owned the entire area, which was now referred to as the "province lands."[3] Residents were allowed to use the Province Lands for wood cutting and any other purpose related to the fishing industry.

Grazing and wood cutting, however, had already transformed much of the area. By 1725, it was described as a desert, with its soils replaced by shifting sand dune formations. Sand from the area silted in the harbor and also blew into fields in Provincetown and Truro, in some cases making them unfit for cultivation. Repeatedly in the eighteenth century, the General Court passed measures intended to mitigate erosion, forbidding grazing and the removal of any trees within a half mile of the high-water mark. Residents were required to plant beach grass (*Ammoph-*

Fig. 2.1. Province Lands, Provincetown, 2003. Photo by author.

ila breviligulata) each spring, and they also planted scotch broom (*Cytisus scoparius*), pines (*Pinus spp.*), bayberry (*Myrica pennsylvanica*), and buckwheat (*Fagopyrum esculentum*). These efforts continued through the nineteenth century, and included federal funding for the planting of beach grass and other measures intended to maintain the viability of Provincetown Harbor. In 1854, the legislature again asserted the state's ownership of the Province Lands, as part of continuing (and futile) efforts to control the wood gathering and grazing that were blamed for erosion.[4] (Fig. 2.1)

The Province Lands was a unique reservation in Massachusetts, with mandated conservation practices and a proscription on most private development. Although Provincetown grew in a strip along the harbor, more than four thousand acres remained undeveloped and under state ownership and (limited) management. (Fig. 2.2) Eventually the Province Lands constituted a significant portion of the Cape Cod National Seashore, when jurisdiction over the area was transferred to the National Park Service.

Other early conservation statutes in Massachusetts affected the landscape of Cape Cod. The Massachusetts General Court protected public access to the colony's "Great Ponds" through ordinances of

Fig. 2.2. Provincetown and harbor, n.d. NPS.

Fig. 2.3. Back Bay Fens, 1910–20. Detroit Publishing Company Collection, LC.

1641–1647, which prohibited private ownership of ponds over ten acres and protected the public's right to use them as common property. The same laws extended the rights of littoral (tidal shoreline) property owners to the mean low-water mark, while preserving the public's right to the use and navigation of tidal waters. The public also retained the right to traverse the area between the high-tide and low-tide watermarks—the "foreshore"—for "fishing and fowling," uses that courts later extended to include general recreational access, except in specific cases. These provisions, interpreted and upheld over the centuries, remain part of Massachusetts water law.[5]

In the nineteenth century, conservationists and landscape architects in Massachusetts began to address the growing need to protect scenic areas specifically for purposes of public benefit and recreation. The public parks movement in Boston gained momentum as the city grew and annexed neighboring municipalities in the 1870s. In 1878, the Boston Park Commission asked Frederick Law Olmsted to design what became the Back Bay Fens, the first of a connected series of parks in Boston and neighboring Brookline that he would design in the 1880s and 1890s.[6] (Fig. 2.3) Olmsted, who in 1881 relocated his home and practice from New York to Brookline, was also a major figure in scenic preservation efforts in the United States, beginning his work in Yosemite Valley in 1865. In the 1880s, he organized the successful campaign to create a New York State reservation around Niagara Falls, and in 1887, he and Calvert Vaux designed a new park there.[7] Olmsted was also involved in the creation of a system of scenic reservations in the suburbs around Boston. In 1879, he visited Lynn Woods with Philip A. Chase, a prominent local manufacturer, and others who advocated maintaining the area as a public park. That year, the journalist Sylvester Baxter published an article in which he described (and named) Middlesex Fells, another scenic wooded area in suburban Boston, and argued for its preservation. Olmsted advised them both on how regional scenic reservations differed from municipal parks, urging their protection to the greatest degree possible (as he had at Yosemite), while making them accessible to the public.[8]

Olmsted's greatest influence on scenic preservation in Massachusetts, however, was through the training and advice he gave his protégé, the landscape architect Charles Eliot. Eliot was an apprentice in Olmsted's office beginning in 1883, and after traveling in Europe he began his own practice in

Boston.[9] In 1890, Eliot organized a distinguished committee of "persons interested in the preservation of scenery and historical sites in Massachusetts" to form The Trustees of Public Reservations, the first private land trust in the world dedicated to this purpose.[10] Established through an act of the state legislature in 1891, the Trustees accepted gifts of land to be held (tax-free) and opened to the public. Although the organization concerned itself with a wide variety of scenic and historic sites, it was immediately concerned with public access to the seashore, which it noted in its first annual reports was rapidly diminishing as more and more waterfront property was being developed for residential and vacation homes. The Trustees commissioned Jonathan B. Harrison, a minister and journalist from New Hampshire, to inventory parks and other public landscapes in Massachusetts shore towns, and to report on the general state of public access to the seashore in the state.

Harrison was a well-known advocate who had worked with Olmsted on the campaign to preserve Niagara Falls. His 1891 report described a critical situation. Of forty-six shore towns surveyed in Massachusetts, only a few had public parks or commons. Instead of public access to the seashore, Harrison found "a great population inland hedged away from the beach" by private holdings "wherever summer people have bought places on the seashore." He noted a strong movement under way of "moneyed people from the cities and towns of the whole country east of the Mississippi River to the shore towns of Massachusetts."

Rather than assuring public access, many towns were selling off properties and commons and actually decreasing the opportunities for public recreation on the shore. On Cape Cod, Harrison reported that Sandwich and Bourne had "no place of public resort" and found similar situations in Barnstable, Yarmouth, Dennis, and Harwich. Falmouth had no public beach access except for the little-used "town landing." In Chatham, the first of the six towns of the Outer Cape, there was "no common or park," although "summer people [were] crowding in." In Orleans, Harrison noted that vacation homes were already dominating the best sites along the shore, and while the time was near when the town could expect large crowds all summer long, there would "not be much more space or freedom for them than convicts enjoy at the State Prison." There was no public beach, and he recommended the town provide one. Eastham, he observed, had an "interesting history" but "no considerable public holdings." Wellfleet was "an attractive town," and again, "much land [had] been bought here by non-residents within a few years." Truro, like the other towns of the Outer Cape, had "no park or common or right on the shore," although the Pamet was noted as a "picturesque region, with qualities to woo the heart of an artist."[11]

Harrison was particularly interested in Cape Cod. "The wonderful 'Cape country,' with its indefinable charm," he wrote, was "the most interesting region in New England, or anywhere," although "most New England people know little more about it than they do about Arizona." Conscious that he was walking in Thoreau's footsteps, Harrison referenced his descriptions in *Cape Cod,* and dared to revise him: "The Cape region is much better wooded, has better soil, and is far more interesting and attractive than his account of what he saw along the beach has led people to believe." Harrison had a more immediate, if prosaic, vision for the Cape, which he expected would "be a paradise for women and children as long as the wildness and freedom remain unspoiled." But, "unless great areas here are made public holdings, free for the people's enjoyment forever, the time will come when the tired dwellers in the cities . . . who are driven by the heat of summer to find rest and new life by the sea, will find here the city all over again."[12]

Harrison's interest in the Cape was driven in part

Fig. 2.4. Province Lands, Provincetown, 2003. Photo by author.

by a fascination with the Province Lands. The potential for public recreation in the large and unique state reservation led him to write an independent second report on the area and its history. Unmoved by the beauty of the shifting dune formations, he believed that "the whole of the desert area might be reclaimed and rendered stable and productive" through an aggressive campaign of revegetation and windbreak planting.[13] (Fig. 2.4)

The Trustees did not acquire any land on the Cape following Harrison's report, but it did petition the legislature to improve the management of the Province Lands. In 1892, the legislature responded by directing the organization to map the reservation and make recommendations for what should be done there. Eliot took on the task of mapping, photographing, and investigating conditions in the area. His 1893 report suggested that only a coordinated reclamation plan, implemented by the town, state, and federal governments, would be adequate to revegetate the shifting dune landscape.[14] As any visitor to the Province Lands can see, such plans were never fully realized. Following Harrison's and Eliot's research and documentation, however, the General

Court acted in 1893 to allow the residents of the occupied portions of the Province Lands (in other words, Provincetown) to receive full title to their properties, while clarifying the boundaries of the remaining reservation.[15] The efforts of The Trustees of Public Reservations in the early 1890s to inventory and plan for seashore access in Massachusetts mark the beginning of modern conservation efforts on Cape Cod—some twenty-five years before the National Park Service came into existence.

The inventory of publicly held land on the Cape also did not tell the whole story of how the region's beaches were already being used, regardless of their status or ownership. In 1892, the town clerk of Chatham responded to an inquiry by Eliot by reporting: "Everybody and his friends goes to the sea beaches for amusement. Most of the beaches are used as common property, though the town would probably claim all not held by private individuals. The beaches are very attractive to summer visitors."[16] By the 1890s, the towns of Cape Cod had begun to assert ownership of any beaches within their boundaries which were not privately owned. Title was based, as with other unowned properties in the towns, on the basis of common ownership—as common lands—a tradition of public ownership dating to the seventeenth- and eighteenth-century establishment of most New England towns. In some cases, extensive shorelines, such as Nauset Beach in the towns of Chatham and Orleans, were "said to belong to no one," as Eliot reported, and so would be available at least unofficially to the public.[17]

Over the coming decades, "town beaches" became important recreational amenities in all the towns on Cape Cod. Based on accessibility and the suitability of specific beaches and shorelines for swimming and other forms of recreation, town beaches became established destinations. This was especially true where town roads ran along or ended at the shore. Roads provided accessibility, and their rights-of-way created an exception to the rule of private property extending to the low-tide mark. Town governments made basic improvements—unpaved parking areas, wooden steps down the dunes and bluffs—to facilitate use by tourists and residents alike.

The availability of public town beaches was an important factor in real estate development by the 1920s, since proximity to accessible beaches was a consideration for vacation homes and tourist accommodations. Larger crowds of summer visitors motivated town governments to begin acquiring beaches by purchase, or in some cases by gift, during this busy decade.[18] Parking fees eventually became a source of town revenues, and restriction on parking privileges could assure town residents and the owners of vacation homes priority access once day-trippers in automobiles began arriving in numbers. All six towns of the Outer Cape developed town beaches (or some form of public access to the shore) in the first half of the twentieth century. The question of their jurisdiction would become an important consideration as national seashore proposals and boundaries were considered beginning in the 1930s.

The creation of the National Park Service in 1916 began a new era in landscape conservation in the United States. As already noted, however, significant proposals for seashore parks only materialized once the park service had greatly expanded its role as the nation's "outdoor recreational planning" agency in 1933. In the meantime, like many states, Massachusetts made efforts to develop its state park system during the 1920s, a decade when public demand for areas suitable for automotive day trips and camping excursions intensified. By 1926, one hundred thousand acres of state forest had been established in Massachusetts, as well as seven "state reservations" and eight "wildlife reservations."

The movement received federal encouragement when Calvin Coolidge convened a national conference on outdoor recreation in 1924, attended by public officials and conservation groups from all over the country. Massachusetts governor Alvan T. Fuller responded by appointing a Committee on Needs and Uses of Open Spaces in 1927. The committee included the state conservation commissioner and other state officials, but was dominated by representatives of the numerous nonprofit organizations that had been leaders in land conservation in the state, including the Appalachian Mountain Club, the Massachusetts Audubon Society, and the Society for the Preservation of New England Antiquities.

The Trustees of Public Reservations had been urging state action since 1925, when they had initiated state planning efforts through their own Committee on Open Spaces. Several board members of the Trustees served on Governor Fuller's committee, including Charles Sumner Bird Jr., as chairman, and the landscape architect Charles W. Eliot II (nephew of Charles Eliot), who in 1926 had already drawn up a mapped inventory of public lands in the state for the Trustees.[19] In their *Annual Report* that year, the Trustees indicated a pressing need for a comprehensive plan for the development of a well-distributed system of state parks, and for better coordination among the agencies responsible for state land. The report noted that certain scenic areas important for public recreation lacked any state reservations, foremost among them "the beaches of Cape Cod."[20]

Neither private reservations nor state parks were forthcoming on the Cape, however. The committee appointed by Governor Fuller observed that Massachusetts had been a "pioneer" in land conservation but now ranked far below other states, such as New York, Minnesota, Pennsylvania, and even New Hampshire, in the creation of state parks. Its response was to propose a basis for expanding and coordinating a system of state reservations. A "Bay Circuit" corridor of connected parks was proposed to form a semicircle around metropolitan Boston, from Duxbury to the south, as far west as Framingham, and back to the North Shore at Ipswich.[21] Three new public beaches were proposed, at Salisbury, Duxbury, and Westport, all intended to serve nearby urban populations. The plan suggested the establishment of thirteen new state parks, but none were on the Cape.[22] Apparently, Cape Cod remained sufficiently remote in the 1920s for state park planners to prioritize other areas in Massachusetts as more immediately critical, in terms of the demand for outdoor recreation and the encroachment of private development.

But residential and tourist development in some towns on Cape Cod, as noted by Jonathan Harrison, was well under way at the time. By the 1920s, the construction of new residential and vacation houses had transformed much of the Upper Cape, and extended to Orleans and Chatham on the Outer Cape. By the end of the decade, boom turned to bust in many parts of the country; but the Great Depression only slowed, it did not stop, the advance of tourism on Cape Cod. During the early 1930s, unemployment was high, tourism dwindled, and the real estate market crashed. For many Americans, however, hard times increased a desire for relatively affordable vacations, and driving to the seashore remained more feasible than other vacation plans.

Above all, the limiting barrier to automobile traffic created by the completion of the Cape Cod Canal in 1914 was removed when parallel highway bridges, at Bourne and Sagamore, opened in 1935. (Fig. 2.5) The new bridges spanned the widened canal and replaced a drawbridge that previously had been the only connection to the mainland. Their construction was supported through the "emergency spending" legislation of Roosevelt's New Deal which was intended to alleviate unemployment. But with state highway improvements also made during the decade, the bridges rendered Cape Cod a more convenient destination for people in cars than ever before. By the middle of the decade, the affordable

Fig. 2.5. Bourne and Sagamore Bridges, postcards, c. 1930–45. BPL.

attractions of the Cape made it a desirable vacation destination, even during hard times.

In 1937, Jeremiah Digges published a guidebook, *Cape Cod Pilot,* which was another New Deal project, one of the American Guide Series funded through the Federal Writers' Project.[23] Filled with historical narratives and colorful details of regional life, the book was the most important guide to the Cape published since Thoreau's day and encouraged an appreciation of the cultural landscape and its historical associations in a new generation of automotive tourists. At the same time, the National Park Service was actively researching the prospect of creating a new "national beach park" at Cape Cod, as it was at Cape Hatteras. But while the North Carolina beaches were still inaccessible and undeveloped, the new bridges and the real estate market on Cape Cod indicated that any proposals for the area would be complicated and expensive.

By this time, the park service had assumed its role in the overall New Deal land-planning initiative. Roosevelt had established a National Planning Board in 1933, which was renamed the National Resources Board the next year. The new agency was under the authority of Roosevelt's cantankerous and effective secretary of the interior, Harold L. Ickes, who also oversaw the various and widespread activities of the new Public Works Administration (PWA) and so controlled a vast amount of New Deal spending. As its name implied, the National Resources Board had a broad mandate to coordinate national resource planning in order to guide the many programs and new agencies being created within the executive branch. Ickes appointed Charles W. Eliot II executive secretary of the new federal planning agency. For expertise in the area of outdoor recreational planning, Eliot drew on the knowledge and experience of landscape architects at the park service, especially Conrad Wirth, who was already organizing the massive expansion of state park systems all over the country which would be accomplished through the labor and funding of the CCC, the PWA, and other New Deal construction programs.[24]

Eliot II issued his agency's first report in 1934, and while many natural resource issues were covered, the nation's need for better opportunities for public outdoor recreation figured prominently. The lack of seashore reservations was noted.[25] This need was also described in the park service's own, complementary report on national land use planning and recreation, which was written the same year. Remarking on the special need of public access to the seashore, Wirth and his planners observed that sea coasts had "a recreational value of unique and matchless character," and that the "recreational value of beaches" was of the "highest order." Although they acknowledged a paucity of ocean frontage in any kind of public ownership, however, they did not yet articulate a vision for national seashore parks.[26] But that idea was now taking shape at the agency.

By the time their first national recreational study for the National Resources Board was completed in 1934, Wirth and his colleagues had initiated their study of undeveloped shorelines along the Atlantic and the Gulf of Mexico. The seashore studies continued through the decade, with the help of the U.S. Coast Guard and other partners. By 1937, they were able to report that little had been done to preserve desirable seashore areas up to that point, and that the development boom of the 1920s had already limited public access in many cases. They urged that coastal areas be included in national and state park system plans, and specifically recommended twelve areas, totaling 437 miles of the Atlantic and Gulf Coasts, that would qualify as new national parks. Another thirty areas were suggested as additions to state park systems. In the meantime, Cape Hatteras proceeded as the pilot national seashore project.[27] By 1941, thirty-four state recreational plans were completed, covering all aspects of the recreational uses of public lands of all types, including wilderness areas, historic and archaeological sites, recreational areas, and more. The plans included data on demographics and economics as well as history and natural resources.[28]

Massachusetts was one of the states featured in the national plan, and in 1941, the state released its own "Park, Parkway, and Recreational-Area Study," which gave a more complete documentation of what had been accomplished by the Massachusetts State Planning Board working with the National Park Service. Considering the decade's achievements in state and local park creation, the Massachusetts planners revealed relatively modest ambitions. "No attempt has been made to achieve the spectacular," they wrote in their foreword, "either in the presentation of the material or in the resulting recommendations."[29]

For several reasons, the state planners did not prioritize extensive new reservations on Cape Cod. They emphasized two salient factors affecting recreational land use planning for the state in the twentieth century: the increased urbanization of the population, which made Massachusetts the third most densely populated state, and the question of how to manage the state's forests, which now covered 60 percent of its area. The two trends were related, both reflecting the abandonment of farmland that had been under way since the nineteenth century. The planners repeated the proposals of the 1927 governor's committee, calling for the development of the Bay Circuit of connected parks around metropolitan Boston, as well as ten additional state parks. The need for public ocean beaches was particularly noted, and four new state park beaches were proposed, including two on the Upper Cape: Scusset and Poponesset beaches. On the Outer Cape, three locations that had been suggested as wildlife sanctuaries by the 1927 committee were again put forward, this time as "alternate" proposed state beaches.[30]

Although the 1941 Massachusetts planners did highlight the need for public "ocean beaches," describing them as the state's "most important income producing natural resources," they apparently still considered the Outer Cape remote enough from centers of population to prioritize other coastal locations for new state parks.[31] Several factors probably affected their considerations. The first was the fact that by the 1930s, towns such as Dennis had acted to acquire and develop town beaches. A second was the creation of a major state park in Brewster in 1934, Nickerson State Park. The former estate of Roland Nickerson, whose grandfather had purchased the property in the 1890s, the 1,700-acre park was a gift from the family after Nickerson's death. The park had no shoreline, but it did have large ponds and extensive pine forests, and state officials developed it as a much-needed automotive camping area.[32]

A third development that may have dissuaded the planners from making any ambitious proposals for Cape Cod was their awareness of the coastal surveys that had identified Cape Cod as a desirable location for a new national park. At the time, the first (and still only) federal park in Massachusetts was the Salem Maritime National Historic Site, established in 1938. The urban park encompassed nine acres in downtown Salem and consisted mainly of historic buildings there. But following the initial park service coastal surveys, Wirth commissioned a private consultant to assemble a comprehensive, if speculative, plan for a national park and parkway on Cape Cod. Completed in 1939 by the landscape architect Thomas H. Desmond, this was the first elaboration of what a national seashore park on Cape Cod might entail.[33]

During the 1930s, hundreds of landscape architects idled by the Depression found work with the National Park Service or with state park agencies. Desmond, who had opened his own practice in Hartford, Connecticut, in 1913, however, was not among them. Unlike many, he managed to keep his office working during the lean years doing a range of projects, including large and small residences, municipal and state park commissions, institutional and commercial development, and town plans. Before he undertook the Cape Cod project, he does not appear to have done any work for the park service.[34] Nevertheless, Wirth, who had scores of landscape architects and planners working for him and an entire bureaucracy of outdoor recreational planners, chose to hire Desmond as a consultant to explore the potential of a national seashore for Cape Cod.

Desmond had a tremendous personal interest in the project, dedicating himself to a broad study of Cape Cod, its history, and the many historic, scenic, and recreational resources that could be incorporated into a comprehensive vision of a national park. The result, titled "A Proposed National Seashore and Historic Parkway on Cape Cod, Massachusetts," was not typical for a park service planning report of the era because it was prepared by a private consultant. Desmond's proposal entailed the acquisition of 38,000 acres, beginning with Duxbury and Sandy Neck beaches and extending to Provincetown. At the center of his plan, a new national parkway—a noncommercial, automotive highway—was to connect Duxbury to Provincetown and all the Cape attractions along the way. Desmond suggested acquiring all the land north of Eastham, except the village centers of Wellfleet, Truro, and Provincetown, at an estimated cost of ten dollars an acre.

Although done under Wirth's supervision, Desmond's report exceeded anything the park service would have likely suggested, even in 1939. By using a consultant, Wirth allowed for an expansive vision to be bruited, without the same authority of one of his own reports and plans. While admirably detailed, Desmond's report was not likely to be realized, and does not seem to have gone far enough toward implementation even to have been a subject of controversy. The 1941 Massachusetts state plan barely mentioned the proposal; it appeared on only one map in that report, as a dotted line labeled "parkway suggested by others." No mention was made of the acquisition of most of the private property north of Eastham. But the interest of the National Park Service in the creation of a large national seashore park had been made evident, and so probably influenced state park planners in their consideration of the region. The experience at Cape Hatteras, however, also had made clear the difficulties of land acquisition for a national seashore, even in that more remote area. Desmond's plan was delivered but, along with the CCC and most of the New Deal bureaucracy, all but disappeared after the country's entry into World War II.

The experience of World War II of course changed many aspects of life on Cape Cod. While travel restrictions ended most regular tourism for the duration, wartime activities in the region had lasting effects on land use, on demographics, and on the relationship of the people and governments of Cape Cod towns with the federal government. The military brought a federal presence to Cape Cod at a grand scale. Camp Edwards and Otis Field (later Otis Air Force Base) on the Upper Cape were rapidly expanded to accommodate and train recruits. (Fig. 2.6) In the 1930s, the state had acquired 25,000 acres for

Fig. 2.6. Camp Edwards, Bourne. Photo by Martin Stupich. HABS.

Camp Edwards in the interior of Bourne, Sandwich, and Falmouth. After 1941, the base became a huge construction site, with hundreds of buildings and required roads and utilities rapidly built. At its peak, Camp Edwards housed thousands of soldiers and a prisoner-of-war camp. Other locations on the Cape were also taken over by the federal government for the war effort, including the Woods Hole navy base, Camp Wellfleet, and the harbor at Hyannis Port, which was a center for North Atlantic shipping convoys. The region's unique geography made it a major center of military activity and intelligence.[35]

In addition to military installations and thousands of new transient and permanent residents, the region was the scene of training exercises, staging areas for shipping, and firing ranges. Monomoy, despite local opposition, was used for aerial bombardment practice. Extending south about eight miles from Chatham Harbor, Monomoy was a stunning, almost ephemeral landscape of sand and low vegetation, separating Nantucket Sound and the Atlantic. (Fig. 2.7) The sandy peninsula had recently been the site of controversy involving another federal agency, the Bureau of Biological Survey (later the Fish and Wildlife Service). In 1928, the state ornithologist of Massachusetts, Edward H. Forbush, with others, had recommended that Monomoy be acquired as part of the Atlantic coastal wildlife refuge system. The lack of accessibility to Monomoy, its limited development, and its importance as a migratory and nesting bird habitat made it both a desirable and a feasible location for the purpose. The biologists who investigated the area in the 1930s noted that there might be other areas on the Cape of greater value as a bird refuge, but land costs put them out of the agency's reach.

Difficulties ensued, however, in determining adequate property titles as well as in finding willing sellers, and local opposition to federal ownership emerged quickly. By 1939, a local committee of town selectmen, hunters, and property owners from Harwich and Chatham had expressed their total opposition to the creation of a wildlife refuge. Although the area was mostly undeveloped, it was accessible by modified automobiles, and it was a popular destination for hunting, clamming, ocean fishing, and other recreational activities. Local opposition stalled the plans until, after 1941, the situation changed dramatically, and the federal government acquired Monomoy for use as a bombing range. Objections to federal ownership, although raised, proved less effective against the war effort. But the experience had organized local constituencies in favor of local control of Cape Cod's beaches, and had involved some individuals, including Edwin F. Eldredge, a local sportsman and selectman, the businessman and civic leader Joshua A. Nickerson, and Chatham resident Robert McNeece, who would later become important voices in the debate surrounding the Cape Cod National Seashore legislation.[36]

The War Department planned to cede management of Monomoy to the Interior to create a wildlife refuge after the war, but military use continued through the 1940s. With federal ownership now a fait accompli, local concerns centered on the delayed creation of the wildlife refuge and the desire for the development of facilities and policies that would allow public recreation to continue. Eldredge insisted that Chatham had been promised a highway, picnic parks, breakwaters, "and all the good things that go with a wildlife refuge."[37] Local opposition to the bombing range finally resulted in the transfer of management authority to the Department of the Interior in 1951. Clearly, there may have been discrepancies between the purposes of the new wildlife refuge and local expectations for outdoor recreation. In any case, automotive access to Monomoy was never fully reestablished after the hurricane of 1944 destroyed a wooden bridge. Without automotive access, recreational use declined, which presumably suited the federal managers of the wildlife refuge.

Fig. 2.7. Monomoy. Photo by author.

Another storm created a breach between Monomoy and Morris Island in 1958, and Monomoy became more isolated under its continued management by the U.S. Fish and Wildlife Service.[38]

By the time Monomoy became the first part of Cape Cod to come under (non-military) federal management, other important trends were changing life on Cape Cod. As postwar development and population growth soared, new concerns arose regarding land use planning and the limitations on development that could be imposed through town zoning ordinances. Land use regulations had become common in the United States since the Supreme Court upheld such municipal laws in the 1920s. By 1930, more than 750 municipalities, including all but a handful of American cities with populations over 100,000, had adopted such codes.[39] Zoning was slower to come to the rural towns of the United States, however, where the pressure to plan growth was less intense. In Massachusetts, the legislature had passed an enabling act in 1920 to allow towns to appoint planning boards and adopt zoning ordinances in 1920, and in 1923, Falmouth became the first town on Cape Cod to create a planning board, and three years later, the first to establish a zoning bylaw. During the prewar period, however, Falmouth was joined only by Barnstable among Cape towns to take such action.[40]

Most of Cape Cod was far slower to adopt zoning. In Chatham, for example, a planning board was established through town meeting in 1936, with Edwin Eldredge as chair. But the next year a zoning bylaw was defeated in town meeting, by an overwhelming majority. In 1938, a weaker proposal was defeated again, and in 1940, the planning board was abolished. By the time Chatham reconstituted the board in 1949, the town was being rapidly developed, but zoning remained a contentious issue in town meeting. Between 1950 and 1955, eighty-five subdivisions with 1,458 individual lots were created, and the town's population increased by about 20 percent. In 1953, the state legislature passed a Subdivision Control Law, but the Chatham planning board still had no control over subdivisions along existing road frontages. "The control of this type of so-called 'ribbon' development," they reported, "comes only when the Town adopts protective ordinances and building codes."

In 1954, the planning board drafted such codes and, in a major turning point, secured a majority vote in favor of them at town meeting. Opponents to the law, however, forced a special town meeting to attempt to overturn the results. After a considerable effort to rally opposition, they did succeed in getting a majority to vote against the new zoning code at the special meeting. They failed, however, to amass the two-thirds majority required by the town's bylaws to overturn the previous vote, and so a zoning ordinance was finally established in the town. But the battles over the content and implementation of land use regulations in Chatham continued.[41]

The dissent over land use zoning in Chatham was vitriolic and not atypical. Similar scenes were played out in other Cape Cod town meetings in the 1940s and 1950s. Like the debates over the disposition of Monomoy, these fights over municipal regulations presaged aspects of the coming storm that would be caused by renewed proposals for the Cape Cod National Seashore beginning in 1955. In Harwich, proposed zoning bylaws were "shouted into oblivion" at a 1938 town meeting, according to the *Harwich Independent,* "in one of the wildest sessions ever held in Harwich, if not the Cape."[42] But by 1955, the impacts of postwar development were becoming apparent.

In 1953, a study of tourism in Barnstable County revealed the extent to which tourism had replaced agriculture and fishing as the region's economic mainstay. The Cape Cod Chamber of Commerce in Hyannis recorded over 200,000 visitors in 1951, and a statistician at the Federal Reserve Bank in Boston estimated the value of the industry to the county at $70 million, compared with $8 million realized from agriculture (mainly cranberry farming), fishing, and manufacturing combined. Agriculture had been in decline, overall, since the late nineteenth century, and only 18 percent of the county was farmed in 1920. After a small increase in agricultural land use during the 1930s, the total fell to 8 percent by 1950. "With its economic re-emphasis the Cape has become a wealthy area," the study concluded, "its landscape is being transformed, and its people are now accustomed to a new way of life, dependent on its existence on a hectic 12-week summer season."[43]

The transformation was significant in many ways. The Town of Dennis was cited as an example of how, thirty years earlier, basic services such as fire and police protection were "barely existent," and schools were "poor." By midcentury, however, professional and centralized fire and police departments had been established, along with a "modern consolidated school." The town's real estate tax valuations rose from $1.5 million to $9.5 million, increasing the taxes raised from about $45,000 to over $360,000. In the county as a whole, property owners paid over $2.5 million in taxes to local towns and villages. Property values were rising quickly, reinforcing the shift away from any kind of agricultural production.[44]

With the postwar boom, other aspects of Cape

culture changed rapidly. Contention in Chatham over the town "blue laws," which kept most businesses closed on Sundays, revealed the degree to which new owners, many of whom were not "natives," had their own priorities and felt less adherence to local traditions. For investors, the languid pace and traditions of Cape Cod summers only hindered the realization of profits. In 1953, the Hyannis train station was demolished and service connecting Cape Cod to New York and elsewhere became sporadic after 1958 (ending altogether in 1964). The social character of summer resort activities, which had been altered radically by the thousands of servicemen stationed there during the war, became noticeably less genteel, at least according to some who decried the "honky-tonk" atmosphere in Hyannis. On the Fourth of July 1955, forty-eight people were arrested during a disturbance in the once "sedate" West End of Hyannis, which that weekend reportedly had resembled "Scollay Square on New Year's Eve."[45]

Increasing awareness of the rapid changes led to the establishment of planning boards by all the towns on the Cape by the mid-fifties. Of special concern was the uncontrolled "ribbon development" of Route 28, along the South Shore, which had a strong impact on the overall experience of the Upper Cape. By the middle of the decade, the combination of a strong market for new residential and commercial development and the inherent limitation of the amount of developable property on the Cape had created what was widely perceived as an "emergency." Together with the construction of shopping plazas, motels, and restaurants along Route 28, the new class of tourists led the older, often more affluent, vacationers on the South Shore and elsewhere to despair the loss of their idyllic summer retreats of the 1920s and 1930s. As the historian Leo Damore relates, early local efforts by "militant garden clubs" and historic preservationists to prevent the felling of street trees and the demolition of historic structures could not "stop the bulldozer."[46] Not only were town meetings calling for zoning regulations, but the Cape Cod Chamber of Commerce campaigned to form a "Regional Planning District" before the "rural seaside charm" that was drawing so many new residents and visitors was completely overwhelmed by subdivisions and roadside sprawl.[47]

This, then, was the social and demographic setting that provided the context for the reintroduction of plans for a national park on the Outer Cape. The population of Barnstable County was exploding upward, from under 27,000 in 1920 to over 70,000 in 1960. The increase varied from town to town, but on the Outer Cape during the same period, the populations of Chatham and Orleans doubled, and that of Eastham tripled. Truro and Wellfleet were approaching the same number of inhabitants they once had in the mid-nineteenth century. Only Provincetown, with its limited area for expansion, had remained relatively stable (and in fact decreased) in its total number of residents.[48] But again, census figures did not account for transient residents and visitors, who swelled the population at least by several times during summer months. (Fig. 2.8) In reaction to this growth, the towns of the Cape had created planning boards and were beginning to implement zoning ordinances, although only after sometimes fierce debate and with limited results. The Cape Cod Chamber of Commerce, representing significant business and real estate interests, had perceived the need for regional solutions to the rapid development that threatened to overwhelm the landscape character of the Cape. Many civic leaders and town selectmen also were aware of a need to act. By the mid-1950s, land development and the need for land conservation on Cape Cod were reaching a critical point, beyond which further proposals for any kind of comprehensive

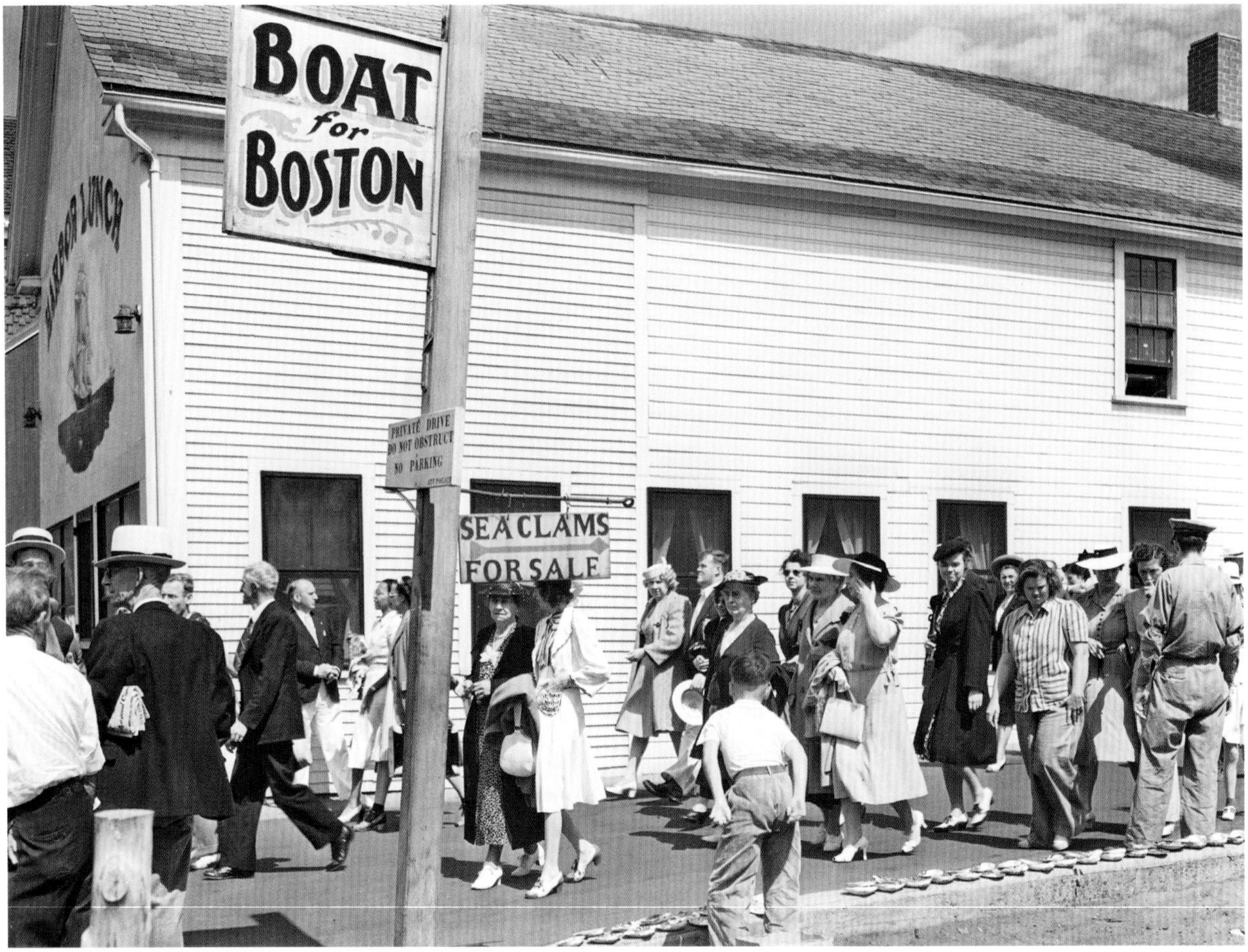

Fig. 2.8. Tourists arriving in Provincetown by ferry from Boston, 1940. Photo by Edwin Rosskam. FSA/OWI.

conservation planning would become impossible to implement, or worse, become irrelevant.

At the state level, planners and conservation groups had been considering Cape Cod since the 1890s, and in the 1950s finally began to become more actively involved. The state's land management agencies were reorganized in 1953, and a new commissioner of natural resources, Francis W. Sargent, initiated plans for a significant expansion and enhanced management of state parks and other lands. An Orleans resident and ardent conservationist, Sargent was particularly concerned with Cape Cod during his productive career. State senator Edward C. Stone, who lived in Osterville and represented the Cape and Plymouth district, was another key figure in state conservation efforts. In 1954, Stone succeeded in having the state acquire 750 acres of the High Head area of Truro, which became Pilgrim Spring State Park.[49] The new park joined the two existing state parks on the Cape, the Province Lands and Nickerson State Park. (Fig. 2.9) Land had also been preserved by private organizations, such as the Massachusetts Audubon Society, which established the 350-acre Wellfleet Bay Wildlife Sanctuary in 1958.[50]

The National Park Service, which had surveyed

Fig. 2.9. Cliff Pond, Roland Nickerson State Park, Brewster, postcard, c. 1930–45. BPL.

and made proposals for a regional approach to land conservation on the Outer Cape since the 1930s, so far had achieved nothing. But as noted in chapter 1, the park service was at a juncture in its institutional history in the mid-1950s. As the Mission 66 planners in Washington assembled their proposals, seashores were a high priority for the expansion of the national park system. With Cape Hatteras National Seashore finally established in 1953, attention now turned to the next most important opportunity for the new national beach parks: Cape Cod. As Wirth later recalled in an interview with Francis P. Burling, the managing editor of the Orleans weekly, the *Cape Codder,* Cape Cod had been passed over in the 1930s as the pilot national seashore project because it was considered "too hard a job to tangle with for the first Seashore." By 1955, however, Wirth and his planners considered the Outer Cape "A-1" on the list of potential projects resulting from the coastal surveys they completed that year.[51] The act finally authorizing the Cape Cod National Seashore in 1961, however, had an eventful and difficult legislative history. Its outcome was by no means certain as the park service reactivated its interest in national seashore plans that had lain dormant since the end of the New Deal.

PART II

Creating the Seashore

Marconi Beach, South Wellfleet. Photo by Carol Betsch.

THREE

The "Birth Throes of a National Park"

When Conrad Wirth described the "birth throes" of the Cape Cod National Seashore in an article written in 1959, he was reporting on a lively evening meeting held in the town hall of Eastham that March.[1] (Fig. 3.1) It had been a difficult session, with many vocal opponents objecting to the ambitious proposals for the acquisition and conservation of land on the Outer Cape that had been discussed since the 1930s. But Wirth never flinched from attending public meetings with sometimes hostile citizens. The Cape Hatteras project, for example, had many opponents and at least one public meeting in 1952 more contentious than anything Wirth experienced on Cape Cod. In Eastham, however, he faced a very different audience, one enflamed by rumors of the taking of private property through condemnation—by which owners would be forced to sell at a market value determined by a court—which provoked widespread anguish.

The history of the Cape Cod legislation is one of the best documented of any national park. Those directly involved were aware of the significance of the precedent they were setting, and they included some of the most prominent local, state, and national elected officials of the day, as well as park service officials, local civic leaders, and journalists. The most important account was written by Francis Burling in 1977.[2] As both a newspaper reporter and editor, he was well informed and directly involved in the events between 1955 and 1961 which culminated in the national seashore legislation. Burling had been stationed at Fort Devens, in central Massachusetts, during the war and settled on the Cape in Orleans in 1945. Elected to the select board in 1953, Burling helped pass the town's first zoning ordinance and supported the acquisition of Nauset Beach as a town beach. Burling was a reporter for the *Cape Codder* when it was purchased by Malcolm Hobbs in 1953, and the new publisher appointed him managing editor that year.[3] In the ensuing years, Hobbs and Burling made their paper the principal local news source for information on the evolving seashore legislation, and their editorial support, although never unqualified, would be a bulwark of reasoned analysis of the often complicated and contentious details of proposed park plans.

The National Park Service renewed plans for a national seashore on Cape Cod as a result of the Seashore Recreation Area Survey begun in 1954 and funded by the Mellon family. Paul Mellon's interest in the Cape was undoubtedly intensified by the fact that in 1948 he had purchased a property in Oyster Harbors, an exclusive community on the South Shore in the town of Barnstable. His neighbor there was Edward Stone, the state senator and conservation advocate.[4] The park service needed little encouragement from either source, however, to prioritize Cape Cod as its next national seashore project. Completed in 1955, the survey suggested the Great Beach as a future national park, a conclusion the National Park System Advisory Board approved, recommending further study.[5] (Fig. 3.2) That year the park service responded with a supplement to the coastal survey specifically on the "Great Beach Area." The report was premature, in a sense, because at that time Conrad Wirth was mobilizing his entire agency to prepare the detailed proposals, or prospectuses, for every park in the system, which would form the basis of his Mission 66 program. (Fig. 3.3) In that context, the 1955 Great Beach proposal was a conservative, quickly prepared plan. Planners suggested a national park of no more than 12,000 to 16,000 acres, restricted to a thirty-three-mile stretch of the Great Beach from Provincetown to Nauset Beach and including only the immediate uplands, extending on average three-quarters of a mile inland. They extolled the qualities of the Great Beach, describing the flora, fauna, and rich history of the region, but they also emphasized the difficulties of land acquisition. They noted that even this limited park would be "one of the most difficult and expensive land purchase projects of its kind yet undertaken," with an estimated cost of $10 million. With the experiences of Cape Hatteras fresh in mind, but the striking budgetary success of Mission 66 not yet realized, the park service staff who initially considered Cape Cod refrained from suggesting anything like Thomas Desmond's 1939

Fig. 3.1. Eastham Town Hall. Photo by author.

Fig 3.2. The Great Beach. Photo by author.

plan or even the less ambitious revised plans for Cape Hatteras.[6]

During the summer of 1956, the National Park Service contacted Edward Stone, a critical partner at both the state and local levels if any plans were to proceed. In a series of communications, regional director Daniel J. Tobin sought the state senator's advice and support in outlining an initial national seashore proposal. Tobin was a former park superintendent who had been assistant regional director in the Southeast Region until July 1955, so he was familiar with the development of Cape Hatteras. He was assisted by the region's chief planner, Allen T. Edmunds, who headed up the park service's Cape Cod planning effort.[7] Tobin had understood the discussions to be preliminary, but that fall Stone arrived unannounced at the Orleans office of the *Cape Codder* and shared the park service's 1955 "Great Beach Area" report with Hobbs and Burling. Presented with such an opportunity, the journalists were not

Fig. 3.3. Conrad L. Wirth dedicating the new Mission 66 visitor center at Carlsbad Caverns National Park, New Mexico, in 1959. NPSHC.

likely to keep the conversation private. They published a summary of the plan, including a map, in November 1956.

Despite the proposal's comparatively circumscribed dimensions, the implied acquisition of private property incited an immediate outcry from wary Outer Cape residents and from town governments jealous of their home rule prerogatives. Joshua Nickerson, president of his family's lumber company, spoke for many when he told the *Cape Codder* that "to take the biggest part of three towns" did not "make sense," although he had no objection to "a National Park on the sand dunes in North Truro." Park service officials soon regretted both the report and the manner of its release. Eivend T. Scoyen, a longtime national park superintendent whom Wirth appointed his associate director in Washington in 1956, lamented the situation in a memorandum to Benjamin H. Thompson, another associate director and chief "land planner" who, like Scoyen, had worked with Wirth since the 1930s. Scoyen rued the publication of the "confidential and very preliminary" report as "inadvertent."[8] The results were indeed unfortunate for the park service. The proposal was ambitious enough to immediately galvanize local opposition, and modest enough to create another problem. As planning for Mission 66 widened the possibilities for congressional support, Tobin and Edmunds were already expanding the boundaries of their Cape Cod park proposal. Inevitably, opponents would later demand, at the very least, that the agency return to its "original," more modest proposed boundaries, as described in the "very preliminary" 1955 document. As years of underfunding suddenly gave way to bipartisan congressional support for increased budgets for national parks, the entire situation was changing.

The apparent potential of Mission 66 to encourage federal park spending was confirmed in January 1956, when Wirth presented the initiative to Eisenhower during a cabinet meeting. The president personally endorsed the program, and that spring Congress indicated a willingness to go along with the initial $700 million ten-year budget by increasing the agency's funding for fiscal year 1957 to $68 million, up from $32 million in 1955.[9] Suddenly the situation was radically different. Tobin and Edmunds abandoned the idea of a narrow park that included only the "Great Beach Area" and put forward what they described in 1957 as the "Proposed Cape Cod National Park."[10]

This time they proceeded more thoughtfully in enlisting state and local support before releasing further plans. Early in 1957, the park service officials asked to meet with Edward Stone, as well as Francis Sargent, who they hoped would facilitate meetings with the selectmen of the six towns of the Outer Cape that would be affected. That March, Stone chaired a public meeting in Orleans. Tobin and Edmunds represented the park service. Sargent represented the state and became the first Massachusetts official to endorse publicly the concept of a national seashore (although at the time he rejected the transfer of jurisdiction of state lands for the purpose). Harry Albro, the state representative for the Cape Cod region, also attended, along with about forty concerned residents. Burling was there for the *Cape Codder,* which was already on record as supporting the idea of a national seashore, and reported that the park service officials came away from the "fairly friendly" meeting encouraged to pursue their plans.[11]

That May, a park service "Cape Cod Study Group" began work on a new national seashore plan. The team of park service landscape architects and planners, under the supervision of Tobin and Edmunds, conducted extensive on-site surveys, researched land titles and real estate prices, and considered the potential of various areas in terms of public recreation, resource conservation, and interpretive programs. They spent the summer exploring the Outer Cape on foot, in cars, with "beach buggies," and through aerial reconnaissance to compile a comprehensive survey of the region's scenic, historic, and ecological resources. They also held further meetings with selectmen and planning board members in the six towns.[12] That fall they returned to the regional office in Philadelphia to prepare the report and accompanying maps.[13] At this stage, Conrad Wirth took a direct interest as the plan was assembled and visited the Cape on "familiarization and appraisal tours." The director's personal approval of the details of such an important report was part of the process.[14]

The study group completed its "Field Investigation Report" in September 1958, but the plan was not made public for another six months. The delay had been caused, in part, by the organization and announcement of the Mission 66 program, an effort that required the mobilization and dedication of park service staff all over the country. Sargent and Stone had also requested that the release of the park service plan be delayed until after the fall 1958 elections.[15] Francis Burling, who had seen the new plan at a meeting in Boston with Wirth, Tobin, Allen, and Edmunds that January, published a summary of it—with an enthusiastic endorsement—in the *Cape Codder* on March 12. This third iteration of a national seashore plan proposed an ambitious park: about 29,000 acres, including almost forty miles of Atlantic shoreline, over six miles of shoreline on Cape Cod Bay, and Harding Beach on the South Shore in Chatham.

But the new park was to contain far more than beaches and associated public facilities. Eight square miles of sand dunes in Truro and Provincetown, twenty freshwater ponds, and "prime examples of the Cape's picturesque rolling heathlands, marshes, river valleys, and forests" were all part of the regional landscape to be included within its boundaries. (Figs. 3.4, 3.5) Moreover, "important historic sites," primarily associated with the early history of the Pilgrims, were described as an important dimension. The national seashore would "emphasize, yet protect, the natural and historic values" of the cultural landscape, while also making provision for "swimming and related activities at appropriate locations." The planners made ample note of the recreational demand on the area, which was at the time within a day's drive for a full third of the population of the United States—the only other national park on the Northeast coast was Acadia, two hundred miles to the north in Maine. But this plan implied more than accommodating the enormous pressure for recreational access and facilities. The report described the Cape Cod National Seashore as an important and much-needed new national park, one that would conserve resources of national

Fig. 3.4. View east from Bearberry Hill, Truro, 2017. Photo by Larry D. Moore. Wikimedia Commons.

Fig. 3.5. Long Pond, Wellfleet. NPSHC.

significance while also providing major recreational opportunities, but only in the context of regional landscape conservation.[16]

The park planners knew that the enormous increase in postwar travel to the Cape had only begun, and that virtually everyone visiting the area, whether for a day trip or for summer vacation, would be doing so in cars. Gone was any suggestion of a new "parkway" that would complement the Mid-Cape Highway (Route 6), however, as the central artery of the Outer Cape. The authors did suggest a system of park roads separate from that highway; but a new "national parkway"—a noncommercial, recreational highway connecting the attractions of the Cape back to Duxbury—was an idea that belonged to the New Deal era. By the 1950s, very different federal highway policies were in the making. In 1956, Congress passed the Interstate Highway Act, which assured that new federally sponsored highway construction would be engineered to serve combined commercial and noncommercial purposes. The act would have an incalculable impact on the American landscape, as the new system of high speed, limited-access highways spread urbanization across the continent in low density, automobile-dependent patterns.

The plans for the Interstate Highway system had been an instigation, and to some degree a model, for Mission 66. Wirth and his staff knew that the new system of highways would make national parks more accessible than ever, and the park service's ten-year modernization plan responded to that reality. Park service officials anticipated that the surge of park visitors in cars had only begun in the first postwar decade, and the basic tenets of Mission 66 planning—and the specific details of the Cape Cod National Seashore plan—were shaped by the expectation of continued dramatic increases of people and cars in virtually every national park. Mission 66 "guiding principles" suggested that the increased numbers of visitors could be accommodated without "impairment" of the parks if a new set of strategies was employed.

National parks were to be planned increasingly for "day-use" visitation, with overnight accommodations, gas stations, and other tourist needs met by private businesses in "gateway" towns. The 1958 proposal for Cape Cod therefore did not include any new park lodges or motels, although it suggested that camping sites would be provided (in part by the inclusion of a private campground in Truro constructed the year before). Since no accommodations were to be built, there were no plans for park concessioners, that is, private investors who would build and operate such facilities in exchange for a monopolistic service contract. Visitor centers (the new day-use visitor service and administration buildings) were proposed for Salt Pond in Eastham and Race Point in Provincetown. (Fig. 3.6) The first would serve as park headquarters and the principal entrance to the park; the second was envisioned as a smaller interpretive center and ranger station. At seven identified beaches, parking, comfort stations, and bathhouses would be built. Off-road vehicles (ORVs), or "beach buggies," were to be permitted subject to restrictions and regulations.[17]

Maps and figures delineated the proposed boundaries of the park. These notably encompassed a "Bayside Region," because the "impressions associated with Cape Cod" would be "incomplete" without representing the very different and "more serene mood" of the landscape extending across the Cape to Cape Cod Bay. Six and a half miles of bayside shoreline, from Jeremy Point in Wellfleet north to Truro were included. Inland from this shoreline, the proposed park comprised "extensive heathlands, dimpled with deep-set glacial kettle holes . . . the Herring River estuary . . . the fresh marshes of Duck Harbor and Bound Brook," and examples of pitch pine and mixed hardwood forests connecting to the ocean side of the Cape. (Fig. 3.7) The diversity of the biological

Fig. 3.6. View from the Salt Pond Visitor Center. Photo by author.

resources and wildlife habitat were documented as desirable and necessary features, along with historical sites adding to the "interpretive possibilities" of programs and walks the park service would conduct. "Recreational values" were, of course, extensively considered as well—but a national seashore clearly was intended from the beginning (conforming with the precedent of Cape Hatteras) to be more than a recreational beach.[18]

In many respects, the 1958 "Field Investigation Report" described the basic outline for the national seashore legislation that would be passed three years later. The visitor centers and six of the seven public beaches (the exception being Harding Beach, which remained a town beach in Chatham) would be realized. The most important single factor that would need to be resolved, however, was the disposition of private land within the proposed seashore boundaries. Land already under federal (military) and state jurisdiction, it was assumed, could be transferred through negotiation over time, depending in part on changing national defense priorities. In Provincetown, almost 5,000 acres (including the Province Lands) were identified as state land to be transferred, and only 70 acres of private land would need to be acquired. In Truro, however, 7,100 acres of private land were identified for acquisition, and in Wellfleet almost 5,800. The private land totals were 3,287 in Eastham, 1,600 in Orleans, and 1,010 acres in Chatham. The rest of the acreage was made up of

Fig. 3.7. Nauset Bay from above Coast Guard Beach. Photo by author.

proposed transfers of jurisdiction for military camps (North and South Truro Air Force stations and Camp Wellfleet, 2,737 acres), the Great Ponds (state owned, 740 acres), state parks and other lands (6,298 acres), and town beaches and landings (1,040 acres). Of the total 28,645 acres, 17,830 were privately owned.

The planners estimated—optimistically—that if long-term and life tenancies were offered to sellers, the total cost of acquisition would be $15.5 million. But the park service, even after a year and a half of investigations, had only a general idea of the complexities land acquisitions would entail. The boundaries had been drawn to exclude towns and most commercial establishments, with the exception of the old Highland House hotel, two small motels, a campground, and "a few isolated groups of cottage rental units of primitive seashore type." (Figs. 3.8, 3.9) The private homes and cottages included were "seasonal in use" and "until recently, widely scattered." But the subdivision and development of land that already characterized the Upper Cape was "rapidly taking its toll" on the Outer Cape, even as their report was being assembled. Some areas that had not been developed had been subdivided or were about to be. In a region that had been settled since the seventeenth century, some land titles were obscure or would become the subject of litigation. The planners made a preliminary count of 98 seasonal homes and 60 year-round homes in Eastham, 185 seasonal and 68 year-round homes in Truro, "5 to 7" seasonal

Fig. 3.8. Highland House, North Truro, 2013. Photo by John Phelan. Wikimedia Commons.

Fig. 3.9. Ruins of pier and new tourist cottages in Provincetown, 1940. Photo by Edwin Rosskam. FSA/OWI.

homes in Chatham, and "about 10" seasonal homes in Provincetown, all within their proposed boundaries. "No accurate account" of the number of private residences was available for Wellfleet.[19]

With the release of the "Field Investigation Report" in March 1959, public discussion and the legislative campaign to authorize the new park began in earnest. The taking of private property would be the salient and contentious single issue that would galvanize the opposition. Many Cape residents had long been reconciled with the concept of some kind of Great Beach park along the Atlantic Coast. They pointed out that over 60 percent of the Great Beach shoreline was already in public ownership, under either state, military, or town jurisdiction. But in 1959 the park service was suggesting something far more significant: a national seashore that would include representative landscapes and protect the cultural and natural resources which would make it a suitable addition to the national park system. A complex negotiation began, in which the park service's contemporary ideas for a national seashore would be reconsidered in the specific social and political contexts of the six towns of the Outer Cape and the long history of landscape conservation in Massachusetts and on Cape Cod.

Wirth scheduled his two evening meetings in Eastham and Chatham as the report was already generating significant controversy. Faced with five hundred "grim-faced Cape Codders" packed into the Eastham Town Hall for what was described as an "explosive" four-hour meeting, Wirth attempted both to allay concerns and to share a vision of what the creation of the national seashore could mean for the future of the region. Real estate developers, businesspeople, and native and seasonal residents alike grilled him until midnight, demanding to know whether eminent domain proceedings would be used to acquire the approximately seven hundred private homes now estimated to be within the proposed boundaries. Local tax rolls would be affected, and town officials warned that the loss of tax-paying properties could mean sharp increases in town taxes for remaining property owners. Beyond these questions, there was a larger and pervasive unease that the creation of a national park would forever change the character of the landscape and its communities by encouraging an increase in the number of day-trippers who would crowd beaches and pressure local services without making lasting contributions to the local economy and tax base.

Wirth had "been through it all before. Not once, but many times." These were people, he knew, who would be asked to make sacrifices and endure change for the sake of the many who would benefit if the "dream of a National Seashore area for the use and enjoyment of all were to become a reality."[20] He was sympathetic, acknowledging the dramatic—and inevitably to some unwelcome—shift in the ownership, use, and management of 29,000 acres of the Outer Cape, but he repeatedly recalled the higher purpose of the proposed park. To remind everyone of what was at stake, he recalled the Miami Beach he had known at the beginning of his career. At that time it was like the Great Beach, still undeveloped and available to all as a seemingly endless resource, but by the 1950s, it was lined with hotels and apartment buildings.[21]

But there were too many questions for which Wirth had no convincing answers. Above all, on the issue of taking property through eminent domain, he could only say that "such things, fortunately, happen only very rarely," and that the park service preferred to rely on negotiations with willing sellers who, if they desired, could receive twenty-five-year or lifetime tenancy rights which would delay the transfer of property to the federal government. When owners asked about their rights to pass their property on to their children, Wirth could only intone that eventual public ownership would be the only effective means to assure that their children—and children of future generations—would be able "to know the Cape as we have." The next evening Wirth faced an even larger, although apparently more sedate, audience in Chatham.[22]

Although Wirth recalled that the two evening meetings went well, in fact, he did not allay the fears of private property owners that their land would be forcibly purchased through eminent domain proceedings, and he did not persuade business and civic leaders that the creation of the national seashore would not have an overall negative impact on tax receipts and the regional economy. Above all, perhaps, the people of the six towns of the Outer Cape felt they had been neither considered nor consulted in the development of the plan—and to a significant degree they had not been.

It was unlikely Wirth had ever encountered audiences quite like the ones assembled to hear him in Eastham and Chatham. Among the "natives" and year-round residents concerned for their properties and their livelihoods were the literary critic Edmund Wilson and the writers Edwin O'Connor and Paul Chavchavadze. The architect Serge Chermayeff argued briefly with Joshua Nickerson, for and against the park, respectively. Robert McNeece, a veteran of the Monomoy wildlife refuge battle, led a group of Chatham residents and selectmen dedicated to keeping as much of that town's acreage as possible (in particular, Harding Beach and Morris and Stage Islands) outside the proposed seashore boundaries. Anthony Duarte, a Truro selectman and a leading figure in real estate, was another significant opponent. The freshman congressman for the Ninth District, Hastings Keith, attended both meetings and maintained a studied ambivalence on the proposal as he gauged the political climate. Replacing Francis Sargent (who had moved to Washington, DC, to direct the federal Outdoor Recreation Resources Review Commission), the new Massachusetts commissioner of natural resources, Charles H. W. Foster, was on hand to confirm the continued support of that agency.[23]

E. J. Kahn Jr., a staff writer for the *New Yorker* who owned a house in Truro within the proposed boundaries, reported on the Eastham meeting in a lengthy essay published that fall. Kahn described the turmoil that both residents and vacationers on the Outer Cape had been suffering since the inadvertent release of the 1955 report. Since then, the revised plan had been anxiously anticipated for almost three years, and during. that time the debate over whether and how the park service should become involved in regional land conservation had "swelled into a storm." Various local individuals and groups had formed factions, staged events, and written letters for and against the park to the *Cape Codder* and other newspapers all over Massachusetts.[24]

At the March meetings, Wirth described the greater good and the long-term conservation of the landscape as eloquently as he could; but many attitudes, for and against the idea, had already hardened. To Kahn, a *Cape Codder* editorial in 1957 had captured the somewhat apprehensive approval of the pro-park constituency on the Outer Cape: "The Cape has a responsibility to itself and to the country in general to preserve what is essentially a national resource. We have concluded that the National Park is the best alternative in keeping with this responsibility." The Provincetown *Advocate* editorialized another characteristic view: "The Cape is not a seashore. It is a quintessence of old New England, and more important, by far, is the imprint of its people, past and present—mostly past." Kahn himself expressed what was probably a widely held opinion that in all the investigations of the "biological, archeological, historical, scenic and interpretive values" of the Outer Cape that had been the basis of the new plan, "the human inhabitants got short shrift, and this omission didn't escape notice." He quoted Joshua Nickerson making the same point, when the local businessman observed, "People are more important than geological formations." Nickerson was a powerful local voice for maintaining the landscape of the Outer Cape under local control. "I have a strong feeling that I represent a certain continuity of a way of life," he stated at the meeting, reminding the audience that his forebears had settled the area in the seventeenth century—and that his family had already donated the land for Nickerson State Park as well as a significant extent of shoreline to the Town of Chatham.[25]

Many community leaders and concerned property owners rejected the idea of a national seashore. Charles E. Frazier Jr., another native Cape Codder and an influential opponent, had been a Wellfleet selectman for twenty years and at the time was assistant attorney general for Massachusetts in addition to being a prominent real estate investor. Francis Biddle, who had been Franklin D. Roosevelt's attorney general, had retired to Wellfleet and now offered his formidable legal skill and connections, pro bono, should they be needed to defeat park legislation in Congress.[26] The historian Jacqueline Mullen describes how Cold War–era fear of government overreach also colored the response of homeowners, who compared taking their property to the "tactics of the Kremlin." The painter Edward Hopper, a longtime homeowner on the Cape, wrote in 1959 that "people turned out of their houses . . . is tyranny and Russia."[27]

Those in favor of establishing a national seashore recognized that some form of federal intervention, despite the sacrifices, would be the only way of preventing the wholesale development of the still-open spaces of the Outer Cape. Massachusetts officials recognized the benefits of federal involvement to the state as a whole and supported at least the idea of a national seashore. The early endorsement of Francis Sargent was followed by a statement of support by Governor Foster Furcolo in January 1958, and then by a resolution in support by both houses of the state legislature the following April. But the influential and increasingly informed residents of Cape Cod would require a great deal of reassurance and convincing—including a significant change in the park service's entire approach—if national seashore legislation were to succeed.

Passage of national park legislation would require the support of the two senators and the representative from the Ninth District who made up the region's congressional delegation—support that would depend in large part, of course, on the wishes of their affected constituents. The legislative process had begun already in April 1957, when Massachusetts Representative Phillip J. Philbin introduced a bill (H.R. 6720) in the 85th Congress to authorize the creation of a "Cape Cod National Park," shortly after seeing the *Vanishing Shoreline* published summary.[28] The bill did not include specific boundaries or authorization amounts. In May 1958, two more Massachusetts representatives, Edward P. Boland and Thomas P. ("Tip") O'Neill (who, like Philbin, did not represent the Cape), introduced identical bills in the House also to create a "Cape Cod National Park." These indicated a park of 30,000 acres within the six towns of the Outer Cape, with 50 percent of the land to be acquired through donations and the rest through purchase.[29] No action was taken on any of this early legislation, however, although Philbin and O'Neill reintroduced their bills early in the 86th Congress in 1959.[30]

These early bills to create a national park on Cape Cod, introduced by Democratic representatives from western and urban areas of the state, were bitterly opposed by the Ninth District's Republican congressman, Donald W. Nicholson.[31] With the implications of establishing a federal park on the Outer Cape still unclear, the early bills also exacerbated tensions among residents and vacationers alike and intensified the initial mostly negative response to the park service's plans.[32]

In April 1959, the legislative situation was made more complex by bills introduced in the Senate. In what was by now a national movement to do something to preserve the nation's seashores, the National Park System Advisory Board recommended that the secretary of the interior report favorably on the pending seashore legislation being prepared by Senator Richard L. Neuberger of Oregon.[33] Neuberger, a Democrat, was leading efforts to conserve the Oregon coastline. His 1959 bill (S.2010) was broadly conceived, with the intent of authorizing $16 million for the Department of the Interior to acquire three shore areas totaling 100,000 acres for park purposes, and to do so without further hearings or public consultation. The idea of taking private property without further public consultation on the boundaries and management policies of the future park was an anathema for a plurality of Outer Cape residents. The proposed legislation outraged even park advocates on Cape Cod and was condemned, for example, by Hobbs and Burling at the *Cape Codder.* Neuberger did more to galvanize national seashore opposition on the Cape than even the formidable local opponents had managed to do at that point.[34]

A second seashore bill (S.2460) was introduced in the Senate that July by James E. Murray of Montana, chair of the Interior and Insular Affairs Committee, with seventeen cosponsors, including Neuberger. The omnibus legislation, named "Save Our Shorelines" ("S.O.S.") called for the creation of ten shoreline parks at a cost of $50 million, but it included a provision for public hearings. It was also prepared with support from the Department of the Interior, which reported favorably on the legislation it had helped instigate. But both the Neuberger and the Murray bills, sponsored by western senators, caused great apprehension on the Outer Cape, in part because the relevant Senate and House Committees on Interior and Insular Affairs were dominated by western legislators in a Democratic Congress. For many in the insular, Yankee, and still overwhelmingly Republican communities of Cape Cod, the taking of private property and the threat to a long tradition of self-governance seemed nothing less than Orwellian.[35]

That summer, the *Saturday Evening Post* published an editorial titled "National Parks Shouldn't Be Set Up by Decree." The magazine's editorial board had clearly been moved by the response among prominent Cape residents to the Neuberger legislation, which the board felt had been promoted by the Department of the Interior to allow it "arbitrarily to take over sections of Cape Cod or any other area regarded by the National Park Service as suitable for a park, with scant regard to local interest."[36] The attack from a publication that had often been a stalwart supporter of national park causes was notable, and it fomented further negative reactions locally. Jacqueline Mullen observes that "influential Cape Cod residents continued putting public pressure on the Park Service to ensure popular support for a Cape Cod National Seashore that included homeowner protections," and that during summer 1959 a number of influential homeowners on the Cape retracted their previous support for the idea of a national park. That August, Francis Biddle and Arthur Schlesinger Jr. were among the authors of a letter to the editor published in the *New York Times* that was a paean to the traditions of private home ownership and cultural life on Cape Cod—a way of life they felt was about to be erased through eminent domain acquisitions.[37]

For his part, Conrad Wirth responded with a long letter to Ben Hibbs, editor of the *Saturday Evening Post,* defending the "basic conservation objectives" of his agency. The park plan they had devised in 1958 described a "national area where not only outstanding ocean recreation activity would be available but a representative portion of all the scenic, natural, and historic elements that go to make up Cape Cod's great significance" needed to be as well. The region was a "complex of many features, bound into a unity by origin, by ecology, and by human experience." The uplands, ponds, and bayside of the Outer Cape were "as essential to the beauty and scientific significance of the Cape as is the beach," and all were "interrelated." The seashore would therefore necessarily include many private homes (not a "minor proposal"); but these acquisitions were intended to preserve the "heart of the charm" of the Outer Cape: its "traditional way of life." Property acquisition could not "crystalize human behavior," he admitted, but it offered the best means of preserving "community character against the undisciplined pressures of development."[38]

But such arguments were no more effective with editors than they had been with Outer Cape residents in public meetings, and that summer the prospect of park service acquisition of the private homes threatened to scuttle the entire project. The two senators from Massachusetts, however, were already at work seeking an acceptable compromise. Their interest had been catalyzed when Francis Sargent met with them both in 1957, again shortly after *Our Vanishing Shoreline* had been published and distributed to key members of Congress. At the time, the two men represented very different backgrounds and eras in Massachusetts politics, but they also had a unique and collaborative relationship. Leverett Saltonstall was the former speaker of the Massachusetts House of Representatives, who had been elected governor of Massachusetts in 1939 and then U.S. senator in 1945. His family traced its roots to the earliest English settlers of Massachusetts, and he embodied the wealthy, patrician, and Republican class of Bostonians that Oliver Wendell Holmes once characterized as "Brahmins."

The junior senator from Massachusetts was also from a prominent family in the state but of a very different heritage. John Fitzgerald Kennedy was the grandson of the former Democratic mayor of Boston, John Francis (Honey Fitz) Fitzgerald, and the son of the millionaire businessman and ambassador Joseph P. Kennedy. Irish Catholic and representing both new wealth and the political power of the state's more urban areas, Kennedy was elected to the Eleventh District of the House of Representatives (which included Cambridge and parts of Boston) in 1947 by capitalizing on his record as a best-selling author and war hero. In 1952, Kennedy ran against Henry Cabot Lodge Jr., the senior senator from Massachusetts (and another Republican "Brahmin"), winning a tightly contested election to replace him.

Although a scion of the state's Democratic political machine, Kennedy remained somewhat aloof from those more populist roots, relying on his father's fortune and connections—and his own extraordinary charisma—to quickly advance his ambitions. Saltonstall and Kennedy cultivated a cooperative and bipartisan approach to representing the state's interests, a relationship enhanced by the political benefit each derived. The older man was even something of a mentor, to the degree that party politics would allow. They met regularly with both their staffs, during a period that Frederick Holborn, Kennedy's legislative assistant at the time, described as a "high water mark in cooperative efforts," in order to strategize on issues and policies of mutual concern. One of the topics they discussed was national seashore legislation, the bills that were being introduced in the House and Senate, and the possibility of introducing a new bill in the Senate that they would cosponsor.[39]

Francis Sargent, then still Massachusetts commissioner of natural resources, was on record supporting the idea of a national park on the Outer Cape and felt he was "on the firing line" as opponents grew more vociferous and organized. Indeed, many on the Outer Cape who saw only a threat to livelihoods and private property had identified Sargent, who had owned a sporting goods store in Orleans since 1946 before being appointed a state commissioner, as a principal instigator of the seashore movement.[40] Kennedy contacted Sargent in 1957 and offered his support for a national park on Cape Cod. It was an easy decision for the Democratic senator, who never had high hopes for winning many votes in the Republican stronghold of Barnstable County. His main constituency was in urban areas, where the prospect of a national seashore was popular. Saltonstall agreed to cosponsor legislation as well, although with more trepidation, since he had already heard from Joshua Nickerson and others on the Cape who had made their feelings clear.[41]

Nickerson also wrote to Kennedy expressing outrage over Neuberger's 1959 seashore bill. Kennedy counseled patience, noting that the legislation was not likely to move forward in the Senate and, further, that if national seashore legislation for the Outer Cape were enacted, "it is probable that the condemnation provisions would be considerably altered" from what Neuberger had suggested—a telling indication of how Kennedy was perhaps already considering a novel legislative approach. For good measure, Kennedy added a testimonial on the motivations of park service officials, in whom he had "noted little arrogance and certainly no calculated effort to steamroll over the rights and views" of his constituents on the Outer Cape. "I personally feel," he concluded, "that this is a subject which can be sensibly approached and gradually solved by reason rather than by the ventilation of sinister charges."[42]

Saltonstall and Kennedy set their legislative aides to the task of investigating the possibilities for drafting a bill. Kennedy assigned Frederick Holborn, who would go on to have a distinguished career in foreign policy at the White House and in academia.[43] Saltonstall assigned David H. B. Martin, who later had a career in the Department of Health, Education, and Welfare. Both men were highly capable political aides, but neither had any experience in land conservation. Martin had never seen the Outer Cape.[44] Their contributions would prove invaluable, however, because they had exactly the political skills, instinct for compromise, and understanding of the dynamics of the legislative process that would be required to successfully sponsor federal park legislation.

In addition to its popularity among his constituents, there were other compelling reasons for Kennedy to take an interest in the proposed national park. His family had spent summers in Hyannis Port since 1926, and both their summer home, and Cape Cod generally, were intrinsic to Kennedy's public identity in ways that the family's other residences (in Brookline, Westchester, and Palm Beach, for example) were not. Images of the photogenic politician sailing, swimming, and enjoying his summers on Nantucket Sound were instrumental in the construction of his political persona as an energetic and youthful counterpoint to the staid Eisenhower era. (Fig. 3.10) They also helped dispel rumors regarding the state of his health. Kennedy used his father's house in Hyannis Port as his official address as a senator and later as a successful candidate for president—and by 1957 he was already exploring the possibility of running for that office.[45] According to Holborn, in fact, he was intrigued at the outset by the possibility that he might introduce Cape Cod legislation as a senator and later sign it as the nation's chief executive. His widening ambition made the controversies in the town meetings of the Outer Cape less relevant as he began to perceive his political constituency as national. Saltonstall was a willing cosponsor, but his Republican affiliation made him at least initially more circumspect when it came to angering fellow state party members on Cape Cod.[46]

Although Kennedy and Saltonstall were already discussing legislation in 1957, the release of the "Field Investigation Report" in 1959 provided the detail necessary for proceeding. From the beginning, the process of developing the bill was atypical. That summer, Holborn and Martin took the lead and conducted a fact-finding field trip, speaking with local elected officials and property owners. While this was a normal approach for legislative aides when considering a new bill, park service staff was not as involved as it often had been in drafting legislation that affected the national park system. Park service planners had provided the basis for the proposed boundaries and other details for the national seashore in their national seashore proposal; but by all accounts the political aides at that point took the initiative to draft a bill independently. Holborn and Martin, in later interviews, offered no insight as to why, or whether park service officials had wanted to

Fig. 3.10. John F. Kennedy, his children, and children of his extended family, at Hyannis Port in 1963. Photo by Cecil Stoughton. NACP.

be more involved. Preparing legislation (although not park bills) was an undertaking they both understood well, and they felt they were following an established approach. For his part, Conrad Wirth had known since the 1930s that establishing a national seashore on Cape Cod would be a politically difficult undertaking. He had just received his boisterous receptions at Eastham and at Chatham and, as indicated by the *Saturday Evening Post* editorial and other negative responses, he was not winning broad support for the park service plan as it stood. With the interest and backing of the state's two powerful senators, he was evidently ready to see what their staffs, working together, could do.[47]

During two trips to the Outer Cape that summer, Holborn and Martin inspected the proposed park boundaries, met with concerned citizens, and consulted with town selectmen and state elected officials, initiating a kind of public outreach that was potentially more responsive to public concerns than the process of the park service had been. But in addition to listening to constituents, they also heeded the park service's desire to create a true national park—a reservation that would be more than beaches and recreation facilities. In short, they needed to draft legislation that would authorize a park that not only met national park standards but would also have a place for the people who lived in it. Those people felt that they had been left out of the 1959 proposal, which had implied that all private property within the park would be acquired. Even if the current owners were allowed to remain through a twenty-five-year or a lifetime tenancy purchase agreement, in the end the park service would have what it traditionally wanted in a national park: no private land within its boundaries. Wirth and his planners considered private properties within a park (or "inholdings") to be management problems, with tremendous potential for future complications that could undermine the basic goals of conservation and public access. The question was, could these conflicting visions and interests be reconciled in a way that would satisfy the communities of the Outer Cape as well as the mandate to "preserve unimpaired" the landscape for future generations?

By the end of the summer, Holborn and Martin had devised a strategy to win over a key constituency on Cape Cod: those who were only moderately opposed to the national seashore because they feared the taking of their private residences through eminent domain. Real estate developers and others who believed that they would benefit from increased commercialization would likely never be in favor of the park. But many of those directly affected by the national seashore proposal were vacation home owners, among them professionals, educators, and cultural figures. They might support the national seashore if it were consistent with their interests, above all, if it allowed them to retain ownership of their properties. Their anxiety for their vacation homes was balanced by an awareness that much of the Outer Cape was in imminent peril of being subdivided and covered in houses and businesses. As Charles Foster observed, "an odd coalition of summer residents and year-rounders was beginning to form—a coalition dedicated to the proposition that some form of major conservation action was essential to the well-being of the Cape."[48]

It would fall to Holborn and Martin, and soon others, to enable that coalition to grow by eliminating the most pressing fear that inhibited it: the anticipated taking of property through condemnation. Their idea was simple, unprecedented, and for the park service, previously unthinkable. They would devise a strategy to leave the private residences (or "improved properties") in which title had been vested before September 1, 1959, as inholdings, but only if they were under local land use restrictions that assured the future integrity of the park. The homeowners within the proposed boundaries could remain, in other words, if town zoning restrictions on their properties assured continued residential, noncommercial use, keeping them in something like their contemporary state. In theory, as long as the properties were not significantly redeveloped in a way that undermined the purposes of a national park, inholdings would not be a threat to the park's future. For the idea to work, however, town governments would need to impose specific zoning regulations ("seashore districts") on the areas of each town within park boundaries. As a matter of constitutional law, the federal government could not directly enforce land use regulations on private property owners, even within the boundaries of a national park.[49] And so Holborn and Martin came up with an effective idea for assuring that the six towns would pass the needed zoning laws. The use of eminent domain would be authorized in the seashore legislation to be used if necessary; but it would also specify that the use of eminent domain would be "suspended" for existing "improved properties" as long as the towns of the Outer Cape created zoning districts for the areas within the seashore's boundaries which imposed restrictions on any future development. As long as the towns enacted their own zoning—based on guidelines distributed by the secretary of the interior—the legislation would guarantee a suspension of the use of eminent domain, and the owners of private residential property within the park who did not want to sell would never have to.[50]

This was the essential feature of what came to be known as the "Cape Cod formula," or the "Cape Cod model." While it is unclear whose idea it was, exactly, those directly involved give credit for the breakthrough to David Martin and Fred Holborn, who, working together, came up with the solution after consulting with the many concerned residents and officials. Their meetings with Sargent, Foster, Burling, Biddle, Nickerson, Frazier, and others persuaded them that a fresh approach was needed for legislation to succeed. Martin, who was a lawyer, drafted the text of the bill. By all accounts the park service was not directly involved, although agency lawyer Frank Harris reviewed the draft language with Martin and Holborn. Martin also corresponded directly with Benjamin Thompson with specific lists of questions regarding the implications of potential provisions in the legislation.[51] There is also no indication that Wirth and his staff actively opposed the idea, even if it represented a major departure for them. Thompson later admitted that although he and Wirth "were never happy with it," they felt it was a necessary compromise.[52]

The unprecedented intent of the legislation was captured in the introduction and the preamble to Section 4 of the final bill:

> The purpose of this bill is to provide for the establishment of a Cape Cod National Seashore so that lower Cape Cod may be preserved in substantially its present condition for the benefit of all the people of the United States and future generations.
>
> Lower Cape Cod cannot be considered solely as a geographical area with certain physical characteristics. The lower cape must also be viewed as a way of life—a culture—which though conditioned by its environment finds its essence in the people who have lived and are living there. This bill seeks to preserve the way of life which these people have established and maintained on the cape.
>
> . . .
>
> [Section 4] together with section 5 may be considered as the heart of the bill for purposes of preservation of the way of life of lower Cape Cod as well as the geographic area to be included in the seashore. The provisions represent an unprecedented innovation in legislation to accommodate the special circumstances of lower Cape Cod. They are designed to assure that the area will be preserved for the purposes set forth in the preamble of the bill in such a way as adequately to safeguard the private and municipal interests in the area.

With its lofty intentions, the 1959 legislation exceeded a merely expedient compromise to allow homeowners—some of whom wielded considerable influence—to retain their houses. At the heart of the entire effort was the notion that there was a "way of life" that contributed to the value of the new park, and that the bill's innovative provisions were intended to "accommodate the special circumstances" of the region, circumstances that found their "essence in the people who have lived and are living there." The drafters of the legislation were outlining new premises for how a national park should be conceived and established, specifically in terms of the relationship of the park, as an institution, to the communities around it—and now, in fact, within it. Those premises, however, remained undefined as long as the "way of life" of the Outer Cape also resisted exact definition. Which people, activities, places, or events were essential to maintain "in their present condition," and which were not or even represented an erosion of the regional "circumstances" identified as worthy of preservation?

In 1959, however, these complexities lay comfortably in the future. The "odd coalition" in favor of the park which Foster had seen forming supported the new national park model, not only because it reduced the proposed taking of private property but because it promised to respect what was for many the most important regional resource of all: its distinct culture and what that implied about the "character" of the Outer Cape.

View over the dunes, Provincetown. Photo by Carol Betsch.

FOUR

Preserving a "Way of Life"

Contentious aspects of the seashore proposal, especially the question of the exact delineation of the new park's boundaries, still needed resolving. Many of these difficult details were of enormous importance to individuals and to individual towns, and it fell to the Ninth District's new representative, Hastings Keith, to sort them out and, ultimately, to decide whether to cosponsor the legislation his senatorial colleagues were about to introduce. Keith had won a tightly contested Republican primary and replaced Donald Nicholson—a staunch and vocal opponent of any kind of federal park proposal—after the 1958 general election. Kennedy won reelection easily; he even carried Cape Cod, the first major Democratic candidate ever to do so (although he did not carry the county two years later in the presidential election).

The election changed the political climate and offered new hope for reaching a consensus on the national seashore. But Keith faced a difficult situation. As a congressman in his first year of office, he occupied a more vulnerable position than either senator. Keith had no statewide constituency (and certainly not a national one) and was directly answerable to the voters on the Outer Cape every two years. He therefore was under some obligation to be more solicitous and responsive to complaints and suggestions about the seashore plan than the senators felt they needed to be. As the third member of the area's congressional delegation, his support was crucial for the park's advocates; others expected him to be responsive to the local concerns of his fellow party members and perhaps follow Nicholson's line. Keith involved himself personally in negotiations and consultations on the Outer Cape far more than Saltonstall or Kennedy. At first he remained uncommitted while he investigated details, moved to make revisions to satisfy constituents, and generally tried to ascertain where the greatest political advantage (or least damage) lay. "I don't want anyone to think I am in league with the National Park Service," he told the *Cape Cod Standard-Times.* "I'm a representative of the people of the Cape and I'm anxious to get their point of view." His legislative assistant, Judy Carberry, collaborated with Holborn and Martin as they went to work that summer, and Keith recognized that the legislative effort had great momentum. But until the summer of 1959 he avoided a specific commitment, and afterward he continued to press for amendments to the Senate bill.[1]

Once the issue of eminent domain was neutralized by Martin and Holborn's "formula," exact boundaries became the principal bone of contention. In drafting their bill, Holborn and Martin were guided by the 1958 park service plan. Keith and Carberry, however, were more receptive to the town selectmen and others who wanted certain areas excluded and the overall size of the park reduced. Four areas of the proposed boundaries incited particularly strong local concern:

Fig. 4.1. Fort Hill area, Eastham. Photo by author.

Fig. 4.2. Monomoy National Wildlife Refuge, 2010. Photo by U.S. Fish and Wildlife Service, Northeast Region. Wikimedia Commons.

the ponds in Truro and Wellfleet; Great Island, Bound Brook Island, and the bay shoreline in Wellfleet; Fort Hill in Eastham; and Monomoy and Morris Islands in Chatham.[2] (Figs. 4.1, 4.2)

The Town of Chatham, and its energetic selectman Robert McNeece, offered the most organized lobbying effort. A majority of participants in Chatham town meeting wanted to make sure Monomoy would not become a major recreational destination and so alter the character of what McNeece described as the "unspoiled little fishing village" of Chatham.[3] (Fig. 4.3) McNeece and others had come full circle. They had originally objected to the wildlife refuge and been in favor of recreational access; but by the 1950s it was clear that the potential level of use of Monomoy was much greater than the local fishing and hunting they once were trying to protect, and the group argued to maintain Monomoy as a relatively inaccessible wildlife refuge. Since that use was consistent with the purposes of the national seashore, the park service planners had left the island out of their 1958 proposal, but it was added in the Senate version of the legislation.

Fig. 4.3. "Fishing Shacks at Chatham," postcard, c. 1930–45. BPL.

In 1961, those in favor of the private development of Morris Island and others in Chatham distributed a mock park brochure, dated 1972, with a map showing extensive recreational facilities, including marinas and boat ramps on Morris Island and a new highway lined with campgrounds and picnic areas along the length of Monomoy. They also included a reprint of a recent *Atlantic Monthly* article by Devereux Butcher, then executive secretary of the National Parks Association, decrying the overdevelopment of national parks under the Mission 66 program. Butcher summarized the fiercest criticism of the park service at the time and, although he made no mention of Cape Cod, he questioned the agency's fundamental commitment to landscape preservation. The Chatham group claimed, based on the essay, that the park service could not be trusted to "hold to their original directions or intentions" to limit recreational development in the town. Francis Burling alerted the park service to what national seashore advocates considered a disinformation campaign and noted that Hastings Keith was now primarily concerned with keeping Morris and Stage Islands out of the national seashore. The *Cape Codder* responded to the campaign with a strong editorial questioning whether the concerns raised in the *Atlantic* essay had any bearing on the pending national seashore legislation, which Butcher knew little about.[4]

McNeece and the Chatham selectmen were by now veterans of conflicts with the Department of the Interior, the military, and the Commonwealth of Massachusetts over the eventual disposition of their beaches. The park service had included Morris Island and Harding Beach in its 1958 plan as a crucial component of the landscape diversity of the proposed park, being the only areas with shoreline on Nantucket Sound. McNeece and his confederates were determined to keep the areas out of the park, the beach to remain under town control and Morris Island to become an exclusive residential development that would boost local tax receipts. In fact, a plan for Morris Island had already been prepared by a landscape architect in Falmouth, Donald Durrell.

Chatham's efforts to exclude as much of the town as possible from the seashore were organized and effective. Jonathan Moore, who replaced David Martin as Saltonstall's legislative assistant that fall, recalled that the Town of Chatham hired lobbyists with close personal and political connections to both Saltonstall and Kennedy. Despite the efforts of the Chatham planning board chair Alice Hiscock and other residents who argued in favor of the proposed park boundaries (as well as town zoning codes), Harding Beach was excluded in the first draft of the Senate bill.[5] Moore delayed the decision on Morris Island, however, believing that if he gave in too soon, other towns would demand similar concessions. But Morris Island ultimately would not be part of the national seashore, either, to the disappointment of Hiscock and others.[6] Debates on boundaries continued over the next two years through a series of congressional hearings and local efforts to make changes right up to the final resolution. And though some changes were made, no other town on the Outer Cape had Chatham's success in influencing the seashore legislation.[7] (Monomoy was included in the first draft of the Senate bill in 1959—a significant addition to the proposed 1958 park service boundaries—but was removed by the conference committee in 1961 and remained a National Wildlife Refuge, which it is today.)

By September 1959, Holborn and Martin were ready to introduce their bill in the Senate. For Hastings Keith, the issue was now being forced, since the senators would proceed with or without his support. But his decision was made far easier after the restriction on the use of eminent domain described in the Senate bill became known and shifted public sentiment. For many former opponents, the question was no longer whether there should be a park but what the exact boundaries and management policies should be. Keith therefore planned to introduce his own bill in the House, mostly identical to the Senate version, with the intention of working out such details—especially the final boundaries—through hearings, amendments, and the rest of the legislative process. By the end of the summer of 1959, the *Cape Codder* reported that both Saltonstall and Keith agreed "in principle" on the establishment of a Cape Cod national seashore.[8] On September 3, bills were introduced by the congressional delegation in their respective chambers. The order of the names for the "Kennedy-Saltonstall" bill (S.2636), "to provide for the establishment of the Cape Cod National Seashore Park," was decided by Holborn and Martin through a coin toss (according to Martin), the results of which reversed the traditional practice of putting the senior senator's name first.[9] (Fig. 4.4)

The introduction of the legislation, sponsored by the members of Congress who represented the affected constituencies, changed the discussion on the Outer Cape and also the format and venues for that discussion. The Subcommittee on Public Lands of the Senate Committee on Interior and Insular Affairs scheduled public hearings to be held in Eastham Town Hall for December 9 and 10. That fall, the Town of Eastham sent out the Senate bill

Fig. 4.4. John F. Kennedy and Leverett Saltonstall, 1959. Photograph Collection, Massachusetts Historical Society.

to all resident and nonresident taxpayers with a survey to measure public reaction. About 80 percent favored a national seashore "in principle." (The battle was hardly over in Eastham, however, where the planning board nevertheless remained opposed to any seashore proposal.) In Truro, selectman Anthony Duarte organized a poll that found the reverse: 80 percent against the establishment of a park. But if the "storm" of the previous four years that E. J. Kahn Jr. had described had not cleared, the weather nevertheless was changing. As the towns of the Outer Cape prepared statements and position papers for the upcoming hearings, even though resentment against the use of eminent domain remained strong, the emphasis was increasingly on altering the proposed boundaries.[10]

Congress held a total of four public hearings on the evolving legislation between December 1959 and March 1961, producing over eight hundred pages of published transcripts. Senator Frank E. Moss, a Utah Democrat, chaired the first two hearings in the Eastham Town Hall, with Leverett Saltonstall and Hastings Keith assisting, as sponsoring legislators. Forty-eight individuals testified and more than one hundred written comments were submitted for the record.[11] The opportunity to be heard generated great interest and resulted in a unique written record of the attitudes and aspirations of the people of the Outer Cape. As the historian David Jenkins has observed, the hearing transcripts recorded a diversity of views and a variety of concerns.[12] They also captured a sense of what Outer Cape residents and public officials hoped the legislation could or should achieve. The transcripts give insight into how these interested parties perceived the "unique cultural, scenic, historic, scientific, and recreational values" that the creation of the park was intended to "preserve and enhance." Almost all of those who testified indicated their interest in preserving the "character" of the Outer Cape, which was described in the legislation as an "irreplaceable part of the Heritage of the United States." But what exactly were the sources and elements of that character? And what boundaries would define an "adequate and representative portion" of the Outer Cape landscape which would achieve the purpose of the national seashore?

The arguments against federal ownership of such a significant proportion of the Outer Cape had been well formulated by then. The unprecedented scope of the Cape Cod proposal did not escape Quincy A. Shaw, whose wealthy Boston family had long owned a large property in Eastham. He felt that the purpose of the national park could be achieved simply by incorporating Great Beach, the true "natural monument" in question, and did not require taking upland homes and farms, which residents should continue to "live on and enjoy, not as a park, but as their own—their homes." Shaw also understood the ecological implications of restricting private inholdings to three-acre plots, the amount deemed "reasonably necessary for the enjoyment of the dwelling." Inholdings of larger acreage, such as Shaw's, would be subdivided and the land in excess acquired by the park service. Shaw observed that during the "halcyon days of the old Cape Cod," the landscape had been open and agricultural, affording scenic vistas and views of the ocean and harbors. He, like other landowners, invested capital and labor to keep the land open and ocean views intact. Shaw correctly foresaw that if such areas passed into public ownership, they would rapidly become a "second-growth wilderness of oak and scrub pine, of poison ivy and briars," dramatically altering the landscape character that the park was intended to preserve.

Other residents emphasized the broader point: the character of the cultural landscape of the Outer Cape depended on the communities that had occupied and managed the landscape for hundreds of years. A park that threatened to dislocate or destroy those communities would, in fact, lead to a deterioration of the "real charm of the Cape," not to its protection. Madelane Winslow worried that traditional practices, such as the harvesting of bayberries, rose hips, and blueberries, would be largely eliminated on land under park service jurisdiction, again with deleterious impact on the true character of the Cape while in addition causing economic hardship for year-round residents who depended on these traditional practices to augment their income. Likewise, Robert McNeece testified: "It is not only the seashore and the dunes and the waves that contribute to something that Cape Cod means to the American people. We believe that an unspoiled little cape town, its little old white Cape Cod cottages, its neatness, its order, its white churches, meeting houses, we believe that the charm of a cape town as a unit contributes a great deal to the heritages that we are trying to preserve for future generations." The Truro select board chair, John Worthington, also noted that many of the private homes in question were hundreds of years old and represented "a culture and a way of life which is unique and a truly significant part of the charm of the cape."

But all of these objections also revealed an acknowledgment, if not an endorsement, of some form of imminent federal park protection. Since the previous spring, the polemics had shifted. Even Joshua Nickerson now concentrated his efforts not on stopping the park, but on assuring strong local influence—through a proposed citizens' advisory commission—on the park's future management. "We, who are direct descendants of the Pilgrim Fathers, and who have lived on this land continuously since they first settled here," he insisted, should be "allowed to give . . . both advice and consent to the essential features of its [the landscape's] future use and development." Francis Biddle, too, now supported the legislation, although with an important rhetorical caveat that would characterize much of the future debate over the specific boundaries and design features of the park. He expressed the need for emphasis on "preservation" rather than "recreation" in future park policy. Too much facilitation of recreation, he felt, would defeat the larger purpose of preserving the landscape character of the Outer Cape. Too many roads, parking lots, public beaches, campgrounds, and boat launches would attract too many of the fifty million Americans who lived within driving distance of the narrow and fragile Outer Cape landscape.[13]

Biddle's concerns were echoed by others, who were on record both for and against the park.[14] Noting the effects of new interstate highways and of improved roads on the Cape, Mrs. Walter P. Chrysler Jr. (who strongly rejected any idea of a national park) warned that day-trippers would have easier access than ever—and, "God help us if they all arrive at the same time." She later testified that, in her view, the park service "talks conservation from one side of its face—and then from the other side comes the real reason for the taking of this acreage on Cape Cod—recreation. These two words should never be used in the same breath and have any honest meaning." She insisted that the "real charm" of Cape Cod lay in the fact that it was "a community, or a way of life." Federal ownership and regulations were inimical to the preservation of the communities that were the true source of the region's landscape character.[15]

The potential threat of greatly increased tourist visitation gave people on both sides of the debate common ground and a shared desired outcome. The architect Serge Chermayeff, for example, insisted that "everything that several people said, and emphatically Mr. Biddle, about limiting the recreational function within [the park] are of the utmost, the most vital importance." He was especially worried about the influx of cars, which if not controlled would defeat the "very conservation which you speak of." (Fig. 4.5) Many who testified in Eastham spoke movingly of the features of the cultural landscape they hoped would be saved through federal legislation. Warren Partridge Jr. described with considerable expertise the varieties of bird and plant life that populated the beach, wetland, and upland ecosystems of the Outer Cape. "Surely such birds, flowers, and trees are a vital part of the charm of Cape Cod," he confirmed, "and only a national park can assure them for future generations." But again, the planning and management of that park would decide its success. "Millions of people seek our national parks," he warned, and overcrowding would destroy the habitats and ecosystems that contributed to the values and significance of the Outer Cape landscape.[16]

The rhetoric of "preservation versus recreation" would continue to frame the debate over how the national seashore should be realized. Hastings Keith, in particular, would use this dichotomy in the coming months to convey his concerns and to advance his desired amendments to the Senate bill. Precedents supported apprehensions about overuse. While an economic report commissioned by the park service and released in March 1960 predicted that the establishment of a park would have an overall positive effect on land values and tax bases (alleviating some fears about increased tax rates and suppression of economic growth in the region), it also made clear that such an effect would be the result of increased tourism that the park would generate. Estimating that about 1.5 million visitors would come to the Outer Cape in 1960, the consultants suggested that the number would double by 1975 if the park were not created; but with the creation of the park, they predicted (based in part on data from the now-open Cape Hatteras National Seashore) that the number would rise to ten million.[17] The specter of millions of new visitors—many coming only for the day—preoccupied those testifying both for and against the park during the public hearings.

Even as they began to support the idea of the national seashore, Francis Biddle, Joshua Nickerson, Charles Frazier, Robert McNeece, and others testified with considerable knowledge and expertise on how the creation of a national park, especially one that served primarily recreational uses, could under-

Fig. 4.5. Herring Cove, Provincetown. NPSHC.

mine the primary purpose of any federal park legislation: landscape preservation. McNeece worried that the "fringe" areas outside the park, especially town centers, would come under great pressure for commercial development and so would lose their "present charm," which he described as "something like a Currier and Ives picture." Charles Frazier predicted that "in attempting to preserve the park area . . . they will destroy the rest of the area outside the park, and certainly that is not consistent with conservation or preservation."

Nickerson went further, objecting to the inclusion within the park boundaries of ocean and bay waters in a one-quarter-mile zone extending from the shore. He believed that the provision was intended to limit commercial fisheries—another vital component of the Cape's character—and likely revealed an intent to build public marinas that would, again, lead to too high a level of recreational use. He also wanted motels and any other "commercial development" within the park to be subject to town approval, and for camping to be under the same restriction. His larger point—one that significantly impacted future policies—was that the proposed citizens' advisory commission should have the power to assure that local concerns would shape park service plans and management. In a letter accompanying his testimony at Eastham, Nickerson summarized the concern of many Outer Cape residents:

> You can turn the lower cape into a summer recreation and amusement area for a million people, but you cannot, at the same time, conserve its natural charm. This can be conserved, however, if emphasis is put on conserving the way of life of the people living in this area, and also on the conserving of the flora and fauna which have been put there by nature.
>
> For 300 years the flora, the fauna, and the people have gotten along with mutual understanding; so successfully, that it is an outstanding characteristic which accounts, to a marked degree, for the charm of the area. This mutuality of understanding between man and nature can best be preserved by preserving both man's way and nature's way.[18]

Others who testified expressed an opposing view that the park service should in fact represent (and protect) the national interest at stake, beyond local considerations. A wide range of state and national conservation organizations expressed their support, including Massachusetts sportsmen's clubs, who appreciated the provisions to allow continued (regulated) hunting and fishing in the park. In general, the strongest support came from people and organizations representing a constituency outside the immediate region. Speaking as the Massachusetts commissioner of natural resources, Charles Foster dismissed concerns that the park would lead to a deterioration of the character of the landscape, observing that "no federal agency would tend to be more sympathetic to pure conservation that the National Park Service." This sentiment was echoed by other park proponents, who emphasized that national park jurisdiction was the surest means available to achieve landscape preservation. Edward Stone believed that the unique history of the Outer Cape and the sites associated with the first Pilgrim landing would finally receive adequate stewardship and interpretation only through park service management. Others recognized the importance of the precedent being set by the national seashore.

At the final set of hearings, in Washington on March 9, 1961, both Udall and Wirth attested to their full support of the legislation, as it had been amended by that time. Udall pointed to the new president's interest in the bill and the "pioneering" opportunity that Udall hoped would lead to similar initiatives elsewhere in the county. Wirth confirmed his support of the "special provisions" of the Cape Cod model and urged Congress to act in the limited time left to save the Outer Cape and, by extension, seashores elsewhere in the country.[19]

The congressional hearings uncovered a complex set of sometimes conflicting aspirations for what the "preservation" of the "character" of the Outer Cape landscape might mean. Those who favored keeping people and their ways of life intact in the landscape frequently showed a sophisticated understanding of how a long history of settlement had shaped not only the physical landscape but its associations and meanings for residents and visitors alike—its "character" and "charm." Those in favor of more complete control by the park service were more impressed by the threats of mid-twentieth-century patterns of development and the endless pressure of people who wanted to build vacation homes. For this group, the ecosystems and natural features that were being staked out by surveyors and leveled by bulldozers were at as great a risk as the cultural landscape. A fundamental dissonance was evident: a failure to agree on not only what preservation meant, but what exactly was to be preserved. How vital were human occupation and activities to the value and character of the landscape? To what degree did the concern for the cultural landscape undermine the imperative to preserve natural systems and features? But this lack of a consensus on the exact terms, definitions, and methods to be employed did not prevent a more general conviction from forming: something should be done to "preserve" the Outer Cape—whatever that might mean to various residents—and some form of national park legislation was increasingly accepted as the best means to achieve it.

Another continuing set of concerns involved boundary decisions. Hastings Keith had endorsed the idea of a national park "in principle" and had introduced his own House bill. His strategy was to use the legislative process to minimize the extent of the park and return it to something more like the 1955 "Great Beach Area" proposal. By 1960, he had a detailed list of areas he felt should be excluded. In Wirth's view, if all the congressman's suggestions were taken, it would so "dismember and impoverish the National Seashore as to make its national significance questionable," and he urged Udall to support the agency's "well considered position." (The park service director was more amenable to Keith's vague insistence that the provision creating a citizens' advisory commission be strengthened.)[20] The proposed boundaries were debated in every town on the Outer Cape.

A group of Provincetown officials hoped to have a significant portion of the Province Lands given back to the town for private development if and when the area was transferred to the federal government. The town manager hired the planners Van Ness Bates Associates to design a resort complex for the acreage they hoped to build on west of the town. An "Emergency Committee for the Preservation of the Province Lands," including Josephine Del Deo, Charles Mayo, Ross Moffet, and Stanley Kunitz, formed to prevent the development and assure the Province Lands remained intact.[21] They testified to Congress and won the day in town meeting; all the Province Lands eventually became part of the national seashore.

Wellfleet, under the leadership of selectman Charles Frazier, advocated for a reduction and modification of the park, not an outright rejection of it. Working with Francis Biddle, Frazier proposed that the amount of land taken in Wellfleet could be greatly reduced if the town established a "buffer zone" that would allow private ownership but prevent undesirable development. While the existing "improved properties" within the boundaries were already to be treated in this way in the pending legislation, Frazier was suggesting that much of the still-undeveloped private property in Wellfleet (which the park service planned to acquire outright) could be protected through similar town zoning restrictions. The result again would mean a return to something like the 1955 proposal. But undeveloped property did not have the inherent constituency of vacation home owners, and Frazier's scheme was unsuccessful.[22]

Some people in Eastham also wanted a reduction in the amount of land taken for the park, particularly the Fort Hill area, which was not included in the 1958 park service boundaries but was in the Senate legislation. Saltonstall and Kennedy had personally requested the addition after viewing the area from a helicopter in August 1959.[23] In this case, Hastings Keith strongly supported removing the acreage (which was already subdivided and very desirable for development) and keeping it on the town's tax rolls. But much to his disappointment, in the negotiations with both House and Senate subcommittees over the next two years, Fort Hill was not returned to Eastham.

The deciding moment occurred in March 1961, during a tour of the Cape by House and Senate subcommittee members who wanted to see the areas being discussed for inclusion. Jonathan Moore and Francis Burling recalled that those on the tour were as impressed by the views from Fort Hill as Saltonstall and Kennedy had been and decided the area should remain within the seashore.[24] At Keith's request, however, the House subcommittee returned other developable acreage to Eastham, as well as to Wellfleet and Truro. As a result, the House bill, as it was amended and passed, was in most regards identical to the Senate bill but described different boundaries and reduced the park's overall size by about 4,990 acres.[25]

Removing developable private acreage from the boundaries was a means of mitigating the effect the park would have on the towns' tax bases. While this was not an important issue in Orleans and Provincetown, where little land would be taken, it was in Chatham and Eastham, where it fueled the debate over whether to include Morris Island and Fort Hill. Truro and Wellfleet had the most to lose, and Keith consulted with town representatives to suggest adjustments in park boundaries that would make some future development possible. There were also measures in the 1959 legislation intended to lessen the economic impact of putting thousands of acres into the public domain. Holborn and Martin included a provision for up to 10 percent of the private land that fell within park boundaries in each town to be set aside for residential development, subject (like the preexisting "improved properties") to the town's special zoning restrictions. Payments in lieu of taxes, to be made by the federal government to town governments to compensate for the loss of tax revenue were also to be authorized for a period of up to twenty-five years. But neither provision would survive the legislative process. The 10 percent clause was considered potentially complicated and difficult to implement, and town officials sought instead simply to have more developable land excluded from the park boundaries in the first place. Payments in lieu of taxes would be expensive, and were not likely to get by the watchdogs of the Congressional Budget Office. Both measures were dropped as the bill was revised in Congress.[26]

Payments in lieu of taxes, the 10 percent clause, and boundary revisions all were attempts to mitigate the anticipated impact of the seashore on towns' economic well-being. In Eastham, although the town's survey indicated that many residents had changed their view, the planning board and a group of park opponents organized as the Eastham Citizens Committee remained firmly opposed to the Senate bill and its proposed boundaries. The planning board hired Blair Associates to prepare an economic analysis, to be presented at a special town meeting held in November 1959, just before the first congressional hearings. The report called for a reduction of eight hundred acres in the land to be taken in Eastham (including, of course, Fort Hill) "to allow sound community development in coming years." The consultants made no further prediction or judgment on the potential influence the seashore might have. At the congressional hearings the next month, the planning board nevertheless registered absolute opposition to the establishment of the seashore in any form. The town's selectmen, however, influenced by the public survey results as well as the economic analysis, supported the creation of the seashore but with boundary changes that reduced the land taken in Eastham. They offered a "buffer zone" scheme, like Wellfleet, to protect the land that would remain in private ownership.[27]

With the seashore's boundaries being contested on economic grounds, the park service hired Economic Development Associates, Inc., from Boston, to complete an independent report on the entire Outer Cape. The study was intended to predict the overall economic impact of the park and compare that situation to an economic forecast for the region if no park were created. It was released March 1960, and generally reassured many on the Outer Cape that the impact of removing thousands of acres of land from private ownership would be mitigated by increased land values and opportunities for development on properties outside the park. Far from depressing the regional economy, the park would stimulate businesses and employment. The analysts noted that both the present and the future economy of the Outer Cape was supported by tourism, and that the creation of the national seashore would benefit, not inhibit, this type of economic growth. They supported phased payments in lieu of taxes, but concluded that any negative effect on local tax receipts would be temporary, and the long-term effect would be positive. They rejected the 10 percent clause and pointed out that excluding certain areas would achieve the same result without the "confusion, conflict, and uncertainties" that were bound to result from allowing continued private development within the park. They also sounded a prescient warning on the need for "coordinated planning" for the Outer Cape. Noting that the establishment of the park would generate increased development outside its boundaries, that activity, "if not properly planned and controlled," would hasten the loss of the "values" the park was intended to preserve. "Should this happen," they warned, "the maximum value of the Park to the Cape towns, and some of the value of the Park itself, will be lost."[28]

One of the most significant aspects of the 1959 legislation introduced in the Senate and the House was a provision to establish a Cape Cod National Seashore Advisory Commission to help set the policies governing the seashore and its future administration. Its ten members were to be appointed by the secretary of the interior from nominations made by the selectmen of the six towns of the Outer Cape, by the commissioner of Barnstable County, and by the governor of Massachusetts. This was a special concern for Keith, who wanted to assure that the influence of his constituents would not evaporate as soon as the legislative process was complete. He tried to extend the commission's authorization to twenty-five years, but it ended up at ten years in the final legislation. Charles Foster, who would be named the first chair of the commission in 1961, later claimed that the park service would never have agreed to such a commission at all, but he probably overstated Wirth's opposition to the idea.

Citizen advisory boards were not unprecedented in the national park system. At Yosemite National Park, a Board of Expert Advisors had been established in 1928, with Frederick Law Olmsted Jr. as its first chairman. The Historic Sites Act of 1935 created the National Parks System Advisory Board, which still advises on many aspects of the national park system. Benjamin Thompson, citing his experience with the Yosemite board, insisted that he and Wirth actually felt the Cape Cod advisory commission would "be a good device" that would give "people locally a voice and knowledge of developing problems."[29] But this was the first time national park legislation would include specific requirements for a citizens' advisory group, another precedent set by the Cape Cod National Seashore. The advisory commission, which was generally considered an important success over the coming years, would become a template for other such committees for national parks and an increasingly common tool used by other federal agencies.[30]

One of the reasons Wirth, Thompson, and other park service officials may have been willing to accept so many precedents—and make significant compromises—at Cape Cod was that the legislation set the most important precedent of all for the park service: it authorized funds for the acquisition of land to establish a new national park.[31] At first $15 million, then raised to $16 million, the amount was obviously low to anyone familiar with the region's real estate market. But as Wirth wrote in his memoirs, he considered this to be one of the most significant steps taken in the history of national parks since 1872, when Congress established Yellowstone National Park. Nevertheless, the provision attracted remarkably little discussion or even notice. Congress's unprecedented move seems to have been not so much a change in policy as a shift in climate

Fig. 4.6. Point Reyes National Seashore, California. Photo by Carol Highsmith. CHA.

Fig. 4.7. Padre Island National Seashore, Texas. Photo by Carol Highsmith. CHA.

in Washington. Park service budget appropriations were increasing by tens of millions of dollars for Mission 66, and at the time other seashore bills were being considered which would have funded land acquisitions for not one but multiple new parks. In this context, congressional deliberations of the Cape Cod legislation, with its relatively low price tag, hardly addressed what was, for Wirth, its single most important component.

The park service minimized the estimated cost of land acquisition intentionally, not because of any delusions regarding real estate prices on the Outer Cape, but strategically. While it might be a standard legislative practice (as Holborn put it, if they made a "good showing" they always "could come back" for additional funding), there was a specific reason the park service did not try to fund the entire project at once.[32] Wirth had ambitions for establishing national seashores in the immediate future at Point Reyes (California) and Padre Island (Texas), where planning had also been well advanced. (Figs. 4.6, 4.7) In the Senate, an amended version of Neuberger's seashore bill (S.2010) was introduced by Republican senator Gordon L. Allot of Colorado in April 1960, shortly after Neuberger's untimely death. The same month, another seashore bill (H.R. 11842) was introduced in the House by John P. Saylor, a Republican from Pennsylvania and ranking member of the House Interior Committee. These bills joined Neuberger's Oregon Dunes proposal with Padre Island and Cape Cod, again with the backing of the Department of the Interior, which reported favorably to Congress on the legislation and issued a press release supporting it.

The omnibus approach would authorize funding for acquisition of all three parks unencumbered by the special provisions of the Kennedy-Saltonstall bill, so a Cape Cod National Seashore would be created without the compromises that Martin and Holborn had devised on their own.[33] This effort made little progress, though—the Senate committee had evidently decided to proceed with the Kennedy-Saltonstall bill and give each seashore its own legislation.[34] But this legislative history indicates that Wirth had not given up on avoiding the concessions he had made by going along with the Massachusetts senators. At the very least, Wirth hoped to fund Point Reyes and Padre Island either with Cape Cod or immediately afterward, and he did not want to lessen his chances for them by including the full cost for Cape Cod (which would end up more than twice the amount authorized). If this was the strategy, it worked; Point Reyes and Padre Island National Seashores were both established in 1962 with authorizations of funding for land acquisition.

At the second set of congressional hearings, held in Washington on June 21, 1960, and again chaired by Senator Moss, proposed boundary changes dominated the discussion. The 1960 economic impact study commissioned by the park service and released that March addressed many of the concerns raised during the first set of hearings. On the Senate side, Holborn and Moore had submitted a revision of the Kennedy-Saltonstall bill, amended in response to comments from the first set of hearings, for the subcommittee to review. On the House side, however, the influential chairman of the Interior and Insular Affairs Committee, Wayne N. Aspinall (a Democrat from Colorado), began the hearings by announcing that the legislation would not come to a vote that year but would be delayed to be taken up by the 87th Congress in 1961. Given the often-observed need to act quickly—surveyors' stakes for subdivisions continued to appear on some of the acreage in question—Aspinall's decision threatened to derail the entire process and inevitably increased the eventual costs of land acquisition.

Although Aspinall did not elaborate on his reasons, Holborn believed that the experienced congressman did not want the bill to leave the committee, as a courtesy, until it had Keith's full support. Aspinall also had a close relationship with Kennedy, who had announced his candidacy at the beginning of the year. Kennedy might well be president when the 87th Congress convened, which would certainly ease the bill's passage. Conrad Wirth, who had excellent relationships with Congress generally, also was particularly close to Aspinall, whose committee often had direct dealings with the park service. The park service director may have wanted to slow down the Cape Cod legislation since the latest omnibus seashore legislation (Saylor's H.R. 11842) was still being considered and might provide a viable alternative. Francis Burling, always an astute observer, understood that the Department of the Interior had delayed reporting to Congress on the Kennedy-Saltonstall bill, and Hastings Keith had expressed reservations while introducing further last-minute amendments in the House. Some combination of these considerations caused Aspinall to delay and have the matter taken up by the 87th Congress.[35]

Delays can be fatal to congressional legislation,

but Kennedy's election that November obviously improved the prospects of the bill he had introduced. Congress was likely to be receptive to the wishes of a new president—who had been a prominent senator—regarding the creation of a national park near his family home. Hastings Keith was not giving up on his constituents' behalf, however, and continued to pursue boundary changes. The House subcommittee held a third set of hearings in December 1960, back in Eastham Town Hall. The meeting was more sparsely attended than the first, and transcripts reveal an incipient new mood. The committee chair, Gracie B. Pfost (a Democrat from Idaho), began by announcing that new versions of both the House and the Senate bills would be introduced on the first day of the new Congress, noting that the president-elect had asserted the importance of the legislation only a week earlier, while announcing the appointment of his secretary of the interior, Stewart Udall.

In January, Kennedy and Udall initiated their agenda of New Conservation, which would result in major achievements and new policies at the park service and other federal agencies within the Department of the Interior. The establishment of national seashores, Udall announced at his first press conference, would receive a high priority under the new administration. On the first day of the 87th Congress, a flurry of identical Cape Cod bills were introduced in the House by Massachusetts representatives Edward P. Boland, Thomas J. Lane, and Hastings Keith. Later, F. Bradford Morse and Silvio O. Conte filed bills as well. Few representatives from Massachusetts, apparently, now did not want to have their names associated with what looked to be a popular and important piece of legislation. In the Senate, Saltonstall and Benjamin A. Smith (who had been appointed to replace Kennedy) introduced a new version of the bill (now S.857), with revised boundaries that reduced the size of the seashore by about 1,500 acres, since the 10 percent provision had been abandoned.

Final hearings on the new bills were quickly organized and held in March.[36] After this last round and, presumably, further consultations on the Outer Cape, Keith introduced a new bill (H.R.5786), which still had most of the same provisions as the Senate bill but described a considerably smaller park of about 23,375 acres. Omitted areas included Morris and Stage Islands and Monomoy in Chatham; most of the Great Pond–Long Pond complex and Griffin Island in Wellfleet; and two areas in northern Eastham.[37] The House subcommittee used Keith's new bill as the basis for further action and began markup. (This was when members of both the House and Senate subcommittees toured the Cape—and decided to include Fort Hill.)

The final Senate bill still described boundaries for a seashore of about 30,370 acres (including Monomoy), but subcommittee markups made several changes, including removing the word "park" from the name of the bill, at the request of the park service. The bill now referred to the "Cape Cod National Seashore," not "Seashore Park." The nomenclature followed the precedent of Cape Hatteras and was also desirable because national "parks" usually prohibited public hunting. It was at this stage that the provision for payments in lieu of taxes was removed, based on an expressed belief (corroborated by the park service economic study) that town tax bases would be increased, not diminished, by the creation of the seashore. The Senate subcommittee then reported the bill favorably to Aspinall's full committee, and on June 27, the Senate passed the bill unanimously.

In the House, Aspinall's committee replaced the text of Keith's bill (while retaining the registration number and title), also removing the payments in lieu of taxes provision and adding back certain areas to the seashore for a total of 25,380 acres. On July 10, the House passed the bill with a large majority.[38] The House then considered and passed the Senate bill, but only after replacing its boundary provisions with those from the House version. If the Senate did not agree to the change, it would be up to a conference committee of legislators from both chambers to resolve the differences between the two bills.

The Senate did not agree, and appointed conference committee members (none of whom were allowed to be sponsors or cosponsors of the subject legislation) would now decide which areas in the Senate version that were left out of the House version would or would not be included in the seashore. The conference was reportedly an "amicable" one, in which the members shared a sense of the importance of preserving the Outer Cape—and perhaps of the wishes of the popular new president. But boundaries were not the "stickiest" of the issues negotiated, surprisingly; the legislation included "advance contract authority" that would allow the Department of the Interior to incur obligations in land purchases in advance of specific appropriations. The measure could have saved a great deal of money by allowing transactions to be made quickly, before prices rose further. The House conference committee members, however, deemed the provision "backdoor spending" that undermined the House's prerogative in appropriating public funds, and so they removed it.[39]

On August 1, the conference committee completed its report. In short, it added about 840 acres that Keith had excluded and removed approximately 3,700 acres that the Saltonstall-Smith bill had originally included. Monomoy and the Massachusetts Audubon property in Wellfleet, both of which were included in the Senate bill, were removed in conference (over 3,000 acres in total). These areas were not in the 1958 park service plan and would be protected whether in the park or not. Morris Island was excluded, as was Harding Beach, also in Chatham. Two strips of developable land in Truro were also removed. But Fort Hill in Eastham and Griffin Island, Great Island, Jeremy Point, and the Great Pond–Long Pond complex in Wellfleet all were included. The result was a national park that encompassed an estimated 26,670 acres of land (a figure that would eventually increase to 27,549 acres in the course of surveys and acquisitions). And if the underwater acreage (extending one-quarter mile from shore) was considered, the total area of the new park was 43,607 acres.[40] In 2007, a calculation based on park land records indicated that 76.8 percent of the area of Provincetown, 67.1 percent of Truro, 58.9 percent of Wellfleet, 29.6 percent of Eastham, 11 percent of Orleans, and 4.8 percent of Chatham eventually came under park service owner-

Fig. 4.8. John F. Kennedy, surrounded by members of Congress, signing the Cape Cod National Seashore legislation, August 7, 1961. Conrad L. Wirth is on the extreme right. Photo by Abbie Rowe. NPS.

Fig. 4.9. Cape Cod sunset. NPSHC.

ship.[41] In the end, the conference committee achieved a balanced compromise that was not too far short of the acreage the park service had originally proposed in their 1958 plan.

The process was now complete. President Kennedy signed the bill (S.857, Public Law 87-126) on August 7, in a White House ceremony, using more than two dozen pens to be handed out as mementos. (Fig. 4.8) He had introduced the first version of the legislation as a senator nearly three years earlier, when he announced that he and Leverett Saltonstall were "trying to achieve a new method of park establishment and operation," in which they were "entering some uncharted areas of park legislation."[42] The *Berkshire Eagle* editorialized that the authorization of the national seashore was "the finest victory ever recorded for the cause of conservation in New England."[43] (Fig. 4.9)

The Great Beach, Truro. Photo by Carol Betsch.

FIVE

The "Cape Cod Model"

Kennedy's election improved the reception of the Cape Cod bill in Congress and perhaps helped assure that the approach his and Saltonstall's staffs had devised—the Cape Cod "formula" or "model"—would be the legislative path chosen, not the omnibus bills backed by Wirth and the Department of the Interior that would have included fewer "special provisions." But there are other reasons to believe that the approach Martin and Holborn had used would be favored. They had done an artful job of building a broad constituency in an area that had a long history of settlement and a complex local political context. In the future, more often than not, new federal park legislation would need to address such complexities, through partnerships, public outreach, and compromises, as well as appropriations for the acquisition of land. The long history of concern for the cultural landscape of Cape Cod among Massachusetts conservation organizations and individuals had shaped the movement to create the seashore. Because of the personal interest of two powerful senators, and above all because of the activism and involvement of the people of the Outer Cape, the Cape Cod National Seashore authorized in 1961 differed from any earlier federal park. But it would not remain unique. The Cape Cod model heralded changes in how land conservation would be accomplished in the United States.[1]

Those changes had already begun in 1958, when Congress established the Outdoor Recreation Resources Review Commission (ORRRC). Composed of members of Congress, government officials, and private citizens, the commission produced its final report, *Outdoor Recreation for America,* in 1962.[2] With the creation of the ORRRC, Congress began consideration of legislation that would replace New Deal–era policies and bureaucracies with new planning organizations and funding methods. Mission 66 had increased congressional appropriations for national park development, but the ORRRC heralded a new willingness in Congress to legislate a more comprehensive approach to the conservation and recreation issues of the day. Francis Sargent, who served energetically as the Massachusetts commissioner of natural resources for ten years, and who had been so instrumental in initiating the seashore movement on Cape Cod, was named ORRRC executive director.[3]

The authorization of Cape Cod National Seashore was the only important piece of conservation legislation Kennedy and Udall were able to pass during the first year of the new administration, but many more were on the horizon. New Conservation under Secretary of the Interior Udall would soon establish an impressive legislative record (including the 1962 bills that created Padre Island and Point Reyes National Seashores) and would change policies and leadership at federal land management agencies. In April 1962, Udall implemented one of the ORRRC's recommendations by creating (through executive action) a new agency within the Interior, the Bureau of Outdoor Recreation (BOR). The new bureau, although it only survived until 1977, assumed many of the national recreational planning duties that Wirth and the park service had performed since 1933.[4]

Wirth opposed the creation of the BOR, and the reorganization began changes at the park service that culminated in the director's resignation in 1964. While many of the planning initiatives of Wirth's Mission 66 continued—including the national seashore program—they did so in a changed bureaucratic and political context and under new leadership. Udall had been a member of Congress before he resigned to become secretary of the interior, and his experience on the House Committee on Interior and Insular Affairs made him a capable shepherd of conservation legislation that the administration supported. During the nine years he remained secretary of the interior, Congress passed the Wilderness Act (1964), the Land and Water Conservation Fund Act (1964), the National Historic Preservation Act (1966), and the Wild and Scenic Rivers Act (1968).[5] His 1963 book, *The Quiet Crisis,* was a best seller and exhorted the public to embrace the environmental movement and the "land ethic" that Aldo Leopold had described in 1948.

Kennedy's election had assured the establishment of Cape Cod National Seashore and the successes that followed for the park service, but it also precipitated changes that set the agency on new paths. By 1960, Conrad Wirth understood that change was coming. Over the previous four years, Mission 66 had achieved a remarkable record of construction and park development, including new and expanded campgrounds, park housing and maintenance areas, road improvements, and new interpretive programs and displays. More than fifty of the new visitor centers were already built, and over fifty more were planned to be completed by 1966. (Fig. 5.1) By the time Udall was sworn in, park service operations budgets had risen dramatically, and Wirth claimed that the national park system, as a whole, was "in the best condition in its history."[6] But the creation of the ORRRC in 1958 had begun to indicate the need for Wirth to adapt the Mission 66 program to reflect the commission's looming recommendations and the changing priorities in Congress which the ORRRC represented. By 1959, revision of Mission 66 was already under way, and Wirth implemented a "top-level review" of the program to be prepared in time for the 1960 elections.[7]

For all of the construction progress during its first half, Mission 66 had been held back from an ambitious expansion of the national and state park systems by Congress's reluctance to directly fund land acquisition for new parks. During the New Deal, a myriad of federal and state agencies had acquired land that was used to create parks; but under Mission 66, much to Wirth's frustration, plans for new national parks—and national seashores in particular—only began to come to fruition with Cape Cod in 1961. By 1962, the ORRRC recommendations, planning efforts under way at the BOR, and Wirth's own revised Mission 66 priorities all em-

Fig. 5.1. Salt Pond Visitor Center shortly after opening in 1966. NPSHC.

phasized the need for major federal land acquisition. The ORRRC did not make recommendations for specific park projects; but Wirth and his municipal and state partners had been making such plans since the 1930s. "Approximately 40 bills were introduced in the last Congress, to authorize the acquisition of national seashores . . . [and] state seashore areas as identified in the seashore survey reports," Wirth's planners reported in 1960. "None of these were enacted."[8] The situation was about to change. Wirth, together with a group of state and local park officials he had organized, met with Udall and Francis Sargent (in his role as ORRRC executive director) early in 1961. He and Benjamin Thompson presented their estimates for a ten-year plan of national, state, and local park system land acquisition by the federal government: 9.6 million acres at a cost of $6.3 billion. Wirth described the new initiative as "Parks For America."[9]

President Kennedy, historians have observed, was not particularly committed to conservation issues, even considering his personal role in establishing the Cape Cod National Seashore. Foreign policy obviously preoccupied him during much of his administration. But his energetic secretary of the interior encouraged him to emulate the "conservation records of the two Roosevelts." A major federal land acquisition program—particularly of seashores and other national parks—was a first priority, followed by the desired passage of the Wilderness Act and the Land and Water Conservation Fund Act (LWCF).[10] Udall was able to exploit the work of the ORRRC, and that of the BOR and the National Park Service, to quickly inaugurate his program of New Conservation. The passage of the LWCF was crucial, in particular, because it offered the means to fund the millions of dollars for land acquisition that Udall considered an imperative. In addition to Padre Island

Fig. 5.2. Oregon Dunes National Recreation Area, 2015. Panoramic photo by Joe Mabel. Wikimedia Commons.

Fig. 5.3. Indiana Dunes. Photo by Carol M. Highsmith. CHA.

Fig. 5.4. Assateague. Wikimedia Commons.

and Point Reyes, Udall sought to acquire land for Indiana Dunes and Sleeping Bear Dunes "national lakeshores," Oregon Dunes, Fire Island, and Assateague Island National Seashores, and many other new national parks. (Figs. 5.2, 5.3, 5.4)

The fruition of Udall's efforts came largely after 1964, under the Johnson administration and the 88th "Conservation Congress." By 1966 (the final year of Mission 66), Congress had authorized nine national seashores and lakeshores. (Fig. 5.5) By 1972, four more national seashores (which had been planned earlier under Mission 66) followed. In all, 718 miles of shoreline were eventually protected through the acquisition of over 700,000 acres.[11] The project that inaugurated this unprecedented federal effort in coastal landscape conservation and validated its underlying approach and premises was the Cape Cod National Seashore. Cape Cod set the precedent for the direct federal acquisition of private land for the creation of new parks, a fact of great significance not only for national seashores but for national parks generally. (Fig. 5.6) From 1961 to 1966, Congress

Fig. 5.5. Cover of an informational brochure for Mission 66. NPSHC.

Fig. 5.6. A Mission 66 construction sign at Cape Cod National Seashore. NPSHC.

authorized fifty-four additional national park areas, and in almost all cases the legislators included money for the purchase of land.[12]

Seen in the context of 1960s federal conservation initiatives and the emerging environmental movement, the implementation of the provisions of the Cape Cod authorizing legislation would be an indicator of the success or failure of an entire new generation of conservation policy. The national seashore was only "authorized" in 1961; the tasks of land acquisition, planning, design, construction, and operation would now challenge the park service to realize the innovative vision for the park that had been contested and elaborated for decades. The sum result would be a new model for national park establishment and operation: the Cape Cod model. But the park service would not be acting alone. The involvement of the many actively engaged residents of the Outer Cape who had shaped the legislation continued under one of the bill's most important provisions: the creation of the Cape Cod National Seashore Advisory Commission (CCNSAC).

The initial appointments to the commission were critical to its subsequent effectiveness. The 1961 legislation specified that ten members would be appointed for two-year terms by the secretary of the interior, who would also designate one member as chair. Six appointments were to come from recommendations made by the boards of selectmen of the Outer Cape towns. Since the towns could recommend only one or two candidates, they exercised considerable influence on who their representatives would be. One member would be suggested by the commissioners of Barnstable County, two by the governor, and one by the secretary of the interior. The group met for the first time on February 16, 1962, at the Department of the Interior in Washington. Barnstable County was represented by Joshua Nickerson and the Town of Chatham by Robert McNeece. The towns sent Arthur Finlay, selectman and chair of the Orleans board of assessors; Ralph Chase, a former Eastham selectman; Esther Wiles, a noted park opponent from Wellfleet; John Dyer, a Truro selectman; and Nathan Malchman, former president of the Provincetown chamber of commerce. Massachusetts was represented by Josiah H. Child, an architect and park supporter from Provincetown, and Charles Foster. Udall appointed Leo Diehl, a state tax official and political aide to Congressman Thomas P. "Tip" O'Neill, and named Foster as the commission's chair.

The formulation of the commission—in part due to the provisions of the 1961 legislation—included members, such as McNeece, Nickerson, and Wiles, who had been among the most vocal opponents of the park; but it was chaired by Foster, an early and influential backer, and included others, such as Chase and Child, who also had been supporters from the outset.[13] Udall made the appointments as recommended by the local governments, but he also consulted with Conrad Wirth, whose agency would be required to work with the group and consider their advice. Wirth was instrumental in having Foster, rather than an Interior official or a political operative, named chair. The choice was a wise one. Foster enjoyed credibility with the selectmen and residents of the Outer Cape because of his role in state government. He was also well known and respected by park service officials for his early and essential support of the national seashore. His leadership would shape the early procedures and activities of the CCNSAC, which had been left vague in the legislation.

The commission had no actual authority; its role was entirely advisory and its members were unpaid. But such a group was bound to have influence, nevertheless. After years of controversy, lobbying, and compromise, its members were organized and equipped with developed positions and opinions on what shape the future of the national seashore should take. Articulate, well connected, and representative of the range of interests of their communities, the commission members would play a significant role in the implementation of park service plans and policies. In the process they would inevitably be drawn into the collaborative and experimental park project taking shape and become personally invested in its success.[14]

Wirth and his new Northeast regional director, Ronald F. Lee, made other personnel decisions that proved fortunate in the coming months and years. Robert F. Gibbs was officially appointed the first superintendent of the Cape Cod National Seashore in April 1962. (Fig. 5.7) But he began his duties earlier, for example, when he attended (as an observer) the first meeting of the CCNSAC that February. He had been superintendent of Cape Hatteras during the early years of its establishment, and so had unique qualifications for implementing the plans for the nation's second national seashore.[15] By all accounts a genuinely affable man who hoped to avoid unnecessary antagonisms, Gibbs was well suited to the delicate diplomacy that lay ahead on the Outer Cape,

Fig. 5.7. Robert F. Gibbs and Francis W. Sargent at the 1966 dedication of Cape Cod National Seashore. NPS.

where many resentments and apprehensions lingered regarding the acquisition of private property.[16]

Gibbs opened the park service's temporary offices in fall 1961, in the Nauset Coast Guard Station (in Eastham), a historic building at the time still under U.S. Coast Guard jurisdiction. (Fig. 5.8) That fall and winter park service staff worked with the Cape chamber of commerce to get out the message that federal park facilities, including public beaches, would not be operational until at least the summer of 1963. In April, the park service issued a press release reminding the public that the national seashore was still no more than "a boundary line drawn on a map," and that the land within that boundary was still private property and should be respected as such. A small visitor contact station was improvised by moving a purchased cottage to a site on Route 6 near the Orleans traffic rotary, the unofficial gateway to the Outer Cape. (Fig. 5.9) That summer park rangers intercepted thousands of visitors and reminded them that no federal beaches or park facilities existed yet.[17]

Fig. 5.8. Robert F. Gibbs (front row, in uniform) and his staff in front of the repurposed Nauset Coast Guard Station. Benjamin Thompson is to his left. NPSHC.

There was much work to do before Gibbs and his staff could begin welcoming the public. Land acquisition loomed ominously as the most important initial task, and the potential for failure was great. Cape Hatteras was only the most recent example of the difficulties that could ensue. At Grand Teton National Park (Wyoming) in the 1920s, and at Shenandoah National Park (Virginia) in the 1930s, the land acquisition process had created ill will that plagued the parks' relations with nearby communities for decades. In these cases, the purchase of properties had been done through private philanthropy and state government, respectively, with the land then given to the federal government. At Cape Cod, the park service itself would administer the process of land acquisition, for the first time entirely with money that was appropriated by Congress for the purpose. The opportunity carried with it considerable risk; a good showing would give the federal lawmakers confidence that the agency was capable of meeting the challenge of completing hundreds of land transactions efficiently, honestly, and without generating a political backlash. The experience at Cape Cod could easily influence future attitudes in Congress.

The legal "establishment" of the Cape Cod National Seashore would only occur when the secretary of the interior determined that "sufficient acreage" (the number of acres was left unspecified) had been acquired to allow the park to be "administered effectively." At that point, which occurred in 1966, the secretary would designate the seashore as a unit of the national park system. It would be more than

Fig. 5.9. The first park information center near the Orleans Rotary. NPS.

twenty years, however, before land acquisitions would be completed (or nearly so). The purchases fell into three periods, dependent on congressional appropriations: two main phases, from 1961 to 1968 and from 1970 to 1974, and a minor phase from 1975 to 1984.

The person initially charged with organizing and completing the land acquisitions was George H. Thompson, a Massachusetts native who had worked for the park service since the 1930s.[18] Thompson (no relation to associate director Benjamin Thompson) had trained as a landscape architect at Massachusetts Agricultural College, where he and Conrad Wirth were both students in the 1920s. In the 1950s he had worked in the Boston office on the national seashore survey and plans, including for Cape Cod, and most recently had been a land planning and acquisition officer in the Philadelphia office under Allen Edmunds. Relocating his family to Orleans, Thompson began his operations in October 1961, working out of the basement of the Eastham Coast Guard building. He spent the following months attending public meetings and giving interviews to reassure anxious residents about the land acquisition procedures he was organizing. He had been warned by colleagues in Philadelphia that he would "run into a hornet's nest" of contention on the Cape, but he later recalled that, in general, relations with property owners were usually amicable. From the outset, Lee, Gibbs, Thompson, and other park officials tried to strike a conciliatory tone, assuring property owners that they expected the use of eminent domain to be rare, and that in most cases transactions would be negotiated with willing sellers, and through transfers of jurisdiction from the state, towns, and the military.[19]

The park service provided Thompson with a staff that soon included ten members, including a lawyer, a surveyor, an appraiser, and clerical help. They prioritized and organized a process that Thompson hoped would "assure an orderly acquisition with the least adverse impact on local residents." The first task was to survey and mark the boundaries of the seashore with concrete monuments. Despite the detailed descriptions in the 1961 legislation, in some areas the survey proved problematic and required adjustments. In Wellfleet, a portion of the boundary followed a twenty-foot contour line (as shown on topographic maps), a situation that Gibbs insisted be corrected so that existing property lines were used to the greatest degree possible. The changes were minor (and could not exceed the legislated extent of the seashore), and the result was the creation of boundaries that were easier to survey and could be more readily perceived in the field.

Surveyors were also hired to produce tract maps of the seashore to provide an accurate basis for appraisals and transactions. Here again there were difficulties surveying tracts that in some cases had not changed hands in generations and relied on deeds with historical or vague boundary descriptions. The work was time consuming but vital. There were estimated to be 3,600 separate tracts of land within the seashore, including undeveloped parcels, about six hundred private homes, and nineteen commercial properties. In some cases the park boundaries described in the legislation split properties in two, even running through existing buildings. All of these problems would need to be resolved for acquisitions to proceed. In total, over 17,000 acres of private land were to be acquired. Some parcels were as small as a twelfth of an acre.[20]

Once properties were adequately defined through surveys, contracted appraisers and title examiners would also need to complete their work before any sales could be completed. Either two or three outside real estate appraisers would be used to establish a market price for a property to be acquired, and Thompson then used that information as the basis for negotiation with sellers to reach a mutually agreed upon price. Thompson also clarified the priorities for the order of acquisition. Undeveloped land would be the first to be surveyed and appraised for purchase. Although not protected from condemnation (since they were not "improved properties"), most sales on undeveloped properties were made through negotiation. Land that was already for sale, along with any areas of particular "scenic, historic, or scientific value," beach areas, and areas immediately needed for the administration and operation of the park were also prioritized.

Thompson responded to anxious inquiries by confirming that for at least for one year from the park's authorization date, no action would be taken on any improved properties in order to give the towns time to approve their "seashore" zoning districts for areas within the park and submit them to the secretary of the interior for approval. Vacant land and some beachfront areas were not protected by the same provisions and were subject to condemnation, if necessary. But Thompson, as well as Saltonstall and Keith, assured the public that "negotiating will be used almost exclusively" in land purchases. "The National Park Service," according to a joint press release, was "reluctant to use eminent domain . . . except as a legal device to clear title, as an emergency device to acquire lands urgently needed for use, or to prevent damage to the authorized park area."[21] From the beginning, the park service prioritized maintaining the best possible relations with private property owners, probably slowing the process of land acquisition to some degree.

In July 1962, with the first tract maps in hand, the land appraisers began their work. The first closing on six acres of vacant land (leaving the homeowner with his cottage and a two-acre lot) was signed that December, much to the relief of regional director Ronald Lee, who was happy to see transactions finally begin. By the summer of 1964, the boundary survey was complete, as was much of the tract mapping: three-quarters of the land to be acquired had been mapped and appraisals of the individual tracts had been made or were under way. Thompson had received 350 authorizations to negotiate purchases covering a total of 3,000 acres, and 225 owners had signed land purchase options, indicating that they had agreed on a price with Thompson and were contracted to sell. Most undeveloped land was acquired in "fee simple" (complete ownership); but in a few cases "less than fee" ownership (types of conservation easements) was negotiated. In Eastham, the threat of condemnation was used to forestall a developer's plan for a tract of undeveloped land. The threat was carried out in Wellfleet to forestall another development scheme. Foster reported that the surprising efficiency of the Wellfleet condemnation discouraged similar plans elsewhere. But despite the progress in surveying and appraising, by 1964 the park service had closed on only 130 properties—a total of 1,400 acres of land.[22] By 1965, about $10 million of appropriated funds had been spent on only 6,700 acres, signaling an imminent and large shortfall in funding.[23]

The range of different types of ownership within the seashore also presented a complex situation. The long history of settlement and private ownership meant that titles to land in some cases were difficult to verify. Public lands within the seashore were under various jurisdictions, complicating the process of transferring ownership. The Coast Guard still owned life-saving stations or lighthouses at Race Point, Wood End, and Long Point in Provincetown, the Highland Light in Truro, and Nauset Light in Eastham. (Fig. 5.10) The military still operated an early warning radar station in Truro, and the decommissioned Camp Wellfleet occupied a prime location vital to future park operations. The state not only owned the Province Lands and Pilgrim Spring State Park but also had jurisdiction over any freshwater ponds of more than ten acres (the Great

Fig. 5.10. The Nauset Coast Guard Station in Eastham that served as the first park headquarters. Photo by author.

Ponds). All six towns owned land within the boundaries—including their town beaches—and the legislation stated that these lands could be acquired only through donation, which would require a two-thirds majority vote in town meeting. Both the state legislature and the town governments would need to act in order to complete transfers of ownership of these areas to the park service. This was an opportunity, at the state and local level, to exert some influence over the federal seashore administration.

Charles Foster, as chair of the advisory commission as well as Massachusetts commissioner of natural resources, was determined to see the transfer of state lands made quickly through the necessary legislative action. But Joshua Nickerson, acting for the Barnstable County commissioners, instigated a delay in hope of gaining concessions from the park service. At this point state senator Edward Stone, the longtime advocate of land conservation on Cape Cod, stepped in and used his considerable influence to move the legislation forward. Compromises were made: the state retained jurisdiction over the Great Ponds in Wellfleet (though not ponds elsewhere) and ceded its jurisdiction over tidal lands (up to one-quarter mile offshore) only in Provincetown and Truro.[24] Provincetown also secured a fifteen-year delay in the transfer of forty acres of the Province Lands, where some town officials still hoped to build a marina. The Emergency Preservation Committee continued its vigilance and eventually prevented the

Fig. 5.11. The Great Beach. NPSHC.

Fig. 5.12. Nauset Light Beach. Photo by author.

development. In fall 1962, the Massachusetts legislature agreed to transfer the Province Lands and Pilgrim Spring State Park, comprising about 7,000 acres, to the park service.[25] The decommissioned Camp Wellfleet military reservation was being prepared for transfer through "decontamination," which was completed by the U.S. Army in August 1962.[26]

The donation of town lands was complicated by other considerations. Town beaches were a particular concern. In Provincetown, Truro, and Wellfleet, the transfer of state and military land would create opportunities for federally administered beaches. Other beaches, such as Coast Guard Beach in Eastham and Nauset Beach in Orleans and Chatham, were town owned and would be desirable to bring under federal jurisdiction for the operation of the national seashore. (Figs. 5.11, 5.12) But the towns had little incentive for donating their beaches. While federal jurisdiction would relieve them of the expense of maintaining the areas, it also would mean giving up local control over access and parking permits. In the case of Eastham, the planned park headquarters and visitor center at Salt Pond did give the park service leverage. Gibbs promised to begin construction on the facilities as soon as possible—once Coast Guard and Nauset Light in Eastham were donated. At its town meeting in March 1963, Eastham agreed to transfer Coast Guard Beach; Nauset Light Beach followed two years later. But in the five other towns, as land acquisitions dragged on (and perhaps the scale of public visitation started to become apparent) decisions were made in town meetings to retain jurisdiction over their beaches.[27]

If the process was slow, it was also notable for its relative lack of animosity. Most properties initially acquired, as Thompson indicated, were undeveloped land and properties already for sale. The "improved properties"—with title vested before September 1, 1959—would not be acquired at all. Owners of these residences (commercial properties did not have the same protection) could request official "certificates of suspension of condemnation" once their town had put approved zoning regulations in place. If they chose to sell, they had a choice of a tenancy agreement for twenty-five years or the life of the owner. Exceptions to the three-acre limitation had to be made in some cases, such as Quincy Shaw's property, in which the residential and outbuildings could not be included without defining a larger parcel to remain in private ownership. Driveways sometimes presented similar problems. But the wording of the law provided some flexibility, and Thompson succeeded in most cases with what he reported to be amicable negotiations when a division of a property larger than three acres was made. The great majority of the improved properties, in any case, were smaller and did not require subdivision. These inholdings would continue to be tax-paying private property, in perpetuity, under the definition of an "improved property" as a "detached, one-family dwelling" and its "accessory structures." In 1964, Thompson estimated that there would be about 500 of them, encompassing around 1,200 acres. This estimate was low; today there are about 610 on just over 1,500 acres.[28]

The suspension of condemnation depended on town governments' enacting the required land use regulations and having them approved. Solicitors at the Department of the Interior were at work drafting standards to distribute to the towns as soon as the seashore legislation was signed. The bill (section 5) specified that the secretary would issue zoning standards and could later amend those standards, if "changed or unforeseen conditions" made a change "desirable." But the bill also protected property owners by making the secretary's initial approval of the town's regulations irrevocable. Once the towns had an approved zoning code, the secretary could not later say that the approved code no longer met the standards, if those standards were later amended. Any new or altered town bylaws, however, would need to meet the current (possibly changed) standards then in effect. The park was protected against future zoning changes by the towns; but the towns were protected from guidelines that might become increasingly restrictive. Other details addressed the issue of zoning variances and noncompliance. Variances would require review and approval by the secretary of the interior or the property would become subject to condemnation. Violations of codes would have the same effect.[29]

Opinions on what the Interior's guidelines should contain were offered as early as 1959, when a group of Harvard Law School students made a study of permissible restrictions. The law students concluded that federal guidelines for zoning of private property within a national park would be held constitutional, but such guidelines for areas in the towns outside the park would not be. The Interior solicitor issued a similar opinion in 1961. The CCNSAC also played a role, and facilitated consultations between Elmer V. Buschmann, a park service lawyer, Louis H. Smith, from the Massachusetts Department of Commerce, the six town governments, and Blair Associates, who were now preparing a regional plan for Barnstable County. Through a collaborative process, they drafted guidelines for the "seashore district" codes for the six towns. The process was democratic and therefore arduous. In Eastham and Wellfleet (which together contained well over half of the improved properties), selectmen and planning boards joined forces and sent Udall their own proposed zoning guidelines in June 1962. The Interior published its guidelines in the Code of Federal Regulations in July 1962. Since the moratorium on the condemnation of improved properties would end on August 7, clearly it would need to be extended, which the secretary agreed to do as long as the towns were working toward ratifying the needed codes "in good faith." It would be almost five years before all the six towns' zoning codes were passed in their respective town meetings. Udall approved the first new bylaws—for Orleans, Chatham, Eastham, and Truro—in August 1963. Provincetown did not receive its approval until June 1966; Wellfleet finally did in March 1967. None of the affected improved properties were condemned despite the long delays.[30]

Based on the published Interior guidelines, the zoning codes for the six "seashore districts" all shared essential language and provisions that led to their approval. Some of that language was contained in the 1961 legislation (section 5), which required that approved zoning would prohibit "commercial or industrial use" but for exceptions specified by the secretary. More generally, the bylaws were required to promote the "preservation and development" of the seashore in accordance with the purposes of the authorizing legislation, and would not be approved if they contained provisions "adverse" to those purposes. Bylaws were expected to employ the means of "acreage, frontage, and setback requirements and other provisions" consistent with Massachusetts state law. The guidelines issued in 1962 expanded minimally on these directions. No moving or enlargement of residences was to be permitted if it violated a fifty-foot setback from the street or twenty-five foot setback from adjacent residences. The guidelines allowed that erosion or other natural processes might diminish the size of a lot or require a relocation of a building, circumstances under which the secretary could approve an exception to the setbacks.

Restrictions were included against "burning of cover, cutting of timber, filling of land, removal of soil, loam, sand or gravel and dumping, storage or piling of refuse," and other actions that would "detract from the natural and traditional seashore scene." Residences were allowed to be used for some personal businesses that were considered "traditional to these seashore communities," as long as they did not alter the primary character of the residence as a dwelling. Specifically this could mean a professional office, an artist's studio, or the use of the premises to make and sell "traditional Cape Cod products." The rental of rooms and serving of meals were also allowed. Signs in such cases were to be limited to two square feet and lit only indirectly. "Traditional" agricultural uses were specifically allowed, although this did not include "objectionable uses such as a piggery" or any commercial livestock farming. "Traditional fishing activities" were similarly allowed as exceptions to the general proscription on "commercial or industrial ventures."[31] (Fig. 5.13)

These were the general provisions of the "seashore districts" (not all towns used this specific term) that the six town meetings subsequently created as part of their zoning bylaws. Different towns had different formats, either a narrative description or a matrix chart, and approaches; restrictions were described in more or less detail. But the setbacks and restrictions on uses were complied with, and the zoning codes received the needed approval. Towns also went beyond the necessary restrictions and anticipated potential enterprises not mentioned in the federal guidelines. Orleans, for example, prohibited summer camps, kennels, and other uses. Other towns imposed additional restrictions and specified various frontage requirements. The fifty- and twenty-five-

Fig. 5.13. Rock Harbor, Orleans. Photo by Carol M. Highsmith. CHA.

foot setbacks required by the guidelines would have no bearing on the size of lots of improved properties, on which houses were already built (and which were surveyed and reduced to three acres where necessary). But any enlargements or modifications of those residences would need to conform to the new regulations. The setbacks also implied a minimum lot size, at least if any new subdivision or building occurred on undeveloped land within the seashore boundaries before the park service was able to acquire the property. Such new construction would need to meet the seashore zoning standards once they were in place.[32]

The basic provisions of the seashore districts established a baseline for how the improved properties within the seashore would be managed in a manner consistent with the purposes of the park's authorizing legislation. By remaining single family, detached residences within a surveyed plot of land, the future of the improved properties seemed both secure (with the "suspension of condemnation" officially certified) and predictable. But soon several problems emerged. The first was that the towns had little incentive to change the zoning regulations for their seaside districts in spite of increasing development pressures that might warrant amendments. The secretary of the interior's approval of their bylaws was irrevocable, unless the codes were amended, and the seashore district provisions remained unchanged for years. Increased property values and changing ownerships, in the meantime, sometimes resulted in ambitious renovations and expansions of residences. The bylaws required minimum setbacks and restricted certain uses but did little more to control how a residence might be expanded. And although significant redevelopment of an improved property required a building permit issued by the towns, there would be little incentive to deny such permission as long as the town's zoning requirements were met. It was up to the towns, not the park service, to impose any additional limitations on the size or height of residences within the seashore, if such regulation were ever deemed desirable. The park service could offer advice but had no power to force towns to reconsider their zoning codes once they had been approved.

In theory, the national seashore legislation allowed the park service to revoke the suspension of condemnation for any improved property developed in a manner "adverse" to the purposes stated in the 1961 act. In practice, this phrasing was vague, while local zoning ordinances were specific. It would be easier for a property owner to demonstrate compliance with zoning than it would be for the park service to demonstrate how a specific house enlargement or renovation was adverse to the purposes of the park. The six towns dutifully enacted approved zoning regulations and so secured the rights of residents to keep their homes, or sell them, or rent them, as they chose. Town governments also issued building permits for renovations and sometimes major expansions of those buildings. Property values continued to rise as it became evident that many of the improved properties enjoyed remarkable settings, protected by the surrounding national seashore from any encroaching development. The pressure to sell and redevelop such exclusive enclaves would soon create an unforeseen threat to the integrity of the park landscape: enlarged year-round residences, visible from afar, replacing what had been modest vacation cottages, nestled comfortably in the landscape.

Over the next twenty years, Provincetown, Truro, Wellfleet, and Chatham did enact height restrictions, between twenty-eight and thirty feet, and Wellfleet and Chatham restricted buildings to 5 percent and 10 percent, respectively, of their lots.[33] But the redevelopment of the improved properties after 1961 would continue to call into the question whether the national seashore landscape had been as fully protected as had been hoped through local zoning restrictions alone. Despite significant alterations to some of the improved properties—which in some cases amounted to a complete rebuilding and significant expansion of an existing residence—none were ever condemned and acquired because of a perceived adverse effect on the purposes of the seashore legislation, or because they detracted "from the natural and traditional seashore scene."[34]

A more immediate problem emerged, however, which was also tied to the power of the towns to issue building permits within the seashore boundaries. After Kennedy and Saltonstall first introduced their bill in the Senate, which specified the cutoff date of September 1, 1959, as part of the definition of an improved property, the six towns continued to issue building permits for new residences on undeveloped privately owned parcels of land within the seashore boundaries. Passage of the legislation was as yet two years away, and the final boundaries were still being debated, adding to the uncertainty about exactly which properties would be affected—if indeed the legislation passed at all. In the meantime, the towns were not restricted from issuing permits for developable parcels. They might, in fact, be subject to legal action if applications were denied without cause. The permit applicants were constituents acting within their rights. The situation eventually created a new class of properties within the final seashore: private residences that began construction after September 1, 1959. These properties did not meet the legal definition of an "improved property" and so would not be shielded from condemnation. Nevertheless, the economics of rapidly increasing property values created strong incentives for proceeding with new construction.

After 1959—and even after the park was authorized in 1961—there was little reason to be in a hurry to sell an undeveloped lot within the seashore. Prices would only rise, and the park service would have to pay an independently assessed amount. If a new residence were permitted and built, the sale price would more than cover the cost of construction. Even after a sale, a twenty-five-year right of tenancy would allow the residents to enjoy their new home (or rent it at a significant profit) for a generation.[35] Considering the rapid rise of property values in the region, the investment potential was considerable. One analysis suggests that between 1961 and 1968 the value of private property within the seashore rose by over 100 percent, a rate of return at least three times what other investments of capital might have been expected to yield during the same period.[36] Developing buildable (but not yet acquired) lots within the proposed boundaries of the seashore after 1959 was less a gamble than it was an easy way to make money.

Between 1959 and 1961, seventy-two new residences were permitted or built within what became the final seashore boundaries, the majority (thirty-three) in Wellfleet. The construction even continued after 1961 and greatly increased the total cost of land acquisition. By 1974, the park service had acquired (most with twenty-five-year tenancy agreements) eighty of what were thought to be eighty-two "non-exempt [post-1959] improved properties." The estimate was low; there were numerous other building permits issued that had escaped the notice of park service staff. The flurry of post-1959 building eventually saddled the park service with the ownership of more than one hundred residences that would need to be either maintained for a park-related use (usually housing for park staff), or demolished, both expensive options.[37]

Already in September 1961, the *Cape Codder* editorialized that "building in the seashore costs all of us." While the building between 1959 and 1961 might have been excusable because of "lack of information," no one could "plead ignorance now."[38] It is easy to see why Thompson prioritized the purchase of undeveloped land within the seashore. He did everything in his power to facilitate the surveys, assessments, and negotiations that preceded the purchase of undeveloped land. But the number of transactions involved assured that the process would take years. In the meantime, opportunities to build within the seashore boundaries continued to be exploited.

By 1968, the initial authorization of $16 million had been exhausted, but land acquisitions were nowhere near complete. Land acquisition activities were brought to a temporary standstill, and Thompson retired that year. The park service had acquired a total of 20,456 acres of land: 6,906 through negotiated purchase; 2,718 through condemnation; and 10,832 (including the Province Lands, Pilgrim Spring State Park, and military properties) through donation.[39] The rapid rise in property values together with the cost of acquiring post-1959 residences increased the overall costs. Congress would now need to act to authorize further funds for land purchases, and any delay would compound the rising expense. During the intervening years, however, enacting the authorized funds had become a more complex undertaking. Cape Cod may have been the first national park to receive significant federal funding for land acquisition, but by 1968, Congress had passed a plethora of park legislation. The national seashore now had significant competition for federal appropriations. Following the assassination of Kennedy in November 1963, Cape Cod remained closely associated with Kennedy's memory. Shortly after the tragedy, for example, Edward Boland and Hugh L. Carey (a Democrat from New York) introduced legislation in the House (H.R. 9256) to rename the seashore the Kennedy Memorial Seashore. The effort never came to fruition, in part because of a reluctance at the park service to rename national parks as memorials.[40] The national seashore nevertheless had lost a chief executive with a direct and personal interest in its progress.

There were also changes at the National Park Service during the same period. In 1962, the ORRRC published its report and Udall established the Bureau of Recreation (BOR). In 1964, Udall replaced Conrad Wirth as director of the National Park Service with George B. Hartzog Jr., a park service concessions lawyer and former superintendent of the Jefferson National Expansion Memorial (the St. Louis Arch). Hartzog was a talented government solicitor with over fifteen years' experience, but he was not Wirth's choice for the seventh park service director. Hartzog's appointment was a turning point in the politicization of the position: Udall chose him because his views were more compatible with the recommendations of the ORRRC, with the activities of the BOR, and with the agenda of New Conservation. Previous park service directors had been "career men," with ties and loyalties to the original group of executives who had established and set the early policies of the agency. Hartzog offered a different set of skills and a new outlook. Over the next nine years his political skills and allegiances facilitated legislative accomplishments that made him one of the most successful directors in the history of the park service.[41] The challenge of more than doubling the authorization for appropriations for Cape Cod National Seashore, however, meant that the amendment to the original act increasing the authorization from $16 million to $33.5 million was not passed until 1970. The additional $17.5 million was the projected cost of the estimated 7,518 acres of remaining private land.[42] But the hiatus meant, of course, that costs had increased. The delay also added to the uncertainty of the entire land acquisition effort, and so also led to further construction of new residences within the seashore.

The administration of Cape Cod National Seashore was changing, as well, during these years. In 1966, Lemuel A. (Lon) Garrison replaced Ronald Lee as regional director, and Stanley C. Joseph replaced the retiring Robert Gibbs as superintendent of the seashore. Both men were longtime park service professionals and were part of the agency's cadre of superintendents. Garrison had been a close associate of Wirth's and at one time was thought to be a possible successor as director. Joseph transferred from Everglades National Park, where he was superintendent, and left Cape Cod in 1968 to take a position in Washington before retiring. He was replaced by Leslie P. Arnberger, who remained until 1974. Arnberger had served for two years as superintendent of Point Reyes National Seashore and would go on to become the superintendent of Yosemite National Park.[43]

After George Thompson's retirement, the second phase of land acquisitions at Cape Cod was directed by land acquisitions officer Fred Meyer. Between 1970 and 1974, 4,524 acres were acquired through purchase and 2,585 through condemnation—including eighty of the post-1959 residences. Only two of the original nineteen commercial properties within the seashore were acquired: a gift shop and the Spink Cottages (motel), both off of North Highland Road in Truro. The other businesses continued to operate through special permits, which had been renewed as funds for acquisition were prioritized elsewhere. Given the situation, undeveloped land and post-1959 residences had to be acquired first, and so the park service had little choice but to renew permits for ongoing businesses.[44] By the end of 1974 more than 28,000 acres were under federal jurisdiction, while over 12,000 acres of state "tidal lands" still awaited transfer. The total area of town land within the seashore was 2,240 acres. Town beaches and roads made up only part of this total; other town lands served various municipal purposes and were the subject of land transfer negotiations with the goal of consolidating ownership within park boundaries. The remaining acreage in the seashore—the improved properties—was private property and would remain so. The major phases of land acquisition for the national seashore were complete. The national seashore's land acquisition office was closed, and the negotiations and litigation for the remaining parcels would be handled at the regional office by Richard Schwartz, who previously had administered the acquisitions program at Fire Island National Seashore.

By 1975, the overall cost of land acquisitions and the continued private construction within the seashore drew increased public attention. In March 1974, the *Provincetown Advocate* had noted that the land acquisition program was "mopping up" the remaining properties in the seashore, mostly post-1959 residences. Almost all of these had agreed to negotiated sales with twenty-five-year tenancy agreements. Condemnation proceedings for the most part involved land in which title remained obscure or for which owners could not be contacted.[45] Some cases required protracted and complex litigation. In 1972, for example, the park service attempted to close on over one hundred acres of wooded land in North Truro, tracts that were in the category of "unknown owners." A Falmouth architect, John R. Hellman, then claimed to have title to the land through "adverse possession" (squatter's rights) dating back to his use of the property since 1948. With a value estimated at over $200,000, other claimants soon appeared, based on their historical use of the property as traditional "wood lots," and in one case on a deed dated 1718. Hellman's case for ownership was initially upheld by the courts, causing both amazement and a scandal, according to the *Boston Globe*.[46]

But it was the post-1959 construction that attracted the most attention—and some outrage—in the press. The *Cape Codder* investigated the situation in 1976 and concluded that the houses had been built with full knowledge, in all cases, of the boundaries of the national seashore. The reporters also discovered that there were more of them than the park service had ever realized. The towns themselves were now investigating the extent of the problem because of concerns that some of the owners had been evading local property taxes. In fact, those post-1959 residences that had been acquired (and occupied under twenty-five-year leases) were legally exempt from property tax, at least until the situation was corrected through state legislation in 1974.[47] Under the original terms of acquisition, residents were supposed to be paying the equivalent of an annual tax rate to the park service, but many had not. The towns were unable to put a lien on what was federal property and eventually abated the back taxes, at least in some cases.

Not only were new houses built without the park service ever knowing, but some were then the subject of extensive expansions. Owners used political connections, according to the *Cape Codder*, to encourage the park service to "look the other way." When Martin Peretz sought to expand his Truro property (a 1967 house he purchased in the early 1970s), for example, he contacted U.S. Representative Herman Badillo (a Democrat from New York), who owned a home in Wellfleet. Badillo contacted then–House Majority Leader "Tip" O'Neill, who turned the matter over to his "administrative assistant," Leo Diehl. Diehl, who had been an original member of the CCNSAC, was, considering O'Neill's position in Congress, undoubtedly able to apply considerable pressure on then-superintendent Lawrence Hadley.

The *Cape Codder* investigated over a dozen such "problem tracts." The park service had its own, longer list. The journalistic inquiry revealed that eighty-five post-1959 residences had already cost taxpayers millions to acquire. The "alteration" of improved properties had turned "shacks into palatial summer homes going far beyond the liberal guidelines set by the Seashore." The paper editorialized that the " 'spirit and intent' " of the original legislation had been "subverted." The incensed editors felt the park service had "slipped into laxness in defense of the area."[48] To be fair, when members of Congress chose to become directly involved in national park management decisions, their influence was difficult to counteract; Congress held the agency's purse strings and controlled the fate of legislative initiatives.

Incited by the *Cape Codder*'s findings, the two senators from Massachusetts, Edward M. Kennedy (Democrat) and Edward W. Brooke (Republican), demanded an accounting of post-1959 construction in the park, which the park service produced at the end of 1976. The report was prepared by staff at the seashore and signed by the new regional director, Jack E. Stark. As requested, it reported on the overall conditions under which new construction had occurred and specifically addressed the "problem tracts" that the journalists had investigated. The agency was in a difficult situation, one that had been created by the original provisions of the 1961 act. Only a greatly accelerated program of land acquisitions could have minimized the problem, and the congressional conference committee had rejected the "advance contract authority" that might have made that possible. The policy of minimizing conflicts with private property owners had further slowed the process. Delays by Congress in appropriating the authorized funds (and then in increasing the authorized amount) undermined the threat of condemnation and created delays and uncertainty. Any attempt by the park service to enforce more "rigid standards" than those described in the approved seaside district bylaws would be subject to legal challenge and might be construed in violation of the 1961 legislation. The writers of the report insisted that "given the legislative mandate and the existing zoning standards," the "spirit and intent of the legislation [had] not been violated." In their view, while there were important exceptions, in the vast majority of cases the existing system of control through local zoning had served its purpose, and that the park had followed its legislative mandate.[49]

The CCNSAC, aware of the issues, unanimously voted to support Superintendent Hadley in further study on the expansion of improved properties and on problems in acquiring the remaining post-1959 residences and other private land still within the seashore. But neither the CCNSAC nor the park service had the legal authority to do more than assess the problem and then make recommendations for better "guidelines" and "definitions." The issue was one of local zoning bylaws and the issuance of construction permits, and so remained firmly rooted in the prerogatives of municipal government and in the town meetings of the Outer Cape. By 1977, with money for acquisitions running out, the *Cape Codder* accurately observed that "power of condemnation [was] a weapon without ammunition." Only Congress could authorize a further increase and appropriate the funds. The park service report therefore concluded that funds for condemnation proceedings should be made immediately available in order to forestall any further construction. A review of zoning standards "to put precise limits on the extent to which existing properties may be enlarged" should also be completed.[50]

It was understandable that the park service would try to defend itself and put the situation in the best possible light. But the agency's response infuriated the editors at the *Cape Codder,* who derided the report as "casuistry and speciousness," which was an insult to deliver to the "the brother of one of the drafters of the legislation." They pointed out that the construction of post-1959 residences, itself, violated "what the bill's drafters intended." Their paper had also documented "case after case in which 'improvements' to the existing legitimate buildings within the Park [improved properties] have abused the Seashore's own original and liberal guidelines." The total effect had been "to create special conditions for the favored wealthy to develop leisure homes." They insisted that they were not asking for "rigid standards" to be imposed, only adherence to the original purpose of the 1961 legislation that the "Seashore be kept 'permanently preserved in its present state.'" But if the journalists had done a great service by investigating the shortcomings of the situation, they did not offer many solutions. They hoped Congress would make appropriations available, and that "advance contract authority" might finally be allowed. Otherwise they could only demand that the Department of the Interior acknowledge the extent of the problem and show "real leadership," which they felt had been lacking.[51]

Kennedy and Brooke introduced legislation in the Senate in January 1977 (S.440) intended to give the park service increased control over zoning standards and to increase the authorized funds for acquisitions. Kennedy, who was elected to his brother's former place in the Senate shortly before the president's assassination, felt that the park service report "raised more questions than it answered" and that there was no "sense of urgency" in the matter at the Department of the Interior. He testified in support of his bill that there was no legal reason that the park service should have offered twenty-five-year tenancy agreements in the purchase of post-1959 properties, and the proposed legislation prohibited the practice. The secretary of the interior was directed to develop "size and design requirements" for seashore district zoning, and the bill called for section 4 of the original act to be amended, making federal approval of local zoning revocable if the bylaws no longer met the revised guidelines. Realizing that condemnation remained the only remedy for noncompliance on the part of private property owners, he asked for the authorization for acquisitions to be raised another $10 million, with an additional $5 million set aside as a "reserve fund." In his testimony, Brooke also suggested that the park service had yielded too much authority to the CCNSAC, granting it the authority of a "policy making body" rather than advisory commission. He believed that "some fundamental changes in land management policies" at the national seashore were required.[52]

Congress apparently did not give the Kennedy-Brooke bill further consideration. Issues such as the secretary of the interior's authority to revoke approval of local zoning bylaws, or whether twenty-five-year tenancies should be granted in purchases, had become somewhat irrelevant in any case. Almost all of the post-1959 residences already had been purchased, and the six towns had begun to address the shortcomings of their zoning codes. Above all, however, the sole remedy of condemnation was increasingly becoming what one legal scholar has described as a "paper tiger" rather than a "sword-of-Damocles."[53] All the park service could do in cases of noncompliance—regardless of how strict the guidelines might be—was condemn and acquire a property; the threat depended on the availability of funding and therefore on the political will in Congress to carry it out. Both would be in increasingly short supply in the coming years.

By the 1980s, the political climate for large-scale park planning and land acquisitions had shifted. The changing mood both in Congress and in the executive branch made it increasingly unlikely that appropriations would be made for the condemnation of private land in a national park. Already in 1979, the U.S. comptroller general had published a report titled *The Federal Drive to Acquire Private Lands Should Be Reassessed.* Made to Phillip Burton, chair of the House Subcommittee on National Parks and Insular Affairs, the report urged Congress to find alternatives to "full-fee acquisition" of private property for park purposes. It included a case-by-case analysis of federal land acquisition efforts that had proliferated over the previous twenty years, noting that "spiraling land values" were drastically increasing costs. The comptroller also noted that in many cases local governments and officials resented the loss of taxable properties and perceived other negative economic effects.

At Cape Cod, the report suggested, the final phase of land acquisition was "unnecessary," since land use zoning within the seashore's boundary could adequately achieve the purposes of the park.[54] In 1982, President Ronald Reagan's secretary of the interior, James G. Watt, issued a policy statement directing federal agencies to seek "cost effective" alternatives to the acquisition of land in fee simple for public purposes. In 1983, Congress did raise the total authorization for acquisitions at Cape Cod to almost $43 million, but that would be the final amount.[55] Thereafter, any condemnation proceedings would need to be funded by taking money from other parts of park service budgets. The last, more minor, phase of land acquisition that had begun in 1975 ended, unofficially, in 1984. In all, some 16,300 acres of private land had been purchased, and the total area acquired was now 26,886 acres. There were remaining small tracts, disputed ownerships, and condemnation awards to be settled; but twenty-two years after its start, land acquisition at Cape Cod was all but finished.

The expanded activities and increased experience in land acquisitions by the park service—now in national parks of many different types all over the country—resulted in consolidation and professionalization of procedures. In 1979, the park service published a "Revised Land Acquisition Policy," and in 1980, the national seashore produced its own, revised "Land Acquisition Plan," as every unit of the park system was now required to do.[56] The plan indeed included more "rigid guidelines," detailing "incompatible uses" that would trigger condemnation proceedings. These included, for undeveloped land, any subdivision or new construction. For developed properties (regardless of their date), the plan specified the following "actions or proposed actions" that were "incompatible with park values" and could result in acquisition: "new separate residences or new residences linked to the existing structure; documented increase in damage to resources, scenery, or the historical scene; replacement of a major structure with one that is substantially larger in size, location or purpose from its predecessor; impairment of an identified historic structure;" and, finally, any "expansion of existing uses to a point where they cause documented increase in damage to the scenic, cultural or natural resources of the area."[57]

The document may have been late; much of the perceived damage and abuse of the system had already occurred. But the struggle to maintain the integrity of the national seashore landscape was far from over. While the new guidelines addressed problems that had been recognized for years, the matter and means of enforcing them remained uncertain. Without new or amended seashore legislation, the park service was still confined to essentially an advisory capacity to the six towns regarding their zoning codes. At issue ultimately was the willingness of the town planning boards and boards of selectmen to impose greater restrictions on the overall size of houses within the seashore zoning districts. Eastham responded to the new guidelines, establishing more restrictive zoning bylaws for its seashore district in the 1980s. But many of the improved properties most vulnerable to redevelopment lay within the boundaries of Wellfleet and Truro, where potential changes to the seashore districts generated significant opposition.

The tide turned in Wellfleet in 2008, when a particularly egregious proposed redevelopment, known as the Blasch House, was approved by the town and survived court challenges brought against it. The new house was a 5,800-square-foot mansion on the site of what had been originally (in 1961) a 500-square-foot cottage. Located on Great Island in a highly visible and sensitive location on the Cape Cod Bay shoreline, the proposed house was far too large, many people felt, and would be a major intrusion on the landscape of the national park. But under existing zoning in Wellfleet, the legal basis to stop the project was insufficient, and so it went ahead. Shocked by the result, a group of Wellfleet citizens, led by Griswold Draz, worked with town government, the Cape Cod Commission, and the park service to develop a more effective seashore district bylaw. They then encouraged their fellow residents to support it. Later that year they succeeded in securing the required two-thirds majority vote in town meeting to enact the new bylaw—a remarkable achievement. It took another nine years for Truro, after a similar process, to revise its zoning restrictions to prevent at least the worst cases of oversized resort homes. By 2017, after decades of advocacy within the towns, supported by park service studies and other data, all the towns of the Outer Cape had imposed more effective building size restrictions for their seashore districts.[58]

Fifty years after the park's legislation was conceived, the long struggle to win the support needed to improve the seashore district zoning codes finally addressed what can be considered, in hindsight, one of the most significant shortcomings of the Cape Cod model. During the same period, however, it also became clear the economic forces transforming areas outside the park's boundaries constituted the greatest impact of all to the cultural landscape of the Outer Cape. Since at least 1959, prescient voices had predicted that the creation of the seashore would only address landscape conservation within the park and would, in fact, exacerbate the deterioration of regional character and natural systems elsewhere in the six towns. The national seashore was a new kind of national park—but perhaps not new enough. Increased numbers of visitors, increased land values, and the removal of about 27,000 acres of land from future development inevitably intensified the pressure to take advantage of development opportunities on private land outside the park. Not all of this growth could be attributed to the creation of the national park; but neither had the park been conceived with any effective mechanism for mitigating the effects of residential and commercial development outside its boundaries.

Few issues would affect the future management of the seashore more profoundly than that of the relationship with town governments, particularly with regard to their powers to regulate land use, not only of the improved properties but of the rest of their area outside (but adjacent) to the park. Whatever the restrictions on the improved properties within the seashore—adequate or not—the preservation of the character of the Outer Cape was not a project that could be accomplished only by managing the land under park service jurisdiction. Neither ecosystems nor scenery stopped at the park's boundaries. The six towns of the Outer Cape had to be partners to achieve the goals expressed for the seashore: the park service needed to consult and collaborate with not only the CCNSAC, but with the people of the Outer Cape and their selectmen and town meetings, if they were to achieve those goals. As postwar patterns of urbanization intensified, almost every national park in the system faced a similar challenge.[59]

In the dunes, Provincetown. Photo by Carol Betsch.

SIX

Designing the Park

The success or failure of the Cape Cod model would depend as much on its planning, design, and construction as it did on the acquisition of land and the enforcement of zoning guidelines. As a national park, the seashore needed to be planned and developed in a manner that would preserve the landscape while facilitating meaningful public enjoyment and appreciation of it. Since the 1930s, the first priority for any national park was to develop a "master plan" that would define—and limit—the overall physical development of the park and outline strategies for resource protection and educational programs. At Cape Cod, the 1958 "Field Investigation Report" and the 1961 authorizing legislation were the starting points for one. The CCNSAC would also influence the development of early planning documents. The commission proved to be both an influential and a vital partner during these years. The park's first master planning efforts covered far more than the physical development of visitor facilities, beaches, and interpretive trails. Park staff and their partners needed to address some of the most contentious aspects of the balance of "preservation and use," the issue most on the minds of Outer Cape residents and property owners as the national seashore was physically realized.

The people of the Outer Cape had let it be known, long before the legislation was passed, that they intended to remain active partners in the planning and management of any new park. Shortly after they first introduced their legislation in 1959, Kennedy and Saltonstall responded to such concerns and requested from the park service a "statement of policy" that would recognize the "special nature of this Park," if it were to be authorized "along the general lines of S. 2636." Regional director Ronald Lee responded in 1960 with a statement that, in a very preliminary way, indicated some of the "tentative" strategies that the park service intended to implement. In addition to general policies that could have applied to any park in the system, such as "halt impairment of natural and historic features," and "provide for the use and enjoyment of the area through properly located facilities," specific priorities were described. The mandate to "protect and preserve the natural features" was complemented by an intention to "retain the life and atmosphere of the seafaring era and historic Cape Cod." Historic preservation, Lee asserted, would be "a prime objective" of park management. The six towns of the Outer Cape received assurance that "disruption of life" would be "kept to a minimum," and that the park service would "cooperate closely" to assure that "the town and park relationship" would be "harmonious." Lee hedged on the matter of campgrounds, pointing out that the park service provided for camping "where it was essential" but was under "no obligation to provide for camping as a purely diversionary activity." Concession developments that would "compete with private industry" would "not be introduced into the park," with businesses outside park boundaries providing "accommodations, lodging, and related services."

The memorandum included few specifics about the physical planning of facilities, but the first park master plan would soon supply many more details. Lee did indicate, however, his concern over the future of Route 6, which would remain the sole arterial automotive route—mostly outside park boundaries and under state highway jurisdiction—for the park and for the six towns. He suggested that the highway should be "redesigned as a limited access highway," with one or two park access points in each town. Such a plan would have had a profound effect on the pattern of roadside development and would have diminished impediments to the flow of traffic. A redesign of Route 6 as a limited access highway would have transformed the experience of entering the park and moving from one park area to another. It also would have done much to preserve the character of the landscape along the length of the Outer Cape.[1] Such an important undertaking, however, would have required a significant commitment from the state, in cooperation with the six towns and the federal government. But this was another case of the

Fig. 6.1. Robert F. Gibbs (center) with park planners. NPSHC.

national seashore being a new kind of park, but not new enough. Route 6 would remain a state highway with almost unlimited access points ("curb cuts") on the Outer Cape, and it would soon be lined wherever possible with commercial development, profoundly affecting the park experience and contributing to inevitable traffic congestion.

During the winter of 1962–63, superintendent Robert F. Gibbs needed to prepare for the following season, when the seashore would become more than "a boundary line drawn on a map," and the park service would welcome visitors for the first time. (Fig. 6.1) The transfer of the Province Lands and Coast Guard Beach in Eastham in the spring of 1963, for example, allowed the park service to plan for public access to several areas, and Gibbs needed to draft the special regulations under which territory coming under park service jurisdiction would be managed.[2] (Fig. 6.2) Hunting was permitted on federal land, under all applicable state laws, with the exception of developed areas and areas identified to have special scientific or historic interest. Fishing, including shellfishing, was similarly allowed under state regulation, except within three hundred feet of bathing areas. Waters were open to swimming, subject to safety regulations, and prohibited where public health, safety, or resource preservation concerns required it.

Fig. 6.2. Coast Guard Beach. NPSHC.

Motorboats were banned on freshwater ponds. Many of the regulations related to the use of motor vehicles, and especially to "oversand," or off-road, vehicles. Such "dune buggies" required a park service permit, available at park headquarters (still situated in the Nauset Coast Guard Station), and were restricted and regulated. Driving ORVs outside designated tracks and areas was prohibited. Pets were to be kept on leashes at all times, and horseback riding was to be limited to bridle trails and unsurfaced roads. "Obscene or indecent exposure" was banned on all federally owned property.[3]

By the time these management policies were submitted to the CCNSAC for comments, park service landscape architects and planners at the Eastern Office of Design and Construction (EODC, located in Philadelphia) had also prepared a "tentative" master plan for the national seashore. A draft was prepared in the summer of 1962 by landscape architect Benjamin Howland.[4] Numerous park service planners, historians, scientists, and landscape architects developed the plan, under the supervision of EODC chief landscape architect Eugene DeSilets. DeSilets made a point of bringing early drafts to the CCNSAC, which now met in the basement conference room of the temporary park headquarters. There he presented the tentative outline of the master plan, and the commissioners had much to say, resulting in a thorough revision of the plan by the end of the year.

The new (still "tentative" and "confidential")

master plan was presented to the commission in April 1963.[5] Charles Foster, as chair of the commission, later wrote that Ronald Lee had personally assured the group that they would be involved in every aspect of the "planning and development program." The commissioners were particularly interested in the stated intention to keep the "disruption" of local communities to a minimum. They also expressed strong, consensus opinions regarding the prioritization of "preservation" over "use" in the master plan. As a group, the commission advocated for the preservation of wetlands and other natural areas, and for the maintenance and interpretation of historic structures. New campgrounds and marinas—popular facilities the park service might once have once considered building—were not featured in the revised 1963 draft plan. Even picnic areas (for day use) were a subject of concern, should they be too extensive or encroach on a natural or historic scene.[6] The revised draft plan, which the CCNSAC found "generally acceptable," did indeed emphasize the limitation of recreational facilities and the preservation of specifically identified natural and cultural resources and areas. The park service had made good on its promise to empower the group, at least in the preliminary planning phases, over which the commission apparently had close to veto power.

The approved 1963 master plan was prepared while land acquisitions were only beginning, and so it included overall statements of the park's purpose, notable resources, policies governing land acquisition, and other general statements and observations culled from the 1958 "Field Investigation Report" and subsequent memoranda and documents. It was divided into four general headings: "Preservation and Use Objectives," "The Land," "The Visitor," and "The Staff," giving summaries of management policies, a description of park resources, the extent of services and interpretation, and suggested staffing levels under each heading respectively. The locations of public beaches, visitor centers, historic sites, interpretive exhibits, and other public areas were indicated on accompanying "base maps," elaborating on the plans drawn up in 1958. The planners emphasized that topography, wetlands, historic sites, and other park resources were represented in their base maps, and that the "general development plan" had been built on this "fundamental data" to assure that "significant resources" would be preserved "for the public benefit."

The overall strategy was to disperse visitors along the length of the Outer Cape to avoid overuse in particular areas. DeSilets and his planners had not given up hope that there could be a "proposed Seashore road," a park road (mostly separate from Route 6) along which visitors in cars could access scenic, recreational, and historic points of interest. They proposed linking existing, secondary roads where possible with new "tour road connections." The proposed connections, mainly in Provincetown and Wellfleet, were shown as dashed lines on the maps and were intended as a "major element of the Seashore circulation" and "a valuable interpretive device." This idea of a secondary means of visitor circulation that would bypass at least parts of Route 6 remained a part of park service plans for years, but it was never realized as such. Already in 1963, the planners noted that bicycling was "considered a desirable recreational activity" and the construction of trails for bicycles should be given "further consideration."[7] When a viable alternative to Route 6 finally took shape, it was in the form of bicycle trails, including the Cape Cod Rail Trail, which followed the right-of-way of the old railroad (under state jurisdiction). (Fig. 6.3) By 1970, park planners had replaced the idea of an alternate road system with a "proposed bike/hike trail."[8]

Other aspects of the 1963 plan identified what would quickly become the basic infrastructure of the new park. No new campgrounds or commercial (concessioner) operations would be introduced within

Fig. 6.3. Province Lands Bike Trail, dedication day. NPSHC.

the park, and day-use areas would be located only where they would not encroach on identified scenic areas and resources. These decisions had been influenced by the CCNSAC, but they were also consistent with Mission 66 master planning principles that Wirth and his landscape architects had developed in the mid-1950s. (Figs. 6.4, 6.5) DiSilets and Howland were longtime park service landscape architects who had worked on major Mission 66 projects, and the Cape Cod plan embodied many of the policies, as well as the overall approach, of a Mission 66 "prospectus."[9] What was different was the emphasis on "close cooperation between the towns, the county, the Commonwealth, other federal agencies, and the Park Service to assure harmonious development of land areas adjacent to the Seashore, and Seashore areas adjacent to the towns."[10] No Mission 66 prospectus had ever been devised in cooperation with a citizens' advisory commission, nor had the need for partnerships with other individuals and organizations been so expressly acknowledged.

The landscape architects left their 1963 plans at a conceptual level and did not produce detailed drawings of developed areas. Each section did include, however, a narrative "Design Analysis," providing general guidance for how buildings, circulation, and utilities were programmed and located. In addition, the analysis explicitly stated some criteria, for example, for siting development, which was another departure from earlier Mission 66 planning. The base maps showed significant identified natural and cultural resources, as well as attractions (historic sites and beaches) that the public would want to visit. Nineteen specific areas were labeled as "only slightly altered natural conditions" and so of particular concern. Cultural sites and historic structures, as well as ecosystems and plant species of note, were included in the descriptions of these areas. Specific sites for exhibits that would allow for the "interpretation of man's experiences on Cape Cod" were identified.[11] The resulting "plan of development" followed the process and overall pattern of the 1958 "Field Investigation Report" but offered more detail. The proposed principal visitor center remained at Salt Pond, in Eastham, with a secondary visitor service area at Race Point, in Provincetown. (Fig. 6.6) Camp Wellfleet now was the proposed site of an administrative headquarters and staff housing.

Fig. 6.4. Quarry Visitor Center (1958), Dinosaur National Monument, Utah, 2008. Photo by Roger Whitacre. HABS.

Fig. 6.5. Flamingo Visitor Center (1958), Everglades National Park, Florida. Photo by Jack E. Boucher. HABS.

Fig. 6.6. Province Lands Visitor Center. Photo by author.

By spring 1963, park staff also had completed an initial "prospectus for interpretive facilities and activities" in addition to individual reports on the interpretive programs to be initiated that summer in specific areas: Race Point; the site of the former Marconi wireless station in Camp Wellfleet; and the Pilgrim Heights area. Guided nature walks were planned for a total of six areas, and evening programs were to be held in a temporary outdoor amphitheater next to the Coast Guard building. Three (federal) beaches were to be open to the public, at the former Provincetown Beach (now called Herring Cove Beach), at Race Point Beach, also in Provincetown, and at the newly acquired Coast Guard Beach in Eastham.[12] (Fig. 6.7)

With acquisitions of many key properties still in the future, plans were indeed "tentative." Consistent with other Mission 66 projects, the 1963 master plan primarily considered development and interpretation. Although it included the work of scientists and historians in the preparatory process, it did not describe a program of scientific research as part of the park's operation. Existing staffing levels would need to rise as the park took shape, but these increases were entirely in the categories of administration, protection, maintenance, public information, and programs and planning. Under central administration (including the position of superintendent) the existing staff of six was to rise to ten. There were four permanent and thirty-five seasonal "protection" rangers and life-

Fig. 6.7. Race Point Beach at sunset, 2005. Photo by Daniel Schwen. Wikimedia Commons.

guards, numbers the planners felt should increase to sixteen and ninety, respectively, in the "long range." Only three permanent and no seasonal "interpretive" rangers were employed in 1963, which they suggested should increase to fourteen and twenty-three. The number of maintenance workers was anticipated to increase from eight permanent and five seasonal to thirty and thirty-one.[13]

The 1963 plan was thoughtful and thorough, if still lacking details, but it would soon be subject to major revision, in any case. The culture and process of planning was changing rapidly at the park service, and within five years a new master plan was taking shape reflecting new policies. During this initial period, however, major construction proceeded based on the 1963 plan—the challenge of receiving and serving millions of visitors could not wait. In 1964, 1,668,854 visits to the seashore were recorded, and the number would double by the end of the decade.[14] The park service moved as quickly as land acquisitions allowed it to build an entire program of "interpretive shelters," restrooms, bathhouses, and two visitor centers. In the process, the agency engaged the residents of the Outer Cape—some of whom were prominent architects—in a discussion of what these new buildings should look like, now that the overall plan for their locations and number was at least tentatively decided.

The landscape architects, architects, engineers, and others at the park service who undertook the "in-house" design effort for the Cape Cod National Seashore had the benefit of having worked on Mission 66 since the mid-1950s. Planning and implementing its thorough modernization of the park system made them uniquely qualified in designing and managing park development projects.[15] In addition, most of the senior administrative staff had been with the park service since the busy days of the New Deal. Regardless of where they received academic training, their most formative professional experience had been working in state and national parks, many of them for decades.[16]

Between 1954 and 1957, Wirth and his cadre of planners and designers developed the idea (and the name) for "visitor centers" as the successors to prewar park museum and administration buildings. The new building type combined many functions into a single large building: park service offices, interpretive display areas, and restrooms, as well as lobbies, information desks, and auditoriums, were all combined in efficient, indoor sequences of spaces that were linked together in plan by a diagrammatic conception of "visitor flow."[17] (Fig. 6.8) Most of these spaces related to functions previously handled in separate park buildings, such as museums, comfort stations, and administration buildings. New audiovisual media and larger numbers of visitors also required larger (even multiple) auditoriums and spacious lobbies that could receive and organize floods of arriving visitors. The buildings were planned in conjunction with extensive parking lots and new or realigned park roads. The visitor center was more than an adaptation of the park museum idea. As the "hub" and "focal point" of a park, visitor centers provided a hub

Fig. 6.8. Salt Pond Visitor Center. Photo by Jack E. Boucher. HABS.

for arrival, orientation, and park interpretation intended to provide virtually all park visitors with a desired level of service. Visitors were more numerous and mobile than ever, often staying in motels outside park boundaries and visiting parks on automotive day trips. The visitor center was intended to assure that even under these circumstances, basic orientation, services, and core interpretive messages would be delivered.[18]

New visitor centers were high on the list of the majority of the prospectuses drafted by park superintendents and Mission 66 planners. Landscape architects and interpretive planners, in the EODC and in individual parks, took the schematic idea for the project and worked it into the overall development context of the park's master plan. Often "secondary" visitor centers—smaller roadside structures or signs—and short "nature walks" near areas of particular interest composed the complementary features of an "interpretive plan." The landscape architects usually established the footprints of proposed visitor centers and designed parking lots, paths, and outdoor amphitheaters that exploited the views of scenery, historic scenes, or other "park resources" in the surrounding landscape. (Fig. 6.9) At that point, architects and engineers (who sometimes never saw

Fig. 6.9. Parking lot and amphitheater, Salt Pond. NPSHC.

the visitor center site) would finish the set of "preliminaries" by developing designs for the building itself.[19]

Mission 66 buildings were also notable because of their contemporary, midcentury modernist design. The "log and boulder" and pseudo-vernacular architecture of the prewar "rustic" era gave way, as early as the 1940s, to new influences. The end of the subsidized labor of the CCC and the changing economics of building materials and technology made new approaches imperative for park service architects. Postwar buildings such as visitor centers also served distinctly new programs and combined functions. As one-stop service centers for day-use visitors, their design was predicated on new assumptions about patterns of use and, above all, on vastly larger numbers of people arriving almost exclusively by car. The new trend in park buildings was quickly criticized, however, by those concerned that "modernistic" and "urban" architecture was creeping into the parks. But for EODC senior architects, such as Donald F. Benson and John Cabot, the new planning principles of Mission 66 required architecture consistent with the materials, construction technology, and perhaps the spirit of the mid-twentieth century.

For a number of projects the EODC architects recruited some of the most talented professionals of the day. For smaller projects (under $200,000 construction costs), the agency provided all design and construction management services. Even for larger projects, this was often still the case (as it would be for the Cape Cod visitor centers). But in notable instances, larger visitor centers were given to architectural consultants for design development and final design. The Quarry Visitor Center in Dinosaur National Monument (opened 1958), for example, was an important early commission for Anshen & Allen, as was the visitor center at Wright Brothers National Memorial (1960) for Mitchell/Giurgola. Taliesen Associates designed the Beaver Meadows Visitor Center and Administration Building (1967) in Rocky Mountain National Park, and Neutra & Alexander completed the Cyclorama Visitor Center (1962) for Gettysburg National Military Park.[20] (Fig. 6.10)

The park service garnered praise from the architectural profession for its innovative work. In January 1957, the critic Emerson Goble dismissed the attitude that "if we must have buildings [in national parks], let's have good, safe, sentimental rustic stuff that everybody associates with scenery." Goble saw the opportunity "for architects in the world's best building sites" to "add something to the nobility of nature in her most exalted moods" and hailed the "courage" of Mission 66 architecture.[21] In 1964, Wolf Von Eckardt, art and architecture critic for the *Washington Post,* concluded that "the Park Service dares

Fig. 6.10. Cyclorama Building at Gettysburg, 2004 (now demolished). Photo by Jack E. Boucher. HABS.

to build well," commending the visitor centers at Wright Brothers and Gettysburg, and unique shade structures Benson and Cabot had designed for Cape Hatteras, as "outstanding contemporary buildings by outstanding modern architects." Quoting at length from a conversation with Cabot, Eckardt compared the park service favorably with the "dreary mediocrity of federal architecture."[22] In 1970, the AIA awarded a citation to the park service as an organization for its "continuing effort to provide excellent design at all levels in our national parks." The next year the *AIA Journal* featured a portfolio of Mission 66 architecture, including the Quarry, Wright Brothers, and Everglades Visitor Centers (among others), which had "serve[d] architecture well" and been the basis of the national award.[23] At least in professional circles, Mission 66 endowed the park service with the highest reputation for architectural design and patronage that the agency has ever enjoyed.

By 1963, the completion of a tentative master plan and the arrival already of more than a million visitors made the construction of a major visitor center in Eastham a priority not only for the park but for the entire park service construction effort. Donald Benson wrote in a letter to Ronald Lee that the main visitor center at Salt Pond was not only a vital project for the national seashore but "possibly the most important building in the 1964 National Park Service building program." He emphasized that the visitor center site, a small rise near the park entrance with scenic views of the pond and direct access to Route 6, was the right choice for the main arrival and public orientation point. (Fig. 6.11) Superintendent Gibbs, however, felt that the building should not attempt to combine all the functions of park administration and maintenance. He believed that the delicate site, which already would need to receive thousands of visitors a day, could not also bear the additional parking and maintenance areas that would be required if it served as the park's headquarters.[24] Gibbs also knew that Camp Wellfleet, now decommissioned and decontaminated, would provide an ideal headquarters area, although it was more distant from the park entrance. He argued that

Fig. 6.11. View across Salt Pond to Visitor Center, 2001. Photo by Jack E. Boucher. HABS.

the building program should be split, with only minor administrative facilities at Salt Pond, leaving Camp Wellfleet to absorb maintenance areas, main administrative offices, and staff housing. Although labeled as a "proposed" idea in the master plan, in fact the decision to follow this advice was made before design work began at Salt Pond.

By 1963, Benson was already at work designing interpretive shelters and bathhouses. The new visitor center was assigned to another EODC architect, Ben Biederman. A newer arrival at the office, Biederman was given explicit instructions on how to proceed. Benson, who was the chief of architectural design at the EODC, had already decided that the national seashore should have an architectural "theme" that would unify all the public facilities in the park, giving them a distinct character and helping build the identity of the seashore. The desire to create a unifying theme was another significant innovation of the emerging Cape Cod model. Working with the architect Robert Hall, who headed the EODC, Benson felt that such a theme could respond to the materials and building types of a given region while also establishing a distinctive idiom that would readily distinguish park buildings.

Early in the spring of 1963, Benson produced designs for the interpretive shelters for the Pilgrim Heights area in Truro and the Marconi site in Wellfleet. In both cases, the shelters featured hexagonal floor and roof plans and unpainted cedar shingles. Construction was a heavy timber wood frame over a concrete platform. The hexagonal plan lent "itself to the many directional views," and "typical Cape Cod materials with contemporary detailing" were intended to suggest both continuity and innovation in the context of the Outer Cape landscape.[25] The Marconi shelter, which interpreted the location of Guglielmo Marconi's successful transatlantic wireless transmissions in 1903, was the first completed that summer, at a cost of $8,600. The shelter housed a scale model of Marconi's wireless station (which was no longer extant on the site) and was included in the cost. Fences, also sided with cedar shingles, bordered the approach path to the shelter and enclosed it on two sides. The second, very similar shelter at Pilgrim Heights was completed in 1964, and the next year a topographic model of the area, where the Pilgrims were purported to have first found a source of fresh water in 1620, was added to it.[26] (Figs. 6.12, 6.13)

John Cabot wrote to Hall that he was very pleased with the "architectural concept" Benson and Hall had devised for both shelters: while it was "definitely indigenous," it was "just as positively a clear cut architectural expression," an aesthetic success that was vital for the first structures in the park. In Cabot's view, the theme begun by the two shelters was "an appropriate interpretation of the environment without imitation or eclecticism," and it established a standard in this regard which future park projects should meet.[27] A third interpretive shelter was completed at Fort Hill in 1965. The later shelter kept the same construction and detailing, but in a

Fig. 6.12. Pilgrim Heights Interpretive Shelter, Wellfleet. NPSHC.

Fig. 6.13. Marconi Interpretive Shelter, Truro. NPSHC.

Fig. 6.14. Lobby, Salt Pond Visitor Center, 2001. Photo by Jack E. Boucher. HABS.

simple square plan rather than a hexagon.[28] The new park service director, George Hartzog, was also impressed with the "architectural theme" of the early Cape Cod designs for shelters and bathhouses, considering them the "most appropriately designed that I have seen in the {national park} areas."[29]

The idea of a theme for the buildings of a given park was not new, although the acquisition of so many new parks after 1961 created an unprecedented opportunity for the park service to explore the concept.[30] Again, Cape Cod would demonstrate initiatives that would be implemented elsewhere in the coming years. Continuing the nascent Cape Cod theme at a larger scale, in summer 1963, Biederman quickly produced drawings for a visitor center at Salt Pond centered on a large hexagonal lobby at the building entrance. (Fig. 6.14) Window walls took full advantage of the immediate view of Salt Pond, Salt Bay, and the surrounding landscape—a particularly scenic area and one that allowed for the interpretation of the varied landscape of the Outer Cape. Two hexagonal outdoor terraces extended the lobby toward the view. On the opposite side (away from the view), a ranger contact desk, a small office, and restrooms were all immediately accessible. Flanking the lobby, in long wings, large spaces for audiovisual presentations and for museum exhibitions completed the composition. (Fig. 6.15) In elevation, the large roof over the central lobby followed the hexagonal geometry and recalled the outlines of the two interpretive shelters already under way. Construction was primarily concrete and masonry, with the roof covered in cedar shingles. The lateral wings, housing uses that necessitated limiting natural light, extended as low, earth-tone masses to each side.[31]

As Biederman realized it, the Salt Pond Visitor Center epitomized some of the best qualities of this building type. It presented a low silhouette, familiar materials and color palette, and no ornamentation. The biggest impact on entering was the view of the landscape—including Salt Pond and the ocean in the distance—beyond the lobby's window walls. Although the building provided for a large and complex program of visitor services, it functioned as an almost-transparent viewing pavilion, making

Fig. 6.15. Interior of museum, 2001. Photo by Jack E. Boucher. HABS.

Fig. 6.16. View across atrium to auditorium, 2001. Photo by Jack E. Boucher. HABS.

the landscape the center of attention and the most memorable impression for visitors. The lobby also allowed "visitor flow" to access key services efficiently, including the lateral spaces of the indoor theater and museum. (Fig. 6.16) The plan solved a central issue created by dual programs: the central lobby was full of natural light while the lateral theater and museum wings were protected from natural light. In other Mission 66 visitor centers, the need for more extensive administrative space was often met by a second level, inaccessible to the public. Because of the anticipated construction of an administration building at Camp Wellfleet, the Salt Pond building was dedicated almost completely to visitor spaces, with only small offices and storage areas for interpretative staff.

As Biederman was working on the Salt Pond project, the CCNSAC became involved in the discussion over what might constitute architecture appropriate to the character of the Cape Cod landscape. The prominent Boston architect Josiah Humphrey Child, who had lived in Provincetown since 1958, originally had not been put forward by the town's selectmen as an advisory commission member. Child was a friend of Francis Sargent, and his early advocacy for a national park may have made him less desirable for the appointment, at least initially. But Child had designed beach facilities for Scusset Beach in the state park system, and based on this experience (and impressive recommendations) Governor John A. Volpe appointed him as a state representative to the commission. Early in 1963, Child became concerned that park service architects would design new facilities in a "Cape Cod Colonial" style, which in his view would not be appropriate for buildings that, considering both program and size, could not be aesthetically successful if conceived as oversized imitations of historical architecture. He wrote to five of his architectural colleagues, "the most distinguished architects in the Northeast," to offer advice that he and the CCNSAC could pass on to the park service architects.[32]

The discussion was well advised, and Child may have been acting on Superintendent Gibbs's advice. Debate on the desirable characteristics for national seashore architecture was foreseeable, in part because of the numerous prominent architects who vacationed on Cape Cod. Walter Gropius, for example, first came to Marion, Massachusetts, for a memorable summer in 1937, shortly after emigrating to the United States and accepting a permanent position at Harvard's Graduate School of Design. He was joined there by Marcel Breuer and numerous other artists and designers, one of whom described their reunion in 1937 as the "Summer Bauhaus," after the design school Gropius had founded in Germany in 1919. The architectural historians Peter McMahon and Christine Cipriani describe how over the next decades a remarkable group of architects, most based in the Boston area, made the Outer Cape their chosen retreat and the site of a memorable group of summer cottages designed in a modern, Bauhaus-influenced style.[33]

Serge Chermayeff, who had purchased property in Wellfleet in 1944, was one of the group and since 1955 had been an active participant in the public meetings and debates surrounding the seashore proposals. Chermayeff responded to Child's request, as did the noted Boston architect and preservationist James Lawrence Jr. The dean of the architecture school at MIT, Pietro Belluschi, declined to offer advice, writing instead that "with so much bad contemporary design being produced, I am getting a little shy about recommending it."[34] Gropius himself, although he did not own a house on the Cape, wrote what Child thought was the best and most concise advice: "The Cape Cod shore is not a museum; it lives, it grows, it changes. It would be against its inherent tradition if we should try to preserve an external 'cosmetic' uniformity. . . . New buildings in this area, therefore, must be invented, not copied."[35]

Gropius's statement captured a strong consensus among the architects consulted that the new architecture for the national seashore should not imitate traditional types, although it should make use of traditional materials, colors, and massing. This was, of course, exactly what the architects at the EODC wanted to hear; it was a description of what they had been doing in national parks for at least a decade. If Child, Chermayeff, and Gropius appeared completely unaware of this, their support was no less welcome. The harshest criticism park service architects had received over the previous years had been not from architects but from preservation groups, such as the National Parks Association, which had questioned why the agency had not taken exactly the course that Gropius and the other architects warned against. Chermayeff, who was never reticent in his criticism of the park service, in fact later stated that the EODC's work at Cape Cod was "rather well done."[36] Early in 1964, Gibbs asked Child for a written assessment of the Salt Pond Visitor Center design, which was then being finalized. Child responded that it had an exterior "designed in the same spirit as the bathhouses and other shelters, which I must say do blend in to the surrounding terrain. The designs are not too Cape Coddy, and yet are not out of character with Cape Cod."[37] (Fig. 6.17)

For Benson, Biederman, and the other architects of the EODC, this was high praise, and the approved design was put out to bid. Land acquisitions of the site (which was in part donated by Eastham) were not begun until early in 1964, and final acquisition of all the needed land was not completed until early in 1965. In the meantime, contractors went to work during the summer of 1964, and funding for the building was made available in September. Construction was completed in September 1965 at a cost of about $380,000. An outdoor amphitheater to replace the temporary one then operating at the Nauset Coast Guard Station was begun during the summer of 1966. At an eventual total cost of more than $67,000, it featured seating for seven hundred, a rear projection system for audiovisual presentations, and new utility lines. Also that summer the parking lot, the redesigned intersection at Route 6, and other site improvements completed development for the area.

Fig. 6.17. Coast Guard Beach bathhouse. NPSHC.

The Salt Pond project had been kept in-house at the EODC for a number of reasons. Benson was already working on the theme for the park's architecture, and that effort would best be served by assigning the project to Biederman, not an outside consultant. By the time the Salt Pond Visitor Center was designed in 1963, Wirth's tenure as park service director was also nearing its end, and the emphasis on Mission 66 was shifting as Udall implemented his New Conservation policies at the Department of the Interior. The quick and successful design of the central visitor center at Cape Cod had therefore been vital, and expediting its progress may have been another reason for keeping it at the EODC.

Twenty miles to the north, the park's second visitor center was also completed by the end of the decade. The Province Lands Visitor Center at Race Point served as a base of operations for rangers in the northern portion of the park. An example of a smaller, "secondary" visitor center, it was designed by another in-house architect, F. Clifford Pearce Jr., loosely following the established architectural theme. It was complemented by a small maintenance area and an outdoor amphitheater, designed by landscape architects DeSilets and Edward H. Abbuehl.[38]

Construction of other structures and road and parking improvements proceeded with alacrity over the next several years, as did landscape improvements, including dune stabilization and road removal. At the renamed Herring Cove Beach, in Provincetown, state authorities had built a bathhouse in the 1950s to serve visitors to the Province Lands. Designed by Mario V. Caputo, it was a simple brick-and-concrete building with restrooms and changing areas. Work on its renovation and expansion began after the end of the 1963 summer season and was completed in 1965 at a cost of about $64,000, including new utilities. The redesigned building featured new restrooms and storage areas.[39]

Other public restrooms were required in the areas now opening to the public. The Pilgrim Heights comfort station was completed in 1964 ($11,200) and established another building type that would be repeated elsewhere in the national seashore. It was constructed of low concrete block walls with a wood frame superstructure over its high, horizontal windows. The pitched, shed roof was again covered in cedar shingles, and the gable ends screened for ventilation. The concrete block was painted a light tan, continuing the earth-tone theme. Horizontal massing, emphasized by the low pitch of the roof and the high band of rectangular windows, further integrated the building into its site. The same contractors completed a similar comfort station for the Marconi area (Camp Wellfleet) at the same time. Following the model, comfort stations were built for the Beech Forest area in Provincetown in 1964 and for Fort Hill, Nauset Light Beach, and the Doane Rock picnic area by 1968. Simple, inexpensive, unobtrusive, and of their time, the park's comfort stations were classic Mission 66 architecture.[40]

Bathhouses were an essential part of the construction program, serving the developed federal beach areas that were the destinations of most park visitors. The buildings again followed the architectural theme of the park, featuring central areas with hexagonal floor plans and roofs, containing restrooms and a women's changing area, and a rectangular wing that served as a screened but partially open changing area for men. Similar bathhouses were completed for the beaches at Race Point, Nauset Light, Head of the Meadow, and Marconi by 1967.[41] (Fig. 6.18) At Camp Wellfleet, now the Marconi area, some buildings were demolished or purposely burned, and others were sold, moved, or salvaged where possible.[42] Two concrete-block maintenance buildings were completed by fall 1965. The simple, flat-roofed buildings featured brick cladding on the exterior and housed maintenance areas, shops, and a fire station. A similar "sub-maintenance" building

Fig. 6.18. Race Point bathhouse. Photo by author.

was built at the same time at Race Point. The administration building at the Marconi site was also completed by the end of the decade, but it did not follow the architectural theme of the park. Perhaps because it served park staff and had no official public contact function, it was designed in a vernacular Cape Cod residential idiom.[43] (Fig. 6.19)

There were many other aspects to the development program of the national seashore, for which $3.6 million was budgeted between 1962 and 1966. Significant new utility and sewage lines at the Race Point and Marconi areas were constructed, and staff housing (including a superintendent's residence) created, usually through the relocation or rehabilitation of existing structures coming under the agency's ownership.[44] Significant road work was required to make the park's new facilities accessible. By 1965, for example, $80,000 was spent on roads, parking areas, and paths in the Pilgrim Heights area around the new interpretive shelter. Roads were also obliterated and replanted, as were 250 feet of graded roadway also at Pilgrim Heights. Park staff acquired assorted site furniture, or fabricated it, during these early years. In 1964, 160 wooden picnic tables were purchased and installed, and the following year fifteen lifeguard stands and twenty benches were built.[45]

Fig. 6.19. Marconi administration building. Photo by author.

The park's operating funds rose from $195,000 to $400,000 during the same period.[46]

Dune stabilization and other landscape rehabilitation work was also part of the early development program. At the Marconi site, between 1962 and 1964 over $70,000 was spent on dune stabilization, a process that employed specialized machinery pulled by a crawler tractor to speed the planting of beach grass, as well as the transplanting of seedling pines. The procedure included fertilizing the beach grass (*Ammophila breviligulata*) by hand and by helicopter. Another $15,000 was spent on planting and installing "sand fences" in various locations in the Province Lands in 1963. In the fall of 1964, extensive planting was completed at Race Point, including rugosa rose (*Rosa rugosa*), beach plum (*Prunus maritima*), inkberry (*Ilex glabra*), arrowwood (*Viburnum dentatum*), and shadblow (*Amelanchier spp.*) The following year more than 1,100 plants of the same species and others were planted at Coast Guard Beach in Eastham. The park reported initial survival rates for the plantings at 95 percent or better.[47]

The official establishment and dedication of the new national park was ready to proceed long before the entire development and landscape rehabilitation program was completed. In the spring of 1966, with the Salt Pond Visitor Center completed and with land acquisitions well under way, the park service was ready to recognize the Cape Cod National Seashore as a unit of the national park system. Memorial Day, May 30, 1966, the day after what would have been John F. Kennedy's forty-ninth birthday, was chosen as the date for ceremonies at the new building. Stewart Udall gave the principal address, and Governor Volpe formally presented the deed to the Province Lands and Pilgrim Spring State Park. The congressional delegation—Leverett Saltonstall, Edward Kennedy, and Hastings Keith—made speeches, and the Outer Cape towns were represented. Udall acknowledged that the seashore was a "pioneer park" that "marked a turning point in conservation" and "began a new era of conservation in America." "The original sponsors" of the groundbreaking legislation, he continued, "had deep roots in this Commonwealth and an abiding love for this Cape." (Fig. 6.20) George Hartzog, who had succeeded Wirth as director of the park service, received

Fig. 6.20. Dignitaries at the dedication ceremony. *Left to right:* Thomas P. "Tip" O'Neill, Hastings Keith, unidentified, Lemuel L. "Lon" Garrison (at podium), Benjamin A. Smith, Stewart L. Udall, Leverett Saltonstall, John A. Volpe, Edward M. "Ted" Kennedy. NPS.

the state land deeds and remarked on the unique history of the Province Lands. His agency was dedicated to helping "the visitor interpret what he sees for himself," and "one of the most successful tools" for accomplishing that end was the visitor center, "like this beautiful building, and the exhibits and orientation programs presented in it." Salt Pond was described as "the newest of the over 100 visitor centers" that the park service had built "over the last several years."[48]

In fact, Mission 66 had begun in 1956 and officially ended that year, 1966, the fiftieth anniversary of the National Park Service. Mission 66 was not celebrated at the Salt Pond ceremonies, however. Udall and Hartzog had moved on to the policies and programs of New Conservation and had no desire to commemorate or even recall Wirth's initiative. That summer, Cape Cod National Seashore recorded more than 2.5 million visits.

PART III

Managing the Seashore

Leaving Head of the Meadow Beach, North Truro. Photo by Carol Betsch.

SEVEN

Recreation and Stewardship

By the time the national seashore was dedicated, land acquisition and development plans had established a successful model—the Cape Cod model—of how plans for national seashores and lakeshores and many other types of new parks could be implemented successfully with Congress's approval and appropriations. The operation of the park now challenged park service officials to balance "preservation" and "use" to the satisfaction of the many diverse constituencies that had as many different ideas of what successful management would entail. From the earliest days of park administration, the stewardship of the unique landscape character and natural resources of the Outer Cape would need to be accomplished while visitation grew from 2.5 million visits in 1966 to more than 4 million less than ten years later. The great question was—and remains—can such levels of recreational use occur without the "impairment" of the "character" the park service was charged with preserving? A new kind of park had been created, and the officials running it would continue to face unprecedented situations as they navigated a sea of social and environmental concerns and pressures. In a delicate and constantly changing landscape, land development would transform the Outer Cape outside park boundaries over the next decades. Moreover, as the Mission 66 era ended, institutional changes at the park service resulted in new laws and policies that altered the agency's priorities and operations.

The essential debate of preservation versus recreation continued to frame the concerns of Outer Cape residents, their elected officials, and the CCNSAC. George Hartzog exacerbated apprehensions on the Outer Cape in 1964 when he attempted to divide the units of the national park system into three categories—recreational areas, historical areas, and natural areas—each with their own explicit "management principles." Undertaken shortly after assuming his position, the initiative was supported by Stewart Udall and was intended to reinforce the park service's mission of "resource management" in response to environmentalists and scientists who had criticized the agency for its failure to incorporate scientific research adequately into park stewardship. By separating the parks into categories, the managers of natural areas could be encouraged to improve natural resource research and conservation, while those of recreational areas would be free to prioritize the needs of their visitors—an idea that had been advocated by early environmentalists for decades. With the Wilderness Act passed in 1964, and Udall now transforming bureaucracies at the Department of the Interior, many advocates felt that the time had finally arrived for increased protection of the ecological integrity of the parks, even at the expense of visitor convenience and experience.

At Cape Cod, however, the problem with the new policy was immediately evident, when national seashores were grouped with national recreation areas in the "recreational" category. Superintendent Gibbs, always aware of the concerns of his advisory commission and other Outer Cape residents, knew that the implied shift to an emphasis on recreation over preservation would alarm many. In the spring of 1965, for example, Joshua Nickerson wrote to Senator Edward Kennedy (who previously had written to assure him the designation would not affect the park's legislative mandate) to suggest that Hartzog had "not read carefully both the Act by which the National Seashore was established, and the Directive . . . with particular respect to the category of recreational areas." There was an essential conflict, he believed, and Cape Cod either belonged in a fourth category or no category at all. At the time Nickerson was vice chairman of the CCNSAC, and his concerns were shared by that group as well as by the Cape's congressional delegation. At issue were the "management principles" for recreational areas, which stated that "outdoor recreation shall be recognized as the dominant or primary resource management objective," a priority that seemed to directly contradict the 1961 mandate that the seashore landscape be "permanently preserved in its present state" with no development that would be "incompatible with the preservation of the unique flora and fauna or . . . historic sites."[1]

The categories promulgated by Udall and Hartzog in 1964, however, did not have a lasting effect, themselves, on park management. Cape Cod was not the only park with carefully crafted authorizing legislation expressing priorities that made categorization difficult. In the fall of 1965, Udall wrote to Hastings Keith specifically assuring him that the "general responsibilities" he and Hartzog had outlined "would of necessity be governed by the legislation establishing the area."[2] Senator Saltonstall addressed the situation in 1966 by attaching language to Cape Cod's appropriation explicitly prioritizing the 1961 legislation over the 1964 policy statement.[3]

But there was no question that the National Park Service had changed under its new leadership, and it did so with the support of Congress, the Department of the Interior, the National Park System Advisory Board, the recommendations of the ORRRC, and numerous conservation organizations. The 1965 management categories were an opportunity to begin to implement the recommendations of the 1963 "Leopold Report," for example, which urged an increase in scientific research and monitoring as a basis for management decisions.[4] Although management policies for the "natural" category were the report's primary subject, all parks with significant natural resources were directed to develop plans and programs in response. During the early years of operation at Cape Cod, Gibbs and his staff were understandably occupied with immediate needs. In 1964, the superintendent's report detailed continued land acquisition, the operation of four public beaches, the ongoing construction program, significant landscape rehabilitation (dune stabilization and other planting), and the initiation of new interpretive programs (with the help of five "seasonal naturalists"). But none of the park's 149 employees (including seasonal) were engaged directly in scientific research.[5]

In 1966, Gibbs summarized the operation of the seashore for the incoming new superintendent, Stanley Joseph. He could point to a growing staff and budget—and, of course, an increased number of visitors. Staff was augmented seasonally by the establishment of the Wellfleet Job Corps Conservation Center at Camp Wellfleet. Arriving in 1965, one hundred "corpsmen" were available to be trained and assist in carpentry projects, bicycle and hiking trail construction, and many other tasks. The federal beaches in operation were Coast Guard and Nauset Light in Eastham, and Race Point and Herring Cove in Provincetown. Head of the Meadow in Truro and Marconi in Wellfleet were soon to follow. Construction was ongoing throughout the seashore, including road improvements, parking lots, and moving and rehabilitating structures for staff housing. Additional planned structures at that time included the secondary visitor center at Race Point. Although commercial operations were not originally envisioned, two existing motels (the Salt Pond Motel in Eastham and the Nauset Knoll in Orleans) continued to be operated through concession contracts.[6] Two more contracts covered refreshment stands at Herring Cove (continuing the state concession there) and at the Nauset Light Beach facility. Several special use permits were also issued, for example, for the operation of the golf course at the old Highland House compound; the campgrounds in Truro also continued to operate as preexisting private commercial properties.[7]

Gibbs's satisfaction with the establishment of the seashore was evident, and the end of his tenure signaled the close of this initial phase. The original group of officials and residents who had seen it through was about to change as well. Joseph remained superintendent only until 1968, when he was replaced by Leslie Arnberger. Charles Foster stepped down from the CCNSAC, and Udall appointed Joshua Nickerson, Barnstable County's representative, as the new chair. But for the commission, the prioritization of "preservation over use" remained a mantra, and it was one that increasingly harmonized with the park service's goal of "resource management." Significant resource preservation initiatives at Cape Cod began to have a regional scope. Debate over the designation of the Monomoy National Wildlife Refuge as a federal wilderness area (under the terms of the 1964 Wilderness Act), for example, began in 1967. Hastings Keith sponsored the successful legislation the next year, with widespread support from the CCNSAC, the Department of the Interior, and conservation and sportsman groups.[8] The advisory commission also took up the matter of potential offshore oil and gas drilling, assigning Robert McNeece to press for state legislation to prevent it. In 1970, the state legislature established the Cape Cod Ocean Sanctuary restricting any offshore mineral development within the state's three-mile limit.[9] Much had changed on the Outer Cape regarding attitudes toward conservation efforts since the contention surrounding the seashore legislation less than ten years earlier.

In 1967, only four years after the completion of first plan for the national seashore, the park service embarked on a revision. The reassessment was imperative for several reasons. The park was approaching three million visits a year, and overcrowding of limited facilities was already an issue. The new mandate for improved resource management necessitated the support of an expanded scientific research program that would provide reliable data on the condition of ecosystems and monitor the impacts of recreational use. Increased regional cooperation would also be needed to anticipate the effects of urbanization in Barnstable County and to coordinate regional recreational opportunities and services if the challenge to protect the character of the Outer Cape landscape were to be met successfully. By 1969, the revision was described as a new "master plan." Published in edited and slightly shortened form under that title the following year, the new plan presaged some of what would soon become new methods and goals in federal park planning.[10]

The National Environmental Policy Act (NEPA) would be signed into law at the beginning of 1970. Because it required an assessment of the environmental impacts of proposed actions (and proposed alternative actions) by the federal government, the act would eventually influence the transition away from the "master plan" to what would be described by the mid-1970s as a "general management plan."[11] The 1970 "Master Plan" for Cape Cod was therefore one of the last of its type, although it already indicated new approaches. As a post-Mission 66, yet pre-NEPA, master plan, the document was an important essay in addressing a new generation of concerns, and in the innovation of appropriate planning methodology.[12]

The planners issued their first observations early in 1968, noting that "the need for coordination" with state and local governments and agencies, as well as private property owners, was "abundantly demonstrated." Traffic, parking, and crowding at beaches was already a major concern. (Figs. 7.1, 7.2) In preparation for the new plan, meetings had already taken place or were planned for park staff, the planning boards of the Outer Cape towns, the Massachusetts Department of Public Works, and the CCNSAC. A number of "special items" were identified that required cooperative management, including the status of fish populations, the protection of estuaries, control of water pollution, the disposal of solid waste, the management of wildlife, and an expanded program of scientific research. The last initiative would require increased participation of universities and oceanographic and conservation institutions. Water rights and adequate supplies of fresh water were already identified as issues, due to the pressing need for new wells in Provincetown.

"Access and circulation" quickly emerged as an inevitable concern. Of three million visitors expected that year, 70 percent arrived between June 15 and Labor Day, the vast majority in cars. Coast Guard and Nauset Light beaches absorbed 63 percent of

Fig. 7.1. Parking at Coast Guard Beach. NPSHC.

Fig. 7.2. Ranger at Nauset Light Beach. NPSHC.

them. Three-quarters of visitors came from four states: Massachusetts (30 percent), Rhode Island, Connecticut, and New York. The planners immediately recognized that a regional inventory and analysis of both transportation patterns and recreational resources would be needed to avoid overdeveloping the limited and fragile landscape of the national seashore to serve the expected increase in visitation. Only coordinated planning efforts would meet the "objective of preserving the quaintness and the charm of Cape Cod throughout the Cape whether inside or outside the Seashore."

For the national park itself, the planners identified several long-term studies be undertaken, not only for the "provision of facilities" but of a "cooperative program for environmental conservation," a system of trails—including the alternative of bicycles routes replacing an internal park road—and careful management of beaches. An "inventory of seashore resources" and a "dynamic plan for research priorities" was to be undertaken "in large measure by personnel of cooperating scientific institutions." A "park capacity" was to be determined, in order to "provide facilities in harmony with and not destructive of the resource being used." While no new campgrounds or concessions would be provided, the existing private businesses would be allowed to continue, and coordination with those providing areas for the purpose outside the seashore would be encouraged. "Beach buggies" would continue to be restricted to specific routes, and these would be reconsidered as impacts on "all natural and historic resources" were studied, including specifically the effects on "bird nesting areas." Overall, the planners prioritized "conservation management through research," the "rehabilitation" of "natural and historic areas," and the prevention or removal of "unnecessary manmade intrusions."[13]

The new spirit of "resource management" infused the park planners' early work. Early in 1969, a draft of the new master plan was already being reviewed by the CCNSAC. In another departure from previous practice, the draft plan was presented at a well-attended public hearing. By the fall, the "Management Objectives Statement" was approved by Superintendent Arnberger and Regional Director Garrison.[14] The master plan published in 1970 set precedents not only in the statement of "management objectives" but also in its methods and recommendations.[15] The plan was drafted at a turning point in the early history of the park, as the first phase of land acquisition ended (with the next phase awaiting funding), and much of the physical development of the park completed.

The first section of the plan described the approved objectives, including a statement assuring that any future park structures would be "so designed as to conform to the Seashore's architectural theme." The next section, "Regional Characteristics and Analysis," indicated how much had changed in how national park plans would be prepared in the future. A "Land Use Map," for example, showed existing land uses for the entire Outer Cape Region, both outside and within seashore boundaries. A precursor of what would become commonplace with the advent of Geographic Information Systems (GIS), the hand-drawn map used different graphic hatching to show zones of industrial, commercial, residential, recreational (public beaches), and other land uses. The accompanying analysis emphasized the degree to which cooperation with town, county, and state governments would be an absolute requisite to achieving resource conservation. The planners noted several "land use trends" that would continue in the coming decades. Increasing numbers of summer visitors would create an expanding market for motels, restaurants, and all other services. In addition to visitors, the Outer Cape was gaining popularity as a retirement destination, meaning that many new or rehabilitated houses were intended for year-round occupancy. The growing population was therefore aging, with a marked increase in residents over age fifty. Another important factor influencing development outside park boundaries was Massachusetts legislation passed in the early 1960s which protected identified wetlands and set up town conservation commissions. "The Cape as a whole and the Seashore face challenges to both," they wrote, "challenges which can be fully met only through close cooperation."[16]

The planners' mapping methodology would become increasingly employed in national park planning. A series of graphically coded maps spatialized data on natural history, natural and fragile areas, history, and historic architecture. This analysis yielded a "general development plan" that incorporated greater protection of the identified and mapped "park resources." The development plan was supported by "land classification" and "zoning" maps that reinforced protections for ecologically sensitive and historic areas. Mission 66 planning had prioritized the lack of adequate infrastructure and facilities, and so the "prospectus" of that era described the rapid construction of, for example, buildings, campgrounds, housing, and maintenance yards. The new plan for Cape Cod was based on the "concept that the resources of Cape Cod National Seashore can be preserved in their present state to the extent that uncontrollable natural forces allow," while allowing for "certain types of outdoor recreation for its visitors." This somewhat tentative endorsement of recreation was further clarified. Planning could provide "fuller *utilization* of the capacity for use of a given resource," but it could not "increase the *innate* capacity for use."[17]

The idea of "use capacity" was given considerable explanation, which was appropriate considering its novelty. "Any natural resource—a marsh, an acre of woodland, a beach—has an optimum use capacity," they wrote, "an ability to be used by a given number of people for a given purpose or purposes without being destroyed." The same was true for the "assemblage of resources" that was the Cape Cod National Seashore.[18] Ecological standards had not yet been developed, however, that could establish what such limits would be. As an alternative, the planners suggested that the "*design load* of the facilities" be used to determine a desirable level of visitation. This number represented "the number of people the facility can serve before it would be overloaded or damaged." The capacity of the physical facilities in the park (as of 1969), they went on to determine, was 33,000 every five hours, a number representing filled parking lots and (private) campgrounds, and with trails experiencing heavy traffic. With a "daily turnover" of two times, the total daily capacity was estimated at 67,000. They predicted that number would be surpassed by 1975, necessitating the consideration of contingencies.

Emphasizing that there was "no *internal circulation system*," the planners noted that the capacity of Route 6—even with anticipated improvements—would soon effectively determine the level of use of both the national seashore areas and the town centers of the Outer Cape. The lack of alternatives to the private car for access was noted. But any amelioration or solution to what was already becoming an overcrowded and at times dangerous roadway would require regional solutions and, again, cooperation with the appropriate state and county planning authorities. By this time, the park service collected parking fees at the five beaches it now operated. Beach parking fees were and would remain the only fees collected in the park. Eleven miles of bicycle trails had already been opened, and plans were under way for a system that would extend throughout the seashore.[19] (Fig. 7.3)

The 1969 draft plan was also notable for including a section on "resource management and visitor

Fig. 7.3. Camp Fire Girls resting during dedication of first bicycle trail, 1967. NPSHC.

Fig. 7.4. American beach grass (*Ammophila beviligulata*). Wikimedia Commons.

protection," a category that acknowledged the impacts of visitors on resources, and combined concern for the well-being of both. Dune stabilization and erosion control, both ongoing activities for most of the decade, were identified as priorities. The planners noted, in particular, the establishment of stands of pitch pine (*Pinus rigida*) on the site of the former Camp Wellfleet, and the extensive planting and fertilizing of beach grass (*Ammophila breviligulata*) in several areas. (Fig. 7.4) Erosion of the bluffs of the Great Beach was observed to be up to three feet a year in areas north of Coast Guard Beach, and the plan called for cooperative study with the Army Corps of Engineers, the U.S. Geological Survey, and the state to see what—if anything—could or should be done to address the dynamic and constant reshaping of the Outer Cape landscape.

Insect control—mainly of mosquitoes and greenhead flies—was the purview of state authorities (a provision of the transfer of state lands), but the planners hoped for a thorough review of "the use of chemicals" in pest management. Another area of special concern was the use of "beach buggies." The park service had succeeded in implementing a permit system and in restricting the ORVs to specific trails and areas, "control measures" that recreationalists reportedly "in most cases supported." But the planners noted that the erosion of dunes and the impacts of "beach buggy travel on dune ecology," as well as the "loss of esthetic values," would require further study. Fire management was another serious concern. The regenerating, stunted forests that characterized much of the Outer Cape could be prone to rapidly spreading fires that threatened private residences as well as park facilities. Here again, it was noted that primary responsibility lay with the towns, four of which had entered into cooperative agreements with the park service, to avoid the need of duplicating firefighting capacities.[20]

The planners also commissioned further research on the economic effects of the seashore on the six towns. Boston consultants Phillip B. Herr & Associates completed the "impact study" in 1969 and found that since 1961 the value of private land near the park had increased overall 106 percent, while regional employment and wages had risen approximately 50 percent. The consultants isolated the economic effects of the national seashore by comparing the Outer Cape to other regions, and by accounting for historical trends. Noting that public ownership and increased regulation had perhaps made the Outer Cape "less attractive to some," it had certainly made the region "more attractive to most," directly stimulating the resort economy to a greater extent than would have occurred otherwise. And while tax rates rose sharply during the decade in most areas of the state, they dropped some 17 percent on the Outer Cape (although assessed values had risen in the six towns on an average of 11 percent annually, increasing average tax bills). By 1969, the park service had spent $16 million acquiring land and over $3 million developing the park, generating some $10 million in the sale of goods and services to visitors. The report found strong positive economic trends that, while they could not be attributed to the national seashore entirely, nevertheless amounted to a confirmation of the projections that had been used nine years earlier (in the 1960 economic study) to assuage concerns over the impacts of putting so much land into federal ownership. The new report also came at the moment when new funding authorization was needed in Congress to complete land acquisitions. Its findings were a cogent response to any remaining doubts regarding potential negative economic effects of the park.[21]

By the late 1960s, park planners were able to express priorities for future ecological studies and management policies that marked a turning point. This shift toward "resource management" epitomized changing attitudes at the park service about what constituted adequate stewardship of a national park—and of the "environment" as a whole. New research programs were shaped by the need for data on the ecologies of the Outer Cape, and perhaps by some of the equally peculiar aspects of the political and social contexts of the park. The members of the CCNSAC, for example, quickly recognized that the science behind improved resource management at the national seashore was useful—even necessary—to encourage the desired emphasis of preservation over recreation.

By 1968, the CCNSAC had established a "scientific advisory committee," at first in response to the issue of beach erosion in Eastham. Josiah Child headed the committee and, as he had in the case of architectural advice, enlisted experts, in this case, twelve scientists who worked in the region and knew its geomorphology and ecosystems. Great Island, which the advisory commission wanted to remain as undisturbed as possible, was an early subject of concern, as were human impacts to the dune areas of Provincetown and Truro, and the deteriorating water quality at Pilgrim Lake (later known as East Harbor) and the freshwater ponds. One of the scientists, Norton H. Nickerson, replaced Child on the advisory commission when the architect retired to Florida.[22] The CCNSAC would remain an important advocate for scientific research in the park, in part because its members recognized the importance of long-term studies and monitoring to the successful preservation of park resources. The commission also represented the residents and homeowners of the Outer Cape who, by definition, were not the transient visitors and recreationalists now arriving by the millions. Science could be a potent ally of preservation when it came to considering what were appropriate levels of use and types of public recreation for the seashore.

Of all the potential conflicts between resource preservation and public recreation that might have been expected to generate contention at the seashore, hunting—of whitetail deer, rabbits, ducks, and pheasants—does not seem to have been one of them. Hunting was a well-established tradition on Cape Cod and was specifically authorized in the park's 1961 legislation. The activity had long been regulated and administered by the Massachusetts Division of Fisheries and Game (MDFG) and the state continued its role, now with national park rangers monitoring within the seashore boundaries. Hunting was almost entirely a local affair, occurring in the fall after summer vacationers had left. But by the 1960s, the increase in year-round (often retired) residents and the density of land development in Barnstable County had reduced the availability of hunting locations on the Cape. The state had ceased stocking ring-necked pheasant (*Phasianus colchicus*) on much of the Upper Cape for these reasons, and opportunities were almost gone in Orleans, Eastham, and Provincetown, as well.[23] This put greater pressure on the remaining areas of the Outer Cape that were undeveloped and would remain so (in other words, were within the national seashore) to make up for the losses of game habitat and hunting opportunities elsewhere. But many areas of the park could not be open to hunting, regardless of the time of year.

One of the park's early administrative actions was to acknowledge that while federal lands would be open to fall hunting, a number of locations would not be, for obvious safety reasons. These at first included the Pilgrim Heights area (the former state park), the Atlantic White Cedar Swamp nature trail, and Camp Wellfleet. In addition, state regulations would apply within the seashore, including hunting season dates and bag limits, required licenses, and a prohibition on hunting within five hundred feet of a building.[24] Park rangers patrolled, coordinated with state officials, and attempted to tally the numbers of animals taken. Overall they reported few problems or violations by hunters.[25] The delineation of areas opened to hunting continued to be adjusted, with more areas put off-limits as other public use areas opened. In 1968, a memorandum of understanding between the park service and the MDFG formalized the cooperative management of hunting on federal land.[26]

In 1971, the MDFG proposed the creation of an "experimental wildlife management area," to be operated jointly with the park service on more than one thousand acres in the southern section of Camp Wellfleet (now called Marconi Station, or the Marconi area). The primary purpose of the management area was to stock pheasant. The state had released the game birds at various locations on Cape Cod since the 1930s, and the national seashore now represented the most important remaining opportunity to continue the practice. The "Marconi Wildlife Management Area" operation began that spring and was closely monitored in terms of the viability of the (farm raised) birds as suitable quarry, the responses of hunters, and the overall public reaction.[27] Various memoranda and reports suggest that the experiment was considered a success, at least initially, and the wildlife management area continued to be stocked for decades, becoming the primary pheasant-hunting location left on the Outer Cape.[28] The practice was curtailed, however, following a 2002 lawsuit asserting that the park service was violating its own policies on the introduction of exotic species (in this case, pheasant) in national parks.

The park service began a court-ordered review,

followed by an environmental impact statement (EIS), analyzing alternative ideas for the continued management of hunting. The result was the selection of an alternative that would improve habitat for native game species, specifically northern bobwhite (*Colinus virginianus*) and wild turkey (*Meleagris gallopavo*), through "adaptive landscape management" that would restore "acres of the . . . landscape to enhance the heathland and grassland plant communities." (Figs. 7.5, 7.6) Mowing and thinning of encroaching trees would maintain successional fields as productive habitat. These native game species hopefully would increase and be hunted instead of pheasant. The stocking of farm-raised birds would

Fig. 7.5. Northern bobwhite quail. Photo by Dick Daniels. Wikimedia Commons.

Fig. 7.6. Marconi site vegetation. Photo by Larry D. Moore. Wikimedia Commons.

Fig. 7.7. Beach buggy at Provincetown. NPSHC.

Fig. 7.8. Surf cast fishing, Provincetown. NPSHC.

be gradually decreased and phased out entirely by 2023.[29]

The principal reason hunting was allowed to continue within the national seashore, despite objections raised by some members of the public over the years, was the explicit intent to allow it expressed in the 1961 legislation. This was one of the provisions of the park's original authorization intended to protect traditional practices as components of the landscape character to be preserved. Sportsmen's groups in Massachusetts also were well organized and would have presented considerable opposition if their interests were not protected. Hunting had been practiced by many generations of Cape Codders, and since it drew mainly local residents, not summer visitors (and took place during the fall hunting seasons), direct conflict between local practices and the values of vacationers and summer residents was relatively slow in developing. The challenge that was finally made in 2002 did not focus on hunting itself, but on the introduction of a nonnative bird species. Other local traditions, however, caused more immediate contention between different groups of park users. This was the case, above all, of "beach buggy," or ORV, use.

Like hunting, driving along beaches in modified automobiles was an established practice on the Outer Cape before 1961, dating back to the 1930s. Early beach vehicles, however, were few in number, two-wheel drive, and (even when modified) needed to stay on the relatively hard-packed sand of the summer "berm crest" (just above the typical high-tide level) and the intertidal zone (foreshore), to avoid getting stuck. After World War II, surplus four-wheel-drive vehicles ("jeeps") became readily available and were capable of far greater mobility, including driving through and over dunes. This type of recreation was not specifically protected in the park's legislation, and in fact it was still relatively new as a popular activity in 1961.

In 1950, the Massachusetts Beach Buggy Association was organized by a group of Cape Cod recreational saltwater fishermen who used their vehicles to reach remote stretches of beach. The state retained responsibility for regulating ocean "surf cast" fishing, and the right to fish within the seashore was never in question. (Figs. 7.7, 7.8) The dune buggy owners who organized in 1950, however, also wanted to protect their right to drive on the beach and even to sleep there in their "self-contained" camping vehicles. The restrictions instituted in the early years apparently satisfied the park service and the ORV drivers, at least to some degree. At first the restrictions were minimal. Nearly one thousand permits were issued in 1965, for example, and all thirty-nine miles of the Great Beach were open to the vehicles, as well as ten miles of bay beach. The park service also maintained twenty-six miles of "sand routes" in the dunes of Truro and Provincetown. (Fig. 7.9) A park service "oversand patrol" enforced rules prohibiting speeding and driving off the allowed tracks, although compliance remained less than complete.[30] By the early 1970s, however, the numbers of ORV permits issued had risen dramatically. As resource management was prioritized by the park service and by much of the public, the damage done by the beach vehicles to dune formations, to plant commu-

Fig. 7.9. Early signs for "sand routes," Provincetown. NPSHC.

nities, and to nesting birds began to be considered in a new light.

The source of that light was expanded scientific knowledge of many aspects of the ecology of the Outer Cape and therefore of the impacts that recreation was having. National seashore superintendents embraced environmental research and monitoring relatively early, and they continued to do so over the following decades. They had the support of George Hartzog, who in 1965 sent out instructions on the "implementation of the Leopold report and guidelines for resource management," making each superintendent responsible for the "development of information and the accumulation of material" needed to draft a "resource management plan."[31] By 1966, the seashore's superintendent, Stanley Joseph, could report on the park's "Natural Sciences Research Program," which had begun the previous year under Gibbs. The program depended on partnerships with universities and nonprofit organizations, including Smith College (studying plant communities of the Outer Cape), the Massachusetts Audubon Society (mortality of tern colonies on Nauset beaches), the Woods Hole Oceanographic Institution (erosion of beaches), and the Wellfleet Job Corps (recording plant and animal species in the Atlantic White Cedar Swamp). Other studies were listed for future priority, including ecological research on the Herring River estuary and the park's kettle ponds, population studies of the black duck and tree swallow, monitoring of game animals (native and exotic), and an investigation of Pleistocene geology.[32]

There were many reasons for the managers of the national seashore to embrace partnerships with the many individuals and institutions eager to set up research projects on the Outer Cape, not the least of which was Hartzog's stated policies for the agency. But research programs were also advocated by the CCNSAC, suggesting support among at least some residents and property owners. With the number of visitors (and ORVs) continuing to rise, the results of ecological research and monitoring quickly became crucial evidence in determining a balance of preservation and recreation. And as the advisory commission certainly understood, the data produced through science could often shift that balance to the former.

By the time the new master plan was published in 1970, several environmental concerns had become significant management issues. These early problems were highly visible and directly linked to recreational activities. The property owners represented by the Great Beach Cottage Owners Association, for example, complained to the park service that they had "watched with horror the constantly worsening destruction of the dunes and dune grass during the past few years" in Provincetown. They blamed increased numbers of people taking shortcuts and walking off trails, and the ORVs and campers.[33] But if some on the Outer Cape were seeking more regulation of ORVs, the members of the Massachusetts Beach Buggy Association were seeking less. In 1970, the group succeeded in having state legislation introduced that would have reduced restrictions at Nauset Beach, the section of the Great Beach in Orleans and Chatham that was under town jurisdiction but within the boundary of the seashore. Both towns then explored the possibility of transferring their beaches to the national seashore, after all, where they would come under park service regulations. The state legislation soon failed, however, and the towns and the park service entered into a cooperative agreement that made the rules for ORVs more consistent across jurisdictions. As motorized recreation increased nationally, the problem was not only a local one. In 1972, President Richard M. Nixon issued an executive order for all federal agencies to review their restrictions on ORV use and to develop coordinated plans for appropriate regulation.[34]

Superintendent Arnberger and park staff were receptive to pleas to improve the situation within the seashore, noting in his response to the Great Beach Cottage Owners Association that new signs urging people to stay off fragile areas were being prepared. He also noted that "the entire subject" would be given "careful study in the coming months."[35] Indeed, that summer the *Provincetown Advocate* editorialized that the Provincetown dunes were "being destroyed" but that the park service was "looking for researchers" to study the effects of people and ORVs on the unique dune formations and their fragile vegetation.[36] Other early environmental concerns included the water quality of the park's kettle ponds, which declined with increasing numbers of swimmers, and the dramatic erosion of beaches and their bluffs, particularly north of Coast Guard Beach. All of these very visible environmental issues were linked. Research into one area would require investigations of others if resource management decisions were to be effective and defensible.

The national seashore found the researchers they were looking for when Paul J. Godfrey and Melinda M. Godfrey relocated from North Carolina to the University of Massachusetts Amherst in 1970. A botanist and a marine zoologist, respectively, the husband-and-wife team had done research at the Cape Lookout and Cape Hatteras National Seashores for the previous six years. At the University of Massachusetts, Paul Godfrey took a position as an assistant professor and from there soon organized and led an interdisciplinary "National Park Service Cooperative Research Unit." Through contracts with the park service over the next decade, the unit completed multiple projects investigating and monitoring the environmental impacts of park visitors and increased urbanization on the Outer Cape.[37] By 1975, projects included investigations on the effects on wetland plant communities of ground water withdrawal (wells) in North Truro; a bacteriological assessment of the freshwater ponds and the potential health effects on swimmers; the "ecological effects" of ORVs within the seashore; and the effects of ORV and foot traffic on the movement of sand and soil biology of the Provincetown dunes. Norton Nickerson, a biologist on the faculty of Tufts University as well as a member of the CCNSAC, also supervised studies of water quality and the effects of foot traffic on dune vegetation and ecology. "The basic goal" of the integrated research program, according to Godfrey, was "to understand all we can about the natural system and what happens when man interferes with it." He hoped that the team would produce the most detailed study yet undertaken on the effects of recreation on the ecology of dunes and beaches.[38]

Successive park superintendents supported scientific research in the park. Lawrence Hadley, who replaced Arnberger in 1974, was from Maine, where his father had served as the superintendent of Acadia National Park, and had over twenty years of experience at the park service. Hadley was replaced in 1978 by Herbert Olsen, a historian by training who previously had managed the Boston area national historic sites. Final conclusions and published papers would take years for the scientists to complete, but the researchers also shared their data with park staff as it was assembled, and the local press published reports on the ongoing investigations. Public interest was high because the results might imply that changes should be made to the seashore regulations. One 1974 headline in the *Cape Cod Standard-Times* made the connection clear: "Park's Study Zeroes in on Dune Buggies."[39]

The scientists assembled data on exactly how the movement of people and vehicles on dunes and beaches affected the vegetative communities they passed over, and their influence on the rate of wind erosion and the collapse of dune formations. The results were hardly surprising: heavy traffic of any kind could destroy vegetation that contributed to the overall stability of dunes and bluffs. Data revealed that salt marshes suffered immediate and long-last-

Fig. 7.10. Bearberry (*Arctostaphylos uva-ursi*). Photo by Jim Kuhn. Wikimedia Commons.

Fig. 7.11. Beach heather (*Hudsonia tomentosa*). Wikimedia Commons.

Fig. 7.12. Dunes, vegetation, wrack line, and beach, Provincetown. Photo by Leonardo Dasilva. Wikimedia Commons.

ing damage from the passage of even low numbers of vehicles. Some species of plants, such as bearberry (*Arctostaphylos uva-ursi*), could regenerate after being run over; but others such as beach heather (*Hudsonia tomentosa,* Thoreau's "poverty grass") did not. On the beach, the "wrack" or "drift" line was the area most sensitive to passing ORVs, which destroyed these accumulations of organic material that acted as nurseries for beach plants and feeding areas for shore birds. (Figs. 7.10, 7.11, 7.12) Even the very initial scientific findings indicated that changes should be made to restrict ORVs to the "summer berm and intertidal zone of the beach," and that the vehicles had "major impacts when driven over stabilized dunes," with the greatest impacts in "intertidal and sand flats and salt marshes." Within two years of beginning their work, the researchers recommended that, at the very least, the number of ORV permits issued not be increased.[40]

Park staff and the members of the cooperative research unit also realized that additional studies needed to be made of the impacts of people, dogs, and ORVs on nesting birds, particularly on the Great Beach. The least tern (*Sternula antillarum*) was an early source of intense concern. (Fig. 7.13) After having been hunted almost to regional extirpation in the nineteenth century, the terns had been

Fig 7.13. Least tern (*Sternula antillarum*). NPSHC.

steadily repopulating the beaches of the Northeast since the Migratory Bird Treaty Act of 1918. But the terns competed for nesting space on the beach with beachgoers, dog walkers, and ORVs, leading to fears that their numbers were again declining. The terns formed nest colonies in the zone between the drift line and the sparsely vegetated "foredunes"—beach space vulnerable to people and ORVs. The birds also laid their eggs in minimal "scrapes" that left them entirely unprotected. The Great Beach was a particularly vital nesting habitat for the recovering species, and at the time it hosted a significant percentage of the total number of breeding pairs on the entire Northeast coast. While some environmental impacts of recreation at the national seashore might be difficult to perceive, the plight of nesting terns—and the evidence of crushed eggs or chicks—was not.

The Massachusetts Audubon Society and local bird clubs first sounded the alarm, and began working with the Outer Cape towns in 1966 to mark tern nesting sites, or "terneries," with signs and fences that alerted the public to the presence of the scrapes and their cryptic eggs, which otherwise were very difficult to see. Beginning in 1972, the Cape Cod Bird Club and the national seashore began marking least tern colonies with minimal (or "symbolic") fences. In 1974, the program expanded with additional educational signs and volunteer "monitors" patrolling the sites.[41] In 1976, the least tern appeared on the National Audubon Society's "Blue List," as a species of special concern. That year a full-time "tern warden" oversaw the fencing and monitoring of the terneries within the seashore. The Great Beach nevertheless remained a hazardous zone for nesting birds, who contended not only with ORVs, foot traffic, and dogs but with a full range of natural predators, including crows and foxes, the most common and efficient nest predator. In an experiment to keep out foxes, fences around the least tern nesting colony on Nauset Beach in Orleans (the largest colony on the East Coast) were electrified. By the mid-1970s, in the view of the seashore's chief naturalist, Richard L. Cunningham, the park's "tern program" had become a model for all federal lands with tern colonies.[42]

By 1978, findings by the ornithologist Bradford G. Blodget of the cooperative research unit suggested that, at least in the case of the least tern, fencing and public education were having the desired effect, and the population of the birds was stable or growing.[43] Since the fencing did not close off beach areas entirely to public or ORV access, the restrictions were relatively uncontroversial and widely respected. There were exceptions, including the willful destruction of terneries. But according to tern warden Dennis Minsky in 1977, the "vast majority" of beachgoers and ORV drivers "enjoyed the spectacle of the terns from a respectable distance."[44]

Private nonprofit organizations and local birders instigated the national seashore's tern protection efforts, and volunteers assisted in its implementation and enforcement. Local birders also sometimes had powerful connections in government. Erma J. Fisk, for example, was the widow of an assistant secretary of commerce. In 1975, she wrote to assistant secretary of the interior Nathaniel P. Reed of her concern for nesting shorebirds on the Outer Cape, where she lived, as well as elsewhere on the East Coast. Fisk, an active birder and bird bander, was conducting a survey of shorebird nesting sites from Florida to Cape Cod. While she found some progress, she was dismayed by the lack of a comprehensive, multiagency federal effort to enforce higher levels of protection wherever possible. Even at the national seashore, "our pilot star" in the effort, she felt that rangers and volunteers were not receiving enough training, funding was falling short, and unleashed dogs and self-contained campers were damaging tern colonies. Having been among the volunteers who had initiated ternery protection measures with the park service in 1972, she was knowledgeable about the situation. Reed wasted no time in pressuring the directors of the park service and U.S. Fish and Wildlife Service to promulgate consistent guidelines (which were drafted by Fisk and Cunningham) across jurisdictions, and to initiate a "prompt remedial response" to the problems Fisk identified. Reed maintained a personal interest in shorebird protection at the national seashore for the remainder of his time in office.[45]

Tern protection efforts included expanded education programs in the park, coordination between park staff and other managers and researchers in the state, and response to a steady stream of letters expressing concern over the fate of shorebirds in the park. Increased public attention was matched by official concern from the Department of the Interior. The Endangered Species Act was signed into law at the end of 1973, and although the least tern was never listed as an endangered species, its parlous situation attracted attention.[46]

While the least tern was of special concern, other beach-nesting birds were also affected by increased recreation. For many observers, ORVs in particular seemed to be an additional danger which the birds should not have to contend with. In 1977, the *Cape Codder* editorialized that it was "obvious that the outer beach—as big as it is—is not big enough for both beach buggies and birds. . . . When any of us goes on the sand of the outer beach, it should be by foot."[47] That year Nixon's 1972 executive order instructing federal land management agencies to review their ORV regulations was amended specifically to require that when "adverse effects" to wildlife and vegetation were officially determined, the affected "areas or trails" be closed to ORV traffic when and where necessary. In July 1978, the park service closed the High Head area of the Great Beach, in Truro, to all ORVs for two weeks to protect least tern chicks. The same year, the towns of Wellfleet and Eastham acted to limit ORV use on their town beaches (which were within the national seashore.)[48] A new phase in the struggle between public recreation and bird conservation had begun.

In 1977, the CCNSAC was drawn into the question of how ORVs should be restricted, one of the most contentious recreation issues the seashore would face in coming years. Charles Foster would later recall that the commission soon had "a bear by the tail." The condition of the Province Lands dunes were of particular concern to a group organized as Save the Dunes, which asked the CCNSAC to look into a range of issues, including noise from the Provincetown airport and the effects of recreation—especially ORVs—on vegetation and wildlife. In 1979, Provincetown resident Mark Primack approached the commission with a proposal for closing the fragile spit of land between Wood End and Long Point to all ORVs. Primack had support from Provincetown town meeting and numerous local editorials, and the commission invited him to their next meeting that spring to make his case. As a result, the commission voted to endorse the idea of vehicle-free zones in principle, but also formed a subcommittee to assess the issue. Commission chair Joshua Nickerson named Clifford H. White to head it. An avid saltwater fisherman and former vice president of the Massachusetts Beach Buggy Association, White had been appointed to the commission in 1976 as the Massachusetts representative.[49] The CCNSAC, as always, balanced opinions from members representing a range of interests and constituents on the Outer Cape.

A well-attended public meeting on the issue convinced the advisory commission that ORV use would indeed be a major issue, one that put deeply held convictions and values of different groups of beach users into conflict. At stake was the character of the Outer Cape landscape; the dispute was over what resources and traditions constituted that character, and so should be protected. Primack and many others believed that there were few opportunities left to experience what Thoreau had: the sublime and undisturbed expanse of the Great Beach. Park managers and scientists compiled their ecological data and responded to new mandates to mitigate harm done to bird species, dune formations, and other resources by recreational use. Beach buggy owners argued that beach access by ORVs and campers for saltwater fishing was a way of life, one pursued by generations of residents and visitors, and so was part of what the creation of the seashore was intended to preserve.

That summer, the advisory commission organized a field trip to the Province Lands and reported that the damage done by ORVs was apparent, as were violations of the regulations for their use. At their October meeting, Paul Godfrey made a lengthy presentation of scientific data assembled by the cooperative research unit. White's subcommittee then recommended a new plan for ORV use, one that would create vehicle-free areas during daylight hours in selected areas of the Great Beach: from High Head to Head of the Meadow Beach in Truro, and from Herring Cove Beach to Long Point in Provincetown. Following later consideration, the proposed limitation was extended to night as well as day.[50] Although it would be for the park service to implement such a recommendation and an environmental review would be required for the action, these were the most significant restrictions on ORV use in the seashore so far proposed. Various ORV and statewide sportsmen's groups responded quickly and arranged to present their views at the spring 1980 advisory commission meeting. The park service, meanwhile, made plans to prepare an environmental assessment (or EA, an expedited alternative to an EIS) under the provisions of the NEPA statute in order to study "management alternatives for off-road vehicle use" at the national seashore.[51]

Required public meetings were scheduled for Boston and on the Outer Cape, and officials at the park and the regional office hoped to have a new ORV management plan in place for the 1981 season. As is often case, the park service found itself trying to find the middle ground between two well-organized camps. Environmentalists wanted to see, ultimately, a complete ban on ORVs in the national seashore. Those representing the ORV owners and fishermen wanted as little regulation as possible. Based on the preferred alternative described in the EA, the new regulations were published and made effective in April 1981. The plan was based on the scientific findings of the University of Massachusetts researchers, which were published in summary form in 1979.[52] The plan banned all ORV use on tidal flats and salt marshes, for example, including Hatches Harbor. Upland areas and dunes, which were also shown to be extremely sensitive to traffic, were closed as well, although with specific tracks where the vehicles would be allowed. The fragile dunes of the Province Lands would become vehicle-free except for a specific route serving the residents of the "dune shacks" and "dune taxis." The beach on the bay side from Hatches Harbor south to Long Point was also closed to vehicles.

But the Great Beach itself, at least in a corridor along the berm crest and the intertidal zone, had been shown to be relatively resistant to ORV impacts. As long as the vehicles moved slowly along the packed sand and did not veer into the wrack line and foredunes, they did not appear to cause erosion or disturb nesting terns any more than people and dogs did. The 1981 plan allowed ORVs to drive the Great Beach, from Race Point to Coast Guard Beach (about thirty miles), except during seasonal high tides and tern nesting seasons, when areas would be closed as necessary. Beaches under town jurisdictions would also be subject to additional local regulation. As for overnight use, one area used by ORV campers was closed, but two in Provincetown were kept open, with a combined limit of one hundred campers per day.[53]

The 1981 ORV plan was based on the science available and it was a compromise. Nevertheless, it caused significant controversy. The users of ORVs would have to live with significant restrictions, even if they did have significant stretches of the Great Beach open to them. Careful ORV drivers who respected park resources felt that they were being punished for the misdeeds of a minority. There existed a deeper sense of injustice as well: a feeling among some that they were being gradually displaced from the seashore landscape in favor of others. One Provincetown resident, for example, was angry that "National Park policy has always been to restrict native use of parkland," by which he meant use by long-time area residents.[54] Environmentalists were not satisfied, either. The Conservation Law Foundation sued the park service as soon as the plan went into effect, seeking a total moratorium on all ORVs until a full EIS was completed.

The district federal court denied an initial injunction, and the plan was implemented. When the court finally ruled in 1984, it did so in favor of the park service. The judge upheld the overall management decisions, noting that they were based on the data provided by the University of Massachusetts scientists and therefore were neither an arbitrary imposition of rules nor an uninformed attempt to protect the park's ecology.[55] The court also found, however, that the park service had not adequately considered a "fair allocation of Seashore beaches between ORV and non-ORV users," and it instructed the agency to continue to improve its plan. Elaborating on the point, the court suggested that the managers had considered ecological impacts but had not adequately deliberated on the "appropriateness" of such widespread ORV use in areas where it would have a negative impact on other, far more popular forms of recreation, including swimming, sun bathing, walking, and bird watching.[56] An amended version of the management plan followed the court's ruling.

Fig. 7.14. "ORV corridor," Provincetown. Photo by author.

The 1985 plan fully closed the Great Beach from High Head (near the Head of the Meadow Beach) south, leaving only the eight-and-a-half-mile "ORV corridor" north to Race Point (and as far as Hatches Harbor) open to ORVs. (Fig. 7.14) Much of this stretch of beach was relatively difficult to access by beachgoers on foot, and it included favorite areas for fishermen. A seasonal closure was also put into effect, banning recreational ORVs on all beaches between November 15 and April 15. Rules for the two areas for campers near Race Point remained unchanged. The Conservation Law Foundation challenged the revised plan, and again the courts upheld the park service, finding that limited ORV use was consistent with the park's legislation as a form of public recreation (even if it had not been specifically mentioned in 1961), and that there was a "rational basis" for the assertion that the park's ORV regulations, as amended, were protecting the ecology of the seashore as well as recreational values.[57]

The story might have ended there, to the partial satisfaction of the groups involved. But by 1985, another ecological impact on the Great Beach and its wildlife had become apparent. Collected data on the least tern suggested that the bird's population had responded to the protection measures that had

Fig. 7.15. Piping plover (*Charadrius melodus*) and chick. Wikimedia Commons.

Fig. 7.16. Girl observing piping plover nest during Massachusetts Audubon educational event, c. 1974. NPSHC.

been implemented, and it was never federally listed as endangered. But there were other species of nesting birds in the national seashore, and at least one was suffering an alarming decline during the same period. The piping plover (*Charadrius melodus*) was a small shorebird that nested in the same fragile zones of the Great Beach as the least tern. (Figs. 7.15, 7.16) As was the case with many shorebirds, its population plummeted in the late nineteenth century and began to recover in the twentieth. But the piping plover was losing the competition over space on busy recreational beaches. Fencing (both symbolic and wire nest "exclosures") could help keep individual nests undisturbed, but the plovers did not nest in colonies, and their chicks became mobile soon after hatching. As the chicks grew and foraged for food, they often ran to the water's edge and back—across the summer berm and intertidal zone—making them more vulnerable to ORVs and any other beach traffic. The issue was not unique to Cape Cod; in 1985, the entire Atlantic Coast population of piping plovers was estimated at only 790 nesting pairs. By 1986, the species was federally listed as "threatened" under the Endangered Species Act.[58]

The plover's legal status mandated that the park service do what it could to reverse the observed population decline. In this case, symbolic fences and educational signage would not be enough. Only closing the beaches to ORV traffic wherever the birds were nesting, at least until the chicks were fully fledged and capable of flight, would mitigate their situation. Officials began doing exactly that, an action that was covered under the 1985 plan that included provisions for closures as necessary during the breeding season of shorebirds. Along the eight-and-a-half-mile ORV corridor on the Great Beach, numbers of pairs of nesting piping plovers were observed, and limited closures to ORV use resulted during nesting season. As the numbers of breeding birds increased, so did the closures. For a period in 1989 for example, all but two miles of the corridor were closed to ORVs due to observations of nesting plovers. Superintendent Olsen was reassigned that year, but the new superintendent, Andrew T. Ringgold, was no less committed to protecting the park's resources. On Fourth of July weekend in 1992, all but two-tenths of a mile of the corridor was closed to ORVs, again causing considerable uproar at a peak time for recreationalists, a situation that occurred again in 1994.

The balance between the protection of a threatened species and recreational use seemed, at least to the ORV owners, to be falling heavily to one side. Environmental groups and many others remained adamant that the protection of the birds should be prioritized. The park service agreed, citing its mandate under the Endangered Species Act and the agency commitment to preventing the destruction of park resources. The contention surrounding the restrictions on ORVs in the late 1980s and early 1990s was one of the most intense conflicts the park service had encountered since the original debates over the park's authorizing legislation.[59]

In the early 1990s, the park service entered into "negotiated rulemaking," a legal procedure made possible through 1990 legislation for producing new federal agency rules on issues subject to public conflict. The goal was to reduce litigation and controversy by bringing all parties into a process in which they could present their cases and hopefully agree to a compromise. Superintendent Ringgold recognized the potential of the new option and initiated the process through preparatory "conflict assessment" meetings with the concerned groups in 1993 and 1994. Maria Burks, who became superintendent in 1995, organized the first rulemaking meetings that fall, making the national seashore the first national park to implement the process. Twenty-three organizations, including federal and state agencies, town governments, and advocacy groups participated in three two-day meetings held in Eastham. The process was not an easy one, as both camps remained committed to their respective positions: increasing ORV access versus eliminating it altogether. The park service continued to seek the best possible compromise. A consensus, required for the negotiated rules to be adopted, was achieved and published in the *Federal Register* in 1997.

Implemented in the spring of 1998, the plan was more complex and also subject to regular modification, depending on observations in the field. The new rules opened additional areas to ORV access but maintained an absolute commitment to closing the ORV corridor to protect nesting birds. High Head to Head of the Meadow Beach was opened for July and August, contingent on nesting activity, and a section of the beach in Truro was opened for night fishing, on the same condition. Limited parking areas would be opened in several strategic locations specifically to provide access for fishing, including night fishing. Self-contained campers would continue to be managed as they had since 1981. The new plan was a more detailed, fine-grained approach that both maintained the closures to protect plovers and offered new opportunities for ORV drivers in places and at times that would not adversely affect the birds. Under the new regulations, campers and fishermen using ORVs maintained their place in the cultural landscape of the Outer Cape; the park service also kept an absolute commitment to protect a threatened species. Some disagreement would continue, but all parties had contributed to the development of the plan and so, at the very least, understood it and hopefully would support and abide by it.[60]

The number of pairs of nesting plovers fluctuated, but increased overall from eighteen within the seashore in 1985 to seventy-four pairs in 2006, indicating that the strategy had a positive effect. Continued scientific research and monitoring was an essential aspect of the plan, since restrictions would be enforced when and where necessary to assure the protection of plover chicks, including another EA for significant alterations to the plan in 2007.[61] But the national seashore's efforts to integrate scientific research and monitoring into its decision making, and the significant efforts made by successive superintendents in conflict resolution and in maintaining traditional recreational uses, deserve to be recognized as one of the first and most long-lived—and reasonably successful—undertakings of its kind in the national park system.

The issue of the environmental impacts of ORVs at the national seashore was instrumental in initiating the park's program of scientific research and monitoring, which continues to this day. The seashore's long history of commitment to continuous ecological study of park resources is notable as an important precedent of science-based national park management. Several factors contributed to encourage this program, including the presence of so many universities and environmental organizations in the region, and the support of the CCNSAC and the interests it represented. The original desire for a park that would prioritize "preservation" over "recreation," expressed by so many Outer Cape residents and officials since the 1950s, created a local constituency in favor of ecological monitoring and protections.

There were also institutional changes at the park service in the 1960s and 1970s, beginning with Hartzog's desire to implement the Leopold Report, that reinforced the policies initiated at the national seashore just as it was finishing its initial phase of physical development and turning toward resource management strategies, as indicated in its 1970 master plan. Ronald H. Walker replaced George Hartzog as park service director at the beginning of 1973. Walker created additional regional offices, including a North Atlantic Regional Office in Boston, which became a significant factor in the development of science programs at the national seashore. The Boston office, whose administration included chief regional scientist Paul A. Buckley and deputy regional chief scientist Michael Soukup, began funding a "regional science program." These officials instituted cooperation and funding for agency science programs that assisted and expanded the work being done at the seashore as well as other parks in the region. The office also helped fund the rehabilitation of the decommissioned MITRE Radar Test Site buildings in South Truro to house the University of Massachusetts cooperative research unit activities. By 1979, the three buildings were known as the Atlantic Coastal Laboratory, supported and directed by the scientists at the regional office.[62]

As scientific programs expanded at Cape Cod, the regional scientists oversaw the seashore projects and coordinated them with studies being done in other parks by numerous institutions. The national seashore cooperative research unit, which periodically opened to competitive proposals from other universities, moved to Rutgers University and then to the University of Rhode Island. In the 1980s and 1990s, the park service built on the science programs initiated at Cape Cod to institutionalize ecological research as part of park operations and decision making. John W. Portnoy, an ecologist who joined the national seashore in 1979 as the first park staff scientist, recalled that over the next decades, science "became integral to the institution." Under the regional chief scientists (Buckley and later Mary Foley), the park began to hire credentialed scientists who completed and published their own research on the seashore's ecology, and coordinated the activities of cooperating university scientists doing research under contract.[63]

In 1999, the park service initiated a national "Natural Resource Challenge," which made increased funding for research available to many parks. At Cape Cod, Portnoy, David Manski, the chief of natural resources, his successor, Michael T. Reynolds, and the new leader of the cooperative research unit, Charles Roman, succeeded in making the seashore one of a half dozen parks in the country to implement an innovative, long term "inventory and monitoring" program. The history of research at the park provided a foundation for an expanded staff of scientists to develop "protocols" for natural resource monitoring procedures, which were later implemented at other parks on the Atlantic and Gulf Coasts. The protocols established methods for long-term studies of water quality, the effects of ground water withdrawal, the ecology of salt marshes, the fire ecology of uplands, and shorebird nesting, among other topics. As Reynolds recalled, the seashore had secured the funds needed to "do things right," including establishing staff positions for a core group of scientists with doctorates in their fields who instituted scientific research that often took years to produce significant results.[64]

In 1994, the park service acquired the decommissioned North Truro Air Force Station, 110 acres of new parkland high on the bluffs overlooking the Great Beach. The station included more than two dozen buildings, some of which were identified for potential reuse. Among the new programs and institutions located in what was now called the Highlands Center were the park's expanding scientific programs, including the Atlantic Research and Learning Center and the national seashore laboratory. The increase in staff and laboratory space allowed scientific inquiry into new topics that had great importance for management but were not directly related to recreational activities, as earlier research had been.

A number of salt marshes within the seashore, for example, were in poor ecological health due to interventions that predated the park. In the early twentieth century, diking and ditching salt marshes was seen as a way to control mosquito populations, an increased concern as the Outer Cape economy became tourism-based. In some cases, railroad and highway construction had contributed to the effect of preventing regular tidal flows through the marshes. The results were degraded water quality and an overall deterioration of ecological systems, as indicated in the studies the seashore was conducting. At East Harbor, for example, what had once been a saltmarsh lagoon had already begun to deteriorate in the nineteenth century when it was cut off from Cape Cod Bay. By the early 2000s, the impairment of the ecosystem, which had become a stagnant freshwater pond with poor water quality, had been the subject of study and monitoring for over a decade. A partial restoration of the tidal flows in and out of the harbor renewed salinity and oxygen levels, improving the habitat for fish and other marine species and beginning a transformation back into a healthy estuarine system.[65]

These landscapes, if ecologically unhealthy, had been familiar to generations of residents, however, and the changes caused public concern. The largest of the salt marshes, the Herring River estuary in Wellfleet and Truro, was studied for decades, but only recently has the proposed reintroduction of tidal flows begun to receive the necessary public support for the project to be realized. (Fig 7.17) In this case, alterations to the estuarine hydrology began in 1909, when the town constructed a dike across the mouth of the river in an (unsuccessful) effort to eliminate mosquitoes and increase hay production. The river was channelized in the 1930s, and some of the former floodplain was made available for development, including a golf course. National seashore scientists documented serious water quality problems, resulting in fish kills and the state's closing of the estuary for shellfishing in the 1980s. Ironically, the conditions were actually favorable for mosquito populations, since the fish that would be a chief predator were largely absent. In 2012, park staff published a draft EIS that sought to reopen the estuary—affecting hundreds of acres including some areas beyond the park's boundaries—to greater tidal flow. The overall goal was an ecological restoration that would improve water quality and reclaim the habitats of fish, shellfish, and shorebirds. For the public to fully understand the impacts of each of the proposed alternatives, years of outreach and collaboration were required. The preferred alternative, recently selected, should provide a flexible framework for continued public outreach and ecological monitoring to determine the best strategies to achieve what will be the largest single landscape restoration ever undertaken on the Outer Cape.[66]

Studies of fire ecology also suggested desirable landscape management practices that could be controversial for a public that sometimes wondered how practices resulting in such significant change could be part of the mandate to "preserve" the Outer Cape. In partnership with University of Massachusetts scientists, the national seashore began research in the 1980s on the role of fire in shaping regional landscapes and ecosystems. Again, long-term scientific research later informed stewardship, in this case the "fire management plan" in the early 2000s, which addressed conditions created by decades of fire suppression and included "prescribed" (controlled) burns to improve specific habitats, reduce fuel loads, and protect structures. In 2008, prescribed burning and mechanical cutting began at the Marconi site, in order to improve habitat for the native quail and turkey that were intended to replace introduced pheasant as game birds.[67]

Only long-term scientific monitoring and research programs could provide convincing data, often presented in public settings, that preservation required such active, as well as passive, management. Partnerships with universities and the numerous nonprofit environmental groups in the region also made possible essential public education and outreach that made the more scientifically based management of the park first understood, and then supported, by much of the public.[68]

Projects like these originated with the concerns of the park's scientific staff and the data collected in the course of long-term monitoring programs. But park managers also at times requested studies to address more specific issues. When Superintendent Ringgold sought the closure of the Provincetown dump, for example, park scientists were able to provide data on its effects on water systems and wildlife, essential to making the case for taking action. Later, when the Herring Cove Beach bathhouse required replacement, data on shoreline erosion was used to determine aspects of the location and design of the new facility. Continued research at Herring Cove will inform the relocation and design of the popular waterfront parking lot in the area, which has been consistently damaged by winter storms.[69] (Fig. 7.18)

As scientific research at the national seashore was institutionalized in the 1990s, the protocols for the inventory and monitoring of natural resources developed there were applied to a network of parks along the Atlantic and Gulf Coasts. The park's staff scientist positions—and the long-term research proj-

Fig. 7.17. View from Great Island near mouth of Herring River estuary. Photo by Christine Harris Bates.

Fig. 7.18 Recent erosion of the Herring Cove Beach parking lot, Provincetown. Photo by author.

Fig. 7.19. The Great Beach. NPSHC.

ects they conducted—continued through multiple changes of management personnel.[70] In 2000, the system of cooperative research units as partnerships with individual universities was replaced by "cooperative ecosystem research units," which allowed multiple universities to be engaged within an identified "bioregion" with related research initiatives. In addition to expanded partnerships with universities, the area's nonprofit organizations, such as the Provincetown Center for Coastal Studies and the Massachusetts Audubon Society, continued their collaborations with many aspects of park science and management. As Charles Roman noted, Cape Cod National Seashore has been at the forefront among national parks in the fields of natural resource research and management for decades, particularly regarding coastal biology and geomorphology.[71] This ongoing legacy is perhaps even more notable for a national park that many worried, at its inception, would prioritize recreation over preservation. (Fig. 7.19)

View to Great Island, Wellfleet. Photo by Carol Betsch.

EIGHT

Camping, Beaches, and Erosion

One reason the controversy over ORVs became so bitter in the 1980s is that it revealed a broad shift in how the Outer Cape was being perceived and enjoyed by a growing and changing public. By the mid-1970s, visitation had reached four to five million visits a year, a level that has remained constant since.[1] As the park planners realized in the late 1960s, the limitations of Route 6 north of the Orleans Rotary and the extent of parking areas established a de facto capacity for the park (one far below the ten million visits once predicted in the 1960 economic study).[2] But five million was still a very large number of people, many of them visiting the park's beaches only for the day. (Fig. 8.1) Barnstable County itself was one of the fastest-growing regions in the state through much of this period, rising in population from about 100,000 in 1970 to over 215,000 in 2005. (Again, a maximum capacity seems to have been reached, with the population remaining at or near that level.)[3]

And as predicted in the 1970 master plan, the population of homeowners on the Outer Cape had grown older, more affluent, and increasingly in residence year-round, not just summers. For those who still remembered the cultural landscape of earlier eras, and the freedom with which lower numbers of people pursued less-restricted forms of recreation (including driving and camping on the beach), the maturing social and economic setting of the Outer Cape meant a demographic shift, changing politics in town meetings, and less isolation during the off-seasons. It was perhaps easy to blame these trends on the creation of the seashore and the implementation of its policies. But these changes were coming regardless, and the national seashore was without doubt the greatest single mitigation of the effects of urbanization achieved in the region.

Another reason for the passionate response to the limitations on ORV use was far less complicated: the paucity of camping opportunities in the national seashore hindered this form of recreation. One of the most vociferous groups of ORV users were those who used their self-contained camping vehicles (often a four-wheel-drive pickup truck with a camper

Fig. 8.1. Coast Guard Beach. NPSHC.

unit in the bed) to drive out on the beaches around Race Point and stay the night or longer. (Fig. 8.2) Night fishing from the beach had always been popular, which is why the self-contained ORVs had first been developed. By the 1970s, often an entire family would enjoy camping on the beach in this manner, with fishing being only one aspect of their activities. Camping in self-contained ORVs was, in fact, the only form of beach camping that the national seashore ever allowed or facilitated. The demand for camping opportunities, in other words, became a major factor in debates over ORV use in the 1980s.

Driving ORVs was not usually allowed in national parks; but the activity did have a history on Cape Cod and therefore a claim to being part of the human dimension of the cultural landscape the park service was attempting to preserve. Camping was the opposite case. There were few forms of recreation more closely associated with the national park experience, but there was little history of camping as a traditional activity on Cape Cod. Although early tourists slept where they could, even Thoreau stayed in private houses and lighthouse stations. The proximity of towns and residences made it easy and affordable for early Cape Cod vacationers to find accommodations or rent a cottage. The park service, however, ex-

Fig. 8.2. Self-contained camper. NPSHC.

celled in campground design and construction, and since the 1920s automotive campgrounds had been major components of park master plans. Automotive camping, and the designed landscapes that made the practice more convenient, figured prominently in the very identity and experience of the national park system for much of the public.

The first national seashore, Cape Hatteras, included the development of campgrounds to serve this typical form of national park recreation. But at Cape Cod, although the earliest planning documents suggested at least the possibility of providing for camping, park officials had already indicated in the 1963 revised draft master plan that new campgrounds would not be built. The three private campgrounds in Truro (within the seashore) would be allowed to continue, but the park service would not be constructing or operating its own areas. The CCNSAC influenced the decision through their review of the first draft master plan. The topic often came up in advisory commission meetings and many possibilities were debated. But over years of discussions, the consensus was that no new park service campgrounds should be planned, although the existing private campgrounds could remain.[4]

This was another case of prioritizing preservation over recreation. The CCNSAC (and most Outer Cape town governments) viewed public campgrounds—like marinas, boat ramps, and even picnic areas—as the types of recreational development that would encourage the overuse of the Outer Cape by day-tripping tourists, to the detriment of vacationers, residents, and possibly the environment. Although Superintendent Gibbs initially argued that campgrounds would need to be provided, by the mid-1960s, the opinion of the advisory commission and town governments dovetailed with the park service's policy emphasis on resource management.[5] New campgrounds, like other forms of overnight accommodations, might be developed outside seashore boundaries, but the park service agreed that no park acreage should be dedicated to the purpose. The Cape Cod model, again, responded to the influence of the CCNSAC and the interests of the residents, vacationers, and town governments it represented.

Public interest in camping at the seashore nevertheless was high. Before the creation of the seashore, camping on the beach was largely unregulated but not widespread. After 1961, national seashore regulations prohibited beach camping, except for the self-contained ORVs.[6] It was soon apparent, however, that a considerable number of visitors expected to be able to camp in the new national park, a situation exacerbated by the fact that overnight accommodations and private campgrounds outside the park were not meeting the rapid increase in demand. One reason for Gibbs's argument that eventually camping would have to be provided for was a 1962 report he commissioned on the subject, which predicted a dramatic increase in visitors looking for campgrounds and documented the very limited number of campsites available on the Outer Cape. The three private campgrounds in Truro had about five hundred sites among them, but were regularly filled to capacity and turned away campers. Outside the seashore's boundaries, there was one private campground (later two) in Provincetown and two (later three) in Wellfleet, but that was all. Nickerson State Forest Park (the nearest state park, in Brewster) had four hundred sites, but already turned away hundreds of cars a day on summer weekends.[7]

Seashore staff continued to study the issue and in 1967 reported to Superintendent Joseph a general "adverse local reaction" to the idea of developing campgrounds and recommended that they not be developed in the park. Indeed, a plurality of residents and business owners of the Outer Cape agreed with the CCNSAC that camping should be restricted. In 1965, the Cape Cod Chamber of Commerce recommended that no new campgrounds be built in the county. In the course of the decade, all six town meetings passed bylaws imposing fines for illegal camping, and all but Provincetown enacted zoning restrictions prohibiting new campground development.[8] In his responses to letters inquiring why no federal campgrounds were available at the national seashore, Joseph and later superintendents emphasized that the decision not to build them was consistent with the mandate of the 1961 legislation to preserve the landscape. Park service policy required new campgrounds only in situations where the private sector could not provide them. Letters in response to camping inquiries also directly cited advice from the CCNSAC.

In 1969, Superintendent Arnberger explained to regional director Lon Garrison, who was concerned about public complaints about the lack of campgrounds, that "camping . . . is a touchy issue here on Cape Cod with many of the local residents of the lower Cape communities. Private campgrounds exist at the sufferance of the towns and new permits for such operations are not being issued in a majority of cases."[9] In the meantime, the three private campgrounds in North Truro were left as private inholdings (not "improved properties"), operating under periodically renewed "certificates of suspension of condemnation for commercial and/or industrial properties." Although nonconforming under the seashore district zoning code of Truro, they predated the code and were allowed to continue.[10]

By the end of the decade, the paucity of available camping opportunities and the influx of visitors created law enforcement problems for both the seashore and the municipalities, especially in Truro and Provincetown. The situation was further complicated by the type, as well as the number, of would-be campers. Camping had become "a controversial matter with stringent regulations in effect," according to Arnberger in 1969, as a result of "indiscriminate camping and trespassing during the summer months." In many cases, he made clear, the campers were "hitch hikers and persons without visible means of support."[11] Camping by young backpackers with no "visible means of support" had become a problem in many parks by the late 1960s. In the summer of 1970, violence erupted in Yosemite Valley when rangers tried to enforce camping regulations on a large group of young people, who clearly represented a new and different public for the park service.[12]

But the problem on Cape Cod was hardly restricted to vagrant hippies. That summer the highway rest area immediately outside the (overcrowded) Nickerson State Park became an ad hoc campground, when dozens of frustrated trailer and camper owners appropriated the area, in defiance of Brewster's bylaws and state highway regulations.[13] At the same time, in Harwich plans for a new state park near Nickerson met with strong opposition from town officials and residents who opposed taking 218 acres of mostly private land to create the park and campgrounds. Hawksnest State Park was developed in the early 1970s only after considerable local opposition was overcome through compromise: there are no campsites in the park.[14]

For the park service, the problem of camping on the Outer Cape came to a head in 1970 in Provincetown. Like Yosemite Valley, the scenic artists' mecca on the tip of the Cape had become a strong draw for young people on vacation equipped with little more than what they carried in their backpacks. The shortage of campgrounds or any other available accommodations promised to create a difficult situation for law enforcement. Perhaps eager to avoid the type of problems Yosemite was experiencing that summer, Arnberger worked with officials in Truro and Provincetown to set up "emergency" campgrounds in the parking lots at Herring Cove and Head of the Meadow beaches. The parking lots were opened for overnight parking for the Fourth of July weekend in 1970 and restrooms were kept open, although tents and fires were not allowed. The contingency greatly assisted municipal efforts to control the crowds and avoided potential disorder. The procedure was repeated for Labor Day weekend. The following summer the crowds coming to Provincetown for holiday weekends were even larger, and an estimated two thousand people took advantage of the two beaches opened for the night on both holiday weekends. Park rangers patrolled the beaches and reported few serious problems.[15]

Provincetown officials were deeply appreciative of the cooperation shown by Arnberger and the seashore staff, and the decision to open the beaches for emergency camping was supported by the park service regional office.[16] Other reactions to the camping situation were more critical. At the end of the summer of 1971, the Truro Chamber of Commerce proposed a series of new measures to control how and where people camped, not only in Truro but throughout the Outer Cape. Their petition appeared in the *Provincetown Advocate* and called for an end to opening national park beaches to campers and strict night closures of highway rest areas along Route 6. They asked all towns to increase enforcement of existing bylaws prohibiting unauthorized camping and sleeping in cars. Finally, the petitioners said that "the solution to this problem" was for the park service "to provide adequate facilities within the National Park or for the respective towns to provide . . . [them] through private endeavor." Understanding park service objections to doing so, the petitioners stated that the "original intent" of the seashore may have been "conservation rather than recreation," but the business community of the Outer Cape now felt that "corrective action" was needed, or both goals would be compromised.[17]

The park service held its ground, however, reiterating arguments that new campgrounds within the seashore would damage natural and cultural resources, particularly the dunes and bluffs in Truro and Provincetown, which were at the time an increasing subject of concern. New federal campgrounds would only be a "temporary solution" to the problem of "too many people coming to the Cape without a place to stay," and only development by the private sector outside the park offered a permanent answer.[18] The options would be discussed in town meetings, at the CCNSAC, and by park staff over the coming years. Editorials for and against campgrounds appeared in local papers.[19] But the number of campgrounds in Provincetown (two outside the park) and in Truro (three within the park) remained the same, and the park service renewed the decision to avoid developing campsites, as stated in its 1970 master plan.

In the end, the "emergency" seems largely to have resolved itself, as towns learned to deal with the problem more effectively and visitors learned to anticipate what accommodations would be available, or not, on summer holiday weekends. Camping never became a major part of the experience of the national seashore for the vast majority of visitors, a significant aspect of the Cape Cod model that differentiated the national seashore from many earlier national parks. This was, again, a precedent; management plans for new national parks after 1961 often did not include campgrounds and instead prioritized landscape preservation and a reliance on surrounding private development to meet the need.

As the national seashore matured, several key characteristics of the Cape Cod model became clear: improved properties rapidly increased in value and were often substantially enlarged private enclaves; limits on recreational infrastructure prevented mass recreation centered on camping, marinas, and other facilities found more typically in "national recreation areas"; motorized recreation and hunting continued but declined; and most recreational visits to the national seashore, especially day trips, chiefly involved using the beach on foot, whether to swim, walk, sunbathe, birdwatch, or simply enjoy the magnificent landscape of the Great Beach.[20]

Using the beach on foot, the primary activity for the great majority of national seashore visitors, usually did not cause the controversy or fear of resource damage that camping and ORV use did. The numbers of visitors was large, but so was the Great Beach. The public's use of developed beach areas was usually restricted not by space on the beach but by available parking, and that remained constant at (or decreased from) the levels described in the 1970 master plan. As the planners then noted, this was an effective means (the "design load") of setting a use capacity for the park service's six public beaches. (Fig. 8.3) The beaches that remained under town jurisdiction had their own limits on the number of parking spaces provided and the number of permits issued. Typically, only town property owners or renters were able to get beach passes, although in some cases other visitors also could pay for a day permit, depending on availability. The number of federal and town-managed beach areas on the Outer Cape spread out visitors effectively. While the parking lots at Coast Guard, Nauset Light, and Herring Cove Beaches might fill by midmorning on peak days and so turn visitors away, the parking lots at Race Point, Head of the Meadow, and Marconi Beaches rarely filled to capacity. (Fig. 8.4) With some extra driving, even with five million recorded visits a year, everyone could get to the beach.

Fig. 8.3. The "sand bowl" parking lot off Route 6 on the Truro-Provincetown line, a former sand quarry used for recreation until 1984. NPSHC.

Fig. 8.4. Nauset Light Beach, 1966. Photo by Earle W. Estes. NPSHC.

There was one important controversy over beach use in the maturing years of the national seashore, however, that was not linked to the operation of the six developed federal beach areas. Nude swimming and sunbathing were traditional activities on the Outer Cape, at least for some, dating back to the less-crowded and less-regulated days before 1961. Since 1963, however, when Superintendent Gibbs promulgated park rules, "obscene or indecent exposure" was at least nominally banned on all federally owned property.[21] Relatively small numbers of enthusiasts continued the practice, nevertheless, on more remote sections of beach or at isolated ponds, where they attracted little notice and no attempts at enforcement by the park service. (Fig. 8.5) The three-mile stretch of the Great Beach between Ballston Beach in Truro and Newcomb Hollow in Wellfleet (both town beaches) was one such area. Remote, undeveloped, backed by high dune cliffs, and out of view for most park visitors, it was conducive to privacy and nude bathing, as were some areas in Provincetown. The park service never attempted to enforce its rule regarding "indecent exposure" because it never had to. There was at least

Fig. 8.5. Great Pond, Wellfleet. NPSHC.

a tacit understanding that if no one complained, there was no reason to interfere.[22]

The live-and-let-live attitude on the subject collapsed in the early 1970s as large numbers of nude beachgoers began to congregate in a specific area in Truro: a stretch of beach about a mile south of the Ballston Beach parking area, known as Brush Hollow. While Ballston Beach was managed by the town, Brush Hollow was owned by the national seashore. Since before the seashore was established, Brush Hollow had been considered a "free beach," where nudity was acceptable, or at least out of view. But the area had now become well known, and the number of nude beachgoers quickly went from dozens to hundreds. This remote and undeveloped portion of the Great Beach was classified in the 1970 master plan as a "natural environment area," in other words with no parking lots, access paths, restrooms, or life guards. By 1973, however, it was experiencing heavy public use. What had been a discreet practice in previous decades became another sign of the times. Damage to dune formations and vegetation was significant. Several improvised pedestrian routes, from South Pamet Road, North Pamet Road, and Collins Road, traversed the dunes from illegal roadside parking to the beach. Truro maintained only eighty spaces for cars at Ballston Beach for those accessing Brush Hollow by walking along the shore. Illegal parking damaged roadsides and involved trespassing on private property. The unplanned pedestrian routes over the dunes destroyed vegetation, encouraged bluff erosion, and damaged the landscape. Without restrooms or waste disposal bins, environmental conditions deteriorated. Illegal parking and traffic congestion affected neighborhoods in Truro, and residents were furious.[23]

That fall, Truro residents and property owners represented by the Truro Neighborhood Association brought the matter to the CCNSAC and the park service, demanding that something be done. For most of those who objected to the situation, the problem was not nudity itself but the developing spectacle that was becoming a destructive nuisance. The issue dominated the advisory commission's 1974 meetings, including two public hearings. Superintendent Hadley told the commission that his principal concern was one of resource management, not nudity. He felt he had two options: accommodate the use or prohibit it. The first would require altering the 1970 master plan (which had precluded any development at Brush Hollow), changing seashore regulations, and creating conflicts with other uses and resource management priorities. The second would lead to enforcement challenges and probably a lawsuit. After lengthy consideration, the CCNSAC supported the second option, even with its shortcomings, as more consistent with the overall purposes of the national seashore and the balance of preservation and recreation.[24]

The following summer, the free beach at Brush Hollow was more popular than ever. On one day, rangers counted 1,200 nudists. On weekends, up to 175 cars were observed daily parking illegally on roadsides, and an entrepreneur had started a jitney service bringing people from Truro Center. On Labor Day weekend, a visitor drowned unnoticed in a crowd of 1,000 beachgoers.[25] Hadley and his staff considered options in consultation with the regional office in order to prepare an environmental assessment of management alternatives. That fall and winter, park service staff assembled an EA that examined eight strategies. The first was to implement a ban on nudity within the seashore, a step that would likely trigger legal and enforcement challenges. The second option was closing all beaches completely for July and August, except for the six managed federal beaches (those with lifeguards, parking lots, and other facilities). The third called for closing the same beaches, but only for swimming, allowing all other activities. Both scenarios would obviously curtail visitor use dramatically and were not likely to be implemented. The fourth alternative called for creating a new managed beach at Brush Hollow, with full facilities, through a concessioner contract or special use permit. The fifth called for a similar level of development, to be done by the park service. Both of these options would involve a major new developed area in a still pristine and scenic natural area of the park, and so were unlikely to be approved when environmental impacts were considered. The sixth option was to accommodate nude bathing at one or more of the existing six managed beaches. Head of the Meadow Beach was considered for this purpose, but local property owners strongly objected that the problem would simply be moved to their neighborhoods.[26] The seventh was to create a beach with minimal facilities (improvised parking, portable sanitation units) provided by the park service, and a last option was to consider providing for the ongoing use at Brush Hollow in a manner consistent with its master plan status as a natural environment area. But these alternatives offered no effective means of mitigating the environmental impacts caused by heavy use of a natural, undeveloped area.

The EA began by describing the problem as one not of nudity but of extensive resource damage. Park staff recognized that nude bathing was a long-established practice on the Outer Cape and that it had continued after 1961. But they also cited estimates that up to four thousand people might be expected on a single day at Brush Hollow if the trend continued. The eight alternatives were considered for their environmental and recreational impacts and their estimated costs. The analysis pointed to the first as the preferred alternative in those terms, a decision already supported that November by the CCNSAC. But despite the nominal park rule barring indecent exposure on federal land, park service lawyers were unable to find an existing federal regulation (one previously published in the Code of Federal Regulations) that would be applicable specifically for enforcing a ban on nudity. Since this option was selected, it required a new federal rule published in the *Federal Register,* to be implemented thirty days later after public comment. With the help of Department of the Interior solicitors, a regulation banning nudity within the seashore was drafted and published in time for the 1975 season.[27]

The Civil Liberties Union of Massachusetts sued shortly after the rule became effective that spring. The controversy became national news, and both local and national nudist advocacy groups organized petitions and wrote letters pointing out that other public beaches in the country were finding ways to accommodate nude bathers. Elected officials, including Senator Edward Kennedy, voiced their disappointment that a compromise had not been found.[28] Public opinion on the Outer Cape (and the comments sent in response to the publication of the new rule) were evenly split for and against. That July, the Federal District Court of Massachusetts upheld the park service ban on nudity at the national seashore. The court affirmed that the plaintiffs had a "personal liberty right, protected by the Constitution, to bathe in the nude at Brush Hollow," but the question was whether the ban "impermissibly infringed on that right."

The judge found that the park service had fully explored its alternatives and had a legal obligation to mitigate the documented environmental damage and the parking and traffic problems that the situation caused. The decision stated that "while the Court found some protection for the right asserted by the plaintiffs, it appears clear that this narrow liberty has been outweighed by the considerations which led the defendants to adopt the regulations."[29] The question was not whether people had a right to swim in the nude but whether the ban on nudity was an acceptable infringement of that right, necessary to address the park's 1961 legislative mandate of landscape preservation. The court ruled that the ban on nudity within the seashore was a justified limitation of personal liberty. That ruling was upheld on appeal and remains in effect today.

With the legal challenge met successfully, enforcement still loomed as a difficult and sensitive task. Organized opposition to the ban was strong, and the nudity advocates knew that no other national park, including the other national seashores, had found it necessary to impose a sweeping ban on nudity. The park service began enforcement by sending out teams of male and female rangers to inform unclothed bathers of the new rule, to issue written or verbal warnings, or simply to ask visitors to put on a bathing suit. Social science researchers observing events that summer reported that almost all encounters were unremarkable, if less than friendly, and that nude bathers usually covered themselves as soon as they saw rangers on the beach.[30] Rangers did have the option of issuing citations for a court appearance, and even of making arrests if visitors insisted on remaining naked. That summer, however, only thirteen citations were issued (resulting in twenty-five-dollar fines) and no arrests were made. Verbal warnings were far more numerous. In August, the Free the Free Beach Committee, a local group of nudity advocates, organized what they called a "clothing-optional beach party," intended as a massive resistance to the new regulation. An estimated 2,600 nudists participated, with another 1,200 clothed spectators also showing up. The park service elected to avoid confrontation and did not attempt enforcement of the ban that day, instead managing parking and traffic in order to maintain public safety. The relatively conciliatory approach to enforcement resumed after the event.[31]

In the following years, the situation continued, and rangers issued warnings and more citations: 153 in 1976 and 139 in 1977, for example. Days of protest coordinated with national nudist advocacy groups were organized, and individual incidents of objection to the ban occurred. A petition with three thousand signatures urging a repeal of the rule was presented to the park service. By the 1980s, however, the movement to "Free the Free Beach" had lost momentum. The controversy faded, although it flares up occasionally, especially in Truro and Provincetown. Rangers continue to enforce the regulation banning nudity at Cape Cod, particularly if complaints are made by visitors. In 2016, they issued only 8 citations resulting in fines of fifty dollars.[32] There continued to be strongly divided public opinion on the Outer Cape, but the problems caused by large gatherings of nude bathers mostly dissipated. Nude swimming returned to being a mostly discreet and relatively private practice.

The national seashore again set a precedent, as the first and only national park to explicitly ban nudity. But in this case the precedent did not influence operations at other parks. The situation that led to the ban on nudity was unique to the specific balance of preservation and recreation that resulted from the relationship of the park service with private property owners, town governments, and the CCNSAC. The park service briefly considered a nationwide ban similar to what had been implemented for the national seashore, but such a measure was soon considered unnecessary and was never attempted.[33]

The single greatest threat to the capacity of the national seashore to provide recreational beaches for millions of visitors, however, was not ORV use, nesting birds, or nudists. It was the Great Beach itself, or rather the geological processes that created Cape Cod over fifteen thousand years ago and have continued vigorously ever since. As Thoreau observed, "Such beaches as are fashionable are here made and unmade in a day . . . by the sea shifting its sands." Formed by retreating glaciers, the Outer Cape remains a remarkably mobile landscape, "made and unmade" both by long-term processes of sand migration and by single storm events lasting only hours.

Since the earliest days of park service administration, the agency sought to understand the geological processes that had shaped the Outer Cape and continued to modify its contours. Cape Cod had been the subject of geological investigations before the park was created, many of them undertaken by the Army Corps of Engineers. The safety of navigation, the economic importance of beaches for the tourist economy, and, above all, the threat to homes and private property have long made the geomorphological processes of Cape Cod and its barrier spits and islands a subject of scientific interest. As with other coastal resort areas, the owners of threatened homes (and the elected officials representing them) often sought government action to armor shorelines to forestall erosion and coastal flooding. In the twentieth century, this usually meant constructing stone riprap walls and dredging sand from the ocean floor to replenish depleted beaches and dunes. Regardless of the unintended impacts of such strategies—and their questionable effectiveness—the value of the real estate involved made government action desirable if not inevitable in many cases.[34]

After 1970, however, the park service would look at the management of the shorelines under its jurisdiction in a very different way. The long-term scientific studies conducted by the seashore and its partners suggested that natural processes should not—and could not—be controlled through engineered interventions. By the mid-1970s, Paul and Melinda Godfrey published their research, based on data assembled at both Cape Hatteras and Cape Cod, indicating that park managers should not attempt to control the natural processes that changed shorelines but rather should adapt plans to the new conditions created by them. The botanists noted that the park service was in the process of adopting the ecological concept of "dynamic stability" as a model for landscape management, and that plant and animal species of the seashore were well adapted to the disturbances of storms and erosion.[35] In 1976, the coastal ecologist Graham Giese and two other scientists, Charles Mayo and Barbara Shuler Mayo, founded the Center for Coastal Studies in Provincetown, which undertook long-term investigation of shoreline geomorphology. This work and that of other partners, including the Woods Hole Oceanographic Institution, would give the park service and the six towns of the Outer Cape data and analysis vital to their decision making in anticipation of future change.[36]

For the park service, the scientific research done by its cooperative research unit and by its partners in the region led to shoreline management strategies consistent with the agency's contemporary emphasis on resource preservation. The land acquisitions that precluded further private development of the Great Beach created the opportunity to allow coastal processes to continue unhampered by concerns for developed properties. In any case, there was no stopping the erosion of the great headlands of Truro, Wellfleet, and Eastham, which faced the full force of the Atlantic every winter. (Fig. 8.6) Nor could the processes of sand deposition and shoreline breaches caused by ocean currents at the north and south ends of the Outer Cape be halted. The rise in sea level, which was already noted in the 1970s, was a contributing factor in rates of erosion, which could only be expected to accelerate with climate change.

But there were potential exceptions to the idea of letting processes of shoreline reconfiguration take their course. The bathhouses the park service built in the 1960s had been sited between 1958 and 1963, just before the anticipation of shoreline erosion had become park policy. Parking lots and bathhouses were placed at accessible points along the shore (as town beaches had been for decades), in most cases quite close to the beaches they were intended to serve. Already in 1966, high tides and erosion had damaged the parking lot and beach access points at Coast Guard Beach in Eastham—the CCNSAC originally formed its scientific advisory committee in response to that situation. That year, the advisory commission consulted with the Army Corps of Engineers and the Woods Hole Oceanographic Institution, and the coastal geologists advised against heavily engineered—and futile—reinforcement, suggesting that the park service instead adapt its facilities to the changing shoreline. By 1970, the future of Coast Guard Beach was in question, and the park service was committed to devising new beach access and services in ways that would be consistent with a strategy of anticipating natural change. Shuttle buses were being considered to bring people to the beach from parking lots at the Salt Pond Visitor Center and the nearby Doane Rock picnic area, but this was not a solution all members of the CCNSAC could endorse. They feared shuttle bus access to the beach would affect the town's economy by deterring visitors to Eastham, who would go elsewhere rather than forego the convenience of having their vehicles (and their supplies for a day at the beach) close at hand.[37]

While the debates continued, however, a series

Fig. 8.6. Heavy surf. NPSHC.

of storms demonstrated the dramatic forces that made the discussion irrelevant. An April storm in 1972 with gale force winds caused damage at several beaches and took away twenty-five feet of shoreline at the site of the Coast Guard Beach bathhouse. The park service made repairs and some attempts at shoreline stabilization, including the placement of concrete slabs. But anyone who witnessed such dramatic events, in which the ocean claimed dozens of feet of shoreline in a matter of hours, could have little doubt as to the fate of the Coast Guard Beach developed area. In Orleans that summer, Superintendent Arnberger addressed a number of contentious beach access issues at a public meeting organized by a state legislative commission. He was blunt on the subject of erosion.

Admitting that the concrete slabs had been a mistake, Arnberger observed that no "engineering measures now known" would stop the erosion of the high bluffs of the Great Beach. The most the towns and the national seashore could do was to control the "human erosion" caused by too much or poorly regulated beach use. While business owners and town governments fretted over the loss of revenue that closing Coast Guard Beach might incur, Arnberger knew there was actually little choice. The conclusion was supported by a consensus in the scientific community. A conference held in Provincetown that fall brought together coastal management scientists from the entire East Coast, and while they no doubt had many discussions and disagreements, they were unanimous on the futility of trying to control erosion on the shoreline in Eastham.[38]

In February 1978, one of the strongest blizzards ever recorded hit the Outer Cape. The nor'easter brought high winds, record tides, and feet of snow. Storm surges breached dikes and dunes at Hatches Harbor and Long Point in Provincetown. On Nauset Spit in Eastham and Orleans, four cottages were swept away, including Henry Beston's "Outermost House," where he lived while writing his 1928 book. (Fig. 8.7) The remains of the houses and other debris ended up at various points along the shore and in Nauset Bay. The storm also settled the question of what to do about Coast Guard Beach. The bathhouse fell into the sea, and its remains were intentionally burned after the storm to prevent the ruins from drifting out to sea and becoming a navigational hazard. (Fig. 8.8) Estimates of the damage of the "great blizzard" of 1978 to national seashore infrastructure were quickly assessed at $600,000, mostly to cover the cost of replacing public services at Coast Guard Beach. When asked by the *Cape Cod Times* whether the beach would be open to the public the next summer, Superintendent Hadley responded that he had "no idea," but that the park service, anticipating the event, had planned not to replace the parking lot and bathhouse. Some of the parking lot was salvaged, but Hadley already had the park service's Denver Service Center working on a new "development concept."[39] An Army Corps of Engineers study of the Outer Cape shoreline begun in 1973 concluded in 1979 that "no beach erosion control project be adopted by the United States . . . along the easterly shore of Cape Cod," on the basis of logistical, economic, and environmental reasoning.[40]

The demise of Coast Guard Beach, just over a decade after it was built, pushed national seashore planners into a consideration of alternative transportation to provide beach access by means other than private vehicles and parking lots. The result was another precedent set at the park. The desirability of a system of bicycle paths independent of automotive roads was already being considered in the early 1960s. In 1967, the park opened the first

Fig. 8.7. Henry Beston's "Outermost House," before its destruction in 1978. NPSHC.

Fig. 8.8. Coast Guard Beach bathhouse during blizzard of 1978. NPS.

Fig. 8.9. Province Lands Bike Trail, 2015. Photo by Giorgia Galeotti, Wikimedia Commons.

"bikeways" built specifically for the purpose in the national park system. Three routes opened that year: the Province Lands trail, an eight-mile loop through dunes, bogs, and forests; the two-mile Pilgrim Heights (or Head of the Meadow) trail, which in part followed the route of the historic King's Highway and was built by Wellfleet Jobs Corps recruits; and the Eastham (or Nauset) trail. (Fig. 8.9) The latter was a two-mile linear trail accessing historic sites near the Salt Pond Visitor Center, including the former Coast Guard life-saving station at Coast Guard Beach and the beach itself. The new trails were dedicated in September.[41] Bicycle use at the national seashore increased rapidly in the 1970s, and for those parking at the visitor center or the Doane Rock picnic area, bicycle access to the ocean beach already existed. The bikeways encouraged the decision to abandon the creation of an internal park road in favor of bicycles, a change that was formally adopted in the 1970 master plan. The system of bicycle paths on the Outer Cape soon expanded dramatically and became a major form of alternative transportation (and beach access), especially after the state acquired rights to the Cape

Cod Railway right-of-way in 1976 and began converting it into a linear bikeway running from Dennis to Wellfleet.[42]

The developed area at Coast Guard Beach was never rebuilt. Instead, the ruins were cleaned up and planted with native vegetation. (Fig. 8.10) Access to the beach shifted to shuttle buses and bicycles from the visitor center parking area. Members of the CCNSAC and the business interests in Eastham still hoped that a way could be found to redevelop the beach, delaying the implementation of any new "development concepts" the park service considered. In the 1980s, the national seashore finally built the Little Creek parking and shuttle staging area, across the road from the Doane Rock picnic area. This became the permanent means of access for visitors to Coast Guard Beach, the first and most popular federal beach of the national seashore.

Coast Guard Beach was the first park facility affected by the dynamics of coastal erosion and storm tides on the Outer Cape, but it would not be the last. The 1978 nor'easter made it clear that the iconic Highland Light in North Truro would soon be imperiled.[43] (Fig. 8.11) Historic life-saving stations, as well as a number of improved properties and park service public facilities, would need to be moved or demolished along the ever-changing Outer Cape shoreline. The Marconi Site interpretive shelter—one of the first structures built by the park service—was removed in 2013, and the Herring Cove Beach bathhouse was replaced (with modular structures farther from the shore) the same year. The bathhouse

Fig. 8.10. Site of the former Coast Guard Beach bathhouse. Photo by author.

Fig. 8.11. Highland Light (before relocation), Highland House, and associated structures, Truro. NPSHC.

at Nauset Light Beach, north of Coast Guard Beach, today is in a situation similar to that of the Coast Guard Beach building in the early 1970s.

More significantly, over the decades, the six towns of the Outer Cape have had to accept dramatic alterations that have at times destroyed homes outside the park and improved properties within it. This is especially true in Chatham, which since 1987 has seen three breaches in the Nauset Spit, which protects the town and harbor from the open sea. Despite millions of dollars spent on shoreline stabilization, dozens of "camps" on the Nauset Spit and substantial homes that lined the inner shore have been lost. In 2014, Superintendent George Price declined to extend the annual permits on some of the last "North Beach camps" on the eroding barrier beach and oversaw their demolition before they could be swept out to sea. The controversial decision was a reminder of the intricate mosaic of public and private property within the national seashore, and of the sometimes complex legal statuses that distinguished improved properties, special use permits, and leased post-1959 properties. Above all, however, Price's action responded to the overwhelming natural processes of coastline transformation on the Outer Cape that—over time or in a single storm—made such considerations irrelevant.[44]

Approaching Head of the Meadow Beach, North Truro. Photo by Carol Betsch.

NINE

The Cultural Components of Character

The environmental movement, which gained momentum around the time the Cape Cod National Seashore was dedicated in 1966, shaped the park's "resource management" policies and scientific research programs during the following decades. Udall's New Conservation was directly associated with Cape Cod, and then with national seashores generally, which were among the most important conservation achievements of the Kennedy and Johnson administrations. The federal environmental legislation of the 1970s reinforced the new approaches to national park operations, epitomized by increased restrictions on public use and scientific research programs at the national seashore. The desire to prioritize "preservation" over "recreation"—now fully shared by the park service, nonprofit partners, the CCNSAC, and many property owners and town governments—led to increased funding for the scientific research needed to inform and implement natural resource management policies.

The central question of the success or failure of the Cape Cod model, however, remained whether the "character" of the cultural landscape of the Outer Cape had been, or could be, maintained to any significant degree through the management actions of the National Park Service. The mandate for conservation in the 1961 legislation explicitly included efforts to maintain the "way of life" in the region. The "special provisions" of the bill—necessary for its passage—were designed in an acknowledgment that the people of the Outer Cape had shaped the landscape and continued to contribute to the essence of its character. The preservation of cultural resources, therefore, was emphatically included in the park's legislative origin. Protecting the natural resources of coastal ecological systems was, of course, also vital. The character of the Outer Cape would not survive if dune formations and their flora were crushed; if nesting shorebirds were extirpated; if campgrounds and parking lots covered too great an extent of the narrow and fragile terrain; or if crowds congregated by the thousands in areas that had been zoned for natural resource protection in the park's master plan. Managing the cultural components of landscape character, however, would be an equally challenging undertaking.

In 1961, the park service had more early inventories and research on the cultural resources of the Outer Cape landscape than it had for its ecological systems. The history of Cape Cod had been the subject of generations of imaginative historical accounts, novels, and architectural restorations during the first half of the twentieth century. The region's cultural heritage—mostly as it had been reimagined and invented—commanded a national audience that was entranced by its windmills and harbor towns, and sometimes actually lived in twentieth-century versions of its cottages. This heritage had been commodified through the development of countless restaurants, motels, and tourist attractions; it formed a cornerstone of the regional identity that was used to promote the market for second homes and vacation destinations. The economics of heritage conservation and interpretation were not lost on the backers of the Pilgrim tercentenary commemorations, or on the regional chamber of commerce, which recognized the significance of historical associations to the tourist-based prosperity of the twentieth century.

For the National Park Service, however, curating the cultural heritage of the Outer Cape would present difficulties that, if usually less controversial than natural resource management problems, were at least as intractable. Controversy over the ecological impacts of recreational use, in fact, fueled the interest in natural resource programs and helped secure funding for them. But cultural resources were usually not affected by the rising numbers of visitors or their activities. Threats to their integrity were less obvious and, at least during the seashore's early years, did not receive the same level of attention or money. The region's rich architectural legacy, for example, was an expensive one to maintain, and the deficiency of funding for the rehabilitation of historic structures was apparent already by the early 1970s. Preserving the historic character of specific landscapes, such as Fort Hill or the Pamet Cranberry Bog, was complicated by plant succession and other natural processes that often accelerated in places that had come under public ownership. Above all, the task of preserving the region's "way of life" would be made nearly impossible by the demographic changes caused by rising home prices, changes in the ownership of improved properties, and a general shift from a rural society to a suburban one in Barnstable County.

As plans for the national seashore took shape in the late 1950s, Ernest A. Connally, an architectural historian then teaching at the University of Illinois, assembled the first comprehensive survey of historic buildings within the proposed park. Connally worked summers directing groups of architects and scholars for the Historic American Buildings Survey (HABS), a program that had begun in 1933 as part of the expansion of the National Park Service under the New Deal. The HABS program began just months after dozens of historic sites and monuments were transferred by executive order to park service jurisdiction, and while the agency also was planning the development of new "national historical parks." Under the overall direction of the landscape architect Thomas Vint, HABS drew on a national network of architects and preservationists, as well as organizations such as the Society for the Preservation of New England Antiquities (SPNEA). Founded in 1910, SPNEA had been, like The Trustees of Public Reservations, a major preservation advocate in Massachusetts for most of the century.[1]

The HABS teams prepared measured drawings, took photographs, and did archival research on selected historic structures. Because of the well-established interest in the preservation of historic structures in Massachusetts, the state was well represented by early HABS projects. During the 1930s, a number of historic houses and other structures (including windmills and a saltworks) were documented in Chatham, Orleans, and Eastham.[2] (Figs. 9.1, 9.2)

After World War II, HABS was reactivated with Mission 66 funding.[3] Beginning in 1959, Connally's HABS researchers and architects began their comprehensive survey of the Outer Cape and compiled a "master list of historic structures" found within the proposed boundaries of the national seashore. The list eventually included eighty-six properties, all but seven of which were privately owned houses that would become improved properties once the park was established.[4] The HABS research and documentation was done specifically to aid in the establishment and early administration of the national seashore, a role that HABS played for a number of new parks at the time (as it had during the 1930s).[5] Connally had a serious scholarly interest in the domestic architecture of the Outer Cape, and he published an influential article on the "Cape Cod house" in 1960. He noted that the characteristics of the Cape Cod house had already been described by Timothy Dwight in 1800, and that the Outer Cape was a particularly rich repository of this vernacular building tradition. The "old ways lasted late and pure"

Fig. 9.1. Chatham windmill, 1934. Photo by Arthur C. Haskell. HABS.

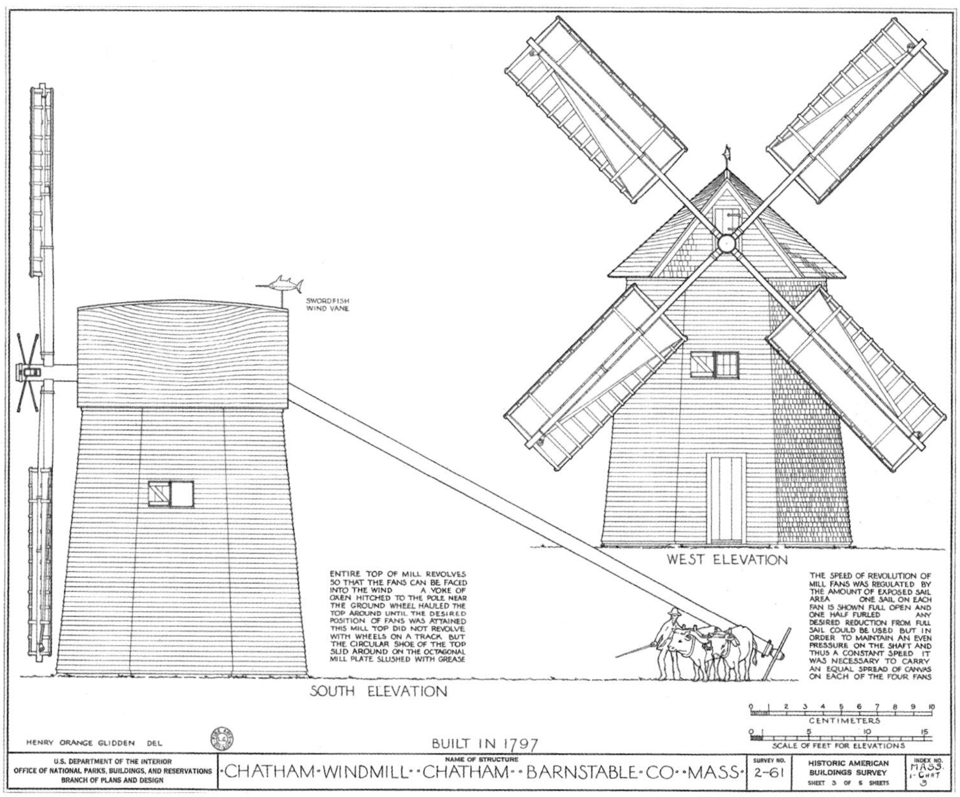

Fig. 9.2. Drawing of Chatham windmill, 1935. HABS.

on this more remote section of the Cape, specifically between 1750 and 1850. By the mid-nineteenth century, there were probably two thousand of the houses in the six towns, representing the historical types of Cape Cod houses: "house, house-and-a half, and double-house." The vernacular design and construction tradition disappeared after the Civil War.[6] The modest cottages were a story and a half, with wooden shake siding and roofs and massive central chimneys. Although many variations existed—projecting dormers, clapboard siding on one or more sides, ell additions—the building type was distinctive and recognizable. Connally estimated that in 1960 half of the Cape Cod houses built on the Outer Cape still existed.[7] (Figs. 9.3, 9.4)

In 1966, Congress passed the National Historic Preservation Act (NHPA), ushering in a new era in historic preservation practice in the United States. Although the act was contemporary to the establishment of the seashore, its implications took several years to become apparent. Ernest Connally became the executive at the National Park Service overseeing the implementation of the legislation nationwide. This included the creation of the National Register of Historic Places, a list of nationally significant historic properties to be maintained by the park service. Under the provisions of the 1935 Historic Sites Act, the agency had already undertaken a survey of nationally significant historic sites. After 1960, the historic sites survey was reactivated as the "national historic landmark" program. A section of the 1966 NHPA automatically listed the previously designated historic sites and national historic landmarks in the new register, and effectively expanded and broadened the earlier surveys to include properties considered to possess local and statewide (as opposed to national) significance. Connally oversaw the organization of this expansion, and he supervised a broad reorganization of cultural resource management at the National Park Service. Although based in park service offices in Washington, the National Register depended on the participation and contributions of

Fig. 9.3. Rowell House, Wellfleet, 1959. Photo by Cervin Robinson. HABS.

Fig. 9.4. David Baker House, Wellfleet. Photo by Cervin Robinson. HABS.

new "state preservation offices" that every state and territory created or designated as partner agencies under the provisions of the NHPA.[8] In Massachusetts, this was the Massachusetts Historical Commission (MHC), an office of state government since 1963.

The Outer Cape's architectural legacy had been a factor in considering the national significance of the region since the 1930s, and Connally's HABS survey of the area of the proposed national seashore amounted to one of the most complete regional assessments of its type at the time. The documentation and research of this "master list" gave the park service a baseline for understanding a unique and significant heritage within the proposed park. Following the passage of the seashore act in 1961, however, the great majority of the houses were and would remain privately owned. The park only came into ownership of the historic houses in the relatively rare cases where owners elected to sell their properties during the acquisition process, or in other special circumstances. In these cases the park would be faced with the task of adapting the houses for administrative purposes or as interpretive museums of some type.

Another option was to "lease back" historic structures for private or institutional use. The question of how these publicly owned and historically significant properties would be rehabilitated, preserved, or otherwise managed loomed as an expensive and complex task. Particularly in cases where the park service and lessees entered into a landlord-tenant relationship, the potential for misunderstanding and antagonism was great. Management issues related to the scores of significant "Cape Cod houses" within seashore boundaries therefore fell into two categories, depending on whether the properties were privately owned or were acquired by the park service. But the entire premise of the Cape Cod model was that most residences would remain private properties, and this included the great majority of historic houses. The question of their preservation—and often their alteration or enlargement—would therefore ultimately rest with town governments, where the power to impose zoning codes and local historic districts resided. This would soon be considered as another shortcoming of the Cape Cod model.

The park service had never elaborated a convincing plan for what would happen to the hundreds of historic houses within the park if they were all acquired. Without the means to adequately maintain them, probably many would have been leased (or sold) for private use, demolished, or just neglected. Only a select few could become museums, and from the beginning the question of what would happen to so many historic houses if they were acquired was a critical one. Even if owners retained life-tenancy rights, the park service could only offer vague assurances that once the houses were vacant the agency would be able to repurpose and maintain them in a comprehensive manner. When the alternative of leaving them in private ownership with zoning restrictions—the Cape Cod model—was put forward, at least initially some perceived it as a potentially more efficient and effective way of maintaining the legacy of Cape Cod houses within the seashore by relying on existing owners to act as the stewards of their properties. (Fig. 9.5) The houses that did come into public ownership after 1961 did indeed present management problems for the park service, most related to the basic challenge of finding adequate funding for rehabilitation and maintenance, and for developing interpretive displays and programming.

Fig. 9.5. "Typical house, Cape Cod." Photo by Carol M. Highsmith. CHA.

Once the National Register was established, another important factor came into play for the management of historic properties within the seashore: the potential listing, or "eligibility" for listing, in the new register. At first it was unclear whether historic structures within national parks should even be included; to some they seemed adequately protected by the legislative mandate of the National Park Service. But it soon became clear that federal agencies in general—including the park service—should not be exempt from the provisions of the NHPA. The period saw the loss of many notable historic structures, and some of them, it turned out, were under federal jurisdiction. President Nixon acted through a 1971 executive order to require that all federal agencies complete surveys of properties under their jurisdiction for potential eligibility for listing in the National Register, a task that was later codified in 1980 amendments to the NHPA (section 110). At the national seashore (as in all national parks), the executive order accelerated the process of determining the eligibility of structures owned by the park service. Listing in the register (or determining eligibility for listing) for federal properties meant that any rehabilitation, for whatever purpose, would be required to meet the secretary of the interior's guidelines for preservation practice. These were general rules that amounted to a method for assuring that the historic character of buildings would be maintained whenever practicable. For private properties, listing in the register had no regulatory implications, although after 1976, owners rehabilitating listed properties could apply for federal tax credits if the proposed modifications were shown to meet the "secretary's standards" for historic preservation.[9]

The matrix of public and private ownership within the national seashore complicated the implementation of the provisions of the NHPA. The 1971 executive order mandated the park service to determine the eligibility of properties it owned, while the MHC (as the state preservation office) was required to perform a statewide survey of private and public historic properties under the original terms of the NHPA. Any regulatory restrictions on the alteration of private properties, however, remained under the zoning authority of local governments, and the park service had no mandate to determine their eligibility for the National Register even if they were within the seashore. Other properties were technically owned by the park service but occupied under the terms of twenty-five-year or lifetime tenancy agreements, or through leases and special use permits. The survey, documentation, and determination of eligibility of historic structures within the seashore boundaries would become a continuous process, particularly as the criteria for determining historical significance expanded in the coming decades.

In 1973, Superintendent Arnberger indicated in a memorandum that park staff was not able to find a complete copy of Connally's 1962 master list of historic houses. The list was provided by the regional office; but the request made it clear that the national seashore had not yet capitalized on the early advantage represented by the inventory.[10] Although this period saw a purposeful increase in scientific research on the Outer Cape, the systematic treatment of cultural resources lagged behind. While natural resources were visibly threatened by higher levels of recreational use, in the case of historic Cape Cod houses owned by the national seashore, deterioration could occur with less notice because it was caused not by too much use but by difficulties in finding any use at all.

The Jedediah Higgins House in Truro was an example. Built around 1800, it was a classic example of a Cape Cod "double house" (or "full Cape" house) that had been researched by Connally and later surveyed by the MHC. The owners chose to sell in 1963 without an occupancy agreement, and the park service began using it for staff housing. By the early 1970s, however, it was no longer considered habitable. The house had a high degree of historical integrity and featured many original features of the type, including a circular brick cellar, post-and-beam construction, and interior wainscoting and plastered lath. (Figs. 9.6, 9.7) Its condition, however, was not good. In other words, many of the architectural features were original, but the roof leaked, the corners

Fig. 9.6. Jedediah Higgins House, Truro. HABS.

Fig. 9.7. Kitchen fireplace, Higgins House. HABS.

of the house had settled into the ground, wiring and utilities were out of date, and windows needed repair or replacement. The house required substantial investment (an estimated $15,000 in 1976) before it would be safe to use as employee housing, and the park service apparently could not find the money. If nothing were done, the condition of the house would worsen to a point that would amount to its destruction.[11] Arnberger therefore sought permission to "sell back" the house in 1972 to any buyer who would be willing to accept a sales contract and deed restrictions requiring that a rehabilitation (to be specified in detail by park service architects) be completed by the new owner. But it proved impossible to find a buyer willing to both invest a substantial sum in the house and accept restrictions on future modifications to safeguard its historic character.

The house sat for years, steadily declining in condition, although the park service funded roof repairs and other stabilization measures in the mid-1970s. The house was also not listed in the National Register. Although regional staff had recommended that all seven of the Cape Cod houses in federal ownership that appeared on Connally's inventory be listed, Arnberger exercised his prerogative as superintendent and demurred from doing so. He wrote to the regional director in 1973 that the advice to list the houses was "directly contrary" to the national seashore's policy at the time. "The whole subject of what belongs on the National Register," according to the superintendent, was "bogging down in confusion and uncoordinated communication." Although he was not more specific, likely he feared that National Register listing would only further restrict his already limited options, making a sale that much more difficult. The superintendent argued instead for loosening the restrictions and lessening the requirements that a new owner of the Higgins House would be required to accept.[12] By 1980, Superintendent Olsen was still unable to arrange a lease or sale. One prospective buyer at the time observed that the "house would slowly go to pieces if it is not lived in." Olsen could only point out that such "freehold conveyances" required careful consideration.[13]

Policy to address situations like these took shape through amendments to the federal tax code in 1976, which authorized federal tax credits to private owners rehabilitating properties listed in the National Register, and the 1980 amendments to the NHPA, which authorized leasing of historic properties in federal ownership for the purpose of preservation (section 111). The problems presented by the Higgins House were all too common throughout the national park system, especially in newer parks that included significant numbers of historic properties. By the 1980s, the option to lease back properties—while assuring uses that would be consistent with park purposes—was encouraged as a means to address the growing "maintenance backlog" for historic structures.[14] Following the 1980 amendments to the NHPA, all parks were instructed to compile lists of historic properties suitable for leasing with provisions that would in some cases require the new occupants to invest in maintenance as well as pay rent. This was eventually the solution for the Higgins House, which is today leased as a private residence, preserving it as one of the finest and most historically accurate examples of its type.[15]

Formal listing in the National Register for the other Cape Cod houses owned by the seashore would take years, although a determination of their eligibility (a much quicker process) could have the same effects. By 1974, the Higgins House, as well as the Ryder House, the Ahearn House, and the Atwood-Higgins House in Wellfleet (all owned by the park service) were considered "eligible." The Higgins House was officially listed in 1984, as was the Ahearn House (also known as the Curran House).

Built before 1851, the Ahearn House was another of the classic Cape Cod houses described by Connally. It was acquired by the park service in the 1960s, and by 1977, it was described as "derelict" and recommended for leasing or "sell back" before its "deterioration {became} irreparable."[16] Like the Higgins House, the Ahearn House today is leased as a private residence and is in good condition.[17]

Leasing historic houses to private residents precluded opening them to the public but did preserve the structures and maintained their overall appearance in the landscape. Leasing was not an option in all cases. The most significant of the Cape Cod houses that came into park service ownership during the process of land acquisition was the Atwood-Higgins House on Bound Brook Island in Wellfleet. (Fig. 9.8) George and Katherine Higgins, who had owned the property since 1919, donated it to the park service in 1961 with a specific restriction that it become a "historic site," open to the public for the interpretation of historic architecture and the "way of life" on the Outer Cape. The oldest section of the house was built by Thomas Higgins (an ancestor of George Higgins) in 1730, and featured the vertical plank construction typical of eighteenth-century Cape houses. Thomas Atwood purchased the house in the early nineteenth century, and additions and modifications to the house at that time included post-and-beam construction, wood paneling, hardware, moldings, and other details of the era. The house was not lived in after the 1880s, and George Higgins purchased it after it had lain vacant for decades. The Higginses fully realized the significance of the building, which exhibited architectural construction from the entire period of significance (1750 to 1850) that Connally identified as the high point of the Cape Cod vernacular tradition. (Figs. 9.9, 9.10) In 1959, Con-

Fig. 9.8. Atwood-Higgins House. Photo by Cervin Robinson. HABS.

Fig. 9.9. Chimney in attic, Atwood-Higgins House. Photo by Cervin Robinson. HABS.

Fig. 9.10. Cellar looking toward stairs. Photo by Cervin Robinson. HABS.

nally described the house as the finest example of the type on the Outer Cape.[18] Higgins and his wife maintained it almost as a museum, restoring it and filling it with period furnishings. (Fig. 9.11) They built a guest house and barn in the 1920s, and in the 1940s they reconstructed a general store and post office, intended to represent a historic New England type. (Fig. 9.12) They hoped the complex would continue to be an important location for interpreting "the way of life existing in the vicinity of the historic site . . . to reflect the . . . past history of the house, its adjoining buildings, and surrounding area as representative of Cape Cod."[19] (Fig. 9.13)

The setting of the Atwood-Higgins complex was also ideal for park interpretation. Although Bound Brook Island was not actually an island, it was isolated by the Bound Brook and Herring River wetlands to the north and south, and by Cape Cod Bay to the west. The area had been inhabited by up to twenty families in the early nineteenth century but since then had reforested and become a relatively remote expanse of naturalized woodlands and wetlands. Its undeveloped condition in the 1950s had made it the suitable point for extending the boundaries of the national seashore over to the bayside—across the peninsula of the Outer Cape—an important goal for park planners who wanted to include a range of representative landscape types and ecosystems in the new park.

As national seashore staff anticipated the public use of the Atwood-Higgins complex in the 1970s, the house itself was listed in the National Register, and an "interpretive prospectus" was drafted. The planners observed that the property's potential for interpreting and displaying the legacy of the "traditional Cape Cod house" was its primary and unique potential. The entire evolution of the region's vernacular building tradition was represented. It was also the logical point for introducing visitors to the cultural and natural history of Bound Brook Island,

Fig. 9.11. Northwest room. Photo by Cervin Robinson. HABS.

Fig. 9.12. Recreated country store interior. Photo by Cervin Robinson. HABS.

Fig. 9.13. Atwood-Higgins House and outbuildings. Photo by author.

a good area for hiking and experiencing the upland landscape that was less frequently visited. The role of the Higginses themselves in maintaining and developing the complex for the benefit of the public would also be presented. The authors noted that the "Cape Cod architectural style" had long been "recognized as one of the major historical themes of the Seashore," and one that was "not dealt with elsewhere in the Seashore or area." Interpreting this legacy at the Atwood-Higgins site would "realize a major Seashore interpretive goal." They suggested that access should be provided by shuttle bus to small groups through a reservation system, and that interpreters could open the house to visitors as part of the scheduled programs.[20]

Despite its potential, it remained difficult to realize the ambition of making the Atwood-Higgins property a major interpretive feature of the park. The nature of the proposed interpretation—through staffed programs on a limited basis in order to protect the site and maintain its integrity—made the plan dependent on having significant time dedicated by the small staff of park interpreters. The house was also relatively remote and so necessitated a shuttle service to avoid building parking lots that would detract from the site. And although the house had fewer problems with its condition than some of the Cape Cod houses acquired by the park service, the buildings nevertheless required significant funds just to maintain them much less to adapt them for programs and public use. The buildings were significantly restored in the 1990s, a process that included archaeological investigations of the site.[21] In 2010, the National Register listing was amended to create a district that encompassed the twentieth-century outbuildings as well as the house, in recognition of the significant role of the Higginses in the stewardship of the property.[22] Open today on a limited basis to the public, the Atwood-Higgins House still requires expensive upkeep. It is fair to say that it has yet to achieve its full potential as a destination for park visitors interested in the architectural legacy of the Cape Cod house.

Another residence acquired by the park service also offered a significant opportunity for public interpretation, although it represented a very different tradition and period in Outer Cape history. Unlike the Atwood-Higgins House, which was ensconced in one of the more remote sections of the park, the Penniman House stood prominently at the entrance to the Fort Hill area in Eastham, close to Route 6 and the Salt Pond Visitor Center. The imposing two-and-a-half story residence was built in 1868 by Edward Penniman, a whaling ship captain. (Fig. 9.14) Penniman grew up in Eastham as one of eleven children on the family farm on Fort Hill. He had gone to sea at age eleven in 1842, and he first captained a whaling ship out of New Bedford in 1860. His wife, Betsy Augusta (Knowles) Penniman, who was born on an adjacent farm in Eastham, then accompanied him on his travels, including two four-year whaling voyages to the South Pacific. Penniman continued whaling into the 1880s, accompanied by his wife and his children, and he was a prominent figure in Eastham until his death in 1913. With a mansard roof covering the entire second story, projecting dormers, and a fenestrated cupola offering views of Fort Hill and the sea, the house expressed the Pennimans' lucrative success in the industry. The interiors featured marble fireplace surrounds, rich wall papers, mahogany balusters, decorated ceilings, chandeliers, carpets, and the first indoor plumbing on the Outer Cape.[23] (Fig. 9.15) The contrast with the Atwood-Higgins House or the other Cape Cod houses (the type of house both Edward and Betsy were likely raised in) could not have been more extreme. The Penniman House was also built at a time of economic depression on much of Cape Cod.

Fig. 9.14. Penniman House, Eastham. NPSHC.

Fig. 9.15. Parlor, Penniman House. Photo by Cervin Robinson. HABS.

The house remained in the Penniman family after Betsy's death in 1920, and one of her daughters lived there until she died in 1957. The property was willed to an aunt and uncle, with the provision that on their death the house would pass to the Town of Eastham for the purpose of creating a public museum. The aunt and uncle, however, paid the town $8,000 in 1960 to gain full title with no such restriction. The park service, recognizing the significance of the house, acquired it in 1963 for $28,000.[24] By that time, much of the interior decoration was gone; nevertheless the potential of the property as a site for park interpretation was manifest. As it was the only "captain's house" within the seashore, park staff soon discovered that something more valuable than original furnishings had survived. Betsy's journal and family letters had been conserved, as well as many personal artifacts. And more than one hundred glass plate negatives of photographs taken on the site by one of the Penniman children provided a visual record of the house and its residents. The trove revealed a detailed and unique record of the family's life and their extraordinary travels all over the world. The park service restored the house in the 1980s, based on the photographic evidence and other investigations. At that point, park interpreters were able to put the archival materials to good use in programs and displays that told the stories of one of the most successful whaling captains in New England, his family, and their remarkable experiences. Opened to the public on a limited basis since then, today the Penniman House is one of the most important interpretive sites in the park.[25]

The fate of other historic houses on the Outer Cape, including the remainder of the Cape Cod houses documented by Connally, depended largely on the willingness of private owners to respect the historic character of their residences. In many cases, such as that of the Higgins and Penniman families, owners included family descendants with a personal understanding of their own heritage who were motivated to be stewards. Others included prominent cultural figures who had been involved in the process of negotiating the park legislation, such as Francis Biddle and E. J. Kahn. Particularly during the early years of the national seashore, many of the proprietors of improved properties were aware of the goals behind the creation of the park. But over time, as the properties increased in value and changed hands, at least some new buyers were less invested in the founding ideas and felt less obligation to maintain the historic and often understated character of what were, for them, merely expensive and desirable summer retreats. Many were unaware of how and why the private properties came to be left within the seashore, and for some, this history perhaps was of little consequence. The park service had no authority to impose their own restrictions (such as the "secretary's standards") on private properties, in any case.

All the towns of the Outer Cape did create historic preservation districts, through their local zoning authority, intended in particular to protect historic town centers in Provincetown, Wellfleet, Eastham, and Chatham. The improved properties within the seashore, however, did not fall under these local historic districts. Listing in the National Register or the MHC state survey of historic properties could improve the situation, since at least some towns enacted additional architectural review for building permits issued for listed structures. For the park service, however, the principal means of stewarding the historic private properties within the seashore was to keep informed of the activities of planning boards, zoning boards of appeal, and town meetings, and when possible to speak directly with property owners to inform them of the special significance of their residences.

Most of the historic Cape Cod houses in private ownership within the seashore today are still not listed in the National Register, even those documented by HABS and surveyed by the MHC. At least some of them would no longer be considered eligible, owing to alterations and enlargements.[26] To a significant degree, the establishment of the seashore was not able to directly affect the stewardship of many of the historic improved properties within its boundaries, because the Cape Cod model never included adequate means for doing so. But over the years, the park service has been able to foster a sense of the importance of the historic preservation of private properties within the seashore through a nonregulatory, collaborative approach with town governments and individual owners.

By the 1990s, the situation also improved thanks in part to the increasingly regional approach to land use issues in Barnstable County. Since the 1950s, the park service, along with the county's chamber of commerce and many other individuals and organizations, had recognized the need for a cooperative approach to issues that could not be successfully managed by the six town governments independently. In 1965, instigated by the pressing issue of adequate drinking water supplies as well as garbage disposal, the state legislature authorized the Cape Cod Planning and Economic Development Commission to coordinate plans for Barnstable County as a whole. By the 1980s, as urbanization continued apace, the pressure on the region's "sole source aquifer" continued to be a matter of great concern. In 1990, the state legislature created the Cape Cod Commission, with the support of a majority of Barnstable County residents as expressed through a regional referendum. The commission's principal mandate was to create an overall "regional policy plan" to guide land use policy for the fifteen towns of the county. Among the powers granted the new county agency was the review of plans to demolish or alter properties listed in the National Register if they fell outside existing town historic districts.[27] In historic preservation, as in many other aspects of national seashore management, the Cape Cod Commission therefore became a vital partner to achieve the overall goal of maintaining the legacy of vernacular domestic architecture on the Outer Cape.

The preservation of the historic Cape Cod houses within the national seashore achieved only mixed success. Private ownership obviously limited what the park service could hope to accomplish. The agency also initially proceeded under the assumption that properties it owned that were under fifty years old would not be found eligible for the National Register, and therefore could be destroyed, moved, or altered with little review or oversight.[28] Some twentieth-century houses that might later have been found to be eligible for the National Register—especially for their associations with the Outer Cape way of life—were demolished as a result. By 1972, what was described as "a large number of buildings less than 50 years old" had been "sold or razed."[29] In the 1970s, in response to the executive order requiring a survey of potentially historic structures owned by federal agencies, the seashore (and all other national parks) began assembling a "list of classified structures," intended to include all buildings owned by the park and considered historically significant.

At first there were fewer than twenty structures on the list. By the 1980s, however, standards for determining historical integrity and significance were expanding to include new historical contexts and new property types, especially those dating to the more recent past. Today there are about seventy-eight individual entries in the national seashore's list of classified structures. They range from historic lighthouses and life-saving stations to Cape Cod houses, the Salt Pond Visitor Center, and residences designed by midcentury modernist architects.[30] But during the early decades of the national seashore's development, buildings and structures not considered historically significant (and therefore not eligible for the National Register) were routinely sold (on the condition of moving them to another site outside the park) or demolished. Since they were not "cultural resources," they were considered intrusions on an otherwise "natural" setting.

Historical contexts and "statements of significance" (essentially researched narratives) were the basis for determining the importance of individual buildings or landscapes and their potential eligibility for the National Register. They also shaped the "interpretive themes" that organized park educational programs. Preserving and interpreting the cultural components of the seashore's character therefore depended to a degree on the historical contexts and interpretive themes described by park service planners, historians, and other staff. First described in the park's earliest master plans and management policies, these themes evolved over the decades to reflect changing understandings of how cultural resources—and the way of life they represented—were construed and assimilated into the park's public programs and management policies.

The development of these histories eventually established a broader definition of the cultural components of the character of the Outer Cape. But most public programs and interpretive exhibits at the park, then as now, presented the natural history Cape Cod: its geomorphology, flora, fauna, and ecology. By the time the first museum displays were finished for the Salt Pond Visitor Center in 1966, for example, four interpretive "nature trails" were opened: Pilgrim Spring, Small's Swamp, Beech Forest, and Atlantic White Cedar Swamp. (Figs. 9.16, 9.17) Evening programs were held in the temporary amphitheater at the Nauset Coast Guard Station and later at the new Salt Pond and Race Point amphitheaters.[31] The growing staff of interpretive rangers was responsible for a wide variety of seasonal activities—including nature walks, evening presentations, and bird walks—that introduced thousands of visitors to the natural history of the Outer Cape.

Fig. 9.16. Atlantic White Cedar Swamp Trail entrance, original signage and logo, Wellfleet. NPSHC.

In the 1970s, the importance of these park interpretation programs to natural resource protection, as well as education, also became apparent. Visitors who were aware of the fragility of dune vegetation and the plight of nesting shore birds could usually be counted on to respect rules regarding beach access or other restrictions that otherwise might be met with greater resentment. Natural resource interpretation became increasingly oriented to the protection of those resources by educating visitors and encouraging people to obey park rules. However, the overall goal of natural resource interpretation still remained, foremost, to enhance the experience of park landscapes by conveying an awareness of natural processes and ecosystems that deepened appreciation. But by the 1980s, natural resource interpretation and signage

Fig. 9.17. Atlantic White Cedar Swamp Trail. Photo by author.

at the seashore (and at many other national parks) prioritized educational messages directly targeted at improving visitor behavior by explaining some of the scientific findings that supported park policies and management actions.

In contrast, the public did not directly threaten the park's cultural resources, at least not to the same degree or in the same ways. But interpreting the cultural history of the region nevertheless was also central to the overall mandate to preserve the character of the Outer Cape. The evolving sense of which historical themes should be developed for public history programs directly influenced how visitors perceived and valued the cultural landscape and helped determine revised priorities for its management.

The architectural legacy of the Cape Cod house was only one of the early interpretive themes of the national park and only one initial category of cultural resources to be preserved and interpreted for the public. The 1958 "Field Investigation Report" included a brief narrative by the regional historian Frank Barnes which emphasized the Outer Cape's Pilgrim history, long a favored subject for research and commemoration in the region. An accompanying archaeological report described the historic sites associated with the Pilgrims in 1620: the "landing site" at Provincetown, for which there was documentary but no physical evidence; "Corn Hill" in Truro, where the Pilgrims may have discovered (and seized) a cache of corn stored by the Wampanoags; the purported "first encounter site," on a bayside beach in Eastham; and "Pilgrim Spring," the area where they found a source of fresh water. All of these sites lacked any physical or archaeological evidence, and all had been memorialized previously by the Pilgrim Tercentenary Commission (established in 1917) based on analysis of contemporary written accounts. The most imposing monument to Pilgrim history on the Outer Cape was erected by the Cape Cod Pilgrim Memorial Association, which sponsored the Pilgrim Monument and museum in Provincetown. (Fig. 9.18) The 250-foot campanile was dedicated in 1910 to the Pilgrims' first landfall and the signing of the Mayflower Compact, and it was by far the tallest structure in the region, visible for many miles.[32] There was no question in 1958 that the story of the Pilgrims' arrival on the Outer Cape would be a prominent interpretive theme for the new park, as it had been for town historical societies and state and national organizations for most of the twentieth century.

Of the identified Pilgrim sites, however, only the Pilgrim Spring area, which had been made a state park in 1954, was incorporated into the national seashore. The 1963 park master plan featured an illustration of an encounter between Wampanoag and English people on its cover sheet, and a "historical base map" of the region identified the sites associated with the events of 1620. Another map in the plan identified the locations of historic buildings (from Connally's list), and a third indicated Native American archaeological areas, as they had been surveyed at that time.[33] A fourth map showed other historic sites, including life-saving stations, lighthouses, shipwrecks, and the Marconi Station site, among others. Taken together, the base maps illustrated what would become the principal interpretive historical themes and points of interest in the national seashore during its early years. Two of the first park structures subsequently built were called for in the 1963 plan: the "interpretive shelters" at Pilgrim Spring and Marconi Station. The Pilgrim Spring shelter was located to provide a vista of the area, and included a topographic model to aid the discussion of the location of freshwater sources the Pilgrims may have used. The Marconi shelter also featured a scale model, in this case of the original array of two-hundred-foot antennae masts erected by Guglielmo Marconi in 1903 to send the first wireless transmission from the United States across the Atlantic. The

Fig. 9.18. Pilgrim Monument, Provincetown, 1959. Erected by the Cape Cod Pilgrim Memorial Association in 1910. Photo by Cervin Robinson. HABS.

station operated at the site, which later became part of Camp Wellfleet, until 1917. It was abandoned and dismantled in the early 1920s. Later the area became a victim of the inexorable erosion of the high bluffs on which the antennae had been sited.[34] The hexagonal shelter housing the model itself was removed in 2013, as its location was also threatened by the same forces.

By 1965, with the first interpretive shelters built and the Salt Pond Visitor Center under construction, park staff assembled a comprehensive "interpretive prospectus." The authors were the chief naturalist, Vernon C. Gilbert, and the park historian, Edison P. Lohr, who elaborated on the themes outlined in the 1963 master plan. They described an ambitious program and a total of four visitor centers, with two to be located at the Nauset Coast Guard Station in Eastham and Griffin Island in Wellfleet, in addition to the Salt Pond and Race Point buildings. The many guided walks, evening programs, and interpretive displays they outlined emphasized the natural history of the region but also integrated topics such as Pilgrim history, historic architecture, commercial fishing and whaling, life saving, and other aspects of past ways of life on the Outer Cape. They acknowledged that walking tours led by rangers would be the most popular and effective activities, regardless of the subject, and suggested expanding the tours and adding guided boat trips.[35] This extensive and integrated interpretive program of natural and cultural history, however, would only be realized in abbreviated form. The two additional visitor centers were never developed, and the 1970 master plan was notable for the brevity with which it treated park interpretation generally, and cultural resource programs in particular.

One of the notable goals of the early interpretive planners was to make the Nauset Coast Guard Station into a "Nauset Life-Saving Museum." In part because of the physical resources associated with them, the historical themes of navigational aids and life-saving efforts on the Outer Cape were among the most important in terms of interpretive programs and the preservation of historic structures. The history of navigational aids in the region was almost as old as that of the Republic. The sand bars, currents, and storms of the Outer Cape had threatened and sometimes destroyed coastal shipping throughout the colonial era. (Fig. 9.19) In 1789, in one of its earliest acts, Congress placed responsibility for the scattered and unreliable lighthouses on the East Coast with the federal government. In 1797, Congress acted to build the first lighthouse on Cape Cod, on the high bluffs of Truro. Known as the Cape Cod Lighthouse, or the Highland Light, it was rebuilt twice in the same area, the last time in 1857. Thoreau stayed at the keeper's residence at the Highland Light during his sojourns. One of the earliest and most prominent lighthouses in the country, Highland became a regional icon. Several other important early lighthouses, built and rebuilt in the nineteenth and early twentieth centuries, also stood as a testaments to the Atlantic "graveyard" offshore and to the general hazard to coastal shipping presented by the Outer Cape and its ocean currents. Congress went on to authorize a pair of lighthouses in Chatham (1808), and three in Provincetown, at Race Point (1817), Long Point (1827), and Wood End (1878). By 1839, the group of three lights above Nauset Beach in Eastham (the "Three Sisters") was also in operation.[36]

In 1961, most of the lighthouses within the seashore, including Highland Light, remained under the jurisdiction of the Coast Guard and were still in use. Two factors threatened their continued existence. First, the opening of the Cape Cod Canal in 1914 and steady improvements in radio communications and navigational equipment made the early lighthouses less essential. Second, in some cases, their locations, necessarily near the shoreline, also

Fig. 9.19. The schooner *Charles A. Campbell* stranded off Truro, 1895. NPS.

made them vulnerable to the encroaching sea. The Highland Light, already listed in the National Register, was recognized as endangered since the nor'easter of 1978 showed that it would be undermined by erosion sooner rather than later. In 1991, Congress directed the Coast Guard to enter into a planning process with the park service to determine a course of action for the historic lighthouse.

The Coast Guard wished to continue to operate the light (by now completely automated) under a special permit, while transferring the property to the park service to take on its preservation and interpretation for visitors. Local advocates, organized by the Truro Historical Society, raised money and awareness of the historical significance of the structure and its place in the Outer Cape landscape. It became clear that moving the Highland Light back away from the eroding edge of the bluff would be a preferable option that would preserve it and allow it to continue to function.[37]

Moving nineteenth-century lighthouses was not only expensive but entailed a danger that the structures might fall over and be destroyed in the process. Finally in 1996, federal and state funds along with money raised by advocates were used to move the Highland Light—very slowly on a set of rails—to a new foundation 450 feet farther back from the edge of the bluff.[38] (Fig. 9.20) Remarkably, the Highland Light was not the only lighthouse moved that year at the national seashore. The Nauset Light in Eastham, which was an earlier (1877) structure moved from Chatham in 1923, faced a similar problem to that of the Truro lighthouse. In this case, the Coast Guard suggested decommissioning it and removing the structure; but an outpouring of public support for preserving—and therefore moving—the lighthouse ensued. The Nauset Light Preservation Society was formed and with park staff received a grant (through federal transportation funding) to move the lighthouse that fall. The following year the Coast Guard transferred the property to the park service, and it was managed by the Nauset Light Preservation Society through a partnership agreement with the agency. The Nauset Light Keeper's House made the

Fig. 9.20. Highland Light, Truro, in current location. Photo by author.

move and rejoined the lighthouse, again through federal transportation funding, the next year.[39] (Fig. 9.21)

Also in Eastham, the "Three Sisters," a group of lighthouses that directed mostly local maritime traffic, became a preservation concern. The Sisters had a complicated history. The original set of three brick lighthouses built in 1839 had been set close together to form an identifiable triple light signal. In 1892, they were replaced by three tapering wood frame towers back from the eroding bluff. The original structures eventually fell into the sea. By 1911, erosion threatened the Three Sisters again. At that point two were decommissioned and the third, which became known as the "Beacon," was moved farther back from the cliff and converted to a single, triple-flash signal. In 1918, Helen M. Cummings purchased the two decommissioned towers at a nominal price with the condition that they be removed, which they were. Two years later Cummings moved them again, and they were incorporated together into her summer home, known as the "Twins." In 1923, the Beacon was, in turn, decommissioned (its function was replaced by the Nauset Light that year), and that structure was also moved and converted into a summer residence. In the 1960s, the park service purchased both the Beacon and the Twins, the latter with a ten-year right of occupancy. Although separated and altered over time, the Three Sisters survived, and were considered possibly the only ex-

Fig. 9.21. Nauset Light and the "French Cable Hut." Photo by author.

ample of a set of triple lighthouses left in the United States. In 1975, with all the Sisters under park service ownership and the right of occupancy expired, the question of what to do with them became central. By 1983, the park service had removed the residential additions to all three towers, stripping them back to the original structures. Then in 1988 the Sisters made their last journey, to a parcel of land off Cable Road in Eastham (near Nauset Light Beach), to be reunited in their original configuration not far from where they first stood in 1892. By the next year restorations were complete, and the Three Sisters were opened for guided tours.[40] (Fig. 9.22)

Lighthouses were only part of the built legacy of life-saving and navigational aids at the national seashore. In 1785, a group of concerned citizens founded the Massachusetts Humane Society for the purpose of aiding shipwrecked sailors by building refuge huts on remote sections of beach. They later established a series of boathouses on the shore from which sea rescues could be launched. (Fig. 9.23) By 1871, the Massachusetts system had more than seventy stations, manned by life-saving crews prepared to go out to sea in the worst conditions to save shipwrecked sailors and passengers. That year, Congress acted to create a federal system of life-saving stations on the East Coast, establishing the U.S. Life-Saving Service, which eventually took over the responsibilities of the Massachusetts Humane Society. The new federal agency compiled a remarkable record of aid-

Fig. 9.22. The Three Sisters in their current location in Eastham. Photo by author.

ing ships in distress over the next forty-five years. (Fig. 9.24) In 1915, the service was merged with the law enforcement activities of the U.S. Revenue Cutter Service and became the U.S. Coast Guard. At that time, there were 203 life-saving stations in all, thirteen of them on Cape Cod. In the twentieth century, as ships switched to steam and diesel power and airplanes and radios were incorporated into rescue efforts, the life-saving stations built along many coastlines became less necessary and were reduced in number. Many were repurposed and survive as reminders of the perils of navigation in the days of sailing ships, and of the history of many heroic efforts to mitigate disasters at sea.[41]

The Outer Cape was, of course, a center of life-saving and Coast Guard activities from the earliest days. As Henry Kittredge wrote in his *Cape Cod: Its People and Their History* (1930), "If all the wrecks that have piled up on the back side of the Cape were placed bow to stern, they would make a continuous wall from Chatham to Provincetown." Shortly after the establishment of the U.S. Life-Saving Service, nine life-saving stations were built on the Outer Cape. Known as the "red house" type (they were painted dark red for visibility), the buildings housed crews and rescue "surfboats" at a regular interval along the shore.[42] The relatively simple structures were replaced or enlarged after 1885 when Congress made funds available for the purpose. The Cahoon Hollow life-saving station in Wellfleet, for example, was expanded and moved to its current site at that time. Many of the old life-saving stations (after 1915 called Coast Guard stations) were replaced during the 1930s. The new construction coincided with a reduction in the number of stations and their shore-based life-saving crews. The Nauset Coast Guard Station in Eastham was built in 1937 (replacing an earlier life-saving station), for example, before being deactivated and becoming the temporary headquarters for the national seashore in 1961. The Race Point Coast Guard Station replaced an 1872 life-saving station in 1931, and has been used as offices by the park service since 1979. The Nauset life-saving station was replaced in 1936, decommissioned in 1958, and transferred to the park service in 1972. Today, the Coast Guard operates out of two modern stations, in Chatham and Provincetown.[43]

Only two of the life-saving stations built in the nineteenth century on the Outer Cape still existed when land acquisition for the seashore began. The Cahoon Hollow station was closed in the 1940s, sold to a private owner, and converted to a restaurant in the 1950s. It was never acquired by the park service and continues to be operated as the Beachcomber

Fig. 9.23. Highland Life-Saving Station, built in 1872, no longer extant. NPS.

Fig. 9.24. "Launching Life Boat, Provincetown," postcard, 1897. New York Public Library.

restaurant. The Old Harbor Life-Saving Station, built in Chatham in 1898, was decommissioned in 1944 and also became private property, in this case a residence. The Old Harbor station was an example of what was called the "Duluth" station type, after the first example built in Minnesota on Lake Superior. (Fig. 9.25) Located on Nauset Beach near what was then the entrance to Chatham Harbor, the building was in imminent peril of being washed away by the early 1970s. Far less altered than the Cahoon Hollow station, Old Harbor presented an opportunity to interpret the neglected history of the U.S. Life-Saving Service; the inherent architectural significance of the building argued for its preservation.

The park service purchased the endangered building in 1973 (with a five-year occupancy clause) and prepared National Register documentation. In the meantime, many ideas for its use and potential new locations for it were discussed. The site chosen after lengthy consideration was Race Point, where there was room (on a beach not threatened by erosion), nearby facilities at the Race Point bathhouse, and easy access for visitors. The site also had been the historical location of the nineteenth-century life-saving station, which the nearby Coast Guard station replaced in 1931. But it was thirty-four miles from Chatham Harbor to Race Point, and moving the massive, shingled building and its observation tower promised to be expensive. Advocates for the move, especially the park service regional architect Marsha L. Fader, had to overcome a shortage of funds as well questions regarding the significance of the building and the feasibility of the project. The decision was made to move the building in fall 1977, in part because it would likely not survive another round of winter storms. Moving it by land would be prohibitive, in terms of both cost and complexity; dismantling it presented similar problems. But the entire building could be craned off the beach (in two pieces) and set directly onto an ocean barge, and that November, it was. (Fig. 9.26) The Old Harbor Life-Saving Station was then towed to Provincetown. The nor'easter of 1978 destroyed the site the building had occupied just months earlier, but the station weathered the winter floating on a barge in the shelter of Provincetown Harbor, where it made an interesting and certainly fortuitously timed spectacle.[44]

That spring the sixty-ton building was lowered onto the beach at Race Point, and work began in the summer to rehabilitate it for use as a museum

Fig. 9.25. Old Harbor Life-Saving Station, Chatham. Built 1898, decommissioned 1944. NPS.

Fig. 9.26. Moving the Old Harbor station in two pieces by barge, 1977. NPSHC.

dedicated to the history of the U.S. Life-Saving Service. As one historian noted, life saving had been the single most prominent activity on the Great Beach for much of the nineteenth century, and that history deserved to be fully interpreted at the seashore. The move, at a cost $120,000, was underwritten by the park service, with still more funds needed to complete the restoration and install museum exhibits. The preservation of the Old Harbor Life-Saving Station demonstrated a strong commitment to preserving the heritage of the Outer Cape by the park service, and especially on the part of the regional and park staff who had been responsible. The park finally had its life-saving museum, and by summer 1979, interpreters and reenactors were at work giving programs interpreting the dramatic activities of life saving on the Outer Cape.[45] (Fig. 9.27)

The establishment of the museum and interpretive programs of the relocated and rehabilitated Old Harbor station were a signal success in the management of cultural resources at the national seashore. By the time Old Harbor was opened to the public, the park had also received its first "historic resource study," an account of the narratives, themes, and physical resources that constituted the cultural resources of a given national park. Written by the historian A. Berle Clemensen at the Denver Service Center, the 1979 study supplied an overview of the agency's priorities and an understanding of what officials believed constituted the cultural heritage of the Outer Cape at that time. The study emphasized the history of early European explorers, who had been drawn to the Cape—as its name had always implied—for its proximity to the cod fisheries of George's Bank. Pilgrim history, and the Outer Cape sites associated with it, were also fully described, as were the maritime industries that followed. The "history of the Cape Cod National Seashore region," Clemensen summarized, "has been one of dependence on the sea for a livelihood." The study viewed the cultural resources of the Outer Cape primarily through this lens. That dependence extended to the history of navigational aids and life saving, important topics that also had physical resources (buildings

Fig. 9.27. Old Harbor Life-Saving Station museum at Race Point. Photo by author.

and structures) associated with them. The growth of historical Outer Cape towns and populations, and their subsequent demise, were determined by historical disturbances to maritime economies.

Clemensen presented the limited agricultural history of the Outer Cape in terms of "white settlement and the destruction of Cape Cod resources," giving a contemporary environmentalist dimension to the old observations of deforestation and the erosion of overworked sandy soils. The 1979 study described a cultural landscape that in many ways Thoreau would have found familiar, as would the generations of vacationers enchanted by "old Cape Cod." But it was a history that seemed to end with the era of twentieth-century tourism. "By the mid-1950s," the region had "succumbed to suburbanization." As the trend intensified, "native Cape Codders could no longer afford the cost" of living there, and "outsiders . . . also tended to own the businesses and take the profits out of the Cape."[46] The history of the Outer Cape, in this sense, ended as the seashore was established.

The underlying implication of cultural resource research and management, up to this point, was that the Outer Cape landscape was a museum to be curated. By the 1990s, with the Old Harbor station restored on its new site and two historic lighthouses moved to theirs, the national seashore reached a stage of maturity in this approach. This heritage—historical Cape Cod—was perceived as the primary concern

Fig. 9.28. Original wayside exhibit: Pilgrim history in Provincetown and Truro. NPSHC.

for cultural resource management, and that responsibility had been significantly addressed. The efforts had required budget commitments for building rehabilitation and maintenance, the management of artifact collections, National Register listings, and the development of interpretive programs. The successes were many, if not complete.

The legacy of Cape Cod houses had been preserved to the degree allowed by the Cape Cod model. The transferred Coast Guard stations were maintained and served new administrative purposes for the park. The lighthouses had also been acquired and were managed through innovative partnerships. Other physical resources were documented, preserved, and interpreted through signage, visitor displays, and staff programs. Despite shortcomings and difficulties, the park had met many imposing challenges. The historical narratives and interpretive themes that had been elaborated (as indicated in the 1979 historic resource study) were finite and clear. (Fig. 9.28) In many ways, they continued the curation of the Outer Cape landscape that had begun with the literary, artistic, and architectural productions of the early twentieth century. But if the Outer Cape "way of life" had been defined through cultural resource management at the national seashore, it had also been limited to a way of life that had long passed. The cultural landscape was conceived as an artifact more than as an ongoing process.

The idea of establishing national seashores had first been conceived during the rich period of New Deal recreational planning. Cape Cod National Seashore was planned under another major period of national park expansion and innovation, Mission 66. The implementation of the national seashore—above all, its unprecedented legislation—occurred through the dramatic changes brought about by the Kennedy administration and Stewart Udall's New Conservation. The subsequent development of management strategies and policies at the park showed the influence of the environmental movement, through increased protection for resources and limitations on recreational activities. The next phase of cultural resource management at the national seashore exemplified some of these developments and included new approaches to preserving aspects of the Outer Cape "way of life" that had been a primary concern since the 1950s.

Starting out on the Dune Shacks Trail, Provincetown. Photo by Carol Betsch.

TEN

Cultural Landscapes and Modern Houses

Archaeological investigations of the Outer Cape began long before the establishment of the seashore. Most of the archaeological research in the region involved its first inhabitants, who over thousands of years left an extensive record of their ways of life, a culture which twentieth-century archaeologists inferred from shell middens, stone tools, pottery, and other types of evidence. Howard Torrey, a Massachusetts amateur archaeologist, collected hundreds of artifacts on the Outer Cape in the 1920s; these objects became the basis of the collection that bears his name at the Peabody Museum in Andover. The noted Provincetown artist Ross Moffet developed a strong interest in archaeology in the 1950s and published numerous articles on his investigations on the Outer Cape. He was hired to perform the survey of archaeological resources that became the base map included in the park's 1963 master plan. Moffet was also a national seashore advocate who, with Josephine Del Deo and others, helped assure the transfer of the Province Lands to the park service in the 1960s. But the establishment of the national seashore—and the provisions of the 1966 NHPA—led to a new generation of professional and comprehensive surveys of the archaeological resources of the Outer Cape. Francis P. McManamon, a park service regional archaeologist who went on to become the agency's chief archaeologist, figured prominently in these efforts.[1]

In 1979, McManamon began a four-year survey of the national seashore intended to document the locations, frequency, and characteristics of archaeological resources. The first volume of the results of this comprehensive effort were published in 1984.[2] Many individual excavations and investigations contributed to the initiative, and by the 1980s, numerous publications provided a full record of early settlement patterns and cultural practices as indicated by the archaeological record. McManamon's work provided new insights into the "prehistoric land use" of the Outer Cape, and also confirmed the general outline of the archaeological base map prepared in 1963 based on Moffet's work. McManamon concluded that early land use on the Outer Cape was "year-round and more diverse" than had been suggested by the "traditional emphasis on coastal shell middens." Settlement was concentrated mainly in a few established areas, with "large, intervening unsettled areas." Archaeological investigations of the national seashore, which have continued since, have provided a substantial understanding of the indigenous land uses and settlements that had been the subject of speculation—based on far less scientific evidence—since the Pilgrims first arrived.

The findings of scientific archaeology also affected other disciplines, including ecology. A more complete understanding of early landscape management practices, resource exploitation, and agriculture made it clearer that human influence on ecosystems did not begin with seventeenth-century settlements. In the 1990s, the park service also sponsored major investigations of the historical (post-1600) archaeology of the Outer Cape, in this case through a partnership with the University of Massachusetts Archaeological Services. The ambitious effort took years and resulted in the most useful and comprehensive history of the region available when it was published as *Historic Cultural Land Use Study of Lower Cape Cod*.[3] Beginning with a thorough review of the literature, the study went on to outline the historical contexts that framed it. A timeline structured a detailed history of economic and social life on the Outer Cape from the seventeenth through the mid-twentieth centuries. Archaeological surveys were conducted to evaluate the connections between the context narratives and the archaeological resources in the park. These included "archaeological reconnaissance" reports for Fort Hill, the Atwood-Higgins site, Higgins Hollow, and Long Point. The *Cultural Land Use Study* went far beyond the "historic resource study," indicating a landscape and environmental history of the region, one that described landscape change over centuries and identified the economic and social forces that shaped it. For the University of Massachusetts historical archaeologists in the 1990s, the landscape itself had become the archaeological site. Their methods combined archaeology and environmental history to produce a holistic historical context for considering the cultural resources of the national seashore.

In one respect, however, the archaeologists working in the 1980s and 1990s continued to see the significant cultural resources of the park in terms of artifacts of the past—a history that ended in the mid-twentieth century. Neither did the park service initiate at this time a significant outreach to the indigenous people who continued to live on Cape Cod, the Wampanoag.[4] This indicated a wider problem with the entire approach to cultural resource management of the period, which remained firmly rooted in its concern for the physical fabric of the region's heritage—its buildings, structures, and archaeological artifacts—and was not conducive to recognizing the ongoing construction of cultural associations and the living nature of the landscape character of the Outer Cape. The period of historical significance for potential cultural resources was never considered to extend beyond the point when the landscape "succumbed to suburbanization" and, not coincidentally, the seashore was established. This focus on the more distant past perhaps made outreach to the tribes of Cape Cod more difficult to consider, but it also placed an inherent limitation on the engagement of people with the park, generally, by creating a barrier between the living communities of the Outer Cape and any building or landscape feature that might be considered a cultural resource of the park.

One way that national seashore staff and other park service professionals began to address the situation was to consider how people and their activities not only had shaped the landscape and its cultural associations for thousands of years but continued to do so. This implied a shift in thinking, particularly in the field of historic preservation, from a concern for individual buildings, structures, and sites to an

Fig. 10.1. "Harvesting Cranberries on Cape Cod," postcard, c. 1930–45. BPL.

understanding of how these resources contributed to a larger landscape. This approach had already been presaged by the work of archaeologists and historians at the seashore. The 1979 historic resource report, for example, included chapters on Bound Brook Island, Fort Hill, and the Truro Highlands, which were short treatments not of individual buildings or structures but of these landscapes and their significance to the cultural heritage contained within the seashore. One chapter was devoted to the history of cranberry cultivation, despite the fact that cranberry farms were never widespread on the Outer Cape but were typically located on the Upper Cape. (Fig. 10.1) But the national seashore had acquired a working cranberry bog in Truro, and park staff needed to decide if indeed it was a cultural resource (in other words, if it was historically significant), and what to do with it in any case.

As Clemensen noted, indigenous people and English settlers appreciated wild cranberries (*Vaccinium oxycoccus*) and made them an important component of their diet. The low shrubs commonly grew in the naturally occurring sandy bogs of the Outer Cape. Commercial cultivation, however, which involved engineering a bog and controlling its water levels, did not begin until the nineteenth century. The first commercial cranberry farm was established in Dennis around 1816, and the crop soon gained economic importance on the Upper Cape. The cranberry farm owned by the park service in Truro, known as the Pamet Cranberry Bog, was actually three bogs, separated by a historic farmhouse, covering a total of about twelve acres (the farm itself was about twenty-seven acres). (Fig. 10.2) The bogs were established in 1888, and were in at least limited production until shortly before they were acquired by the seashore in 1963. But federal ownership meant the end of active farming on the site, and herbaceous weeds and soon woody growth rapidly encroached and covered the bogs. In the 1970s, the possibility of reactivating at least one of the bogs was still apparent, and the potential for interpreting the history of cranberry farming in the region attracted the attention of park interpretive staff. The old farmhouse, which had been converted to housing for laborers and space for cranberry processing, could potentially could serve as a small museum. By 1978, the park's chief of interpretation, Glen Kaye, was organizing public tours and overseeing the partial clearing of the site. He pointed out that more research of both the farm and the farmhouse was needed and that new exhibits and trails would need to be designed and built if the landscape were to become an effective interpretive feature of the park.[5]

But a cranberry bog, like any agricultural landscape, needs to be worked if it is to maintain its basic appearance and distinctive features as a landscape. Even partially clearing the vegetation that had spontaneously covered the bogs was difficult and expensive, and only a temporary solution. As a result, the initial effort to maintain the Truro bogs as a cultural resource, to be open to the public as a demonstration of the history of cranberry production, made no progress despite the enthusiasm for the project. In addition, neither the house (which had at its core an 1830s Cape Cod house but had been significantly

Fig. 10.2. Pamet Cranberry Bog, Truro. Photo by author.

altered to serve its agricultural function) nor the landscape were listed in the National Register. This meant that at least nominally they were not cultural resources, and park managers dedicated budgets to other priorities—such as the Old Harbor station and the ambitious archaeological surveys—that did treat identified resources in the park and required significant funding.

There were also natural resource management concerns. If the cranberry bog was not a listed cultural resource, then it was a regenerating wetland, with a suite of successional native plants establishing the types of plant communities and ecosystems that might have once existed there. From this point of view, the correct treatment alternative would be to remove any invasive exotic plant species, but otherwise to allow succession to take place. In 1980, Michael E. Whatley, chief interpretive ranger and park historian, expressed to Superintendent Olsen (who was himself trained as a historian) some of his frustration with what he felt were shortcomings in the park's cultural resource efforts. While the successes of the Old Harbor station and the archaeological survey were admirable, the overall cultural significance of the Outer Cape landscape was being missed by the public, and indeed was not being adequately presented by the park. The Pamet Cranberry Bog was one missed opportunity, but so was the Atwood-Higgins site, which very few visitors ever saw. Park staff struggled to get the maintenance and attention many other historic houses and structures deserved. Whatley believed that the park was "one of the most culturally significant historical units of the National Park Service," comparable, for example, to Tidewater Virginia in its history of continuous settlement since the seventeenth century. But while that region had a number of national historical parks (and Colonial Williamsburg) dedicated to regional historic preservation, Cape Cod had only the national seashore, which Whatley felt could have qualified as a national historical park itself, had it not been designated a national seashore. The seashore was not doing enough to maintain and interpret its many and various cultural resources, despite (and perhaps because of) the emphasis on expensive but singular projects such as the Old Harbor station and the archaeological surveys.[6]

What Whatley saw missing—and what he felt the public was missing—was a more general appreciation of the unique significance of the overall cultural landscape of the Outer Cape, as it could and should be conveyed through management policies and interpretive programs. By the 1990s, the park began to address this challenge. In 1992, the park service established the Olmsted Center for Landscape Preservation (OCLP) in its North Atlantic regional office. At first housed in the Frederick Law Olmsted National Historic Site (Olmsted's home and office) in Brookline, Massachusetts, the OCLP was an interdisciplinary group of landscape architects, historians, and park planners assembled to provide technical assistance to national parks struggling with sites, like the Pamet Cranberry Bog, that were not being adequately understood or considered. In the 1990s and thereafter, superintendents Ringgold, Burks, and Price successively brought the OCLP to the national seashore to complete studies and planning reports on its historically significant cultural landscapes.

The term "cultural landscape" was now being used by the park service and the OCLP to refer to a specific property type: a historically significant (that is, eligible for the National Register) landscape that could be defined, studied, and managed based on "cultural landscape reports" prepared by the OCLP (or others) which would be analogous to the "historic structure reports" that the park service had long relied on to guide the treatment of historic buildings. The OCLP (and the cultural landscape program started in the Washington office at around the same time) expanded the agency's consideration of historic resources beyond buildings and structures to research and document significant landscapes within the national park system. The first step for this initiative was to inventory parks and determine which areas should be considered significant landscapes that might require a cultural landscape report. Like a historic structure report, the landscape study could then be used as the basis for National Register documentation and to develop preservation strategies for the identified characteristics and features that conveyed the property's historical significance.

At the national seashore, there were some obvious candidates to consider, including the Pamet Cranberry Bog, which received a "cultural landscape inventory" (an abbreviated form of cultural landscape report) in 1995, although it was never restored as a working cranberry farm.[7] Another was the Truro Highlands, the area around the site that had been selected for the Highland Light in 1796. The high bluffs in north Truro had relatively good soils that attracted early settlers. Situated directly above the Great Beach, the highlands also commanded panoramic views of the Atlantic. The government purchased ten acres for the Highland Light from Isaac Small, who had been born on the family farm there and was appointed the first lighthouse keeper. (Fig. 10.3) His son James inherited the position and also began to provide lodging for visitors drawn to the farm by the lighthouse and the excellent vistas. Thoreau was an early customer, and his positive account of his stay probably increased business in the coming decades.

It was James's son, Isaac Morton Small, who developed the family farm into a small but successful resort, particularly once the railroad was extended to Provincetown in 1873. By 1893, his son Willard took over the growing complex, and in 1898, he laid out a golf course and soon added an indoor bowling alley and other recreational amenities. In 1906, the Smalls added a new forty-room hotel, the Highland House, and over the following decades additional guest cottages were built, lining Highland Road leading to the Highland Light. (Figs. 10.4, 10.5) The resort stayed in the Small family until 1947; changes

Fig. 10.3. Small family farm, North Truro. NPSHC.

Fig. 10.4. Highland House, Truro, c. 1935. NPS.

Fig. 10.5 Highland Light, 2012. Wikimedia Commons.

in ownership and some subdivision of the property followed. Some of the guest cottages were sold or demolished, and by the 1950s, the new owners adapted much of the business to serve day-tripping tourists. The park service acquired the property in 1964 with a provision that allowed the business to continue until 1969.[8]

The park's 1970 "development concept plan" for the area called for the preservation of the Highland House, the continuing operation of the public golf course (under a special use permit), and the repurposing of one of the cottages. The planners also anticipated the transfer of jurisdiction (but not yet the relocation) of the Coast Guard's Highland Light facility. But otherwise plans called for demolishing most of the remaining buildings, or selling them on the condition they be removed. The Highland House and the golf course were recognized as potentially eligible individually for the National Register. The intention to restore a natural scene around those features, however, outweighed any sense of the overall significance of the history of the Small family's early resort development, and so the removal or demolition of buildings continued through the first decades of park service management.

Beginning in the 1990s, a series of reports by the OCLP documented the history of the development of the Truro Highlands and described it through historic base maps and comparisons to existing conditions. The impending move of the lighthouse provided additional reason for considering the potential significance of the landscape. As a result, a National Register nomination was prepared for an eighty-five-acre historic district that included the existing listed properties (the Highland House, the Highland Light, and the golf course) and added the remaining structures of the family compound and existing landscape features and characteristics that told the story of early resort development. This research opened the opportunity for new interpretive themes: the site was a rare survival of railroad-era tourist development on the Outer Cape, for example. The new historic district also acknowledged the importance of the people involved in shaping the Outer Cape landscape and the public's experience of it. This was a more holistic way of considering what consti-

Fig. 10.6. Penniman house and barn, Eastham. Photo by Cervin Robinson, 1962. HABS.

Fig. 10.7. Fort Hill, Eastham. Photo by Ross Moffett from "Archaeological Overview, Cape Cod National Seashore," 1960. NPS.

tuted the "cultural resource" in question, one that more directly acknowledged the importance of the regional "way of life" as part of what the park service was intended to preserve and interpret. The cultural landscape approach put people back into the landscape, at least in the consideration of the historical significance of the Truro Highlands.

The Fort Hill area in Eastham was another early and logical choice to document as an individual cultural landscape within the national seashore. A cultural landscape report was prepared in 1995, and further reports followed. As a result, a one-hundred-acre "rural historic district" was entered in the National Register in 2001.[9] In addition to being the site of the Penniman House and barn (already listed), two distinct farmsteads had shaped the still-agricultural landscape over two centuries. (Fig. 10.6, 10.7) The district also encompassed an archaeological area that had been designated a National Historic Landmark in 1993. Nauset Bay was, in fact, one of the most important centers of Wampanoag settlement and agriculture for thousands of years. When Samuel de Champlain sailed into the bay in 1605, he described and mapped extensive villages and agricultural fields and fishing operations. The Pilgrims who had settled in Plymouth repeatedly returned to the important center of Nauset to trade and negotiate with the people there. A group of English settlers came back to the area in 1644 to found a new town, Nauset (later Eastham), to take advantage of its farmland and marine resources.

The soils of Fort Hill made it more conducive to agriculture than much of the Outer Cape, and it was farmed continuously almost until its acquisition by the park service. The Knowles family came into ownership of much of Fort Hill in the early eighteenth century and retained significant property there for the next two hundred years. The Pennimans, related by marriage, were the other principal landowners. The Knowles family sold their property in the 1940s, and the new owners continued to farm it, maintaining much of its historic character including nineteenth-century field patterns. By the 1950s, however, new owners had already subdivided the property and were preparing to develop it with thirty-three residences. Surveyors' stakes and initial road construction added urgency to the debate over whether to include Fort Hill within the seashore. It was acquired through a series of transactions between 1963 and 1965. Park development consisted of an access road and parking area, an interpretive shelter, and hiking trails.[10] (Fig. 10.8)

As the OCLP reported in 2007, "maintenance of the open landscape" at Fort Hill was "an ongoing challenge" for the park service.[11] Once again, it proved difficult to manage an agricultural landscape that was no longer a working farm. Mechanical mowing could not prevent all encroaching woody growth, especially in wet areas, and the extent of open fields gradually declined. New management practices were introduced, including continued mowing and prescribed burns. Without active farming, however, the landscape might remain mostly open, but it would gradually change in character as field patterns were obscured and small ponds succeeded into woody swamps. The views of Nauset Bay and the surrounding marshes, a principal characteristic of the landscape, would be in danger of disappearing without continuous maintenance.

The history and analysis provided by the OCLP again provided new themes for interpretation and an enhanced understanding of the significance of the Fort Hill landscape and the people who had shaped it. The National Register designation acknowledged the importance of the landscape as a cultural resource. But maintaining the overall character of the landscape at Fort Hill, as at the Pamet Cranberry Bog and elsewhere in the seashore, would remain difficult without the active engagement of a new generation of farmers to work agricultural areas as they had been

Fig. 10.8. Fort Hill Trail. Photo by author.

in the past. Managers of many national parks and other protected landscapes have recognized this, and in many cases they have been successful in bringing back active production through partnerships, leasing, and specific arrangements suited to individual cases. The limited spaces and large numbers of visitors on the Outer Cape made the implementation of such strategies problematic (but perhaps not impossible) at the national seashore. In any case, following the recommendations of the OCLP, Fort Hill continues to be maintained through mowing, burning, and other practices intended to preserve its agricultural character without reintroducing farming. (Fig. 10.9)

The most innovative series of park service investigations, however, involved not past land uses and historical associations but ongoing activities and contemporary cultural significance. The people who made Cape Cod a center of literary and artistic production in the course of the twentieth century included those who chose to live in a simple, even Thoreauvian, way in improvised "shacks" on the beaches and among the dunes of Truro and Provincetown. In fact, living in improvised shelters along the Great Beach dated back to early days of English settlement, when fishermen and hunters built them as needed. The initiation of life-saving efforts in the nineteenth century formalized the practice, in a sense, by establishing refuge huts and life-saving stations along the length of the Outer Cape. As the life-saving network was gradually replaced by more

Fig. 10.9. Fort Hill landscape. Photo by author.

modern Coast Guard stations in the twentieth century, most of the earlier shelters disappeared, but not all. Some were moved, repurposed, and inhabited by a new generation of dune dwellers with very different motivations for seeking out simple and isolated retreats in the visually stunning landscape of shifting sands.

The decline of organized life-saving on the Outer Cape coincided with the rise of the region as a seasonal cultural center. As Provincetown's reputation as a summer haven for writers, artists, and intellectuals grew, so did fascination with the landscape of the Outer Cape dunes and the shacks nestled among them. Artists and writers drawn to Provincetown pioneered a new traditional activity by adopting existing structures, or building new ones, where they could find inspiration in their remarkable surroundings. Eugene O'Neill took up residence in the Peaked Hill Bars life-saving station (built in 1872 and named for particularly treacherous sandbars just off the Great Beach near a large dune formation known as Peaked Hill) between 1919 and 1924 and wrote some of his most important plays there. The poet Harry Kemp moved into a "dune shack" in 1920 and lived there for the next forty years, becoming known as the "poet of the dunes." Additional shacks were built in the 1930s, and by the 1940s they constituted a colony of artists and writers, including Ross Moffet, John Grillo, Jan Gelb, and Philip Malicoat among many others. The dune shacks, owned or rented, became emblematic of the cultural life of the Outer Cape, and particularly of Provincetown.[12]

World War II brought an end to most shack construction, and many of the structures changed hands within families or went to new owners. The harsh conditions required continual upkeep—sometimes complete reconstruction—of the fragile shacks, which were also built to be moved if the shifting terrain necessitated it. Most were on private land used by permission of the owner or by paying ground rent. By the 1950s, the value of the shacks (and the land they occupied) began to rise substantially, while their use by artists and their families continued. The popularity and atmosphere of Provincetown attracted a new generation of artists, writers, and actors, some of whom retreated from the busy town to occupy or visit the isolated shacks. When Pilgrim Spring State Park was established in Truro in 1954, a number of the shacks on that side of the town line were acquired, although the state did not immediately remove them. Some shacks had always been located on state land, within the boundaries of the Province Lands. But after 1961, all of the remaining dune shacks would fall within the boundaries of the national seashore.

Controversy was assured because the structures would not qualify as improved properties under the terms of the park legislation. Their occupants could claim ownership of the structures themselves, but not of the land beneath them. Since it did not consider the shacks cultural resources, once the land came into federal ownership the park service intended eventually to remove them and restore, to the degree possible, a natural scene.[13] The dune shack owners, however, were well organized and had the support of many people in Provincetown and Truro, who recognized the significance of the ongoing cultural tradition they represented. The Great Beach Cottage Owners Association (which later advocated for preserving the dunes by limiting ORV access) was first formed in 1962 with the goal of preventing park service acquisition of the shacks from going forward. Nevertheless, the park service proceeded with appraisals and acquisition of the structures, with provisions for leases or rights of tenancy for set periods, depending on the individual case. On the whole, these transactions were carried out in the 1960s and early 1970s, with some going into litigation.[14]

Most dune shack owners continued to use and maintain their property through leases with the park service, an arrangement that existed for many other properties within the seashore which were not classified as improved properties. By the 1980s, however, as leases and tenancy agreements began to expire, concern over the eventual disposition of the remaining dune shacks intensified. A longtime dune shack dweller, Charlie Schmid, died in 1982, and the park service demolished his shack two years later. In 1985, the Peaked Hill Trust was established with the mission of preventing further demolitions. The Truro Historical Commission also wrote to the MHC that year suggesting that the dune shacks were worthy of preservation. By 1989, the MHC agreed (against the position of the park service) and found the dune shacks eligible for the National Register.[15] The basis of their finding was rooted in the artistic and literary associations of the properties and the way of life they embodied. Under most circumstances, properties that had been heavily maintained (or effectively rebuilt) or moved from their original locations might not meet the requirements for historical integrity necessary for National Register eligibility. In the case of the dune shacks, however, the cultural significance of the tradition represented met "criteria considerations" that made them eligible anyway. The final National Register documentation was completed in 2011, and the 1,900-acre Peaked Hill Bars Historic District was listed. It encompassed nineteen remaining

Fig. 10.10. Dune shack, Peaked Hill Bars Historic District, 2010. Wikimedia Commons.

shacks and their associated landscape—much of the dune area that stretched across Provincetown and Truro just inland from the Great Beach.[16] (Fig. 10.10)

The 1989 determination of eligibility required new attitudes and proposals for managing the dune shacks. As cultural resources and tangible evidence of an ongoing tradition of historical significance, they became an important test for how a distinctive way of life on the Outer Cape could be preserved without compromising other park service management goals and policies. Almost all of the dune shacks had been acquired with various provisions that allowed occupants to remain for set periods of time. National Register eligibility, however, meant that demolishing or removing the remaining structures (although not completely prohibited) would no longer be considered a favorable option once those arrangements expired, especially by those charged with managing the park's cultural resources. In 1993, the Provincetown Community Compact, a nonprofit dedicated to "advance the cultural well-being" of the town, and in partnership with the park service, assumed management of the Cohen shack and later the Fowler shack. In 1995, another nonprofit was founded, the Outer Cape Artist in Residence Consortium, for the specific purpose of working with the park service to create an artist-in-residence program for the Margo/Gelb shack and for others, as they became available. The Peaked Hill Trust continued in its preservation role and as the managing entity of the consortium.

By the end of the decade, a model for preserving the shacks had taken shape, through partnerships between nonprofit organizations, residents, and park service staff, in particular the park historian William Burke. The CCNSAC endorsed the approach through a report made by a subcommittee, stating that "the National Seashore should maintain the essence/spirit of the District's historic association with the development of the arts and literature, and its traditionally simplistic lifestyle."[17] The eighteen shacks owned by the park service today are used for the artist-in-residence program and as summer dwellings through various leases, permits, and agreements. After years of work and numerous studies, in 2011 the OCLP produced a definitive history of the dune shacks landscape in its *Cultural Landscape Report for Dune Shacks of the Peaked Hill Bars Historic District.* Combining the previous work of architects, ethnographers, and historians, the report documented the shifting landscape over time, and the deep cultural tradition that developed roughly from 1920 to 1991.[18] As Superintendent George Price wrote in his introduction to the report, the OCLP's work helped the park to achieve its mandate of "preserving the way of life or 'culture' established by people who have lived on the Outer Cape."[19] (Fig. 10.11)

Although the dune shack issue instigated decades of argument and litigation, changes in the practice of historic preservation and in the management of cultural resources helped avert continued strife and the potential loss of a major resource. The recognition, study, and documentation of the cultural landscapes of the national seashore helped make this transition possible and suggested management alternatives that were both more productive and more pragmatic than remaining committed to the demolition of all structures that were once perceived merely as intrusions in a natural landscape.

Another aspect of this shift in how cultural resources were perceived and treated was an increased sense that people—and their activities in the landscape—potentially contributed to landscape character not only in the historical past but up to the present. In 2002, superintendent Maria Burks sponsored a study undertaken by the University of Massachusetts Department of Landscape Architecture and Regional Planning in partnership with the OCLP. Published in 2004 as *People and Places: A Landscape Character Study,* the report integrated the work of faculty and graduate students in planning, landscape architecture, and history to document the combined "places and activities . . . identified as significant components of the cultural landscape of the Outer Cape." Public meetings, or "Cape conversations," were organized to elicit the contributions of residents about how landscapes and people interacted in the past and in the present to define the "landscape character" that had been, since the idea of the national seashore had first been broached, the purported main object of federal preservation efforts. The study presented a process more than a plan, and

Fig. 10.11. Dunes and dune shack. Photo by author.

indicated how much had changed in the methods and priorities of the park's cultural resource managers. People—of the present as well as the past—were part of the landscape, and efforts to manage and interpret the significance of the national seashore needed to acknowledge that fact.[20]

Another change in approach in cultural resource management by the 1990s including an increased awareness of the significance of the recent past, particularly buildings and structures of the postwar period that until then had been routinely dismissed as ineligible for the National Register based mainly on the fact that they were less than fifty years old. Again, the park service was drawn into a controversy over the fate of a group of houses that it owned and that did not qualify as improved residences, in this case because they were built after 1959. The houses were identified by architectural historians as significant examples of residential design by midcentury modernist architects who had been drawn to the

Outer Cape beginning in the summer of 1937, when Walter Gropius with friends and colleagues had enjoyed their summer in Marion. Between the 1930s and 1970s, over one hundred modernist houses were built on the Outer Cape by architects including Marcel Breuer, Serge Chermayeff, Olav Hammarstrom, and Nathaniel Saltonstall. Many of these architects spent their summers in these houses and, with houseguests that included prominent artists and writers, together they established a distinctive cultural community. As the architectural historians Peter McMahon and Christine Cipriani observe, as a group these houses captured ideals of period residential architecture: houses carefully sited to maximize views and that integrated interior and exterior spaces. Most were not large or imposing and employed inexpensive wood construction that blended well with their settings. They offered a mid-twentieth-century version of the classic Cape Cod cottage, one particularly suited to the creative pursuits of their inhabitants. Together the houses comprised an identifiable "regional variation of the modern movement," which the historians describe as "Cape Cod modernism."[21]

The design of these houses by a group of important midcentury modernist architects suggested their potential eligibility for the National Register. Residents and architectural historians began to advocate for the recognition, and again were met initially with some skepticism by the park. The post-1959 residences built within the seashore's boundaries already had been an onerous and unanticipated burden, one that only became more problematic as twenty-five-year tenancy agreements started expiring. The tenancy agreements for post-1959 properties had greatly facilitated sales agreements at the time but only postponed to the 1980s and 1990s the emotional and sometimes bitter business of actually transferring the properties. There were only seven significant examples of the "Cape Cod modern" houses within the seashore, however. All were in Wellfleet, and by 2012 all were owned by the park service and had been found eligible for the National Register.[22] (Fig. 10.12) Removal or demolition were no longer appropriate alternatives for what were now important cultural resources. Other management strategies were called for, but there was little park service money available to adapt, or even maintain or remove, the houses, some of which remained vacant after the termination of tenancy agreements.

As Superintendent Price remarked in 2012, the situation was a "wonderful opportunity" to work with a nonprofit partner, which would be the "best way to keep [the houses] preserved." Following discussions with park historian Burke, architect and historian McMahon established the Cape Cod Modern House Trust in 2007 for the specific purpose of being that partner. The partnership required a reappraisal of what constituted the cultural resources within the park. As Burke wrote regarding the modern houses: "Where does one draw the line between past and present? There is no clear line of demarcation, but we now know that excluding much of the 20th century from the past was a mistake. A strong continuum between the past and the present makes the past seem more relevant to our own lives."[23] By 2014, the trust had leased three of the houses and funded their restoration to make them suitable as "functioning homes for artist and scholar residencies," awarded to architects, artists, and writers on the basis of competitive applications. "Buildings and landscapes bear cultural memories," McMahon wrote, and the trust sought to encourage a "wide range of people to see the value of their modernist legacy" by "reintroducing the ideas embodied in the work of these . . . visionaries." The goal was to "extend the lives of the buildings . . . and to carry on the tradition of freethinking problem solving to nurture new creativity."[24] The result has been a successful

Fig. 10.12. Weidlinger House, designed in 1953 by the architect Paul Weidlinger. Photo by Bill Burke. NPS.

strategy for preserving another aspect of the way of life of the Outer Cape, not by curating the houses as museums but by assuring that they continue to be used to perpetuate the cultural tradition and activities that were the basis for determining their significance as cultural resources.

The recognition and study of cultural landscapes and the architecture of the recent past were major steps in the recognition of how people—historically and up to the present—contribute to the overall "landscape character" and the legacy of cultural resources the park service was charged with preserving and interpreting for the public. The challenges of maintaining the "way of life" of the Outer Cape, however, extended beyond these examples of creative resource management. Since the seashore legislation was first debated and written, there has been a shared conviction that the region's way of life was an important component of what the seashore was intended to perpetuate and protect. But there has never been a full consensus on exactly which activities and resources were vital to maintain in that effort.

What was the Outer Cape way of life, and had it survived the first fifty years of the park's existence in any meaningful sense? The improved properties

Fig. 10.13. Provincetown tourist, 1940. Photo by Edwin Rosskam. FSA/OWI.

(whether they maintained their original appearance in the landscape or not) had often changed hands and had universally increased dramatically in value. Barnstable County had become one of the fastest-growing regions in the state, rapidly increasing in density, population, and affluence. Those concerned for the future of the Outer Cape often emphasized the fragility of its ecosystems and resources, including the single-source aquifer on which residents depended for water. Indeed, as the planners and landscape architects from the University of Massachusetts and the Cape Cod Commission observed by the 2000s, the region had reached limits in the degree to which development could be intensified any further. But the society of the Outer Cape was fragile as well. The less crowded and less regulated setting of prewar vacation idylls could not be recaptured by the postwar experiment in landscape preservation that was the national seashore. (Figs. 10.13, 10.14) Neither could a national park revive cultural traditions of old Cape Cod, which had been relegated to memory and imagination long before 1961.

What the national seashore could do was establish more meaningful engagement with the communities, individuals, governments, and advocacy groups of the Outer Cape, and enlist them in the continued task of defining as well as preserving some of the salient moments, experiences, places, buildings, and landscape features that constituted its commonly valued landscape character. This became

Fig.10.14. Picnic on the beach, Province Lands, 1940. Photo by Edwin Rosskam. FSA/OWI.

a central task of the next and last phase of national park planning at the seashore, which was published in 1998 as a "general management plan," *Forging a Collaborative Future.*[25] This was the third major elaboration of the park service vision for the seashore, following the master plans of 1963 and 1970. Its methods, emphasis, and findings indicated another turning point in how park service superintendents and staff perceived the essential nature of their mandate, and the degree to which they realized that the engagement of the people of the Outer Cape was central to their success.

Wellfleet Harbor. Photo by Carol Betsch.

Conclusion

As the Cape Cod National Seashore celebrated its fiftieth anniversary in 2016, the National Park Service marked the centennial of its establishment. Fifty years earlier, the agency completed Mission 66, its billion-dollar capital investment and park expansion program, the same year it established a new kind of national park on Cape Cod.

The commemorations of 2016 provided an occasion for retrospection; but park service director Jonathan Jarvis assured that the agency's programs and events that year would emphasize outlooks for the future more than ruminations on the past. Jarvis had originally trained as a biologist and had served as a superintendent at Mount Rainier National Park and as director of the Western Region during his long park service career. Appointed director of the National Park Service in 2009, he developed new priorities and concerns for the agency that complemented the commitment to resource management which had characterized both his career and park service policy since the 1970s. The theme of the centennial was "Find Your Park," an overall outreach to the American public encouraging people to discover and appreciate the more than four hundred units of the national park system, not all of which received the visitation they merited. Of special concern were the young and members of immigrant and minority communities, groups who were underrepresented among park visitors.

Since its creation, the park service had worried that the national parks would be "loved to death" and overwhelmed by the constantly increasing numbers of people and their cars. The agency had evolved from the early concern for the scenic quality of park landscapes to a broader mandate to protect the integrity of ecosystems and historic resources. (Fig. C.1) The challenge of trying to facilitate ever larger numbers, however, while keeping the parks "unimpaired" for the enjoyment of future generations, remained a constant throughout the twentieth century. Another threat became clear with the new millennium. The parks could also be ignored to death, at least if new generations of a more diverse American public remained unconvinced of

Fig. C.1. Footbridge into marsh toward Barnstable Harbor. Photo by Carol M. Highsmith. CHA.

their significance. The popularity of national parks may have been a threat to their integrity since 1916, but it also was the basis of a constituency that led Congress to maintain and invest in the system. Public engagement and outreach had emerged as central challenges for the agency's next one hundred years by the time of its centennial.

At the Cape Cod National Seashore, historical developments in how national parks were planned and operated in the United States put the fragile and narrow landscape of the Outer Cape in the vanguard of the implementation of new ideas. The Cape Cod model, from the beginning, indicated an awareness of the need for experimentation in the entire relationship between property owners, communities, and governments both within and adjacent to the park. The resulting mosaic was a physical one, with private inholdings—the improved properties—appearing throughout the public reservation. But it was a social fabric as well, with the threads of private, town, and federal interests interwoven throughout. In this sense, it was truly a new model; but it was one that would never be completed, because it described processes and relationships more than a single, static plan. This model had been determined by the 1961 legislation, which was a turning point that influenced almost all future national park bills considered by Congress. The model was then shaped by two influential planning efforts: the 1963 master plan, which had determined the basic development of buildings, roads, parking lots and programs; and the master plan published in 1970, which initiated an era of protective management of both natural and cultural resources. Both plans set precedents and made the park something of a showcase of contemporary priorities and directions in the national park system.

The third comprehensive iteration of the federal vision for the national seashore was initiated in the 1990s. The "general management plan" had at its core a continued commitment both to public recreation and to the protection of natural and cultural resources which had developed over the previous forty years. But the title of the plan also indicated that further success would depend on a renewed and profound collaboration with the people and governments of the Outer Cape. Archaeologists, the OCLP, and park staff all contributed to a sense of the importance of people in the landscape—in the past but also up to the present. The "way of life" of the Outer Cape could not be understood, much less fostered or protected, without a plan for a fully collaborative future for the park.

The plan that was published in 1998 as *Forging a Collaborative Future* was accomplished only after considerable effort and struggle within the planning culture of the National Park Service. Andrew Ringgold, who became superintendent in 1989, began to work with Denver Service Center planners and regional staff on a new general management plan in 1991. The existing master plan was over twenty years old, and clearly new issues—and methods for addressing them—had arisen since 1970. Visitation had leveled off far below the most dire predictions but remained considerable in the context of the size, staffing, and budget of the park. By the 1990s, the national seashore had settled into a pattern of visits (four to five million per year), of annual budgets (around $3 million), with about one hundred full-time positions. In terms of numbers of visitors served, these figures put the seashore among the national parks doing more with less. In 1995, the historian Dwight F. Rettie compiled a "cost per visit" analysis that yielded a figure of $0.58 per visit that year for the national seashore, compared, for example, with $3.71 for Fire Island, $2.48 for Padre Island, and $1.05 for Point Reyes National Seashores.[1]

Statistics can be misleading, and Cape Cod National Seashore has less acreage than some of the other examples; the efficiency of its operation in terms of the sheer number of visitors, however, put it in a small group of national parks and far ahead of any other national seashore. But in the 1990s, what might have been considered inadequate maintenance and personnel budgets were not necessarily the first concern for planners. They recognized that the park was indeed a special case, an "experiment" in conservation, and that the park service was a "relatively recent partner" in the effort. The "precious and fragile resource" that was the Outer Cape landscape overlaid six established communities, and the 1961 legislative mandate "sought to perpetuate interwoven patterns of human activities and the natural environment." The park continued to face challenges—most involving relationships with the people and communities of the Outer Cape—that again required a reconsideration of the best methods and process for assuring a "collaborative future."[2]

The 1998 plan was initiated through the Denver Service Center, but as it evolved, responsibility for leading the project shifted from the DSC to the regional office and park staff, a move strongly supported by superintendent Maria Burks when she replaced Ringgold in 1995.[3] While the park had entered a mature and stable phase of its operations, the need for improved outreach to the six towns and all the residents of the Outer Cape—by then recognized as the necessary next step—implied that revised approaches to park planning should be instituted. Closer to the Cape and staffed with personnel with long experience with the national seashore and its constituencies, the regional office and the park were in a better position to create the venues and processes for more effective public engagement. They also had more experience with the planning and land use issues specific to Massachusetts, knowledge that was useful in improving the partnership with the six towns.

Sarah Peskin, chief planner at the DSC, recalled that developing a new general management plan for the seashore was one of the most challenging tasks they faced, and that the "complexity and deep history" of the park and the region required a new approach led by the regional office and Superintendent Burks rather than the DSC. The CCNSAC continued in its role as an active partner throughout the effort and formed a subcommittee for the purpose. The Massachusetts Office of Coastal Zone Management, created through state legislation in the 1970s, and the Cape Cod Commission, established in 1990, were two other important partners in the planning effort.[4]

In some ways, the planning process followed procedures that had been well established since the 1970s, following "two interrelated efforts—public involvement and the development of technical data through research studies, interviews, analysis, and mapping." Certainly the amount of scientific data available (and the technology for spatializing it through GIS mapping) was far greater than anything available for the previous master plan. The headings under which natural resource management goals were listed indicated what the planners called a "more holistic and integrated management approach." Goals for resource management, for example, now included a concern for "air resources" and "cooperative regional efforts to improve air quality." Another heading covered "coastal processes" with the goal of allowing "natural shoreline processes to take place unimpeded," while mitigating "human-caused disturbances." Water quality was another category that involved "ground and surface water quality and quantity, as well as adjacent wetlands." The restoration of estuaries "in consultation with affected municipalities" was specified as an ongoing goal. The priority expressed for managing vegetation and wildlife was to allow "natural processes to continue unimpeded" for the benefit of "native biotic resources," except in those cases where endangered or threatened species required protection through "selective management" of other species. The document was an impressive summary of all that had been learned through the ecological research and monitoring at the park over a period of decades, and a mature statement of park service "general management plan" philosophy and management strategies. The natural resource planners noted that they were not advocating "dramatic changes or shifts in policy," and that many "policies and operating procedures" instituted under the 1970 plan were "functioning well."[5]

The emphasis in the plan on "cultural heritage and ethnographic resources," however, was notable, and once again put the national seashore on the leading edge of trends in park planning. The 1998 GMP revealed the change then under way in how the general category of "cultural resources" was being construed at the park, and how cultural resource management increasingly was seen as part of the mandate to preserve the Outer Cape's "way of life." Superintendent Burks felt that legislators, advocates, and park service staff over the years had "missed the boat" in failing to reach a better consensus on what exactly the Outer Cape way of life meant and how the operation of the seashore could do more to preserve it. (Fig. C.2) Burks took an active role in moving the plan for forward with her staff and with Peskin and the other planners at the regional office. She understood that management issues that caused conflicts with visitors and residents were never solved so much as they were "managed" through ongoing consultation and compromise—the kind of process exemplified by the "negotiated rulemaking" governing ORV use which she organized in 1995. At that point in the history of the national seashore, the superintendent needed a process of meaningful community engagement that could yield improved relations with the towns and people of the region: a framework for decision making, not a static plan.[6]

After a first round of public meetings, a draft of the plan was released in 1996, eliciting hun-

Fig. C.2. "Decorative Map of Cape Cod," 1940, drawn by Colonial Craftsmen, Attleboro, MA. Wikimedia Commons.

dreds of comments. More public meetings followed. Seashore staff met individually with town governments and concerned nonprofits to review their specific suggestions. The CCNSAC subcommittee was particularly involved in the process and subsequent revisions. The advisory commission as a whole received the results of these efforts as a final draft GMP in 1997, and at the same time the accompanying draft environmental impact statement (two thick volumes) was made available for review. The EIS presented three alternatives: essentially continuing park operations without significant change ("no action"); a more aggressive approach which implied a more "capital intensive" and "active role" in directing "intensive protection and management efforts"; and a third alternative that promised a middle way, achieving more than "no action" but working within the realm of practicable steps to improve management and "preserve natural and cultural resources." Not surprisingly, the park service chose the middle path, a decision formalized in 1998 immediately before the official publication of the plan.[7]

It is worth noting that the GMP/EIS process for national parks, was, generally, by this time lengthy, onerous, and expensive. In recent years, the entire process has been called into question as the park service reconsiders what the most effective means of providing its parks with comprehensive plans is. But in 1998 the new GMP for the national seashore was another watershed in the history of the park because of the emphasis on new approaches in defining and managing cultural resources, and because of Superintendent Burks's insistence that one important result of the process, at least, would be an increased quality of public engagement in the management and interpretation of those resources. Under the heading of "cultural resources," for example, the plan stated that "the Outer Cape has a distinctive pattern of human activity that is inextricably linked with the land and the sea. This heritage draws from the prehistoric culture of native people, from the arrival of the Pilgrims and settlement by Europeans, from the whaling and fishing industry, from Portuguese and Cape Verdean migrations, and from artists and writers who have lived and worked on the Cape." Ethnographic research and other cultural resource initiatives had "identified the range of cultural use patterns of seashore resources and their value to both traditionally associated and contemporary neighboring people."

Cultural resources, the planners acknowledged, could be either "tangible" or "intangible," the latter expanding the category from buildings and sites to "arts, skills, folkways, and lifeways." If not a full working definition of the "way of life" of the Outer Cape, the statements were the most ambitious attempt the agency had made so far to define what exactly that phrase might mean. The goals expressed for management began with the intention to work "in concert with local communities [to] explore, define, and maintain the components of the distinctive cultural heritage and pattern of human activities that make the character of Cape Cod unique."[8]

The cultural resource initiatives of the 1990s and 2000s described in chapter 10 were guided by this broadened sense of the heritage of the living cultural landscape of the Outer Cape. They built on the promise of a new era of public engagement in national park management contained in the 1961 national seashore legislation. Most of the "interpretive themes" laid out for the park in 1998 were familiar, but others were new. The third theme, for example, stated that "the people of Cape Cod have intensively affected the land, and they continue to interact with the land and surrounding waters. Cape Cod is the continuing saga of human events etched onto the landscape." Another read: "As both a haven and a subject, Cape Cod has drawn artists and authors for more than a century," a continuing tradition embodied, for example, in the dune shacks and modern houses within the national seashore.[9] Overall, the 1998 general management plan was imbued with a new spirit, just as the 1970 master plan had been. People had been part of the landscape for thousands of years and, perhaps more important, continued to be in the present. The cultural landscape was an ongoing process, and the GMP presaged a new kind of national park plan that actively sought processes of engagement which acknowledged that fact.

The next superintendent, George Price, described the national seashore as a "work in progress" that required continued new responses to the continuous environmental and social changes. Price observed that as the park reached its fiftieth anniversary, it might have been considered to "be on autopilot," with many of the early challenges and policy decisions already made and implemented. He had no such illusions about the Cape Cod National Seashore, where new issues, environmental problems, and conflicts over sometimes unfamiliar types of public use constantly arose, among a community of residents and vacationers who could sometimes be passionately engaged in almost every aspect of park operations.[10] In a landscape understood as a process, not an artifact, park management also needed to be an ongoing process and a framework for engagement, not a list of questionable solutions to problems and issues that might not yet have even been correctly identified. In many ways, the 1998 GMP aspired to the fulfilment of the original intentions of the national seashore.

The Cape Cod model, in other words, continued to adapt to the changing context of the cultural landscape of the Outer Cape, and the understandings of what constitutes that landscape and the "way of life" associated with it. From the beginning of the federal effort to create the national seashore, the preservation of the character of the landscape and of the society that inhabited it had been the stated mandate for the agency charged with its management. The great success of the national seashore has been its ability to adapt and change its management principles—from 1963, to 1970, to 1998—to address that mandate. But if the "model" has repeatedly been modified, was it then a success or a failure? Was it an example to be emulated, or an essay requiring significant reconceptualization over the years? Has the model been successfully applied in the creation and operation of other national seashore parks, or was it too seriously flawed to be a "model" at all, and so would perhaps be better characterized as an "experiment" from which valuable lessons, positive and negative, might be drawn?

The questions are linked by the inherent nature of the Cape Cod model, the genius of which was the successful fostering of effective partnerships with the residents and six town governments of the Outer Cape. The model was a success, in this sense, but specifically because it was tailored to the social, historical, and environmental contexts of Cape Cod. As such, it was never likely that simply repeating the "formula" would produce the same results elsewhere. The formula, in a sense, was to be more than formulaic; to adapt national park legislation to the sometimes complex exigencies of local communities and landscape. The Cape Cod model, then, succeeded because it was not really a model, at least not one that could or should simply be repeated. Denis P. Galvin, the former deputy director of the park service who had also been deputy director of the North Atlantic Regional Office during the 1970s as well as the head of the DSC, was adamant when asked about the success or failure of the Cape Cod model: it was not simply a formula that could be successfully applied elsewhere, as the experience (and difficulties) of the Fire Island National Seashore established in 1964, for example, demonstrated. The Cape Cod National Seashore succeeded—with fewer and less contentious controversies than most other new seashores and parks—because the legislators and others involved devised a unique response to the very difficult and complex issues they encountered on the Outer Cape. The working relationships with the six towns, the CCNSAC, and property owners were the source of any success the national seashore could claim; those results should be emulated, but the specific legislative provisions of 1961 should not be taken blindly as the solution for other areas.[11]

Another way of putting this might be to observe that the Cape Cod model succeeded because it was on Cape Cod. In other cases, the regional social, legal, historical, and ecological conditions needed to be considered. This observation highlights the importance of the individuals and communities of the Outer Cape in the construction, operation, and, ultimately, the relative success of the entire project. The Cape Cod model was the result of the long involvement of a remarkable generation of Cape Codders who influenced their congressional delegation, the park service, and their neighbors to create an unprecedented approach to landscape conservation. Many of them were prominent cultural figures and politicians or traced their genealogies to early English settlers. But most were just concerned property owners and business people who overcame strong initial reservations about the proposed national park and eventually both supported and shaped it.

Through the institution of town meeting, the history of the active engagement of the people of the Outer Cape in determining the fate of their own communities was centuries old. The people who came forward in the mid-twentieth century to form a new partnership with the federal government were following in Thoreau's footsteps, as Jonathan Harrison and The Trustees of Public Reservations had at the beginning of the century. The greatest hope of current park administration, then, would be to further enable this tradition of stewardship, and to encourage and expand local participation in the park project. If the Cape Cod model succeeded, it did so because it encouraged a fruition of the special relationship of people and places on the Outer Cape. The preservation of natural resources and archaeological and historic sites and structures would be empty victories unless the people of the Outer Cape continued to evince the concerns and build on the achievements of their predecessors. The cultural landscape cannot be successfully curated as an artifact of the past; it requires the full partnership of its current inhabitants to maintain its integrity.

The many and prolonged controversies described in this book might suggest that the experiment in conservation that began in 1961 was not so successful, after all. At times the restrictions on private inholdings, ORV use, public nudity, the disposition of historic structures, and many other contentious aspects of park administration have generated antagonistic situations in which the national park was at odds with its surrounding communities. Variations of these situations developed in most of the national parks and seashores that followed Cape Cod, and in many cases the conflicts became far more bitter and intractable. But the most important legal challenges the Cape Cod National Seashore faced in the course of its administration resulted in judicial decisions that strongly supported the courses of action the park service had taken. Controversies over restrictions on ORVs and nudity (among many other issues) certainly continue, but they have waned in intensity, indicating that decisions made, if unpopular at the time, also recognized longer and inevitable trends in public recreation as well as the requirements of resource preservation. The national seashore, as the first of its type, has also turned out to be one of the least fraught by internecine strife within its own public. This was, again, because of the long tradition of productive engagement of the people of the Outer Cape in shaping the future of their region, and the degree to which those communities have had a decisive and continuing role, especially through the work of the CCNSAC, in the actions of the park. This has not always been the case for other national parks, more or less modeled on Cape Cod, in other regions of the country.

This book has also shown, however, that Congress and the National Park Service failed to respond quickly and effectively to some of the shortcomings of the 1961 authorizing legislation, problems that were already evident during the first decade of the park's operation. Congress failed to make timely and adequate appropriations for land acquisition (through eminent domain if necessary), and never authorized the "advance contract authority" that would have reduced costs and eliminated some of the most egregious examples of post-1959 residential development. As it became clear that local zoning codes were not sufficient to stop the construction of large mansions in sensitive areas of the park landscape, it took decades for the park service to persuade town governments to remedy the situation. And the park never had an effective means of addressing the commercial development and traffic congestion that soon abutted park boundaries. The Cape Cod Commission was established through state legislation in 1990 as a somewhat belated means to address these and other regional planning issues.

Ultimately, however, the question of the success or failure of the Cape Cod National Seashore over its first fifty years should be answered by even a brief consideration of what the future of the Outer Cape would have been without it. The private development that was overwhelming the region in the 1950s intensified in the following decades and only recently has shown any sign of abating. Whatever its shortcomings (and these have not been overlooked here), the partnership that began at midcentury created a very different future for the region than would have occurred otherwise. There are many experiences—overlooking the Atlantic from the Truro Highlands, walking through the Penniman house, standing on top of Fort Hill, swimming in an isolated kettle pond—that exist only because the national seashore does. The uninterrupted expanse of the Great Beach still inspires awe today as much as it did for Thoreau. Nesting shorebirds and thousands of beachgoers exist together, if not always in perfect harmony. Visitors are able to gain whatever benefit, enjoyment, and inspiration they can, whatever their interests and predilections, in one of the nation's greatest public parks. (Fig. C.3)

These are moments when the success of the overall effort of the establishment and administration of the Cape Cod National Seashore should be acknowledged, even when considered against the goals expressed in 1961 that were never entirely attainable. No national park has ever been "permanently preserved in its present state," certainly not a cultural landscape as complex as the Outer Cape. While the sentiment is clear, the reality is that landscapes are alive, and living things change. "Permanent preservation" then starts to sound rather ominous, and perhaps not at all consistent with the actual intention of the phrase. The "preservation of the way of life of lower Cape Cod" also was more than any piece of legislation could deliver. Life in Barnstable County as a whole has changed radically over the last fifty years and, if a renewed commitment to regional planning solutions has been made evident since 1990, it is unlikely that any national park could have ever been a comprehensive solution for the challenges of the era, on Cape Cod or anywhere else.

But the novelty and audacity of the Cape Cod

Fig. C.3. Nauset Light Beach, Eastham. NPSHC.

National Seashore deserve recognition despite any perceived shortcomings in the ultimate results. The National Park Service and the six towns of the Outer Cape initiated an unprecedented chapter in conservation, one that held great significance for what became a generation of ambitious new kinds of national parks, seashores, and recreation areas. The effects of population growth, social change, and environmental degradation challenged the viability of the national seashore—and perhaps of the national park system itself—after 1961. This history has traced the official, administrative actions that advanced and developed the national park idea on Cape Cod as a vital and beneficial response to the critical environmental and social issues of the era. The significance of the Cape Cod model, above all, has been its contribution to the continued vitality and relevance of the national park in American life.

Archives and Abbreviations

BNA	Boston National Archives, Waltham, Massachusetts
BPL	Tichnor Brothers Collection, Boston Public Library.
CHA	Carol M. Highsmith Archive, Prints and Photographs Division, Library of Congress
CCNSA	Cape Cod National Seashore Archives, Salt Pond Visitor Center, National Park Service
HFC	Harper's Ferry Center, National Park Service
NACP	National Archives, College Park, Maryland
NPS	National Park Service
NPSHC	National Park Service History Collection, Harper's Ferry Center
FSA/OWI	Farm Security Administration / Office of War Information Photo Collection, Prints and Photos Division, Library of Congress
HABS	Historic American Buildings Survey, Prints and Photographs Division, Library of Congress
HAER	Historic American Engineering Record, Prints and Photographs Division, Library of Congress

Notes

Introduction

1. S.857 Public Law 87-126, Cape Cod National Seashore Act, August 7, 1961. "Outer Cape" is used throughout to refer to six towns in Barnstable County, Massachusetts: Chatham, Orleans, Eastham, Wellfleet, Truro, and Provincetown. These towns make up the narrow, north-south peninsula of Cape Cod at its eastern extremity, and they all had some portion of their territory included in the Cape Cod National Seashore. The region is also sometimes described as part of the "Lower Cape."
2. See Bryant F. Tolles Jr., *Summer by the Seaside: The Architecture of New England Coastal Hotels, 1820–1950* (Lebanon, NH: University Press of New England, 2008), 1–14.
3. For a full account of Native American and early English habitation of the Cape, see Richard D. Holmes, Carolyn D. Hertz, and Mitchell T. Mulholland, *Historic Cultural Land Use Study of Lower Cape Cod: A Study of the Historical Archeology and History of the Cape Cod National Seashore and the Surrounding Region* (Lowell, MA: U.S. Department of the Interior, National Park Service, n.d.). Also see Massachusetts Historical Commission, *Historic and Archaeological Resources of Cape Cod and the Islands: A Framework for Making Preservation Decisions* (Boston: Massachusetts Historical Commission, 1986).
4. Barnstable County includes all the towns of the Upper (see n. 10) and Outer (or Lower) Cape. See Kittredge's chapters "Whaling" and "Fisheries," in Henry C. Kittredge, *Cape Cod: Its People and Their History* (Boston: Houghton Mifflin, 1930; 2nd ed., 1968), 164–207. By 1900, Eastham, Wellfleet, and Truro had lost more than half of their populations. The overall population of Cape Cod fell from 35,990 in 1860 to 26,670 in 1920 (Holmes, Hertz, and Mulholland, *Historic Cultural Land Use,* 39–40, 170–75).
5. For a summary of early tourism on Cape Cod, see James C. O'Connell, *Becoming Cape Cod: Creating a Seaside Resort* (Hanover: University of New Hampshire, 2003).
6. John R. Stilgoe, *Alongshore* (New Haven: Yale University Press, 1994), 309–10.
7. "Great Beach" is used here to describe the Atlantic beach that extends from Chatham to Provincetown. The beach extends about thirty-nine miles. Henry Beston described it as the "great beach" in 1928 in his influential and popular account, *The Outermost House: A Year of Life on the Great Beach of Cape Cod.* In 1963, John Hay published another classic of Cape Cod literature, *The Great Beach.* The Great Beach has also been described as the Outer Beach, the Outer Shore, and perhaps more correctly as the Back Side, a name that indicates the importance of the harbors and resources of the opposite, Bay, side of Cape Cod for early residents.
8. Henry David Thoreau, *Cape Cod* (1865), Riverside Edition, vol. 4 (Boston: Houghton Mifflin, 1893), 2.
9. Thoreau only rarely mentions the true "first people" of Cape Cod, the Wampanoags who had lived there for

thousands of years and had shaped their own cultural landscape through agriculture, forest and brush burning, and other practices. As was the case with almost all early landscape tourists in the United States, the extent to which Native Americans had inhabited and shaped North American landscapes went unrecognized. For an account of this earlier landscape history of the Cape, see Holmes, Hertz, and Mulholland, *Historic Cultural Land Use.*

10. "Upper Cape" is used throughout to describe nine towns of Barnstable County: Bourne, Falmouth, Sandwich, Mashpee, Barnstable, Yarmouth, Dennis, Brewster, and Harwich. The last two towns are often considered part of the "Lower Cape" (together with the six Outer Cape towns, described in note 1). Planners also refer to the towns of Barnstable, Yarmouth, and Dennis as a separate "Mid-Cape" region.
11. Thoreau, *Cape Cod,* 25.
12. Ibid., 74.
13. Ibid., 20, 162.
14. Dona Brown, *Inventing New England: Regional Tourism in the Nineteenth Century* (Washington, DC: Smithsonian Institution Press, 1995), 204.
15. William Cullen Bryant, ed., *Picturesque America: Or, The Land We Live In* (New York: D. Appleton, 1874).
16. O'Connell, *Becoming Cape Cod,* 4–8.
17. Thoreau, *Cape Cod,* 329–30.
18. By the 1880s, over seventy-five resort hotels existed, mostly on the South Shore. John Braginton Smith, "Tourism and the Economy: Inns of the First Two Centuries," in *Three Centuries of the Cape Cod County, Barnstable, Massachusetts, 1685–1985* (Barnstable, MA: Barnstable County, 1985), 191–203. See O'Connell, *Becoming Cape Cod,* 11–44.
19. Jeremiah Digges, *Cape Cod Pilot* (New York: Modern Pilgrim Press and Viking Press, 1937), 2–3; Gregory Bryant, "Transportation: Surface," in *Three Centuries,* 205–14; Brown, *Inventing New England,* 204–5.
20. O'Connell, *Becoming Cape Cod,* 47.
21. Holmes, Hertz, and Mulholland, *Historic Cultural Land Use,* 35–40.
22. See O'Connell, *Becoming Cape Cod,* 47–58.
23. See Lee W. Baldwin, "The Art Colony," and Philip A. Jenkin, "Literary Arts," in *Three Centuries,* 261–85.
24. Some principal examples are Henry C. Kittredge, *Cape Cod: Its People and Their History* (1930); Elizabeth Reynaud, *The Narrow Land: Folk Chronicles of Old Cape Cod* (1934); Joseph C. Lincoln, *Cape Cod Yesterdays* (1935), and many novels set on the Cape; Katherine Smith and Edith Shay, *Down the Cape* (1936); and Jeremiah Digges, *Cape Cod Pilot* (1937). Picture books documented the visual appeal of regional architecture and landscapes, for example, Samuel Chamberlain, *Cape Cod in the Sun* (1937). See O'Connell, *Becoming Cape Cod,* 63–77.
25. Quoted in O'Connell, *Becoming Cape Cod,* 75–76.
26. Bryant, "Transportation: Surface," 212–13.
27. Public Law 87-126, S. 857, 87th Cong. (August 7, 1961), 9.
28. Frederick Law Olmsted, "Preliminary Report on the Yosemite and Big Tree Grove" (1865), in *The California Frontier, 1863–1865,* vol. 5 of *The Papers of Frederick Law Olmsted,* ed. Victoria Post Ranney (Baltimore: Johns Hopkins University Press, 1990), 500.
29. Thoreau, *Cape Cod,* 331.

1. National Parks and National Seashores

1. See, for example, William Cronon, *Changes in the Land: Indians, Colonists, and the Ecology of New England* (New York: Hill and Wang, 1983); Norman L. Christensen, "Landscape History and Ecological Change," *Journal of Forest History* 33, no. 3 (July 1989): 116–25; William M. Deneven, "The Pristine Myth: The Landscape of the Americas in 1492," *Annals of the Association of American Geographers* 82, no. 3 (September 1992): 369–85.
2. Hillory A. Tolson, *Laws Relating to the National Park Service and the National Parks and Monuments* (Washington, DC: Government Printing Office, 1933), 296.
3. Ibid., 9–10.
4. Stephen T. Mather, "The Ideals and Policy of the National Park Service Particularly in Relation to Yosemite National Park," in *Handbook of Yosemite National Park,* ed. Ansel F. Hall (New York: G. P. Putnam's Sons, 1921), 77–86.
5. See Ethan Carr, *Wilderness by Design: Landscape Architecture and the National Park Service* (Lincoln: University of Nebraska Press, 1998); Linda Flint McClelland, *Building the National Parks: Historic Landscape Design and Construction* (Baltimore: Johns Hopkins University Press, 1998).
6. Barry Mackintosh, "The National Park Service Moves into Historical Interpretation," *Public Historian* 9, no. 2 (Spring 1987): 51–63.
7. See Barry Mackintosh, *The National Parks: Shaping the System* (Washington, DC: U.S. Department of the Interior, 1991); Ronald F. Lee, *Family Tree of the National Park System: A Chart with Accompanying Text Designed to Illustrate the Growth of the National Park System, 1872–1972* (Philadelphia: Eastern National Park & Monument Association, 1972).
8. The General Authorities Act of 1970 (an amendment to the 1916 National Park Service Organic Act) states: "Congress

declares that the National Park Service, which began with establishment of Yellowstone National Park in 1872, has since grown to include superlative natural, historic, and recreation areas in every major region of the United States, its territories and island possessions; that these areas, though distinct in character, are united through their inter-related purposes and resources into one national park system as cumulative expressions of a single national heritage; that, individually and collectively, these areas derive increased national dignity and recognition of their superb environmental quality through their inclusion jointly with each other in one national park system preserved and managed for the benefit and inspiration of all the people of the United States; and that it is the purpose of this Act to include all such areas in the System and to clarify the authorities applicable to the system." For this and other primary documents related to U.S. national parks, see Lary M. Dilsaver, ed., *America's National Park System: The Critical Documents* (Lanham, MD: Rowman & Littlefield, 1994).

9. For an account of the influence of the New Deal on the National Park Service—and the reciprocal degree to which the agency shaped the programs and values of Roosevelt's public works programs—see Carr, *Wilderness by Design,* 249–301.
10. William E. Warne, *The Bureau of Reclamation* (New York: Praeger, 1973), 13–14, 27, 64, 256.
11. Harlan D. Unrau and G. Frank Williss, *Administrative History: Expansion of the National Park Service in the 1930s* (Washington, DC: Government Printing Office, 1983), 153–55.
12. U.S. Department of the Interior, National Park Service, *Procedure for Park, Parkway, and Recreational-Area Study* (Washington, DC: Government Printing Office, 1937), 1, 6–8.
13. U.S. Department of the Interior, National Park Service, *A Study of the Park and Recreation Problem of the United States* (Washington, DC: Government Printing Office, 1941).
14. U.S. Department of the Interior, National Park Service, *Our Vanishing Shoreline* (Washington, DC: Government Printing Office, [1955]), 9; Conrad L. Wirth, *Parks, Politics, and the People* (Norman: University of Oklahoma Press, 1980), 192–93.
15. Unrau and Williss, *Administrative History,* 267–69; John C. Miles, *Guardians of the Parks: A History of the National Parks and Conservation Association* (Washington, DC: Taylor & Francis in cooperation with the National Parks and Conservation Association, 1995), 86–95, 124.
16. Conrad L. Wirth, "Parks and Their Uses," in *American Planning and Civic Annual,* ed. Harlean James (Washington, DC: American Civic and Planning Association, 1935), 156–61.
17. Cameron Binkley, *The Creation and Establishment of Cape Hatteras National Seashore, The Great Depression through Mission 66* (Atlanta, GA: National Park Service, 2007), 13–14.
18. Ibid., 13–15.
19. Mackintosh, *National Parks,* 42, 61.
20. Binkley, *Creation and Establishment of Cape Hatteras,* 16, 20–23.
21. Ibid., 17–19.
22. Quoted ibid., 35.
23. The texts of legislation related to Cape Hatteras National Seashore appear in appendix B, ibid., 215–23.
24. Mackintosh, *National Parks,* 23.
25. Binkley, *Creation and Establishment of Cape Hatteras,* 65–95.
26. Ibid., 97–99, 121–22; Wirth, *Parks, Politics, and the People,* 55–58, 192–97.
27. In 1955, as Mission 66 planning began, there were 50 million visits to the national park system (compared to 17 million in 1940). By 1961 there would be over 80 million, and in 1966, the year Mission 66 was completed, there were more than 130 million "recreational visits" to the national park system. Visitor statistics are available from the National Park Service through the agency website. See https://irma.nps.gov/Stats/Reports/National. Also see Dwight F. Rettie, *Our National Park System: Caring for America's Greatest Natural and Historic Treasures* (Urbana: University of Illinois Press, 1995), 250–51.
28. Newton B. Drury, "The Dilemma of Our Parks," *American Forests* 55, no. 6 (June 1949): 6–11, 38, 39.
29. Binkley, *Creation and Establishment of Cape Hatteras,* 136–45.
30. See Ethan Carr, *Mission 66: Modernism and the National Park Dilemma* (Amherst: University of Massachusetts Press in association with Library of American Landscape History, 1998).
31. See Binkley, *Creation and Establishment of Cape Hatteras,* 159–66, for an account of the development of Cape Hatteras under Mission 66.
32. U.S. Department of the Interior, National Park Service, *Seashore Recreation Area Survey of the Atlantic and Gulf Coasts* (Washington, DC: National Park Service, 1955).
33. National Park Service, *Our Vanishing Shoreline;* Wirth, Parks, *Politics, and the People,* 55–58, 192–93.
34. "Parks for America Is Our Common Concern," June 8, 1961, DOI press release, National Park Service History Collection, Harpers Ferry Center (NPSHC).
35. Wirth, *Parks, Politics, and the People,* 198–99.

2. Early Land Conservation on Cape Cod

1. For an overview of land conservation efforts in Massachusetts, see Charles H. W. Foster, "Environmental Conservation in Massachusetts: A Twentieth-Century Overview," in *Twentieth-Century New England Land Conservation: A Heritage of Civic Engagement,* ed. Charles H. W. Foster (Petersham, MA: Harvard Forest, 2009): 175–215.
2. *Mourt's Relation, or Journal of the Plantation at Plymouth,* with introduction and notes by Henry Martyn Dexter, Library of New England History, no. 1 (Boston: John Kimball Wiggin, 1865), 10.
3. J. B. Harrison, "The Province Lands at Provincetown," in *First Annual Report of The Trustees of Public Reservations, 1891* (Boston: George H. Ellis, 1892): 63–68.
4. *Second Annual Report of The Trustees of Public Reservations, 1892* (Boston: George H. Ellis, 1893), app. III; Richard D. Holmes, Carolyn D. Hertz, and Mitchell T. Mulholland, *Historic Cultural Land Use Study of Lower Cape Cod: A Study of the Historical Archeology and History of the Cape Cod National Seashore and the Surrounding Region* (Lowell, MA: National Park Service, n.d.), 57–58; William Cronon, *Changes in the Land: Indians, Colonists, and the Ecology of New England* (New York: Hill and Wang, 1983), 149.
5. Heather J. Wilson, "The Public Trust Doctrine in Massachusetts Land Law," *Boston College Environmental Affairs Law Review* 11, no. 4 (1984): 849–52.
6. Ethan Carr, Amanda Gagel, and Michael Shapiro, eds., *The Early Boston Years, 1882–1890,* vol. 8 of *The Papers of Frederick Law Olmsted* (Baltimore: Johns Hopkins University Press, 2013), 13–16.
7. Charles E. Beveridge and Carolyn Hoffman, eds., *Writings on Public Parks, Parkways, and Park Systems,* vol. 1 of *The Papers of Frederick Law Olmsted, Supplemental Series* (Baltimore: Johns Hopkins University Press, 1997), 46–53.
8. Carr, Gagel, and Shapiro, *Early Boston Years,* 13–15.
9. See Charles W. Eliot, *Charles Eliot: Landscape Architect* [1902] (Amherst: University of Massachusetts Press in association with Library of American Landscape History, 1999).
10. The claim is based on the fact that in Britain, the National Trust for Places of Historic Interest or Natural Beauty (the National Trust) was founded along analogous lines in 1895. The Trustees of Public Reservations is known today as The Trustees of Reservations.
11. J. B. Harrison, "A Report Upon the Public Holdings of the Shore Towns of Massachusetts," in *First Annual Report of The Trustees of Public Reservations, 1891* (Boston: George H. Ellis, 1892): 21–62.
12. Ibid., 48–49.
13. Harrison, "The Province Lands."
14. *Second Annual Report of The Trustees of Public Reservations, 1892* (Boston: George H. Ellis, 1893), app. III; Eliot, *Charles Eliot,* 345–48.
15. *Third Annual Report of The Trustees of Public Reservations, 1893* (Boston: George H. Ellis, 1894), 12.
16. *Second Annual Report of The Trustees,* 43.
17. *Third Annual Report of The Trustees,* 43.
18. James C. O'Connell, *Becoming Cape Cod: Creating a Seaside Resort* (Hanover: University of New Hampshire, 2003) 119.
19. Charles S. Bird Jr., *Report of the Governor's Committee on Needs and Uses of Open Spaces* (Boston: Commonwealth of Massachusetts, 1929), 1.
20. *Thirty-Sixth Annual Report of The Trustees of Public Reservations, 1926* (Boston: Wright and Potter, 1927), 5–7.
21. Bird Jr., *Report of the Governor's Committee,* 6. The plan, which continues to be implemented today, was Charles W. Eliot II's expansion of the Metropolitan Park Commission system that his uncle and Sylvester Baxter had succeeded in seeing carried out in the early 1890s. Forming a concentric ring in the suburbs closer to Boston, that metropolitan system of reservations had in turn been inspired by the original "ring" of parks, the Emerald Necklace municipal park system, designed by Olmsted in the 1880s.
22. Among ten wildlife sanctuaries proposed, three were on the Cape: Barnstable Neck (later Sandy Neck town beach), Pilgrim Lake (or East Harbor, now part of the national seashore), and Monomoy Island (later a National Wildlife Refuge). Ibid., 6–7.
23. Jeremiah Digges, *Cape Cod Pilot,* American Guide Series (New York: Modern Pilgrim Press and Viking Press, 1937).
24. For more on the New Deal and national seashore planning, see Douglas W. Doe, "The New Deal Origins of the Cape Cod National Seashore," *Historical Journal of Massachusetts* 25, no. 2 (Summer 1997): 139–56.
25. National Resources Board, *A Report on National Planning and Public Works in Relation to Natural Resources and Including Land Use and Water Resources, with Findings and Recommendations* (Washington, DC: Government Printing Office, 1934).
26. U.S. Department of the Interior, National Park Service, *Recreational Use of Land in the United States: Part XI of the Report on Land Planning,* 1934 (Washington DC: Government Printing Office, 1938), 43.
27. U.S. Department of the Interior, National Park Service, *Our Vanishing Shoreline* (Washington, DC: Government

Printing Office, [1955]), 9; Conrad L. Wirth, *Parks, Politics, and the People* (Norman: University of Oklahoma Press, 1980), 192–93; Harlan D. Unrau and G. Frank Williss, *Administrative History: Expansion of the National Park Service in the 1930s* (Washington, DC: Government Printing Office, 1983), 156.

28. U.S. Department of the Interior, National Park Service, *A Study of the Park and Recreation Problem of the United States* (Washington, DC: Government Printing Office, 1941).
29. Massachusetts State Planning Board, "Park, Parkway, and Recreational-Area Study," unpublished report (Boston: National Park Service, January 1941).
30. Ibid., ix, xii, 46.
31. Ibid., ix, xii, 17.
32. O'Connell, *Becoming Cape Cod,* 117–19.
33. Thomas H. Desmond, "A Proposed National Seashore and Historic Parkway on Cape Cod, Massachusetts," unpublished report for National Park Service, 1939.
34. "Thomas H. Desmond, December 19, 1884–May 20, 1950: A Biographical Minute," *Landscape Architecture* 41, no. 2 (January 1951): 78–79.
35. O'Connell, *Becoming Cape Cod,* 62; Leo Damore, *The Cape Cod Years of John Fitzgerald Kennedy* (Englewood Cliffs, NJ: Prentice-Hall, 1967), 62.
36. Douglas W. Doe, "The Road to Monomoy: Chatham, Massachusetts, and the Cape Cod National Seashore," master's thesis, University of Massachusetts Boston, 1995, 33–44.
37. Quoted ibid., 45.
38. Ibid., 46–49. Doe describes in detail the controversy in the 1950s over access to (and therefore increased recreational use of) Monomoy, including unrealized state plans to create a major recreational beach (69–96).
39. Mel Scott, *American City Planning since 1890* (Berkeley: University of California Press, 1969), 152–63.
40. League of Women Voters of Falmouth, "Land Use," http://lwvf.org/LandUse.html; O'Connell, *Becoming Cape Cod,* 112.
41. Doe, "Road to Monomoy," 50–57.
42. Quoted in O'Connell, *Becoming Cape Cod,* 112.
43. Lewis M. Alexander, "The Impact of Tourism on the Economy of Cape Cod, Massachusetts," *Economic Geography* 29, no. 4 (October 1953): 320–26.
44. Ibid.
45. Damore, *Cape Cod Years,* 133–35.
46. Ibid.
47. O'Connell, *Becoming Cape Cod,* 112–13. Zoning ordinances were not necessarily approved, however. Truro, for example, did not have such a law until 1960, and the subject remained controversial thereafter. Richard F. Whalen, *Truro: The Story of a Cape Cod Town* (Charleston, SC: History Press, 2007), 199–200.
48. Holmes, Hertz, and Mulholland, *Historic Cultural Land Use,* 170–75.
49. Francis P. Burling, *The Birth of the Cape Cod National Seashore* (Plymouth, MA: Leyden Press, 1978), 5–6.
50. O'Connell, *Becoming Cape Cod,* 114, 118–19.
51. Burling, *Birth,* 6.

3. The "Birth Throes of a National Park"

1. Conrad L. Wirth, "Birth Throes of a National Park," *Think Magazine,* June 1959, 26–30.
2. Francis P. Burling, *The Birth of the Cape Cod National Seashore* (1978; Fort Washington, PA: Eastern National, 2000). Also see Peter F. Healey, "The Legislative History of the Cape Cod National Seashore Act: How a Federal Agency Assisted in Resurrecting and Expanding a Dormant Public Policy," master's thesis, Georgetown University, 1967, and Jacqueline Alyse Mirandola Mullen, "Coastal Parks for a Metropolitan Nation: How Postwar Politics and Urban Growth Shaped America's Shores," PhD diss., University at Albany, State University of New York, 2015. For the legislative history as it related to Eastham and Chatham, respectively, see Thad L. Beyle, "The Cape Cod National Seashore: A Study in Conflict," PhD diss., University of Illinois, 1963, and Douglas W. Doe, "The Road to Monomoy: Chatham, Massachusetts, and the Cape Cod National Seashore," master's thesis, University of Massachusetts Boston, 1995.
3. Burling, *Birth,* x.
4. Doe, "Road to Monomoy," 99.
5. The board, known at the time as the Advisory Board on National Parks, Historic Sites, Buildings, and Monuments, had been created through the 1935 Historic Sites Act and consists of prominent experts appointed by the secretary of the interior.
6. U.S. Department of the Interior, National Park Service, "Great Beach Area, Cape Cod, Massachusetts," 1955, unpublished report, CCNSA.
7. Hillory A. Tolson et al., *Historic Listing of National Park Service Officials* (Washington, DC: Government Printing Office, 1991), 13, 19, 22, 37, 135.
8. Doe, "The Road to Monomoy," 103.
9. Ethan Carr, *Mission 66: Modernism and the National Park Dilemma* (Amherst: University of Massachusetts Press in association with Library of American Landscape History,

1998), 103–16. Further increases led to annual budgets greater than $100 million by 1962.

10. U.S. Department of the Interior, National Park Service, "Progress Report—Proposed Cape Cod National Park Study, September 30, 1957," unpublished report, CCNSA.
11. Burling, *Birth,* 9.
12. Beyle, "Cape Cod National Seashore," 1–13.
13. The work was directed by supervisory landscape architect E. C. Martinson and park landscape architect W. C. Applegate. The other members of the planning team were principal naturalist B. T. Gale, regional historian Frank Barnes, and regional archaeologist J. L. Cotter. Two University of Massachusetts Amherst scientists, William E. Randall Jr. and William G. Vinal, undertook a "biological investigation" of the study area. Other park service staff participated and advised on the study, including Benjamin Thompson, Leo J. Diederich, and Andrew G. Feil. Conrad Wirth also took a direct interest in the plan as it was assembled and visited the Cape on "familiarization and appraisal tours."
14. Burling, *Birth,* 10; U.S. Department of the Interior, National Park Service, "Cape Cod: A Proposed National Seashore Field Investigation Report," [1958], unpublished report, CCNSA (hereafter cited as "Field Investigation Report").
15. Doe, "Road to Monomoy," 115.
16. "Field Investigation Report," 1–2.
17. Ibid., 14–17.
18. Ibid., 17–19.
19. Ibid., 11–12, 19.
20. Wirth, "Birth Throes," 26–29.
21. "Cape Cod Discussed at Public Meetings," *National Parks Magazine* 33, no. 141 (June 1959): 12.
22. Wirth, "Birth Throes," 26–29.
23. Burling, *Birth,* 13–15. Other prominent homeowners on the Outer Cape included Arthur P. Schlesinger Jr., Elliot Richardson, Charles Eliot II, Nathan Saltonstall, among others, comprising "a veritable who's who of 1960s politics, academia, art, and architecture." The group would have a "disproportionate say in the types of coastal parks the NPS created throughout the nation" because of their influence over the legislative provisions of the Cape Cod National Seashore. Mullen, "Coastal Parks for a Metropolitan Nation," 61–70.
24. E. J. Kahn Jr., "An Irreplaceable Treasure," *New Yorker,* September 19, 1959, 101; Mullen, "Coastal Parks for a Metropolitan Nation," 70–74.
25. Wirth, "Birth Throes," 26; Kahn Jr., "Irreplaceable Treasure, 108, 114, 116."
26. Kahn Jr., "Irreplaceable Treasure," 102–4.
27. Quoted in Mullen, "Coastal Parks for a Metropolitan Nation," 40, 54. Mullen provides analysis of how postwar fears of communism shaped a perception of the national seashore legislation as an assault on the American home and family (54–70).
28. Philbin first introduced a bill to create a federal park on land in Bourne along the Cape Cod Canal, which was under the jurisdiction of the Army Corps of Engineers. When that bill was sent to the park service for comment, Conrad Wirth sent Philbin a copy of *Our Vanishing Shoreline* and suggested he sponsor legislation for the national seashore instead. Healey, "Legislative History," 24.
29. H.R. 12449 and H.R. 12456. Boland and O'Neill also included a provision for in-lieu-of-taxes payments and the offer of twenty-five-year tenancy agreements for residences taken through eminent domain. Healey, "Legislative History," 25–26. Boland had attended the dedication of Cape Hatteras National Seashore that spring, where he had met Wirth and Paul Mellon, prompting his action.
30. The park service also did not report to Congress on these early bills, a necessary step for them to advance. Any legislation would have needed to have the approval of the Department of the Interior, and that was not forthcoming. Ibid., 30.
31. Nicholson, however, had earlier introduced a bill similar to Philbin's to establish a Cape Cod Canal park in Bourne, which he supported. Ibid., 28.
32. Ibid., 30.
33. Ibid., 31.
34. In his home state, however, Neuberger's bill eventually resulted in the creation of the Oregon Dunes National Seashore (under U.S. Forest Service jurisdiction) in 1972.
35. Burling, *Birth,* 11–12; Kahn, "An Irreplaceable Treasure," 122; Healy, "Legislative History," 34.
36. Editorial, "National Parks Shouldn't Be Set Up by Decree," *Saturday Evening Post,* July 18, 1959.
37. See Mullen, "Coastal Parks for a Metropolitan Nation," 61–74; Francis Biddle, Marcel Breuer, Phyllis Duganne, Waldo Frank, George J. Higgins, Edwin O'Connor, Arthur Schlesinger Jr., Herbert Wechsler, Edmund Wilson, John C. Worthington, "Park Plan for Cape Cod: Legislation Criticized as Failing to Weigh Communities' Problems," letter to the editor, *New York Times,* August 30, 1959.
38. Conrad L. Wirth to Ben Hibbs, August 26, 1959. NACP, RG 79, Administrative Files, 1949–1971.
39. "Interview with Frederick Holborn, November 4, 1975," transcript, 4, CCNSA.
40. Beyle, "Cape Cod National Seashore," 112.

41. "Interview with Francis W. Sargent, November 4, 1975," transcript, 1–2, CCNSA.
42. John F. Kennedy to Joshua A. Nickerson, July 21, 1959, CCNSA.
43. Joe Holley, "Foreign Policy Guru Frederick Holborn Dies," *Washington Post,* June 9, 2005.
44. "Interview with David H. B. Martin, November 13, 1975," transcript, 1, 36, CCNSA.
45. See Damore, *Cape Cod Years.*
46. "Interview with Frederick Holborn," 3–5.
47. Wirth and Benjamin Thompson insisted that allowing the congressional delegation to take the initiative in drafting the bill was not unusual; but most accounts indicate that in the case of Cape Cod, because of the personal interest of Saltonstall and Kennedy and the contention surrounding the proposal on the Outer Cape, the park service was less involved in the process than it was in most national park legislation. "Interview with Benjamin Thompson," transcript, 12–13, CCNSA; "Interview with Frederick Holborn," 8, 12; "Interview with David H. B. Martin," 14.
48. Charles H. W. Foster, *The Cape Cod National Seashore: A Landmark Alliance* (Hanover, NH: University Press of New England, 1985), 5.
49. State governments can make "state cessions" to the federal government when a national park is created in order to allow (constitutionally) the federal government to exercise jurisdiction and enforce laws in the parks. These cessions can legally include authority over land regulation of any private land within park boundaries, but only if the state chooses to cede that authority. This was not the case at Cape Cod, and apparently was never envisioned as part of the formula developed by Holborn and Martin. See Joseph L. Sax, "Helpless Giants: The National Parks and the Regulation of Private Lands," *Michigan Law Review* 75, no. 2 (December 1976): 239–74.
50. This was the first instance of what Joseph Sax describes as "sword-of-Damocles" provisions in national park legislation. Ibid., 242.
51. Benjamin H. Thompson to David B. H. Martin, August 10, 1959, NACP, RG 79, Administrative Files, 1949–1971.
52. "Interview with Frederick Holborn," 8, 12; "Interview with David H. B. Martin," 14, 16, 21; "Interview with Benjamin Thompson," 13; Burling, *Birth,* 16–19.

4. Preserving a "Way of Life"

1. Francis P. Burling, *The Birth of the Cape Cod National Seashore* (1978; Fort Washington, PA: Eastern National, 2000), 18; "Oral History Interview with Hastings Keith, June 2, November 4, 1976," transcript, CCNSA; Thad L. Beyle, "The Cape Cod National Seashore: A Study in Conflict," PhD diss., University of Illinois, 1963, 120, 127.
2. "Oral History Interview with Jonathan Moore, October 29, 1975," transcript, 25–26, CCNSA.
3. "Oral History Interview with Robert McNeece, October 7, 1975," transcript, 2, CCNSA.
4. Devereux Butcher, "Resorts or Wilderness?," *Atlantic Monthly,* February 1961, 45–51; Benjamin H. Thompson, "Phone Call from Frank Burling," memorandum, March 3, 1961, Mrs. E. F. Hiscock to Conrad L. Wirth, March 1, 1961, and "Cape Cod National Seashore Park, Season of 1972, Morris-Monomoy Area," NACP, RG 79, Administrative Files, 1949–1971; "The Best Way to Meet Pressure—Don't Collapse," editorial, *Cape Codder,* March 23, 1961.
5. See Douglas W. Doe, "The Road to Monomoy: Chatham, Massachusetts, and the Cape Cod National Seashore," master's thesis, University of Massachusetts Boston, 1995, 137–66; Allen T. Edmunds to Mrs. E. F. [Alice] Hiscock, March 6, 1961, NACP, RG 79, Administrative Files, 1949–1971.
6. Hiscock had expressed her "delight" to Wirth when Morris and Stage Islands were included in the first Senate bill and wondered if the Chatham selectmen remembered that the areas had only become accessible after the construction of a federally funded dike provided a causeway earlier in the century. Mrs. E. F. Hiscock to Conrad L. Wirth, February 16, 1961, NACP, RG 79, Administrative Files, 1949–1971.
7. For a detailed analysis of Chatham's successful efforts to influence the boundaries of the national seashore, see Doe, "Road to Monomoy."
8. Beyle, "Cape Cod National Seashore," 130.
9. "Oral History Interview with David H. B. Martin, November 3, 1975," transcript, 31, CCNSA; Burling, *Birth,* 20–21.
10. Beyle, "Cape Cod National Seashore," 134–35; Burling, *Birth,* 23.
11. *Hearings on S.2636, before the Subcommittee on Public Lands of the Committee on Interior and Insular Affairs, December 9 and 10, 1959, Eastham, Mass.,* 86th Cong., 1st sess. (Washington, DC: Government Printing Office, 1960).
12. David Jenkins, "Culture of Preservation: The Cape Cod National Seashore Hearings, 1959–1961," unpublished report, 2006, CCNSA.
13. Ibid., 4, 6, 8–9.
14. Arthur P. Schlesinger Jr. joined Biddle in changing his

position to support the park. Jacqueline Mullen describes the conversion of Biddle and Schlesinger—through the special provisions of the Cape Cod legislation—in detail. Jacqueline Alyse Mirandola Mullen, "Coastal Parks for a Metropolitan Nation: How Postwar Politics and Urban Growth Shaped America's Shores," PhD diss., University at Albany, State University of New York, 2015, 82–89.

15. Quoted in Jenkins, "Culture of Preservation," 32.
16. Ibid., 5, 10–11, 13.
17. Economic Development Associates, Inc., "An Economic Study Relating to the Proposed Cape Cod National Seashore Park, 1960," unpublished report, CCNSA, 315–16. In fact, the actual number of "recreation visits" recorded in 1975 was just over five million, a level first achieved in the mid-1970s and which has remained fairly constant since then. See https://irma.nps.gov/.
18. Quoted in Jenkins, "Culture of Preservation," 17, 19, 28, 30–31.
19. Ibid., 7, 34, 40.
20. Conrad L. Wirth to Stewart Udall, "Boundary Amendments for Cape Cod National Seashore Legislation," memorandum, NACP, RG 79, Administrative Files, 1949–1971.
21. In December 1960, Van Ness Bates completed an ambitious proposal, "The Cape and the Park," for the Massachusetts Improvement Association. The study was intended to be the basis of a "Happy Medium solution to the Cape Park problem—between the natural resources conservational point of view of the National Park Service and the community conservational or 'way of life' point of view" of the Outer Cape towns. Bates proposed taking less land (22,000 acres) and building a "scenic coastal parkway" connected to an entire new system of regional parks and parkways in southern New England. The proposal included a "bridgeway and parkway" across Cape Cod Bay from Provincetown to Plymouth, among other visionary ideas, none of which attracted significant support. Van Ness Bates Associates, "The Cape and the Park, December 7, 1960," unpublished report, CCNSA.
22. Burling, *Birth,* 23–24.
23. Beyle, "Cape Cod National Seashore," 131.
24. In 1960, the Fort Hill area was sold to developers who subdivided it and began constructing access roads. See Lynn Kneedler-Schad, Katharine Lacy, and Larry Lowenthal, *Cultural Landscape Report for Fort Hill: Cape Cod National Seashore* (Boston: National Park Service, Olmsted Center for Landscape Preservation, 1995), 46–47.
25. Hastings Keith, "Washington Report, June 6, 1961," press release, CCNSA; "Oral History Interview with Jonathan Moore," 24–25; Burling, *Birth*, 53; Peter F. Healey, "The Legislative History of the Cape Cod National Seashore Act: How a Federal Agency Assisted in Resurrecting and Expanding a Dormant Public Policy," master's thesis, Georgetown University, 1967, 109.
26. Burling, *Birth,* 20–21, 51–52; "Oral History Interview with David H. B. Martin," 33.
27. Beyle, "Cape Cod National Seashore," 135–37.
28. Economic Development Associates, "Economic Study.".
29. "Oral History Interview with Benjamin Thompson, November 4, 1975," transcript, 16, CCNSA.
30. Congress clarified procedures for federal citizens' advisory groups in the 1972 Federal Advisory Committee Act. See Kenneth A. Smith, "Citizen Advisors and National Parks, October 1976," unpublished report, CCNSA.
31. To be clear, Congress had previously funded the acquisition of land for park purposes. During the New Deal, numerous agencies acquired many thousands of acres that in some cases became units of the national park system; funding for the acquisition of inholdings in established parks was also sometimes made available. But in 1961, Congress for the first time established a new national park with significant funding authorized specifically to acquire the land needed to create it.
32. "Interview with Frederick Holborn, November 4, 1975," transcript, 16, CCNSA.
33. Healey, "Legislative History," 55; Burling, *Birth,* 32–33.
34. When he first introduced his legislation in 1959, Kennedy himself urged that the Cape seashore be separate from any omnibus bills. Although it was "obviously related to other proposals now pending," he felt that the Cape Cod bill "should be considered on its own merits in its own setting," since "seashore park legislation is a relatively new field of legislation, in which there is not a large reservoir of experience or precedent." He was particularly concerned that local hearings be held so that the "concrete evidence of local officials and citizens" could be considered. 105 Cong. Rec. S17887 (daily ed. September 8, 1959).
35. "Interview with Frederick Holborn," 21; Burling, *Birth,* 34–40; Healey, "Legislative History," 57.
36. Burling, *Birth,* 42–46.
37. Keith listed his desired boundaries in a detailed memorandum to park service staff. "Interview with Representative Keith on Cape Cod Legislation Amendment," memorandum, June 15, 1960, NACP, RG 79, Administrative Files, 1949–1971. He also provided a summary of his involvement in the legislative process in his June 1961 "Washington Report," in which he expressed the hope that the congressional conference committee would adopt his (the House) version of the legislation, following what

he anticipated would be the passage of both bills in their respective houses, CCNSA.

38. Burling, *Birth,* 47–52.
39. Healey, "Legislative History," 103–4.
40. As of 2015, the park service lists 27,113 acres of land owned in fee simple, 404 acres held in less than fee ownership, and 32 acres in "other federal fee" ownership, for a total of 27,549 acres of land within the seashore boundaries. In addition, there are 14,556 acres of "other public areas" (including offshore), and 1,502 privately owned acres, for a total of 16,058 acres. The total area of the seashore, with water areas and the private "improved properties," is listed at 43,607 acres. National Park Service Land Resources Division, "Listing of Acreage," pdf available at https://irma.nps.gov/Stats/FileDownload/107.
41. Michelle E. Portman, "Coastal Protected Area Management and Multi-Tiered Governance: The Cape Cod Model," *Journal of Coastal Conservation* 11, no. 2 (2007): 121–13. Also see Fabio Ausenda, "The Cape Cod National Seashore: Land Acquisition, Land-Use Control, and Relationships with Surrounding Communities," master's thesis, Cornell University, 1988.
42. Burling, *Birth,* 52–54; Healey, "Legislative History," 107–11; *New York Times,* August 8, 1961; 105 Cong. Rec. S17887 (daily ed. September 8, 1959).
43. *Berkshire Eagle,* editorial, August 3, 1961.

5. The "Cape Cod Model"

1. The park service uses a cutoff date of July 1959 to distinguish between "old and new parks." Before that date, only 32,000 acres of inholding existed in a park system of many millions of acres. See Joseph L. Sax, "Buying Scenery: Land Acquisition for the National Park Service," *Duke Law Journal,* no. 4 (September 1980): 709–40.
2. Outdoor Recreation Resources Review Commission, *Outdoor Recreation for America: A Report to the President and to the Congress,* Washington, DC, January 1962.
3. Later, Sargent served as Massachusetts public works commissioner. He was elected lieutenant governor in 1966 and became governor in 1969 when John Volpe was appointed to the Nixon cabinet; he was elected governor in 1970.
4. See Edwin M. Fitch and John F. Shanklin, *The Bureau of Outdoor Recreation* (New York: Praeger, 1970).
5. Robert M. Utley and Barry Mackintosh, *The Department of Everything Else: Highlights of Interior History* (Washington, DC: Department of the Interior), 1989, 43–44.
6. "MISSION 66 Progress Report," draft, April 1961, box A8213, NPSHC; Department of the Interior, *1959 Annual Report,* 323–24; Dwight F. Rettie, *Our National Park System: Caring for America's Greatest Natural and Historic Treasures* (Champaign: University of Illinois Press, 1995), 251; "National Park Service Officials to Hold Planning Conference at Grand Canyon," DOI press release, April 23, 1961, box A8213, NPSHC.
7. Department of the Interior, *1959 Annual Report,* 324; Herbert Maier, "Half-way Point Evaluation of MISSION 66," September 6, 1957, box 7, Conrad L. Wirth Collection, University of Wyoming, American Heritage Center (CLWC).
8. "Parks of the Future (Discussion Paper)," October 31, 1960, NPS, HFC; "Parks for America, Organizational Meeting," October 31, 1960, minutes, box 22, CLWC.
9. "PARKS FOR AMERICA, The Committee of Fifteen, Minutes of December 5, 1960 Meeting, Washington, DC," box 22, CLWC; "Parks For America," *Parks & Recreation* 43, no. 12 (December 1960): 528–29, 541–43.
10. See Thomas G. Smith, "John Kennedy, Stewart Udall, and New Frontier Conservation," *Pacific Historical Review* 64, no. 3 (August 1995): 329–62.
11. Conrad L. Wirth, *Parks, Politics, and the People* (Norman: University of Oklahoma Press, 1980), 192–200.
12. "An Analysis of the MISSION 66 Program Made by C. L. Wirth at a Meeting at the Grand Canyon in 1961," May 27, 1974, box 33, CLWC; Wirth, *Parks, Politics, and the People,* 198–200.
13. "Cape Cod National Seashore Advisory Commission Appointed," DOI press release, January 9, 1962, CCNSA.
14. Foster's book on the early years of the CCNSAC is an invaluable first-person account of the group's activities, based in part on the published minutes of their meetings. See Charles H. W. Foster, *The Cape Cod National Seashore: A Landmark Alliance* (Hanover, NH: University Press of New England, 1985).
15. Hillory A. Tolson et al., *Historic Listing of National Park Service Officials* (Washington, DC: Government Printing Office, 1991), 72.
16. When Gibbs first arrived at the Cape, he found that the owner of the house he had rented had posted a sign informing him he was not welcome there. Nevertheless, Gibbs insisted that he had a warm reception from Outer Cape residents and that the area was the "friendliest place" he had ever seen, an indication of his determined equanimity. He served until 1966, the year the seashore was officially dedicated, and in his retirement continued to play an active civic role in the region on park issues. Foster, *Cape Cod National Seashore,* 12–14.

17. Ibid., 15; "Cape Cod National Seashore Not Ready for Visitors This Year," DOI press release, April 15, 1962, CCNSA.
18. "George H. Thompson Appointed Acquisition Officer," DOI press release, October 12, 1961. CCNSA.
19. "Interview with George Thompson," n.d. [1975], transcript, CCNSA.
20. Ibid.; Foster, *Cape Cod National Seashore,* 68; Fabio Ausenda, "The Cape Cod National Seashore: Land Acquisition, Land-Use Control, and Relationships with Surrounding Communities," master's thesis, Cornell University, 1988, 28–29.
21. George H. Thompson, "Land Acquisition," memorandum, June 7, 1964, CCNSA; "Interview with George Thompson"; "Questions and Answers," joint press release, Offices of Leverett Saltonstall, Benjamin A. Smith, and Hastings Keith, August 21, 1961, CCNSA.
22. Thompson, "Land Acquisition"; Foster, *Cape Cod National Seashore,* 18–19; "Annual Narrative Report," May 28, 1963, BNA, RG 79, CCNS, Administrative Correspondence Files, 1960–1981, box 1.
23. Ausenda, "Cape Cod National Seashore," 29.
24. In 1984, the Commonwealth of Massachusetts ceded "concurrent legislative jurisdiction" over the entire Cape Cod National Seashore, enhancing the park service's potential authority in enforcing laws and promulgating regulations that would be effective "regardless of landownership on all lands and waters within the national seashore." U.S. Department of the Interior, National Park Service, *Forging a Collaborative Future: General Management Plan, Cape Cod National Seashore,* 1998.
25. Provisions were made for the continued operation and expansion of the Provincetown airport and a town dump. "Authorization of Conveyance of Commonwealth Lands," Massachusetts House of Representatives General Court, Chapter 777, Commonwealth of Massachusetts, Approved July 26, 1962.
26. Thompson, "Land Acquisition"; "Questions and Answers"; Robert F. Gibbs to Ronald F. Lee, April 23, 1962, CCNSA; Foster, *Cape Cod National Seashore,* 20.
27. "Land Acquisition"; "Questions and Answers"; Gibbs to Lee; Foster, *Cape Cod National Seashore,* 24.
28. Thompson, "Land Acquisition." In 2015, the number was about 610 private properties covering 1,502 acres. National Park Service Land Resources Division, "Listing of Acreage," pdf available at https://irma.nps.gov/Stats/FileDownload/107. In 2007, Michelle E. Portman compiled an improved property tally of 612 distributed as follows: Chatham, 19; Eastham, 115; Orleans, 1; Provincetown, 1; Truro, 219; Wellfleet, 257. The total has varied slightly over the years. Portman, "Coastal Protected Area Management and Multi-Tiered Governance: The Cape Cod Model," *Journal of Coastal Conservation* 11, no. 2 (2007): 126.
29. "Questions and Answers."
30. The constitutionality of the federal zoning guidelines was not challenged at Cape Cod but was later at Fire Island National Seashore (New York), where it was upheld. "Suggestions Relating to the Zoning Provisions of a Bill to Provide for the Establishment of Cape Cod National Seashore Park," Harvard Student Legislative Research Bureau, December 1, 1959, CCNSA; Dyer Justice Taylor to Conrad L. Wirth, "Condemnation Provision in Bill for Establishment of Cape Cod National Seashore Park," February 10, 1961, NACP, RG 79, Administrative Files, 1949–1971; Joseph L. Sax, "Helpless Giants: The National Parks and the Regulation of Private Lands," *Michigan Law Review* 75, no. 2 (December 1976): 247–48; Charlotte E. Thomas, "The Cape Cod National Seashore: A Case Study of Federal Administrative Control over Traditionally Local Land Use Decisions," *Boston College Environmental Law Review* 12, no. 2 (1985): 225–72; Town of Eastham Selectmen to Stewart L. Udall, June 1, 1962, CCNSA; Foster, *Cape Cod National Seashore,* 20–21, 88–89.
31. Code of Federal Regulations, Title 36, Part 27, FR 6714, July 14, 1962.
32. For a comparative analysis of the seashore districts of the six towns, see Thomas, "Cape Cod National Seashore," and Portman, "Coastal Protected Area Management."
33. See Portman, "Coastal Protected Area Management."
34. Ausenda, "Cape Cod National Seashore," 44, 141.
35. Initially, the "Inwood formula" was used to calculate the depreciation and rental value of a property over the period in which a seller retained tenancy rights. For each $25,000 of property value, an "owner-interest" value of $8,000 over a twenty-five-year period, for example, would be used to reduce the amount paid for the property. A negotiated property price of $50,000 with a twenty-five-year tenancy agreement would result in a $34,000 sales price. Later the "1 percent" formula was used, in which 1 percent of the value of a property was deducted for every year of continued tenancy that was negotiated: a 25 percent reduction in the case of a twenty-five-year tenancy agreement. "Park Service Seeking Public Views on Land Acquisition Procedures," DOI press release, January 14, 1977, CCNSA.
36. Ausenda, "Cape Cod National Seashore," 37–38.
37. "Post-1959 Properties," memorandum, Cape Cod National Seashore, 1972, CCNSA.

38. "Building in the Seashore Costs All of Us," editorial, *Cape Codder,* September 14, 1961.
39. "Land Status as of July 1, 1974," memorandum, CCNSA.
40. Office of Representative Hugh L. Carey, press release, December 2, 1963, CCNSA.
41. See Ethan Carr, *Mission 66: Modernism and the National Park Dilemma* (Amherst: University of Massachusetts Press in association with Library of American Landscape History, 1998), 309–12.
42. "Statement of Witness for the Department of the Interior before the House Committee on National Parks and Recreation," March 1970, CCNSA.
43. Tolson et al., *Historic Listing,* 11, 28, 64, 72, 94, 113, 161.
44. Foster, *Cape Cod National Seashore,* 32, 36.
45. "Park Land Grab in Last Four Months," *Provincetown Advocate,* March 28, 1974, 8.
46. Anne Kirchheimer and Robert Turner, "Award of Land Worth $200,000 to Squatter Amazes Cape Town," *Boston Globe,* September 27, 1973.
47. Foster, *Cape Cod National Seashore,* 33.
48. Greg O'Brien, "New Homes in the Park: Thick and Fast They Came . . . ," *Cape Codder,* October 7, 1976; "The Seashore: What Has Happened to the 'Spirit and Intent,'" editorial, *Cape Codder,* October 14, 1976.
49. 123 Cong. Rec. S1378–82 (daily ed. January 25, 1977).
50. Charles C. Robb, "Bill to Correct Abuses in Park Filed by Solons," *Cape Codder,* January 27, 1977, and "NPS Report Backs Park Management, Blames Development on $$ Shortage," *Cape Codder,* January 6, 1977.
51. "The Seashore Problem Cannot Be Exorcised," editorial, *Cape Codder,* January 6, 1977.
52. 123 Cong. Rec. S1378–82 (daily ed. January 25, 1977); Robb, "Bill to Correct Abuses."
53. Thomas, "Cape Cod National Seashore," 254–55.
54. United States Comptroller General, *The Federal Drive to Acquire Private Lands Should Be Reassessed* (Washington, DC: General Accounting Office, 1979).
55. By 1970, $33.5 million had been spent, and by 1983, $42,917,575 was the total. By the 1990s, all funds for land acquisition had been spent. "Fact Sheet: Land Acquisition Program, 1970–1974," internal memorandum, CCNSA; National Park Service, *Forging a Collaborative Future,* 12; Thomas, "Cape Cod National Seashore," 254.
56. National Park Service, Land Acquisition Policy, 44 Fed. Reg. 24,790 (1979); see Sax, "Buying Scenery."
57. "Land Acquisition Plan," March 27, 1980, CCNSA; Thomas, "Cape Cod National Seashore," 252–55; Ausenda, "Cape Cod National Seashore," 30–36.
58. Lauren McKean, personal communication, November 6, 2017. See http://wellfleetseashoreowners.org; http://www.savetruroseashore.org; Brent Harold, "Blasch and Lawyer Win; World Loses," *Cape Cod Times,* July 15, 2008; Mary Ann Bragg, "Truro Pushes Limits on House Size," *Cape Cod Times,* February 8, 2017. Portman concludes in her study of the effectiveness of Cape Cod seashore district zoning that up to that point towns generally had met their requirement to report zoning variance applications to the park service, but that park service comments often (up to one-third of the time) did not influence subsequent planning and zoning board decisions. She points to the failure of the original authorizing legislation to include an effective means of instigating "intermittent zoning revision processes" ("Coastal Protected Area," 127–30).
59. See Sax, "Buying Scenery."

6. Designing the Park

1. "Proposed Cape Cod National Seashore Tentative Statement of Policy," March 1960, CCNSA.
2. See Code of Federal Regulations, Title 36, Part 7, in which the special regulations governing individual units of the national park system are promulgated.
3. "Cape Cod National Seashore, Special Regulations, Confidential Pending Approval," February 6, 1963, CCNSA.
4. "Master Plan for the Preservation and Use of Cape Cod National Seashore: Interim General Development Plan," August 17, 1962, CCNSA.
5. "A Tentative Plan for the Development of the Cape Cod National Seashore," April 26, 1963," CCNSA; "The Master Plan for Preservation and Use, Cape Cod National Seashore," draft, 1963, CCNSA.
6. Charles H. W. Foster, *The Cape Cod National Seashore: A Landmark Alliance* (Hanover, NH: University Press of New England, 1985), 16–17.
7. "Tentative Plan"; "Master Plan," draft.
8. U.S. Department of the Interior, National Park Service, *Master Plan: Cape Cod National Seashore, Massachusetts* (Washington, DC: National Park Service, 1970).
9. Ethan Carr, *Mission 66: Modernism and the National Park Dilemma* (Amherst: University of Massachusetts Press in association with Library of American Landscape History, 1998), 80–85.
10. "Tentative Plan."
11. The sites were: in Provincetown, Long Point, Pasture Pond, the Dunes; in Truro, Pamet Valley, Bearberry scrub barrens, the Hollows, High Point; in Wellfleet, Herring River, Bound Brook, Herring River estuary,

Duck Harbor–Merrick Island, Great Island–Jeremy Point, Pineland Kettles, Atlantic White Cedar Swamp; in Eastham, Eastham Bogs, Nauset Marshes; in Orleans, Sampson and Pochet Islands. Interpretive exhibits were planned for the Provincetown whale oil factory and Civil War fort, Pilgrim Heights, Highland Light, Little Pamet historic structures, Pamet Valley historic houses, the Oysterman's House (referenced by Thoreau), Marconi Station, Camp Wellfleet, Nauset Lighthouse, Penniman House, and the Outermost House (Henry Beston's cottage). "Master Plan," draft.

12. "Annual Narrative Report," May 28, 1963, BNA, RG 79, CCNS, Administrative Correspondence Files, 1960–1981, box 1.
13. "Master Plan," draft; "Annual Narrative Report."
14. "Cape Cod National Seashore Operation, Visitation," memorandum, September 29, 1976, CCNSA.
15. Most of this massive planning and design effort was handled at two central offices, the EODC in Philadelphia and the Western Office of Design and Construction (WODC) in San Francisco, both of which had been established in 1954. The park service's Northeast Regional Office (then "Region V") was also in Philadelphia, where regional director Ronald Lee was headquartered and where most of the early master planning for Cape Cod was done. In Washington, Thomas Vint remained overall chief of design and construction, assisted by chief landscape architect Bill Carnes and chief architect Dick Sutton. The EODC was headed by Edward Zimmer, with Harvey H. Cornell and John B. ("Bill") Cabot in the same respective roles. In 1961, the architect Robert G. Hall replaced Zimmer. By that time, there were several hundred employees working at the EODC and the WODC.
16. Vernon L. Hammons, "A Brief Organizational History of the Office of Design and Construction, National Park Service, 1917–1962," unpublished report (Washington, DC: National Park Service, n.d.), 3; "Interview with A. Clark Stratton," conducted by S. Herbert Evison, March 1, 1962, transcript, 2, NPSHC.
17. Sarah Allaback, *Mission 66 Visitor Centers: The History of a Building Type* (Washington, DC: Government Printing Office, 2000), 17–21.
18. U.S. Department of the Interior, National Park Service, "Visitor Center Planning: Notes on Discussions Held in EODC, November 18–22, 1957, and WODC February 4–6, 1958," unpublished report, National Park Service, Denver Service Center Library; Allaback, *Mission 66 Visitor Centers,* 222; Barry Mackintosh, *Interpretation in the National Park Service* (Washington, DC: National Park Service, 1986), 49–51.
19. Carr, *Mission 66,* 127–48.
20. Ibid., 150–74. In 2001, the Quarry Visitor Center (no longer extant) and the Wright Brothers and Beaver Meadows Visitor Centers were all declared National Historic Landmarks for their significance in U.S. architectural history. See Allaback, *Mission 66 Visitor Centers.*
21. Emerson Goble, "Architecture (?) for the National Parks," *Architectural Record* 121, no. 1 (January 1957): 173–85.
22. Wolf Von Eckardt, "The Park Service Dares to Build Well," *Washington Post,* March 29, 1964.
23. Robert E. Koehler, "Our Park Service Serves Architecture Well," *AIA Journal* 1 (January 1971): 18–25.
24. Tracy J. Stakley, *Cultural Landscape Report and Historic Structure Report: Salt Pond Visitor Center* (Boston: National Park Service, 1999), 4, 9; Donald F. Benson to Robert G. Hall, June 5, 1963, BNA, RG 79, NPS CCNS Correspondence, 1955–1971, box 2; Eugene R. DeSilets to George Hartzog, August 21, 1964, NACP, RG 79, Administrative Files, 1949–1971.
25. Robert E. Smith to Robert G. Hall, April 18, 1963, BNA, RG 79, CCNS Correspondence, 1955–1971, box 2.
26. The Marconi shelter was demolished in 2013.
27. John H. Cabot to Robert G. Hall, May 17, 1963. BNA, RG 79, CCNS Correspondence, 1955–1971, box 2. "Construction of Interpretive Shelter," completion report, August 22, 1963, ibid., box 11.
28. "Interpretive Shelter and Exhibits," completion report, October 24, 1963; "Interpretive Signs and Markers," completion report, January 20, 1966, ibid., box 11.
29. George Hartzog to John B. Cabot, July 27, 1964, NACP, RG 79, Administrative Files, 1949–1971.
30. Thematic architecture in parks has precedents in European parks of previous centuries, as well as American municipal parks in the nineteenth century. The idea was used to great effect by Mary Elizabeth Jane Colter for the Santa Fe Railroad buildings at South Rim of the Grand Canyon, and by Louis W. Hill for the Great Northern Railroad buildings at Glacier National Park, to name just two early national park examples. The "rustic" era of National Park Service design developed architectural themes in parks—featuring pseudo-vernacular construction and historical references—throughout the national park system beginning in the 1920s.
31. The drawings are reproduced in Stakley, *Cultural Landscape Report.*
32. "Interview with Josiah H. Child, October 6, 1975," transcript, 4, CCNSA.

33. Peter McMahon and Christine Cipriani, *Cape Cod Modern: Midcentury Architecture and Community on the Outer Cape* (New York: Metropolis Books, 2014), 9–14.
34. Pietro Belluschi to Josiah H. Child, January 24, 1963, BNA, RG 79, CCNS Correspondence, 1955–1971, box 2.
35. Walter Gropius, "On the Desirable Character of Design for the Cape Cod National Seashore," n.d. [January 1963], ibid. The other architects consulted included Marcel Breuer, Heyward Cutting, Gregory Kepes, Olav Hammarstrom, Gordon Robb, Richard S. Gallagher, and Francis B. Sellew.
36. "Interview with Serge Chermayeff, October 20, 1975," transcript, 4, CCNSA.
37. Stakley, *Cultural Landscape Report,* 6–11; Josiah H. Child to Robert F. Gibbs, March 11, 1964, BNA, RG 79, CCNS Correspondence, 1955–1971, box 2.
38. Foster, *Cape Cod National Seashore,* 35; "Massachusetts Historical Commission Inventory Form, Mission 66 Buildings," n.d., CCNSA. The Province Lands Visitor Center was dedicated on May 25, 1969, in a ceremony that featured now-governor Francis Sargent, former senator Leverett Saltonstall, and newly appointed secretary of the interior Russell Train.
39. Ronald F. Lee to Robert G. Hall, May 3, 1963, BNA, RG 79, CCNS Correspondence, 1955–1971, box 2; "Rehabilitation of Provincetown Beach Bathhouse," completion report, September 10, 1965, and "Parking Area Expansion and Access Ramp," completion report, March 3, 1965, BNA, RG 79, CCNS Reports, 1955–1971, box 11. The Herring Cove bathhouse was demolished and replaced in 2013.
40. "Picnic Area Development, Pilgrim Heights," completion report, September 10, 1965, and "Miscellaneous Beach Facilities, Marconi Station," completion report, August 31, 1965, CCNS Reports, 1955–1971, box 11.; "Massachusetts Historical Commission Inventory Form, Mission 66 Buildings," n.d., CCNSA. In the 1980s, the Nauset Light comfort station was demolished and the Doane Rock comfort station was replaced.
41. "Progress Report, Cape Cod," memorandum, January 1964, BNA, RG 79, CCNS, Administrative Correspondence, box 1; "Massachusetts Historical Commission Inventory Form, Mission 66 Buildings," n.d., CCNSA. The bathhouse at Head of the Meadow was destroyed by arson in the 1980s, and the bathhouse at Coast Guard Beach in Eastham was destroyed by a 1978 storm.
42. "Demolition of Undesirable Structures, Camp Wellfleet," completion report, September 21, 1965, BNA, RG 79, CCNS Reports, 1955–1971, box 11.
43. "Roads, Parking Areas, Walks, Pilgrim Heights," completion report, January 11, 1965; "Demolition and Grounds Improvement, Pilgrim Heights," completion report, August 16, 1965; "Construct Main Maintenance Building, Marconi, Sub-Maintenance Building, Province Lands," completion report, September 22, 1965; "Picnic Area Development, Province Lands," completion report, January 20, 1966, all BNA, RG 79, CCNS Reports, 1955–1971, box 11.
44. See General Correspondence of the Assistant Director for Design & Construction, 1965–1968, NACP, RG 79.
45. "Picnic Tables, Park General," completion report, April 23, 1964; "Miscellaneous Beach Facilities," completion report, September 7, 1965, both BNA, RG 79, CCNS Reports, 1955–1971, box 11.
46. Conrad L. Wirth to George B. Hartzog, "Progress Report, Cape Cod National Seashore," memorandum, December 31, 1962, BNA, RG 79, CCNS Correspondence, 1955–1971, box 2.
47. "Stabilization of Sand Dunes," completion report, September 10, 1965; "Stabilization of Sand Dunes," completion report, March 16, 1964; "Demolition and Grounds Improvement Planting," completion report, September 21, 1965; "Planting, Coast Guard Beach," completion report, January 17, 1966, all BNA, RG 79, CCNS Reports, 1955–1971, box 11.
48. "Press Release, May 26, 1966, Memorial Day Ceremonies to Mark Establishment of Cape Cod National Seashore," CCNSA.

7. Recreation and Stewardship

1. Joshua A. Nickerson to Edward M. Kennedy, April 16, 1965, CCNSA; George B. Hartzog to WASO and All Field Offices, "Statement of Management Principles," memorandum, May 15, 1964, BNA, RG 79, CCNS, Correspondence, 1955–1971, box 2.
2. Stewart Udall to Hastings Keith, November 3, 1965, quoted in "Master Plan Studies," 1968, CCNSA.
3. Charles H. W. Foster, *The Cape Cod National Seashore: A Landmark Alliance* (Hanover, NH: University Press of New England, 1985), 29. The policy of dividing the national park system into three categories was officially discontinued in 1970 through the National Park Service "General Authorities Act." Richard West Sellars, *Preserving Nature in the National Parks* (New Haven: Yale University Press, 1997), 245–46.
4. Authored by A. Starker Leopold, "Wildlife Management

in the National Parks" (known as the Leopold Report) was followed by another investigation by the National Academy of Sciences. Both reports criticized park service wildlife management and the lack of adequate scientific data on which to make decisions. See Sellars, *Preserving Nature,* 192–217.

5. Robert F. Gibbs to Ronald F. Lee, "Operating Report, Statements of Accomplishment," memorandum, June 18, 1964, BNA, RG 79, CCNS, Reports, 1955–1971, box 11.
6. Foster, *Cape Cod National Seashore,* 22–23.
7. "Area Information, CCNS, Prepared for Supt. Joseph, January, 1966," CCNSA.
8. "Monomoy Proposal Debated at Hearings in Chatham," *Cape Cod Standard-Times,* January 12, 1967; "Keith Files Bill to Preserve Monomoy," *Cape Cod Standard-Times,* May 5, 1968; "Wilderness Status Given Monomoy," *Cape Cod Standard-Times,* July 11, 1968.
9. Foster, *Cape Cod National Seashore,* 33.
10. By that time, the EODC and WODC had been reorganized into three "planning and service centers" in Philadelphia, Washington, and San Francisco. By 1971, these offices would be reduced in size and combined to create the Denver Service Center (DSC) in Lakewood, Colorado. U.S. Department of the Interior, National Park Service, "Denver Service Center," 1977, unpublished report, Denver, Technical Information Center; Harlan D. Unrau, "A History of the Denver Service Center," 1999, unpublished draft report, Denver Service Center; George B. Hartzog, *Battling for the National Parks* (New York: Moyer Bell, 1988), 100.
11. John J. Reynolds, a landscape architect with a significant role on the 1970 Cape Cod master plan team, recalled that a number of creative national park planning initiatives were occurring during this period, eventually resulting in the official "general management plan" procedures he and others developed and named in 1975. He also observed that the Cape Cod master plan "presaged both analysis and issues at Yosemite several years later," when he and Arnberger (who had transferred to become superintendent of the national park) were reunited in the effort to produce what became an extremely influential GMP for Yosemite, published in 1980. Reynolds went on to direct the DSC and to serve as park service deputy director, among other positions during his long career. John J. Reynolds, personal communication, September 25, 2017.
12. "Cape Cod National Seashore: A Master Plan," draft, February 12, 1969, CCNSA. The participants were drawn from park staff and planners based in both Philadelphia and Washington. The team was headed by David A. Kimball, working with engineer Kenneth L. Smith and landscape architect John J. Reynolds, all out of Washington. Other participants included landscape architects and "resource managers" working from Philadelphia, as well as superintendents Joseph and Arnberger, and staff at the park.
13. "Master Plan Studies," February 29, 1968, memorandum, CCNSA.
14. "Master Plan," draft, CCNSA; "Statement for Management and Planning (Management Objectives)," October 20, 1969, BNA, RG 79, CCNS, Administrative Correspondence Files, 1960–1981, box 2.
15. U.S. Department of the Interior, National Park Service, *Master Plan: Cape Cod National Seashore, Massachusetts* (Washington, DC: Department of the Interior, National Park Service, 1970).
16. "Master Plan," draft, 10–12.
17. Ibid., 25.
18. Ibid., 25–26. The echo of Garrett Hardin's "Tragedy of the Commons," published while the Cape Cod plan was being prepared, was probably not coincidental. Garrett Hardin, "The Tragedy of the Commons," *Science* 162 (December 1968): 1243–48.
19. "Master Plan," draft, 28–30, 36.
20. Ibid., 43–53.
21. Phillip B. Herr & Associates, "Final Report: Cape Cod National Seashore Impact Study," unpublished report, September 1969, CCNSA.
22. Foster, *Cape Cod National Seashore,* 34.
23. "Operational Plan for Developing Experimental Wildlife Management Area," n.d. [1971], BNA, RG 79, CCNS, Administrative Correspondence, box 13.
24. "Hunting is permitted on federally owned land . . . ," press release, October 17, 1963; "Deer hunting on federally owned lands . . . ," press release, November 12, 1963, both BNA, RG 79, CCNS, Correspondence on Wildlife and Forestry, box 8. The area restrictions cited applied to upland game and waterfowl—deer hunters had these area open to them, with five-hundred-foot safety zones around public facilities.
25. "Report on Deer Hunting 1963 Season," memorandum, December 10, 1963, BNA, RG 79, CCNS, Correspondence on Wildlife and Forestry, box 8.
26. "Memorandum of Understanding . . . Relating to Wildlife Management in the Cape Cod National Seashore," December 30, 1968, BNA, RG 79, CCNS, Administrative Correspondence, box 13.
27. For example, "Field Observations of Game Management Unit, Marconi Area—1971," memorandum, December 1,

1971, BNA, RG 79, CCNS, Correspondence on Wildlife and Forestry, box 8.

28. "Operational Plan for Developing Experimental Wildlife Management Area," n.d. [1971], BNA, RG 79, CCNS, Administrative Correspondence, box 13. Pheasants were also released in the Bound Brook area (Wellfleet) and Hatches Harbor (Provincetown). By 2002, these were the only areas left on the Outer Cape being stocked with pheasant. U.S. Department of the Interior, National Park Service, *Cape Cod National Seashore Hunting Program Final Environmental Impact Statement* (National Park Service, 2007), 12.
29. National Park Service, *Cape Cod National Seashore Hunting Program.* The authors of the EIS note that while in recent years some had questioned whether hunting should be practiced in a national park at all, it was a "traditional activity," part of the "cultural heritage of Cape Cod," and specifically protected in the park's authorizing legislation (1).
30. "Area Information, Cape Cod National Seashore," unpublished report, January 1966, CCNSA.
31. "Howard Baker to All Field Offices," memorandum, October 14, 1965, BNA, RG79, CCNS, Reports, 1955–1971, box 11.
32. Stanley C. Joseph, "Annual Status of Natural Sciences Research Program," April 1, 1966, memorandum, ibid.
33. Jan Gelb Margo to Leslie P. Arnberger, August 16, 1971, BNA, RG 79, CCNS, Administrative Correspondence, box 13.
34. Foster, *Cape Cod National Seashore,* 38; John J. Lopez, "The Use of Negotiated Rulemaking in Piping Plover / Off-Road Vehicle Management at Cape Cod National Seashore," master's thesis, University of Rhode Island, 1998, 11–12.
35. Leslie P. Arnberger to Jan Gelb Margo, August 25, 1971, BNA, RG 79, CCNS, Administrative Correspondence, box 13.
36. "The Dunes Are Being Destroyed," *Provincetown Advocate,* August 12, 1971.
37. The team included geologist Alan Niedorada, head of the Coastal Research Center at the University of Massachusetts, and scientists Stephen P. Leatherman and Paul Barrett, as well as numerous graduate students in botany and other disciplines who used their research as subjects of theses and dissertations.
38. Paul J. Godfrey, "Investigators Annual Report," March 3, 1976, BNA, RG 79, CCNS, Administrative Correspondence, box 13; "Cape Cod Seashore Lists Research Projects," *Cape Cod Standard-Times,* May 11, 1974.
39. "Park's Study Zeroes in on Dune Buggies," *Cape Cod Standard-Times,* September 8, 1974.
40. Godfrey, "Investigators Annual Report."
41. [Erma J. Fisk, Richard L. Cunningham], "Guidelines for Tern Colony Management," n.d. [1975], BNA, RG 79, CCNS, Administrative Correspondence, box 12. Tern colonies were studied and protected to a significant degree in the 1970s. Both Massachusetts Audubon and The Trustees of Public Reservations had active tern research and protection programs for other coastal areas in Massachusetts. See, for example, Nan Jenks-Jay, "A Study and Census of Terns at Great Point and Coaskata-Coatue Wildlife Refuge," Trustees of Public Reservations, 1978, BNA, RG 79, CCNS, Administrative Correspondence, box 13.
42. "Program on Cape Shore Seeks to Protect Terns," *New York Times,* July 27, 1974; "Fox-foxing Fence to Protect Terns," *Cape Cod Oracle,* June 7, 1979. A permit was also issued to the park service to shoot at least one black-crowned night-heron, another suspected predator, at Nauset Spit. Herbert Olsen to Town of Orleans Selectmen, June 11, 1978. BNA, RG 79, CCNS, Administrative Correspondence, box 12. On Monomoy, the U.S. Fish and Wildlife Service poisoned over 2,000 great black-backed gulls because they were suspected predators of Arctic and roseate terns on the island. The action was justified by the growth of gull populations that benefited from open landfill sites. Robert Shemeligian, "No Poisoned Sandwiches Planned for Monomoy Gulls This Spring," *Cape Codder,* November 7, 1980.
43. Bradford G. Blodget, "The Effects of Off-Road Vehicles on Least Terns and Other Shore Birds," master's thesis, National Park Service Cooperative Research Unit, University of Massachusetts Amherst, May 1978.
44. Minsky reported on the destruction of a ternery by ORVs in 1977, for example, and also made detailed reports on the effectiveness of the fence barriers. "Scene of Destruction," letter to the editor, *Provincetown Advocate,* August 4, 1977; Dennis Minsky, "Report of the Tern Warden: Season of 1977," BNA, RG 79, CCNS, Administrative Correspondence, box 13.
45. Erma J. Fisk to Nathaniel P. Reed, June 16, 1975; Nathaniel P. Reed, "Protecting Atlantic Coast Shorebirds and Their Nesting Sites," memorandum, July 2, 1975, both BNA, RG 79, CCNS, Administrative Correspondence, box 12.; [Fisk, Cunningham], "Guidelines for Tern Colony Management."
46. For example, "People, Buggies, Dogs, Nature Put Terns on the Danger List," *Cape Codder,* August 26, 1977.
47. "By Foot Alone," editorial, *Cape Codder,* August 26, 1977.

48. "Seashore Closes Beach Because of Tern Chicks," *Cape Codder,* July 21, 1978; Lopez, "Negotiated Rulemaking," 14.
49. Foster, *Cape Cod National Seashore,* 42, 46; Lopez, "Negotiated Rulemaking," 14.
50. Foster, *Cape Cod National Seashore,* 52–54; Lopez, "Negotiated Rulemaking," 15–16.
51. U.S. Department of the Interior, National Park Service, "Analysis of Management Alternatives (Including Environmental Assessment) for Off-Road Vehicle Use, Cape Cod National Seashore," 1980.
52. The University of Massachusetts cooperative research unit had completed thirteen technical reports by this time. After 1976, Stephen P. Leatherman led the effort. Stephen P. Leatherman and Paul J. Godfrey, "The Impact of Off-Road Vehicles on Ecosystems in the Cape Cod National Seashore, Final Report,." University of Massachusetts, 1979.
53. U.S. Department of the Interior, National Park Service, "Cape Cod National Seashore, Environmental Assessment, Options for Managing ORV Access," 2007; U.S. Department of the Interior, National Park Service, "Off-Road Vehicle Activity Report, Cape Cod National Seashore," 2016.
54. Quoted in Brendan Murphy, "Riding Cape Sand," *New York Times,* July 27, 1981. Also see Eileen Mueller, "Surfcasters and Off Road Vehicle Use at Cape Cod National Seashore: An Ethnographic Report," unpublished report, CCNSA.
55. Leatherman and Godfrey, "Impact of Off-Road Vehicles."
56. U.S. District Court for the District of Massachusetts, Conservation Law Foundation of New England v. Clark, 590 F. Supp. 1467 (D. Mass. 1984), June 27, 1984.
57. Exceptions and permitted activities allowed some ORVs beach access for specific nonrecreational purposes. U.S. Department of the Interior, National Park Service, "Off-Road Vehicle Activity Report, Cape Cod National Seashore," 2016; "Memorandum Decision," Conservation Law Foundation of New England v. Clark; Lopez, "Negotiated Rulemaking," 22–26.
58. Edwin M. Hoopes, "Breeding Ecology of Piping Plovers Nesting at Cape Cod National Seashore," unpublished report, National Park Service, Cape Cod National Seashore, October, 1996; Scott M. Melvin, Anne Hecht, and Curtice R. Griffin, "Piping Plover Mortalities Caused by Off-Road Vehicles on Atlantic Beaches," *Wildlife Society Bulletin* 22, no. 3 (1994): 409–14.
59. "Cape Cod National Seashore; Off-Road Vehicle Use," *Federal Register* 63, no. 36, February 24, 1998; Lopez, "Negotiated Rulemaking," 27–28.
60. Lopez, "Negotiated Rulemaking," 64–77; Jennifer Caddich, Kari Jermansen, Jill Mastrotataro, and Susan Senecah, "Conflict Assessment and the Cape Cod National Seashore," *Mediation Quarterly* 17, no. 1 (Fall 1999): 21–40.
61. U.S. Department of the Interior, National Park Service, "Cape Cod National Seashore, Environmental Assessment, Options for Managing ORV Access," 2007.
62. Godfrey, "Investigators Annual Report"; Paul J. Godfrey, "Discussion Paper on Operational Plans for Coastal Research Laboratory (Old MITRE Site)," April 3, 1977; "Atlantic Coastal Laboratory," memorandum from regional director, BNA, RG 79, CCNS, Administrative Correspondence, box 12.
63. For a full account of scientific research at the seashore as of 1987, see Patricia G. Claxon, "Bibliography of Scientific Research for Cape Cod National Seashore," and "History of Scientific Research at Cape Cod National Seashore," unpublished reports, 1987, CCNSA.
64. "Oral History Interview with John W. Portnoy, August 25, 2016"; "Oral History Interview with Michael T. Reynolds, August 9, 2016"; "Oral History Interview with Charles Roman, August 8, 2016," transcripts, CCNSA.
65. U.S. Department of the Interior, National Park Service, "East Harbor Tidal Restoration Project," 2015.
66. Cape Cod National Seashore and the Herring River Restoration Committee, "Herring River Restoration Project, Draft Environmental Impact Statement / Environmental Impact Report," October, 2112, CCNSA.
67. Robert W. Eberhardt et al., "Conservation of Changing Landscapes: Vegetation and Land-Use History of Cape Cod National Seashore," *Ecological Applications* 13, no. 1 (February 2003): 68–84; U.S. Department of the Interior, National Park Service, "Fire Management," brochure, 2011.
68. "Oral History Interview with John W. Portnoy"; "Oral History Interview with Charles Roman."
69. Mary Ann Bragg, "Repairs Planned for Herring Cove Beach Parking Lot," *Cape Cod Times,* May 24, 2017.
70. Michael Soukup went on to serve as associate director for natural resources in the Washington, DC, office, where his experience at Cape Cod and the North Atlantic region influenced the implementation of science policies nationally.
71. "Oral History Interview with Charles Roman."

8. Camping, Beaches, and Erosion

1. NPS Stats, Visitor Use Statistics, https://irma.nps.gov/Stats/.

2. Economic Development Associates, Inc., "An Economic Study Relating to the Proposed Cape Cod National Seashore Park, 1960," unpublished report, CCNSA.
3. https://www.census.gov/quickfacts/table/.
4. Charles H. W. Foster, *The Cape Cod National Seashore: A Landmark Alliance* (Hanover, NH: University Press of New England, 1985), 28. For examples of the discussions on campgrounds, see "Minutes of the Cape Cod National Seashore Advisory Commission, Thirtieth Meeting," December 4, 1964, 8–12; "Minutes . . . , Thirty-second Meeting," February 16, 1965, 2–14; "Minutes, . . . Fifty-sixth Meeting," April 14, 1967, 31–39.
5. See "Minutes . . . , Thirty-first Meeting," January 8, 1965, 8–21.
6. Exceptions were occasionally made for small groups seeking a wilderness experience on the Great Beach during the off-season, such as Outward Bound excursions. Norton M. Bean to Ed Marakovitz, October 13, 1971, BNA, RG 79, CCNS Administrative Correspondence, 1960–1981, box 11.
7. Lewis A. Carter, "1962 Report on Camping in Barnstable County," October 16, 1962, ibid.
8. Camping Committee to Stanley C. Joseph, memorandum, April 11, 1967, ibid.
9. Leslie P. Arnberger to Regional Director, May 20, 1969, ibid.
10. Stanley C. Joseph to Regional Director, memorandum, May 12, 1967, ibid.
11. Leslie P. Arnberger to Harold Baughan, November 7, 1969, ibid.
12. Arnberger corresponded with Yosemite officials to see how they were dealing with the demand for camping areas among the influx of young visitors. In 1971, Yosemite set up a special, temporary campground at a reduced rate, with reduced law enforcement, which separated their "liberated friends from the 'straight' public." Lynn Thompson to Leslie P. Arnberger, December 16, 1971, ibid.
13. "Brewster Rest Area Becomes a Campsite," *Cape Codder,* July 23, 1970.
14. "Hearing Provokes Verbal Donnybrook," *Cape Codder,* October 29, 1970; "Harwich Planning Board Opposes State Park Plan," *Cape Cod Standard-Times,* November 4, 1970.
15. Leslie P. Arnberger, "Overnight Emergency Use, Fourth of July Weekend," memorandum, July 2, 1971; Richard Strange, "Fourth of July Weekend," memorandum, July 7, 1971, both BNA, RG 79, CCNS Administrative Correspondence, 1960–1981, box 11; "Weekend Camping Allowed," *Provincetown Advocate,* September 9, 1971.
16. Frank Barnes, "Camping, Cape Cod," memorandum, November 23, 1971, BNA, RG 79, CCNS Administrative Correspondence, 1960–1981, box 11.
17. "Chamber Wants Restrictions on Sleeping Outside," *Provincetown Advocate,* November 11, 1971.
18. Barnes, "Camping, Cape Cod."
19. For example, the *Cape Codder* backed the park service's commitment to preventing the environmental impacts that campgrounds would have: "An Idea Whose Time Is . . . Never!," *Cape Codder,* November 25, 1971.
20. During the 1970s, the national seashore also came under considerable political pressure to build public boat ramps, a feature hunting and fishing advocates wanted and the state Department of Natural Resources backed. The CCNSAC was consulted and Herring Cove Beach was studied as one of the only areas with the room for parking and other facilities. But it was decided (with the advisory commission concurring) that safety and logistical issues made a public boat ramp unfeasible. "Seashore, DNR in Classic Juxtaposition," *Provincetown Advocate,* May 9, 1974; Jack E. Stark to Edward W. Brooke, December 8, 1977; James C. Killian, "Boat Launching Facility," memorandum, May 8, 1978, both BNA, RG 79, CCNS, Administrative Correspondence, box 4.
21. "Cape Cod National Seashore, Special Regulations, Confidential Pending Approval," February 6, 1963, CCNSA.
22. Nina Fortin, Meryle Sufian, William Kornblum, and Terry Williams, "Preliminary Report, Visitor Use and Social Problems at Cape Cod National Seashore," Cooperative Research Unit, City University of New York, August, 1975, BNA, RG 79, CCNS Administrative Correspondence, 1960–1981, box 13.
23. Grace DesChamps, "Truro Bombs Park on Nude Beach," *Provincetown Advocate,* August 29, 1974; Linda Charlton, "Nudity Ban Aimed at Cape Cod Shore," *New York Times,* March 8, 1975; Stephen Williams et al. v. Stanley K. Hathaway et al., Civil Action No. 75-2050-F, United States District Court, District of Massachusetts, July 11, 1975.
24. Foster, *Cape Cod National Seashore,* 41–45.
25. Lawrence C. Hadley to Eduardo G. Villacorta, October 16, 1974, BNA RG79, CCNS, Administrative Correspondence, box 3.
26. "Oral History Interview with Denis Galvin, August 25, 2016," transcript, CCNSA.
27. U.S. Department of the Interior, National Park Service, North Atlantic Regional Office, "Environmental Assessment: Management Alternatives Addressed to Nude Bathing and Related Concerns, Cape Cod National Seashore, Massachusetts," BNA, RG 79, CCNS Administra-

tive Correspondence, 1960–1981, box 12; Williams et al. v. Hathaway et al.

28. Besides local papers, stories appeared in the *New York Times* and *Time* magazine. See Linda Charlton, "Nudity Ban Aimed at Cape Cod Shore," *New York Times,* March 8, 1975.
29. Williams et al. v. Hathaway et al.
30. Fortin, Sufian, Kornblum, and Williams, "Preliminary Report."
31. Foster, *Cape Cod National Seashore,* 44–45; Williams et al. v. Hathaway et al.; Susan Milton, "Nudity a Defining Seashore Issue," *Cape Cod Times,* August 7, 2011.
32. Leslie Reynolds, personal communication, September 30, 2017.
33. Milton, "Nudity a Defining Seashore Issue."
34. See Graham S. Geise, Rachel B. Geise, and Patricia B. Morse, *The Eroding Shores of Outer Cape Cod* (Orleans, MA: Association for the Preservation of Cape Cod, 1994); Paul J. Godfrey and Melinda M. Godfrey, *Barrier Island Ecology of Cape Lookout National Seashore and Vicinity, North Carolina* (Washington, DC: National Park Service Monograph Series Number Nine, 1976).
35. Paul J. Godfrey and Melinda M. Godfrey, "Dunes and Beaches in the East: Let Nature Do It," draft article, 1974, BNA, RG 79, CCNS, Administrative Correspondence, box 12; Godfrey and Godfrey, *Barrier Island Ecology.*
36. See, for example, Woods Hole Oceanographic Institution, *Beach Studies in the Cape Cod Area Conducted during the Period January 1, 1956–June 30, 1956* (Woods Hole, MA: Woods Hole Oceanographic Institution, 1956); John M. Zeigler, Sherwood D. Tuttle, Graham S. Giese, and Herman J. Tasha, *Residence Time of Sand Composing the Beaches and Bars of Outer Cape Cod* (Woods Hole, MA: Woods Hole Oceanographic Institution, 1965).
37. Foster, *Cape Cod National Seashore,* 30–31, 34, 40–41.
38. "Erosion—Live With It—Says Seashore's Arnberger," *Sunday Cape Cod Standard-Times,* June 25, 1972; "Conference Assesses Erosion: Sea Winning Beach War," *Cape Cod Standard-Times,* October 17, 1972.
39. "Storm Damage Along Seashore Near $600,000," *Cape Cod Times,* February 9, 1978; "Tide, Time Bring Beach Landscape Full Swing," *Cape Cod Times,* February 27, 1978; Vern E. Hurt, "February 1978 Storm," memorandum, and Stephen P. Leatherman to Paul A. Buckley, February 23, 1978, both BNA, RG 79, CCNS, Administrative Correspondence, box 3; Foster, *Cape Cod National Seashore,* 50.
40. Quoted in Geise, Geise, and Morse, *Eroding Shores,* 12.
41. Dr. Paul Dudley White and the Committee for Safe Bicycling that he headed advocated for the trails and led a celebratory ride at their dedication, with many cyclists and a troop of Camp Fire Girls participating. U.S. Department of the Interior, National Park Service, "Press Release," September 7, 1967, NPS History Collection, Harpers Ferry Center, HFC-01261, CACO.
42. George A. Palmer to Edward M. Kennedy, August 18, 1970; William P. Jensen to Raymond Kelleher, December 22, 1972; James C. Killian to Jane Bernstein, July 31, 1973, all BNA, RG 79, CCNS, Administrative Correspondence, box 11.
43. "Landslide Erodes Cliffs at Cape Cod Light," *Provincetown Advocate,* September 21, 1972.
44. K. C. Myers, "Cottages Demolished on Eroding North Beach in Chatham," *Cape Cod Times,* September 17, 2014; Tim Wood, "After Thirty Years, the Breakthrough Still Shapes Chatham," *Cape Cod Chronicle,* January 4, 2017.

9. The Cultural Components of Character

1. See James Michael Lindgren, *Preserving Historic New England: Preservation, Progressivism, and the Remaking of Memory* (New York: Oxford University Press, 1995).
2. Historic American Building Survey, *American Place: The Historic American Buildings Survey at Seventy-five Years* (National Park Service, 2008), 4–15.
3. Ethan Carr, *Mission 66: Modernism and the National Park Dilemma* (Amherst: University of Massachusetts Press in association with Library of American Landscape History, 2007), 195–97.
4. Ernest A. Connally, "Master List of Historic Structures in the Cape Cod National Seashore," September 6, 1962, BNA, RG 79, CCNS, Administrative Correspondence, box 5. Three Cape Cod houses owned by the national seashore are currently listed in the National Register of Historic Places—the Ahearn House, the Atwood-Higgins House, and the Jedediah Higgins House—as is the privately owned John Newcombe House.
5. Historic American Building Survey, *American Place,* 36.
6. Ernest Allen Connally, "The Cape Cod House: An Introductory Study," *Journal of the Society of Architectural Historians* 19, no. 2 (May 1960): 47–56. The "house, house-and-a-half, and double house" are more commonly described today as half, three-quarter, and full Cape houses.
7. Today the Massachusetts Historical Commission lists 1,013 houses with dates of 1850 or earlier in the six towns of the Outer Cape. See Massachusetts Cultural Resource Information System (MACRIS), http://mhc-macris.net/.
8. John H. Sprinkle, *Crafting Preservation Criteria: The Na-*

tional Register of Historic Places and American Historic Preservation (New York: Routledge, 2014), 6–20.

9. John M. Fowler, "The Federal Preservation Program," in *A Richer Heritage: Historic Preservation in the Twenty-First Century,* ed. Robert E. Stipe (Chapel Hill: University of North Carolina Press, 2003), 35–79.
10. Leslie P. Arnberger to Northeast Regional Office Director, memorandum, February 12, 1973; Chester L. Brooks to Northeast Regional Office Director, memorandum, March 6, 1973, both BNA, RG 79, CCNS, Administrative Correspondence, box 6.
11. Henry J. Magaziner, "Field Trip Report—Architect Henry J. Magaziner, February 12–14," memorandum, May 4, 1973, ibid., box 5.
12. Leslie P. Arnberger, "Sellback—Jedediah Higgins House," memorandum, January 11, 1973; "Jedediah Higgins House," memorandum, May 11, 1973, both ibid.
13. Herbert Olsen to LeRoy Morgan, October 16, 1980; LeRoy Morgan to Herbert Olsen, October 22, 1980, both ibid.
14. At least some authority to lease historic, federally owned properties was originally included in both the 1935 Historic Sites Act and the 1966 NHPA. "Sell back" and "lease back" authority was also specifically granted to the park service in the 1968 reauthorization of the LWCA, with the stipulation that contracts would be "subject to such terms and conditions as will assure the use of the property in a manner consistent with the purposes" of the park. Section 111 of the 1980 amendments to the NHPA also included leasing provisions. This authority was expanded in the 1998 National Parks Omnibus Management Act. U.S. Department of the Interior, National Park Service, *Administrative Policies for Recreation Areas of the National Park System* (Washington, DC, 2007); National Trust for Historic Preservation, *Historic Leasing in the National Park System: Preserving History through Effective Partnerships* (Washington, DC: National Trust for Historic Preservation, 2013).
15. Herbert Olsen, "Properties Eligible or Potentially Eligible for Section 111 of the NHPA," memorandum, February 13, 1981, BNA, RG79, CCNS, Administrative Correspondence, box 5.
16. Marsha L. Fader, "Trip Report, CACO, January 17–19, 1977," memorandum, ibid.
17. National Register of Historic Places listing and nomination form available at https://www.nps.gov/nr/.
18. "Atwood-Higgins House, Bound Brook Island Road, Wellfleet, Barnstable County, MA," HABS documentation, 1962, https://www.loc.gov/item/ma0080/.
19. Katherine Higgins continued living in the house under a special use permit until 1975. "Interpretive Prospectus, Atwood-Higgins Complex, Cape Cod National Seashore," 1977, BNA, RG79, CCNS, Administrative Correspondence, box 5.
20. Ibid.
21. Richard Chilcoat, "Atwood-Higgins House Preservation, Completion Report," 1994, unpublished report, CCNSA.
22. National Register of Historic Places listing and nomination form available at https://www.nps.gov/nr/.
23. A. Berle Clemensen, *Historic Resource Study, Cape Cod National Seashore* (Denver: National Park Service, 1979), 73–77; "Historic Structure Report, Captain Edward Penniman House," unpublished report, 1985, CCNSA.
24. "Captain Edward Penniman House, Fort Hill Road, Eastham, Barnstable County, MA," HABS documentation, 1962. https://www.loc.gov/item/ma0017/.
25. "Frank Ackerman, Oral History Interview, August 26, 2016," transcript, CCNSA.
26. By 1998, sixty-two properties within the national seashore had been found eligible for the National Register, and approximately 240 "historic" privately owned buildings had been "identified" by HABS. U.S. Department of the Interior, National Park Service, *Forging a Collaborative Future: General Management Plan, Cape Cod National Seashore* (1998), 48.
27. Cape Cod Commission, *Cape Cod Regional Policy Plan* (Barnstable, MA: Cape Cod Commission, 2002).
28. In 1968, George Hartzog issued a policy statement ordering that the proposed demolition of any building, including those less than fifty years old, be reviewed by regional or Washington staff. The policy apparently had little effect at the national seashore, which moved or demolished these buildings following perfunctory findings of noneligibility. BNA, RG79, CCNS, Administrative Correspondence, box 5.
29. Norton M. Bean, "Removal of Buildings," memorandum, November 3, 1972, ibid.
30. See "List of Classified Structures," CCNSA.
31. "Area Information, CCNS, Prepared for Supt. Joseph, January, 1966," CCNSA.
32. U.S. Department of the Interior, National Park Service, "Cape Cod: A Proposed National Seashore Field Investigation Report," [1958], unpublished report, CCNSA.
33. See Ross Moffett, "A Review of Cape Cod Archaeology," *Bulletin of the Massachusetts Archaeological Society* 19, no. 1 (1957): 1–19; Ross Moffett, "Archaeological Overview, Cape Cod National Seashore," 1960, CCNSA.
34. "The Master Plan for Preservation and Use, Cape Cod National Seashore," draft, 1963, CCNSA; Edison P. Lohr, "The Marconi Station," [n.d.], unpublished report, BNA,

RG79, CCNS, Administrative Correspondence, box 6. The Marconi Station site and interpretive shelter were rededicated in 1973, when a commissioned bronze bust of Marconi was unveiled. "Superintendent's Annual Report, 1973," ibid., box 1.

35. Vernon C. Gilbert Jr. and Edison P. Lohr, "Interpretive Prospectus for Cape Cod National Seashore," CCNSA.
36. Ernest A. Connally, "HABS Documentation, Highland Lighthouse" (MA-750), 1962; Henry C. Kittredge, *Cape Cod: Its People and Their History,* 2nd ed. (Boston: Houghton Mifflin, 1968), 310–11; Peggy A. Albee et al., "Highland Lighthouse and Keeper's Dwelling, Historic Structure Report," unpublished report, 1994, CCNSA; see James W. Claflin, *Lighthouses and Life Saving along Cape Cod* (Charleston, SC: Arcadia, 2014).
37. A similar solution was being proposed for the Cape Hatteras Lighthouse (1870), the tallest in the United States, which was under a similar threat, and which after years of planning and debate was moved in 1999.
38. U.S. Coast Guard, "Highland Light: A Strategy for Preservation and Public Access," unpublished report, 1992; U.S. Department of the Interior, National Park Service, "Preliminary Resource Assessment, Highland Light (Cape Cod Lighthouse)," unpublished report, 1992, both CCNSA.
39. Lance Kasparian, "U.S. Coast Guard Nauset Station," unpublished report, 2008, CCNSA.
40. A. Berle Clemensen et al., "Historic Structure Report: The Three Sisters Lighthouses," unpublished report, 1986, CCNSA; Peter J. Frawley, "Park to Restore and Re-locate the 'Three Sisters of Nauset,'" *Cape Codder,* November 15, 1977; Superintendent's Annual Report, 1988, NACP, RG 79, Superintendents' Annual Narrative Reports, 1980–2000.
41. Claflin, *Lighthouses and Life Saving,* 6–8.
42. Quoted ibid., 15, 26–27. The nine built on the Outer Cape were at Race Point, Peaked Hill Bars, Highland, Pamet River, Cahoon's Hollow, Nauset, Orleans, Chatham, and Monomoy.
43. Maureen K. Phillips, "Race Point Coast Guard Station, Station House, Historic Structure Report," unpublished report, 2005; Lance Kasparian, "U.S. Coast Guard Nauset Station Dwelling and Boathouse, Historic Structure Report," unpublished report, 2008. CCNSA.
44. Peggy A. Albee, "Old Harbor Life-Saving Station," unpublished report, 1988, CCNSA; Leslie P. Arnberger, "Old Harbor Life Saving Station, Chatham," memorandum, September 7, 1973; E. Blaine Cliver, "Transmittal of Specifications for Relocation of Old Harbor Life Saving Station," August 15, 1977, BNA, RG79, CCNS, Administrative Correspondence, box 5.
45. Peter Hartley, "Old Station Gets New Look," *Cape Codder,* October 31, 1978; Susan Areson, "Exhibits, Rescue Demonstrations Set for Old Harbor Boathouse," *Provincetown Advocate,* March 22, 1979.
46. A. Berle Clemensen, *Historic Resource Study: Cape Cod National Seashore, Massachusetts* (Denver: National Park Service, 1979).

10. Cultural Landscapes and Modern Houses

1. See Digital Archaeology's records, which include Cape Cod archaeological reports, at http://core.tdar.org/. McManamon was appointed director of Digital Archaeology in 2009.
2. See Francis P. McManamon, "Prehistoric Land Use on Outer Cape Cod," *Journal of Field Archaeology* 9, no. 1 (Spring 1982): 1–20; Francis P. McManamon, ed., *Chapters in the Archeology of Cape Cod: Results of the Cape Cod National Seashore Archeological Survey, 1979–1981,* Cultural Resources Management Study no. 8 (Boston: National Park Service, 1984).
3. Richard D. Holmes, Carolyn D. Hertz, and Mitchell T. Mulholland, *Historic Cultural Land Use Study of Lower Cape Cod: A Study of the Historical Archeology and History of the Cape Cod National Seashore and the Surrounding Region* (Lowell, MA: National Park Service, n.d.)
4. Wampanoag people today are enrolled in two federally recognized and four state recognized tribes. See http://www.mashpeewampanoagtribe-nsn.gov/.
5. Elise Brett, "Seashore Staff to Restore 19th Century Berry Bog," *Cape Cod Times,* October 10, 1978; Susan Areson, "Seashore Plans Working Museum, Truro Cranberry Farm Being Restored," *Provincetown Advocate,* October 12, 1978; Hillary Quarles, "Cultural Landscape Inventory, Summary Report, Pamet Cranberry Bog," 1995, unpublished report, CCNSA.
6. Michael E. Whatley, "Archeology and the Cultural Resource Preservation Program," memorandum, November 4, 1980, BNA, RG79, CCNS, Administrative Correspondence, box 5.
7. Quarles, "Cultural Landscape Inventory."
8. Larry Lowenthal and Katherine Lacy, *Cultural Landscape Report for Truro Highlands Historic District* (Boston: National Park Service, Olmsted Center for Landscape Preservation, 1995); Michael Commisso, Jan Haenraets, and Margie Coffin Brown, *Condition Report and Treatment*

Plan for Truro Highlands Historic District (Boston: National Park Service, Olmsted Center for Landscape Preservation, 2007).

9. Lynn Kneedler-Schad, Katharine Lacy, and Larry Lowenthal, *Cultural Landscape Report for Fort Hill: Cape Cod National Seashore* (Boston: National Park Service, Olmsted Center for Landscape Preservation, 1995); "Cultural Landscape Inventory, Fort Hill Rural Historic District, 2000, Revised 2008," unpublished report, 2008. CCNSA; Jan Haenraets, *Condition Report for Fort Hill Historic District* (Boston: National Park Service, Olmsted Center for Landscape Preservation, 2007).
10. Kneedler-Schad, Lacy, and Lowenthal, *Cultural Landscape Report for Fort Hill.*
11. Haenraets, *Condition Report for Fort Hill Historic District,* 2.
12. Emily Donaldson, Margie Coffin Brown, and Gretchen Hilyard, *Cultural Landscape Report for Dune Shacks of Peaked Hill Bars Historic District* (Boston: National Park Service, Olmsted Center for Landscape Preservation, 2011), 43–50.
13. Ibid., 77–81.
14. With the exception of the Malicoat shack, which stood on land the family owned, almost all of the transactions had been completed by 1980. The case involving the Bessay property continued until 1991, giving it some notoriety as the "Jarndyce and Jarndyce" of American law: the longest-lasting suit ever brought against the federal government.
15. Superintendent's Annual Report, 1988, NACP, RG 79, Superintendents' Annual Narrative Reports, 1980–2000.
16. Donaldson, Coffin Brown, and Hilyard, *Cultural Landscape Report for Dune Shacks,* 8–9, 80–90.
17. CCNSAC, "Cape Cod National Seashore Advisory Commission Report on the Preservation and Use Plan / Environmental Assessment for the Dune Shacks of the Peaked Hill Bars Historic District, July 2010," unpublished report.
18. See Robert Wolfe, "Dwelling in the Dunes: Traditional Use of the Dune Shacks of the Peaked Hill Bars Historic District, Cape Cod, 2005," and Robert Wolfe and T. J. Ferguson, "Traditional Cultural Property Assessment, Dune Shacks of the Peaked Hill Bars Historic District, 2006," unpublished reports, CCNSA.
19. Donaldson, Coffin Brown, and Hilyard, *Cultural Landscape Report for Dune Shacks,* xv, 93–94.
20. University of Massachusetts Amherst and National Park Service, *People and Places on the Outer Cape: A Landscape Character Study* (Amherst: University of Massachusetts, 2004).
21. Peter McMahon and Christine Cipriani, *Cape Cod Modern: Midcentury Architecture and Community on the Outer Cape* (New York: Metropolis Books, 2014), 16.
22. A multiple-property nomination listed five of the houses in the National Register in 2014. They included the Hatch House on Bound Brook Island, designed by Jack Hall in 1961, and the Kugel House, designed by Charlie Zehnder in 1970. The Kuhn House (Nathaniel Saltonstall, 1960), the Sirna Studio (Victor Civkin, 1960), and the Tisza House (Olav Hammarstrom, 1960) were also part of the nomination, as was the Weidlinger House (Paul Weidlinger, 1954), which was donated to the park by the Weidlinger family. Mary Ann Bragg, "Trust Offers New Life for Old Houses," *Cape Cod Times,* August 14, 2012.
23. William Burke, "I Don't Understand It, It Doesn't Look Old to Me," n.d., park brochure, CCNSA.
24. Mary Ann Bragg, "Trust Offers New Life for Old Houses," *Cape Cod Times,* August 14, 2012; McMahon and Cipriani, *Cape Cod Modern,* 263–65.
25. U.S. Department of the Interior, National Park Service, *Forging a Collaborative Future: General Management Plan, Cape Cod National Seashore,* 1998.

Conclusion

1. See https://irma.nps.gov/Stats/Reports/National for visitor statistics and the appendixes in Dwight F. Rettie, *Our National Park System: Caring for America's Greatest Natural and Historic Treasures* (Urbana: University of Illinois Press, 1995), for comparative budgets.
2. U.S. Department of the Interior, National Park Service, *Forging a Collaborative Future: General Management Plan, Cape Cod National Seashore,* 1998, 7.
3. DSC regional office staff initially involved were deputy regional director Terry Savage and chief planner Sarah Peskin, as well as Ellen Carlson, a planner hired by the region to begin the planning process at the park. Lauren McKean and other park staff took a direct role in producing the plan over the coming years. The DSC sent the landscape architect Mark Tabor to Cape Cod and provided other support and personnel from their Colorado office.
4. "Oral History Interview with Sarah Peskin, September 6, 2017," transcript, CCNSA. The authors of the GMP included much of the staff of the national seashore at the time, beginning with superintendents Ringgold and Burks. Deputy superintendent Linda Canzenelli, Ellen Carlson, and Lauren McKean as well as Frank Ackerman

and Mike Reynolds all contributed to the GMP. At the DSC, planner Linda Dahl, historian Berle Clemensen, and landscape architects Jeff Heywood, Mark Tabor, and Kimball Koch did as well. Northeast regional director Marie Rust supported and approved the results.

5. National Park Service, *Forging a Collaborative Future*, 21–22, 27–41.
6. "Oral History Interview with Maria Burks, August 25, 2016," transcript, CCNSA.
7. National Park Service, *Forging a Collaborative Future*, 139–44, 182–91.
8. Ibid., 42.
9. Ibid., 70–71.
10. "Oral History Interview with George Price, August 23, 2016," transcript, CCNSA.
11. "Oral History Interview with Denis P. Galvin, August 29, 2016," transcript, CCNSA.

Index

Page numbers in italics refer to illustrations.